INTERNATIONAL SALES LAW

A PROBLEM–ORIENTED COURSEBOOK

By

John A. Spanogle
William Wallace Kirkpatrick Professor of Law
George Washington University

Peter Winship
James Cleo Thompson Sr. Trustee Professor of Law
Southern Methodist University

AMERICAN CASEBOOK SERIES®

WEST GROUP

ST. PAUL, MINN., 2000

COPYRIGHT © 2000 By WEST GROUP
          610 Opperman Drive
          P.O. Box 64526
          St. Paul, MN 55164–0526
          1–800–328–9352

ISBN 0–314–23358–X

TEXT IS PRINTED ON 10% POST
CONSUMER RECYCLED PAPER

We dedicate this book to:

Sharon, Kathryn and Tim
Grant Andrew and Brynne
Verity and Adam

*

Preface

The law applicable to sale of goods transactions between the United States and many other countries has been federal law, not UCC Article 2, for a dozen years as of the date of this book. The federal law is contained in the provisions of the Convention on Contracts for the International Sale of Goods (CISG), a self-executing treaty which was ratified by the United States in 1986 and entered into force on January 1, 1988. When it is applicable, as federal law, CISG preempts any competing state law on the subject, including UCC Article 2. At the time it entered into force, it was the applicable law in transactions between the United States and ten other countries. Now, it is the applicable law in transactions between us and fifty-five other countries, including Canada and Mexico, our number one and number three trading partners, respectively.

However, there is little knowledge of this federal law among the bench and bar. A recent survey of the Florida bench and bar by Professor Gordon in the 1998 American Journal of Comparative Law shows that only one third of the *international* practitioners surveyed thought that they had a "reasonable" knowledge of CISG, which means that two thirds of such international practitioners believed they were deficient in their knowledge of this law. The bench had even less knowledge of it. Most judges, including the ones which handled international contract cases, were unfamiliar with CISG, and some believed that "CISG must be a federal law which is applicable in federal *courts*, not in state courts." So much for the Constitutional preemption doctrine.

The purpose of this book is to reduce this lack of knowledge by creating teaching materials which have CISG as their primary focus. The materials present a systematic examination of the difficult issues that arise out of the international sale transaction. In addition to analyzing the usual litigation situations, the materials also present issues concerning lawyers as problem-solvers—planning and structuring transactions so as to allocate risks and avoid litigation.

The book is designed for a two credit hour course and is built around a series of problems which systematically examine the various provisions of CISG. CISG cases, both U.S. and foreign, are also set forth. However, since many of the foreign cases are not in English, they are often available only as abstracts through UNCITRAL (CLOUT cases) and UNILEX. We therefore present the CLOUT and UNILEX abstracts, which are copyrighted by UNCITRAL and the Rome Institute, respectively, and reprinted with permission. Since CISG is a composite of both civil law and common law concepts, we also include readings that explain these civil law concepts, where they arise in CISG. There are also "Legislation Notes" which explain the UCC Article 2 concepts, when the CISG and the UCC are markedly different. However, the focus throughout is on CISG, and the civil law and UCC readings are explanatory.

The coursebook is divided into five chapters. The first chapter introduces students to the basic concept of comparative law and the civil law of contracts and to the basic transaction pattern, then analyzes the scope of application of CISG. The organization of the other four chapters will be familiar to both students and teachers of either contracts or domestic sales law. They take the reader through the formation and performance of contracts, and both formal and informal remedies for non-performance. Chapter Two examines formation issues in the informal, often unwritten contract, the battle of forms, the standard form contract and the very formal, long term "deal." Chapter Three on performance analyzes both the buyer's and the seller's duties under a contract, and excuse of performance by an "impediment." Chapter Four examines the remedies available to an aggrieved party that can be exercised without going to court, such as suspending its own performance, rejecting the goods and avoiding the contract, and reducing the price. Finally, Chapter Five analyzes the remedies available through litigation and the tension between provisions for specific performance and those providing for damages.

There is a Documents Supplement prepared especially for use in this book. References are made in each problem to those provisions in the Documents Supplement which are necessary to an analysis of that problem. The Documents Supplement includes CISG and its associated convention on prescription periods (statute of limitation). It also includes several multilateral conventions on choice of law and choice of forum issues. Finally, it includes selected provisions from UCC Articles 1 and 2.

Neither of us was interested in undertaking this project for the sake of producing a "casebook". We believed rather that a problem-oriented approach and the organization outlined above would offer a different perspective for law faculty teaching in this area.

The book is designed to be supplemented by the instructor's own materials in areas where further depth is desired. Professors of international sales law often have extremely diverse concepts of what the course should include. Not everyone will agree to all of our choices of problems or subject-matter. But we hope that this provides a useful structure on which to hang your own ideas, as well as providing a comprehensive background.

Prior editions of the materials have been used by many people at many schools. We have incorporated many of their suggestions and are very grateful for them. We look forward to receiving and using further suggestions from future users of the book. There is an accompanying Teacher's Manual to help faculty use this book.

JOHN A. SPANOGLE
PETER WINSHIP

November, 1999

Acknowledgments

We wish to acknowledge that in writing this book we have been aided by numerous colleagues and students. Special appreciation is due several persons who have thoughtfully commented on individual problems. They are: Don Clifford of the University of North Carolina, Richard Cummins of George Washington University, Larry Garvin of Florida State University, Clayton Gillette and Steven Walt of the University of Virginia, Peter Hay of Emory University, Robert Hillman of Cornell Law School, Genevieve Saumier of McGill Law School, and John Wladis of Widener University. We also thank the United Nations Publications Board and Joachim Bonell at the Rome Institute for their permission to use their copyrighted abstracts of CLOUT and UNILEX cases, respectively. We also give particular thanks to the many foreign colleagues abroad with whom we have worked over the years and who by adding to our knowledge in international sales law have helped make this volume possible.

*

Summary of Contents

——————————

*

Table of Contents

CHAPTER 1. INTRODUCTION

CHAPTER 2.   FORMATION OF THE SALES CONTRACT

CHAPTER 3. PERFORMANCE OF THE CONTRACT

Table of Cases

The principal cases are in bold type. Cases cited or discussed in the text are roman type. References are to pages. Cases cited in principal cases and within other quoted materials are not included.

*

INTERNATIONAL SALES LAW

A PROBLEM–ORIENTED COURSEBOOK

*

Chapter 1

INTRODUCTION

After that magic day when you have graduated, a second magic day when you have found an employer or "just the perfect spot" to hang out your shingle, and the third magic day when the bar examiners notify you that (of course!) you passed the bar with flying colors—after all that, a potential client walks into your office, says that she is about to sell 500 electronic notepads to a buyer in France, and announces that she wants you to "set up" the transaction for her. What do you do? Read on.

* * *

R. FOLSOM, M. GORDON & J. A. SPANOGLE, INTERNATIONAL BUSINESS TRANSACTIONS
33–34 (4th ed., 1999)*

Many of the aspects concerning international transactions are different in degree from some domestic transactions (*e.g.,* a sale of goods from New York to California), but others are novel and have no counterpart in any domestic transaction. These factors are illuminated by examining the risks arising out of such a transaction, and whether these risks are heightened by the fact that the transaction is international. Once a transaction is identified as international, it will usually involve distance between the parties, and therefore require transportation of the goods. It will also involve more than one legal system, and could involve different currencies. In addition, it is more likely that buyer and seller do not know each other, and do not wish to trust each other or to rely upon litigation (especially in a foreign legal system) for protection.

The primary risk to seller is of not being paid after shipping the goods. Thus seller wants some assurance of payment, as long as the goods are shipped, and that payment will be made in seller's nation. Buyer, on the other hand, will have several different worries. First, buyer will not want to pay unless assured that the goods have arrived, or at least have been shipped. Second, buyer will worry about whether the goods meet the quantity and quality requirements of the contract. For this reason, buyer prefers to pay only after inspecting the goods. Howev-

1

er, where buyer and seller are at a distance from each other, and the goods must be transported, it is impossible both to have seller be paid upon shipment and to allow buyer to delay payment until after inspection after arrival of the goods. Intermediaries must be enlisted.

Payment also causes problems. Currencies fluctuate in value relative to each other. In addition, seller usually wants the funds to be available in seller's nation and in its currency, for its costs are more likely to be incurred in that currency; while buyer may not be able to pay in any currency but its own. Thus, the sales contract must specify the currency to be used for payment and assign the risk of currency fluctuations to one of the parties. In addition, when dealing with a buyer from a "soft currency" nation, seller must carefully ascertain whether buyer is authorized to pay in a "hard currency" or not. A simple declaration from buyer may not be sufficient and much extra paper-work may be required even when such payment is authorized. Finally, if seller relies upon foreign sources for payment, unforeseen events can always interrupt the expected orderly flow of funds—as events in Iran, and then in Iraq and Kuwait, have demonstrated. Thus, seller prefers a creditor located within its jurisdiction and subject to its legal system.

In this day of "long-arm jurisdiction," both buyer and seller must worry about the cultural and legal system of the other party. It may be difficult to determine what law governs the contract—the domestic law of seller's state, the domestic law of buyer's state, or if there is a treaty or multilateral convention applicable. Regardless of what law is applicable, extra regulations may be imposed upon international contracts—*e.g.*, license requirements on exports, customs duties or even quotas on imports. In addition, different rules may be provided for international contracts than for domestic ones. For example, in the United States, instead of consulting Article 7 of the UCC on Documents of Title (including bills of lading), the appropriate statute for regulation of bills of lading will be the Federal Bills of Lading Act, (49 U.S.C.A. §§ 80101–16) and for regulation of contracts with carriers may be the Carriage of Goods by Sea Act (COGSA, 46 U.S.C.A. §§ 1300—1315). The Convention on [Contracts for the] International Sale of Goods (CISG) may govern the sales contract itself, rather than UCC Article 2, unless expressly excluded. If foreign law is applicable to the transaction, the substance of such law may be very difficult to ascertain, both in the sense of sources being difficult to find in available law libraries, and also in the sense that these sources often lack the precision necessary to answer detailed questions. Further, your training is as a common law attorney, and not as a civil law attorney.

* * *

This first chapter is organized to discuss three different topics. First we look at the concepts of comparative law—comparing U.S. or Common Law with other legal systems. Second, we look at one type of transaction which is used in sales of goods across borders. It is more complex than many international sales transactions, but if you understand how the transaction should occur, then it will be easier to understand the rules that are used to govern that complex transaction. Third, we look at different ways in which the difficulties of different legal regimes may be reduced for the merchant who sells across national borders, and introduce the U.N. Convention on Contracts for the International Sale of Goods (CISG) as a way of reducing those difficulties. Finally, we discuss the scope of application of CISG, and analyze some of the problems which arise in interpreting the scope provisions of CISG.

After Chapter 1, the organization of this casebook should be familiar to anyone who has taken a course on either Contracts or Sales. Chapter 2 concerns the formation of contracts under CISG, and is divided into informally-formed contracts, contracts involving printed forms or standard terms, and negotiated long-term contracts. Chapter 3 concerns the performance of contracts under CISG, and is divided into sellers' obligations, buyers' obligations and excuse of performance under force majeure and similar concepts. Chapter 4 concerns non-judicial remedies for non-performance, including suspension of performance, rejection of the goods and avoidance of the contract, and reduction of the price for non-conforming goods. Chapter 5 concerns judicial remedies, including specific performance and damage awards.

* * *

A. OTHER COUNTRIES HAVE DIFFERENT LAWS THAN WE DO—FOREIGN LAWS AND COMPARATIVE LAW

If your potential client had negotiated to sell 500 electronic notepads to a buyer in Missouri, she and the buyer are unlikely to have bargained hard, if at all, over what law governs the sales contract. Drawing on your knowledge of Article 2 of the Uniform Commercial Code you will realize that the risk of surprise or disadvantage is slight. Article 2 will almost always govern and, with limited exceptions, the parties' agreement will displace the Code's provisions, as will the usages of the electronic notepad trade. If you are asked to memorialize the transaction, you will discover that your study of contract law, the Uniform Commercial Code, and all those legal writing exercises in Law School now pay dividends.

When, however, your potential client wishes to sell the same notepads to a buyer in France, the risks of surprise and disadvantage are higher. UCC Article 2, after all, is not the law outside the United States, no matter what your sales law instructor thought. Consider the expectations of the parties when the contract does not designate the law applicable to the contract. Your client undoubtedly expected that the contract would be governed by the UCC, if they thought about that problem at all. On the other hand, the French buyer expects the contract to be governed by French law. Is it different from the UCC, and the basic Common Law of contract? Why would the French law be different?

Most of you have spent your careers in law school studying many aspects of a single legal system. If you have studied the law of the United

States, for example, you will find the legal principles and rules of the Mexican legal system to be "foreign." To study the contract law of a Mexico is to study that system's legal principles and rules governing contracts as if you were a native of Mexico. To make a comparative study of Mexican contract law, you might compare the Mexican law with that of your own legal system. If you were trained in the methods of comparative law, you would typically look beyond formal legal concepts. You might look, for example, for functional equivalents or for an analysis of how each legal system solves a single hypothetical case.

* * *

R. DAVID & J. BRIERLY, MAJOR LEGAL SYSTEMS IN THE WORLD TODAY
17–29 (3d ed. 1985).*

SECTION II—THE IDEA OF A FAMILY OF LAWS

14. *Diversity of Contemporary laws*

Each political society in the world has its own law, and it often happens that several laws co-exist within the same state. Thus, in addition to a federal law there may be laws of states, provinces or districts as in the United States, Canada or Switzerland. There are moreover laws of communities that have no political organisation at all, such as Canon law, Muslim law, Hindu law and Jewish law. There is as well international law which attempts to govern relations between states and international commerce on a world-wide or regional scale.

The purpose of this book is to supply a guide for a first examination of these many laws for those who, whatever their reason, wish to be introduced to a particular foreign law. The very diversity of laws poses a problem which at first sight may appear insurmountable; since the laws of the world are expressed in many different languages and forms, and since they have evolved in societies where the social organisation, beliefs and social manners are so very different, how can they be satisfactorily presented in a work of this limited scope? There is a factor which simplifies the task. In law, as in other sciences, one can detect the existence of a limited number of types or categories within which this diversity can be organised. Just as the theologian or political scientist recognises types of religions or governmental regimes, so too the comparatist can classify laws by reducing them to a limited number of *families*. Without therefore attempting to explain the detail of each individual law, our objective can be carried out by limiting the discussion to those general characteristics of the several legal families to which, in the end, all contemporary laws belong. The idea of a family of laws and the definition of contemporary legal families in the world today must therefore be explained.

* * *

* * * What is asked, or should be asked, of the law student is not that he learn, by heart, and in all their detail, all the rules in force during his time as student: that will be of little service to him in his later professional life when many of those rules will have changed. Of far greater importance to the student will be a knowledge of the structure within which the rules and concepts are organised, the meaning of these categories and concepts, and the relationship of the rules among themselves. The legislators may, indeed, with a stroke of the pen modify the actual legal rules, but these other elements and features nonetheless subsist. They cannot be so arbitrarily changed because they are intimately linked to our civilisation and ways of thinking. The legislators can have no more effect on them than upon our language or our reasoning processes.

Despite changes in the rules as they exist at any moment, then, there is a continuity in the law which draws upon a range of elements subjacent to those rules. The work of the American Roscoe Pound (1870—1964) has made this especially clear. The sense of historical continuity which these elements engender enables us therefore to consider law as a science and makes possible the teaching of law.

16.   *Criterion for the classification of laws into families*

When endeavouring to determine the families into which different laws can be grouped, it is preferable to take into consideration these constant and more fundamental elements rather than the less stable rules found in the law at any given moment. There is agreement among comparatists on this point. The classification of laws into families should not be made on the basis of the similarity or dissimilarity of any particular legal rules, important as they may be; this contingent factor is, in effect, inappropriate when highlighting what is truly significant in the characteristics of a given system of law.

These characteristics can be identified by examining those fundamental elements of the system through which the rules to be applied are themselves discovered, interpreted and evaluated. While the rules may be infinitely various, the techniques of their enunciation, the way in which they are classified, the methods of reasoning in their interpretation are, on the contrary, limited to a number of types. It is therefore possible to group laws into "families" and to compare and contrast them when they adopt or reject common principles as to substance, technique or form.

This grouping of laws into families, thereby establishing a limited number of types, simplifies the presentation and facilitates an understanding of the world's contemporary laws. There is not, however, agreement as to which element should be considered in setting up these groups and, therefore, what different families should be recognised. Some writers base their classification on the law's conceptual structure or on the theory of sources of the law; others are of the view that these are technical differences of secondary importance, and emphasise as a more significant criterion either the social objectives to be achieved with the help of the legal system or the place of law itself within the social order.

* * *

SECTION III–LEGAL FAMILIES IN THE WORLD TODAY

17. *Outline*

What, then, are the major contemporary legal families found in the world today?

There would appear to be three at least which occupy an uncontested place of prominence: the Romano–Germanic family, the Common law family and the family of Socialist law. These three groups, whatever their merits and whatever their extension throughout the world, do not however take into account all contemporary legal phenomena. There are other systems, situated outside these three traditions or sharing only part of their conception of things, which prevail in a large number of contemporary societies and in their regard too a number of observations will be made.

18. *Romano—Germanic family*

A first family may be called the Romano–Germanic family. This group includes those countries in which legal science has developed on the basis of Roman *ius civile*. Here the rules of law are conceived as rules of conduct intimately linked to ideas of justice and morality. To ascertain and formulate these rules falls principally to legal scholars who, absorbed by this task of enunciating the "doctrine" on an aspect of the law, are somewhat less interested in its actual administration and practical application—these matters are the responsibility of the administration and legal practitioners. Another feature of this family is that the law has evolved, primarily for historical reasons, as an essentially *private* law, as a means of regulating the private relationships between individual citizens; other branches of law were developed later, but less perfectly, according to the principles of the "civil law" which today still remains the main branch of legal science. Since the nineteenth century, a distinctive feature of the family has been the fact that its various member countries have attached special importance to enacted legislation in the form of "codes."

The Romano–Germanic family of laws originated in Europe. It was formed by the scholarly efforts of the European universities which, from the twelfth century and on the basis of the compilations of the Emperor Justinian (A.D. 483–565), evolved and developed a juridical science common to all and adapted to the conditions of the modern world. The term *Romano–Germanic* is selected to acknowledge the joint effort of the universities of both Latin and Germanic countries.

Through colonisation by European nations, the Romano–Germanic family has conquered vast territories where the legal systems either belong or are related to this family. The phenomenon of voluntary "reception" has produced the same result in other countries which were not colonised, but where the need for modernisation, or the desire to westernise, has led to the penetration of European ideas.

Outside Europe, its place of origin, these laws although retaining membership in the Romano–Germanic family nonetheless have their own characteristics which, from a sociological point of view, make it necessary to place them in distinct groups. In many of these countries it has been possible to "receive" European laws, even though they possessed their own civilisations, had their own ways of thinking and acting and their own indigenous institutions, all of which ante-date such reception. Sometimes the reception has left some of these original institutions in place; this is particularly clear in the case of Muslim countries where the reception of European law and the adhesion to the Romano–Germanic family have been only partial, leaving some legal relations subject to the principles of the traditional, local law. The old ways of thinking and acting peculiar to these countries may also mean that the application of the new law is quite different from what it is in Europe. This question is particularly important in the case of the countries of the Far East, where an ancient and rich civilisation existed long before the reception of western law.

Finally, with respect to the countries of Africa and America, it will also be necessary to ask whether their geographical conditions and population distribution, creating conditions entirely different from those in Europe, have not led to the development of laws substantially different from their European models.

19. *Common law family*

A second family is that of the Common law, including the law of England and those laws modelled on English law. The Common law, altogether different in its characteristics from the Romano–Germanic family, was formed primarily by judges who had to resolve specific disputes. Today it still bears striking traces of its origins. The Common law legal rule is one which seeks to provide the solution to a trial rather than to formulate a general rule of conduct for the future. It is, then, much less abstract than the characteristic legal rule of the Romano–Germanic family. Matters relating to the administration of justice, procedure, evidence and execution of judgments have, for Common law lawyers, an importance equal, or even superior, to substantive legal rules because, historically, their immediate preoccupation has been to re-establish peace rather than articulate a moral basis for the social order. Finally, the origins of the Common law are linked to royal power. It was developed as a system in those cases where the peace of the English kingdom was threatened, or when some other important consideration required, or justified, the intervention of royal power. It seems, essentially, to be a *public* law, for contestations between private individuals did not fall within the purview of the Common law courts save to the extent that they involved the interest of the crown or kingdom. In the formation and development of the Common law—a public law issuing from procedure—the learning of the Romanists founded on the *ius civile* played only a very minor role. The divisions of the Common law, its concepts and vocabulary, and the methods of the Common law lawyer, are entirely different from those of the Romano–Germanic family.

And as with the Romano–Germanic family, so too the Common law has experienced a considerable expansion throughout the world—and for the same reasons: colonisation or reception. The observations made with respect to the Romano–Germanic family apply with equal value. But here again a distinction between the Common law in Europe (England and Ireland) and that outside Europe must be made. In certain extra-European countries, the Common law may have been only partially received as in the case, for example, of certain Muslim countries or India; and where it was received, attention must be given to its transformation or adaption by reason of its co-existence with the tradition of previous civilisations. A different environment has, in any event, created differences between the Common law of the countries where it originated and that of those into which it was imported. This observation is particularly true with respect to the Common law family because it groups some countries such as the United States and Canada where a civilisation different in many respects from that of England has developed. The laws of these countries enjoy a largely autonomous place within the family.

20. *Relations between these two families*

Over the centuries there have been numerous contacts between countries of the Romano–Germanic family and those of the Common law, and the two families have tended, particularly in recent years, to draw closer together. In both, the law has undergone the influence of Christian morality and, since the Renaissance, philosophical teachings have given prominence to individualism, liberalism and personal rights. Henceforth, at least for certain purposes, this reconciliation enables us to speak of one great family of *western* law. The Common law retains, to be sure, its own particular structure, very different from that of the Romano–Germanic system, but the methods employed in each are not wholly dissimilar; above all, the formulation of the legal rule tends more and more to be conceived in Common law countries as it is in the countries of the Romano–Germanic family. As to the substance of the law, a shared vision of justice has often produced very similar answers to common problems in both sets of countries.

* * *

22. *Other systems*

* * *

In non-western societies the governing social principles to which reference is made are two types. On the one hand law is fully recognized as being of great value but the law itself is framed in a different concept than it is in the West; on the other, the very notion of law is rejected, and social relations are governed by other extra-legal means. [The author then discusses Muslim, Hindu and Jewish laws as examples of the former, and Far Eastern, African and Malagasy societies as examples of the latter.]

NICHOLAS, INTRODUCTION TO THE FRENCH LAW OF CONTRACT

Contract Law Today: Anglo–French Comparisons,
7–15 (D. Harris and D. Tallon, eds., 1989).*

SOME CHARACTERISTICS OF FRENCH LAW

1. *Civil Law and Common Law.* If an English lawyer sets out to identify the characteristics which differentiate French law from his own system, he is likely to start from the proposition that French law belongs to that family of legal systems to which he habitually attaches the name "Civil Law". As a matter of history the name indicates a common inheritance from Roman law. Although the inheritance was never more than partial and was greatly attenuated by the interposition of the Napoleonic codification in 1804, it still constitutes, particularly for the Common lawyer, who lacks any similar inheritance, an important identifying feature. Its importance is seen at two levels. The framework or conceptual structure of French law, as of other Civil Law systems, is obviously Roman, both at the general level of the division into the law of persons, property, succession, and obligation and more particularly (but to a varying extent) within each part. The Roman contribution is indeed largest in the part with which this volume is concerned; the law of contractual obligations, for the codification of which Napoleon's compilers relied heavily on Pothier.

* * *

2. *Codification.* The second characteristic to which the English lawyer is likely to point is that French law codified. It has been remarked above that the Napoleonic codification stands between modern French law and its (partially) Roman origins, and 1804 did indeed mark the beginning of a new era in the sense that all previously existing sources of law became of historical interest only. But in a more fundamental sense the character of the law was not changed by the codification. A codified system differs from the Common Law in that in principle the whole law is to be found in the codification (and such supplementary legislation as may be enacted), whereas the Common Law is never complete, but is in a state of continuous creation. In this sense French law suffered no abrupt change in 1804. The previous law had been seen as in principle complete-embodied in Justinian's *Corpus iuris civilis* and the relevant customs (which had for the most part been set down in writing) and legislation. It was in principle a law embodied in a book. What changed in 1804 was the nature of the book.

This view of the law as in principle complete manifests itself in other characteristic features. The Holmesian view of the Common Law as predictions of what the courts will do contains an element of truth, as a reading of opinions given by counsel will demonstrate, but it is quite alien to the tradition of French law, which sees the law as a set of universally valid precepts, not as a mosaic of solutions to particular disputes. This can equally be expressed in the familiar contrast between a system of rules and a system of remedies. Neither system of course thinks exclusively in terms of one or the other, but the emphasis is clear, and when the Common Law does think in terms of rules, they are seen as generalizations from the solutions of particular disputes, not as independently valid precepts.

3. *"Doctrine."* The contrast between "book-law" and "case-law" is reinforced by a difference as to how the creative function in law is seen and where it is located. The only directly creative function in French law is, it is true, located in the legislature (or, under the constitution of the Fifth Republic, in the rule-creating power of the Executive), but the indirectly creative function of interpretation is conventionally located in *doctrine* or the body of writing about the law by those learned in it. As the literal meaning of the word would suggest, *doctrine* originated in the teaching of the universities from the Middle Ages onwards and it is still overwhelmingly the province of academic writers. It Is they who expound, elaborate, and develop the law and, at the level of the particular instance, it is often to them that recourse will be had by practitioners for an authoritative opinion. Their standing in the scale of authority is therefore quite different from that of their counterparts in England. * * * [I]f one looks merely at the text itself, one sees that the very simplicity and brevity of the Code and its lack of the kind of rigorously exact (and therefore technical) language which is used by, for example, the German Civil Code could only enlarge the need for creative interpretation which exists in any body of law. Not only are rules usually set out in very loose and general terms, but the structure of principles which the rules presuppose is either left to be inferred or very highly sketched in. * * *

4. *Case–Law.* It has been remarked above that at the particular level of the giving authoritative opinions the function of the doctrinal writer in France is exercised by counsel in England. At the general level of the articulation and elaboration of the law in authoritative writings, the doctrinal function is to a considerable extent discharged in England by the courts in their lengthily argued judgments. That the courts do not play a similar part in France is attributable, on the one hand, to the standing in the scale of authority which has been attributed to them since the Revolution and, on the other hand, to the form in which their judgments are cast.

One of the legacies bequeathed by the Revolution to French constitutional thinking has been a vigorous rejection of "government by judges", whether in the form of judicial review of legislation or of administrative action or in the form, which here concerns us, of the power to make law by judicial decision. Article 5 of the *Code civil* lays down that: "The judges are forbidden to make pronouncements or a general and normative kind *(prononcer par voie de disposition générale et réglementaire)* on the cases brought before them." It is in accordance with this rule that constitutional theory still declares that judicial decisions *(la jurisprudence)* cannot be a source of law. Until quite recently the treatises of doctrinal writers would state the law as a matter either of interpreting legislative texts or of reasoning from the web of principle which is seen as underlying those texts and would advert to the decisions of the courts in order to note the extent to which they were or were not in harmony with the law which had been so stated. The modern style is much closer to that to which an English lawyer is accustomed, in the sense that the *jurisprudence* is included among the data of which account must be taken in any statement of the law, but the primacy still lies with the texts and their doctrinal interpretation. And the proposition that *jurisprudence* is not a source of law still has practical consequences. Some are formal or technical. A court may not cite as the justification for its decision a previous decision or line of decisions, even though every lawyer knows that that is in fact the justification and indeed that the previous decisions were cited in the argument of the case. Conversely, when the Cour de cassation quashes a decision as being in conflict with its own *jurisprudence,* it will nevertheless make no reference to that *jurisprudence,* but will simply cite the text or principle on which the *jurisprudence* was based. A more practical consequence is found in the attitude to precedent or the courts themselves. Whereas an English judge accepts that he is bound by the decisions of the courts above him and that he will be justifiably criticized if he departs from them, the French judges' attitude is different. They will accept that it is desirable that precedent should be followed, if only because it is important that the law should be stable and predictable, but their overriding duty is to apply the law and the law cannot, in view of article 5, be contained in the decisions even of the Cour de cassation. If therefore the judges of a lower court are convinced that *the jurisprudence* of the Cour de cassation is wrong, they will ignore it, and they will be regarded as justified in so doing. (As to the powers of the Cour de cassation in such circumstances, see below, para. 8.) Such resistance by lower courts, though exceptional, is not very uncommon and may lead to a change of heart by the Cour de cassation itself.

The doctrinal function of articulating and elaborating the law is therefore in principle denied to the courts by their constitutional position since the Revolution, though the creative importance of *jurisprudence* in practice is now fully recognized. But even if the courts were inclined to usurp the doctrinal function, they could not do so without radically changing the form in which their decisions are cast. This form is the polar opposite of that of the digressive, argumentative English judgment, directed to assessing the arguments put before the court and justifying by reasoning from authority and from policy the decision reached. The French judgment *(arrêt)* takes the vigorously pruned form of a single (even if lengthy) sentence which, after citing one or more legislative texts, states a principle from which, by syllogistic reasoning applied to the facts, the decision is then logically derived. The principle is, ostensibly at least, derived from the text or texts, but it is presented as self-evident and usually no attempt is made to justify or explain the act or derivation or to relate the decision reached to other decisions in apparently analogous situations. Thus, in the extreme case in which the Cour de cassation is reversing a previous line of decisions, the only sign of the change may be found in some alteration of the formulation of the governing principle. Similarly, even where there is no question of a reversal, some small change in the formulation of a principle which has served perhaps through dozens or hundreds or previous *arrêts*, or some particular emphasis in the way in which the facts are stated, may reveal a development in the thinking of the court. The interpretation of *arrêts* calls therefore for skill, experience, and an eye for the nuances of language. The application of these qualities is, again, a function of *doctrine*. In particular, those decisions which are reproduced in the published reports are often accompanied by quite lengthy and elaborate "notes", written by academics or sometimes by practitioners or even judges.

* * *

5. *The primacy of legislation.* This is related to, but not identical with, the character of French law as a codified system. The English lawyer admits the primacy of legislation in the sense that, where legislation conflicts with the Common Law, legislation must prevail, but legislation is nevertheless seen as an exception to or suspension of the Common Law. For the French lawyer, however, legislation has a much more fundamental primacy. For him law is typically a body of enacted rules. He has no conception of a residual, all-pervading common law as the presupposition of any legislation.

This difference of approach has two consequences which will strike an English lawyer. In the first place the restrictive method of interpretation traditionally adopted by the English courts has no place in France and, as a corollary of this, the style of drafting is usually much freer and less detailed than the English (a characteristic found also in the legislation of the European Community, as the English courts have had occasion to notice). On the other hand, it may be that more detail is consigned to administrative enactments. The second consequence is that the French lawyer sees the enacted law (as the English lawyer sees the Common Law) as having an intellectual coherence and fertility of its own. In the Codes, for example, an article will be interpreted in the light not only of its place in the whole plan of the Code, but also of the meaning or purpose of particular articles in a quite different part. In the traditional view legislation is seen as a manifestation of the will of the State and as having therefore an appropriate unity of intention. Nor is this approach confined to the Codes. Interpretation of more particular legislation may extrapolate from the specific instance expressly provided for to other related instances or may infer some underlying principle or policy.

6. *Fact or law, discretion or rule.* We have seen that French law is in principle a complete system embodied in rules which are typically expressed in broad and general terms, whereas the Common Law is the result of a continuing process of evolution from particular cases (and, for the reason set out immediately above, statutory rules also are usually detailed). This difference in the scales on which the rules are formulated is reflected in a difference in the areas appropriated to fact and law respectively in the two systems. The *Code civil*, for example, contains no rules on offer and acceptance. The detailed rules which the English courts have evolved have as their counterpart in the Code simply article 1108, which lays down that the consent of the party to be bound is one of the essentials of a valid contract. Whether or not in a particular case there has been the requisite consent (and when and where it was given) is a matter for the judges of fact to decide: and since the Cour de cassation, whose function it is to maintain the uniformity of the law, has no jurisdiction in matters of fact, there is no scope for facts to harden into law, as happens in a case-law system. This at least is the position in principle, but the Cour de cassation does not always remember the restriction on its jurisdiction.

7. *Conceptualism or pragmatism.* * * * The English lawyer is inclined to believe that the French are excessively "logical" in the sense that they are given to what in recent years has come to be labelled, rather misleadingly, formalism. This is an approach which applies principles to cases regardless of the practical consequences or rather which is unwilling to re-examine the established interpretation of those principles in the light of the consequences or of changed perceptions of the desirability of the consequences (in other words, of changes in policy). The form of the French judgment does indeed lend support to this view, since it appears to apply a principle mechanistically without consideration of consequences or policy; but the form is misleading: the considerations which moved the court are simply not expressed. * * *

* * * Because French law, at least as presented in the *Code civil*, is a complete and internally coherent system, any part of which may, as we have seen, illuminate any other part, and because the principles or rules are broadly formulated and therefore call for more elaborate ratiocination when they are applied, the French lawyer undoubtedly sets greater store by the intellectual coherence of his system and by the elegant manipulation of large-scale concepts than does his English counterpart.

8. *The court system.* The French system of courts is markedly different from the English. It is, in the first place, much less centralized (and there are many more courts). * * *

This brings us to the second main difference. A *cour d'appel* re-examines the whole case before it (a proceeding which is greatly facilitated by the predominantly written character of French procedure), but the Cour de cassation can review only questions of law and can only either reject the complaint (*pourvot*) or quash the decision of the court below. It may not substitute its own decision. If it quashes the decision, the case is remitted to another court of equal jurisdiction. If that court takes the same view of the law as the original court and there is a renewed *pourvot*, the matter goes before a special sitting of the Cour de cassation at which all chambers are represented. This *Assemblée pléniére* may (if the issues are the same as in the original hearing) either decide the case or remit it to a third court, which is then bound by the view of the law taken by the *Assemblée*. The primary function of the Cour de cassation is therefore to ensure a uniform interpretation of the law and for this reason any litigant is free to bring his case to the court on a point of law; no leave is required. In consequence the court has to deal with an annual flood of cases (and is able to do so only because the proceedings are almost entirely written) and is, in the opinion of its critics, severely hampered in its other function or guiding the development of the law.

A third difference lies in the "collegial" character of all courts except those tribunals of first instance which deal only with cases involving small sums. An old maxim says "juge unique, juge inique", and courts consist of at least three judges (at least five in the Cour de cassation). They are, moreover, collegial also in the sense that the decision is that of the court: dissenting opinions are unknown and the secrecy of the voting is strictly maintained. This in turn is related to another feature which may be called the anonymity of the French judiciary. The collegial character of the courts' decisions and the extreme economy of the form in which they are expressed offer no scope for the identification of particular judges with particular views. And this "low profile" is in keeping both with the constitutional position of the judiciary and with its social position. The judicial career, begun after graduation from a university and proceeding by orderly promotion, is not unlike that of a civil servant (with the important qualification that a judge enjoys a constitutional guarantee of irremovability). Moreover, collegiality, coupled with the large number of courts, calls for a great many judges.

As far as the volume and the cost of litigation are concerned, no statistically reliable comparison with England and Wales is available, but an impressionistic conclusion is that small claims are more frequently litigated in France.

2. MAIN DIVISIONS OF FRENCH LAW

* * *

10. *Public and private law.* Public law regulates the organization of the State (constitutional law) and the relations between the State—and institutions deriving from it—and private individuals (administrative law). The practical importance of the distinction between private law and administrative law lies not only in the differences in their content, but, more fundamentally, in the fact that they are in principle applied by two entirely separate hierarchies of courts. It is one of the lasting

legacies of the Revolution that the ordinary courts are forbidden to interfere with the activities of administrative authorities and it was in order to fill the gap thus left in the rule of law that there evolved the administrative jurisdiction or the Conseil d'État and the courts deriving from it.

In the present context the important consequence is that contracts to which a public body is a party and which satisfy certain other requirements as to their public character are governed by public law Public law is almost entirely based on the decisions or the Conseil d'État. * * *

11. *Civil and commercial law.* This division is less far-reaching. No single statement of the scope of commercial law can be accurate, but it applies in principle to commercial transactions (*actes de commerce*), of which the *Code de commerce* contains a list (e.g. contracts of sale if the subject-matter is bought for resale; the hiring out of moveables by way of business; banking, brokerage, and discount operations; bills of exchange), and it applies also to other transactions entered into by merchants (defined as those who make it their profession to engage in *actes de commerce*), provided that the transactions are accessory to their commercial activities.

* * *

Commercial litigation is the province at first instance of special commercial courts, composed of unpaid lay judges, elected for two-year periods by, and from among, the members of the local community of merchants. There is not, however, a totally separate hierarchy of courts. Recourse from the *tribunaux de commerce* is by the ordinary route to the *cours d'appel* and the Cour de cassation (which, as we have seen, has a commercial chamber).

Nor is commercial law a separate and self-contained system. The *Code de commerce* regulates some *actes de commerce*, lays down some special rules for all such *actes*, and imposes some particular duties on merchants, but otherwise the applicable law will be the ordinary civil law. A commercial contract of sale, for example, is in general governed by the same rules as a non-commercial sale. The important consequences of the distinction between civil law and commercial law are now in fact mainly to be found in the jurisdiction and simplified procedure of the *tribunaux de commerce* and in the readier admission of oral evidence of commercial transactions. Nevertheless, doctrinal writing observes the distinction, and the treatment of the principal commercial contracts usually therefore finds no place in the treatises or courses on the civil law which form the centre-piece of the exposition of the private law. The French student's introduction to contract is not therefore, as is his English counterpart's, in terms of the typical business contracts, but looks rather to the transactions of everyday life.

J. BELL, S. BOYRON, & S. WHITTAKER, PRINCIPLES OF FRENCH LAW
310–14 (1998).*

Article 1108 of the Civil Code requires four conditions for the validity of an agreement:

(1) the consent of the party undertaking an obligation;

(2) his capacity to contract;

(3) a certain *objet* which forms the subject matter of the undertaking

and

(4) a legal *cause* of the obligation.

We shall look at each in turn (except capacity) but add a brief discussion as to the role of formality. At this stage it should be noted that there is no conceptual and (arguably) no functional equivalent of the doctrine of consideration.

A. Consent and Agreement

In French law, it is customary to distinguish two elements here: that there be a meeting of minds of the parties—an *accord de volontes*—whose aim is the creation or modification of contractual obligations and, secondly, that each party's consent be free from defect.

* * * [W]e find French texts explaining that agreements should be If analysed in terms of offer and acceptance and these elements have (to a common lawyer) recognizably familiar definitions: an offer is said to be a firm and sufficiently detailed indication of a willingness to contract (as contrasted with an invitation to treat); an acceptance to be its recipient's free, informed and unqualified acquiescence (as contrasted with a rejection or counter-offer). Despite French law's concern for the parties' actual or subjective intentions (*volontes internes*), at this stage in their analysis the jurists accept that what is required are *manifestations* of these intentions, whether oral, in writing or by conduct: only if there is discordance between a manifested and an actual intention does the latter become potentially significant. However, differences do exist on a closer look.

As regards offers, French law does not possess *rules* dictating whether, for example, an object displayed in a shop-window at a price does or does not constitute an offer for its sale: it *may* constitute an offer and often will, subject to any evidence as to the intentions of the parties. It is, moreover, clear that an offer is capable of acceptance during any period for which it is so expressed or, in the absence of such expression, for a reasonable period in the circumstances. The position as regards revocation of offers is less clear. Some jurists say that an offeror is obliged to maintain an offer for any expressed time or, in its absence, for a reasonable time and that therefore it may be accepted despite any attempted revocation; others that this result should occur only where the period for reply is expressed, in other cases the offeree being restricted to a claim for damages for delictual fault, and others that a prematurely revoked offer should give rise only to such a claim for damages. For a common lawyer, these views are most striking in their assumptions that a promise to keep an offer open should be adhered to in the absence of any return (so as to provide consideration) and that (absent contract) liability in delict may play a supporting role.

As we have said, a court may find that a person has accepted an offer where he has made clear his unqualified acceptance of it and the time when this occurs may be affected by custom in the particular context. It is noticeable, however, that although French lawyers recognize the special difficulties which arise in relation to acceptance of offers made *inter absentes* and whether an offeree's silence may constitute acceptance, the courts have not established any firm legal rules governing these situations. Thus, as regards acceptances made *inter absentes,* the Cour de cassation has generally accepted that the time or place of acceptance (whether at posting or receipt at the offeror's address) is a matter for the *pouvoir souverain d'appréciation* of the *juges du fond.* Having said that, however, there seems to be a preference both in the courts and the jurists for placing acceptance at the time and place of sending.

On the other hand, it is clear that in general French law does not allow an offeree's silence to constitute acceptance, but it *may* do so in some circumstances where it "in the context as a whole indicates a view which is capable of interpretation." This is clearest where the parties have had relevant previous dealings or where the custom of the context in which they contract allows silence to constitute assent. Most controversially, however, the Cour de cassation has on the odd occasion (and they have on occasion been rather odd) allowed the lower courts to find that an offeree's silence *was* acceptance where the offer was made "in his exclusive interest", an approach which has been called infrequent, contested and artificial and paradoxically cannot apply to offers of gifts which the Civil Code requires must be expressly accepted.

It has been said that the acceptance must be "informed", but this does not mean that the offeree must actually know *all* the terms of the offer before a contract is made or before these terms form part of the contract, but rather that they should be brought effectively to the offeree's attention, the courts taking a hostile view to terms on the reverse of documents or in documents appended. So, French law accepts in principle that a person who signs a contractual document without reading it is bound by its terms, but makes exceptions where the terms are unusual or not clearly portrayed, notably in standard-form contracts.

* * *

3. *Agreements which are not contracts*

Although contracts are agreements in French law, not all agreements are contracts, but only those which create or modify a person's *obligations*. It is for this reason that it excludes purely social agreements, such as an accepted dinner invitation, from contract (termed *actes de courtoisie*). More difficult, however, are cases involving the gratuitous performance of services, such as giving a person a lift in one's car or giving a person first-aid (even if one is a doctor). Generally, the courts have refused to see these types of case as contractual, with the result that any claims for harm caused by the provider of the service are a matter for delict. On the other hand, the courts have sometimes found that a person who rescues another from danger or attempts to catch an escaping thief does so under a "contract of help" (*convention d'assistance*) though it is often argued that these sorts of cases are also better dealt with either through delict or "unrequested intervention" (*gestion d'affaires*). Finally, the status of "gentlemen's agreements" is uncertain in French law, for although the courts have accepted that agreements which are expressed to be binding in honour only will not be treated as contracts when made between members of a family or between friends, in other circumstances they nevertheless enforce them, seeing them as an illegitimate attempt to escape the legal consequences of agreements which have been made.

NICHOLAS, INTRODUCTION TO THE FRENCH LAW OF CONTRACT
Contract Law Today: Anglo–French Comparisons,
15–19 (D. Harris & D. Tallon, eds. 1989).*

3. MAIN FEATURES OF THE LAW OF CONTRACT

13. *Obligations*. Obligations are those rights *in personam* (and their correlative duties) which are of economic value, as opposed, for example, to conjugal or parental rights. Together with rights *in rem*, which are the subject matter or the law or property (*biens*), they constitute a person's patrimoine or economic assets. Obligations derive from four sources: contract and quasi-contract, which cover roughly the same area as in English law, and delict and quasi-delict, which correspond to the law of torts (excluding of course those aspects which concern the law of property). To a greater extent therefore than in English law contract and tort are seen as forming one category and on occasion it may not be clear whether a decision of a French court is based on one or the other. The blurring of the distinction is made easier by the fact that liability under both heads can be seen as resting in principle on fault (see below, para. 16). On the other hand, in one respect the distinction is made more sharply in French law: a party to a contract may not in general opt to sue in delict for damage arising out of the contractual relationship.

14. *Autonomy of the will and* consensus ad idem. The classical French treatment of contract is in terms of free will. Just as legislation is a

manifestation of the will of the State, so also a contract is a particular law made by the parties for themselves by the conjunction of their wills. The function of the general law is to give effect to this particular law, subject only to such restrictions as are necessary in the public interest. It is evident that this doctrine or the autonomy of the will has affinities, though at a less abstract level, with the classical English doctrines of *consensus ad idem* and *laissez-faire*. In France, as in England, the doctrine has been attacked, but without giving place to any clearly established alternative.

As far as the Code is concerned, what is required (by article 1108, above. para. 3) is "the consent of the party who places himself under an obligation" (the other requirements being capacity, an object, and a cause, as to which see below, para. 17). In the typical bilateral or synallagmatic contract, of course, both parties are under an obligation. So far there is no significant difference from English law, but the English lawyer will find that the French give a more subjective meaning than he does to the requirement of consent. In the analysis of offer and acceptance, for example, French law is more likely to see an offer than an invitation to treat in displays of goods in shop windows or in catalogues or on the shelves of supermarkets. The argument for this view is that the display indicates a continuing intention to sell and therefore that the buyer's manifestation of a will to purchase must immediately complete the contract. English law, by contrast, invokes arguments from convenience for delaying the moment of completion. Similarly, in the matter of revocation, the decision in *Dickinson v. Dodds*, which causes difficulty in English law, is easily acceptable to the French. Again, in the law of mistake the test applied is subjective. "Substance" is defined as those qualities which determined the consent of the mistaken party.

15. *Nominate and innominate contracts.* Although French law starts from a definition of contract in terms of consent, it also inherits from Roman law a system of specific or named contracts (sale, hire, etc.), the normal incidents of which are laid down by law. Thus, the *Code civil* devotes 121 articles to regulating the contract of sale and another 124 to different varieties of the contract of hire. But the doctrine of the autonomy of the will emphasizes the individual's freedom to make other "innominate" contracts, the terms of which derive, in principle, entirely from the parties' wills. The "nominate" contract, however, is the norm and the French lawyer's first step in interpreting a contract is to "qualify" or characterize it, i.e. to determine whether it falls within the limits of one of the nominate contracts. Even when it does not precisely correspond to any of those contracts, the court may well interpret it by analogy to one or more of them.

The existence of these standard rules for the most common contracts is reconciled with the principle (above, para. 14) that the parties are free, subject only to restrictions in the public interest, to make any contract they wish, by recourse to a distinction between rules which apply only in the absence of contrary intention by the parties (*lois supplétives*) and those which concern the public interest and therefore cannot be excluded (*lois impératives*). The great majority, of course, fall into the former category.

English law frames what are in substance *lois supplétives* as implied terms (e.g. in the Sale of Goods Act) and this reflects a fundamental difference of approach. Whereas French law begins by "qualifying" a contract in order to discover the rules applicable to it, English law starts from the general principle and, even where it has isolated typical contracts, such as sale or partnership, it expresses what are in substance their rules as implied terms.

16. *Fault liability and absolute liability.* It can indeed be said more generally that where English law resorts to the device of the implied (or imputed) term, French law is likely to have recourse to a rule. Liability in contract in French law rests, at least on one view, on fault whereas in the Common Law it is in principle absolute, in the sense that, subject to the qualifications deriving from the law or frustration, a party is liable for failure to perform regardless of whether the failure was in any way attributable to him. In practice, however, the two systems reach much the same results. Fault liability is introduced into English law via an implied term requiring due care and French law limits the role of fault by classifying contractual obligations broadly under two heads. A contract may impose on a party either an obligation to take reasonable steps to perform what he has undertaken (*obligation de moyens*) or an obligation to achieve the result which he has promised (*obligation de résultat*). Thus, a doctor is not under an obligation to cure his patient, but is bound only to do his best to that end, whereas it is settled that a contract of transport imposes on the transporter an *obligation de résultat* to carry the person or goods safely. (It must be added, however, that the obligation is still not absolute: the party bound can escape liability by showing that his failure was due to a cause outside his control, but the burden is on him. The parallel to the absolute liability of the Common Law is found in a third category, the *obligation de garantie*, which is imposed, for example, on a seller for latent defects.)

17. *Absence of a doctrine of consideration.* The most obvious difference between the two systems lies in the absence from French law (as, of course, from all non-Common Law systems) of any requirement of consideration for the validity of a contract. In principle any seriously intended agreement is binding, even if it consists only of a gratuitous promise by one party, accepted by the other. Similarly, a contract may be discharged or modified by simple agreement. Nor is the place of consideration taken by any general requirement or formality. There is, it is true, a requirement that a *donation* (i.e. an agreement for the gratuitous transfer of property, including money) shall be made in a formal document drawn up by a notary, but the rule does not apply to gratuitous promises generally and the original reason for it was a desire to protect the family patrimony from the generosity of its present owner, not a general hostility to gratuitous contracts. (The courts have largely deprived the rule of practical effect.) In so far as there is any general

restraint on the enforceability or gratuitous promises, it seems to reside in the imprecise requirement that the agreement must be seriously intended.

It is sometimes thought that the doctrine of cause (for the exposition of which there is no space here) performs a function akin to that of consideration in determining whether or not an agreement is binding in law. This is, however, a misconception. Cause serves rather the purposes of denying validity to those contracts which pursue an illicit or immoral purpose and of ensuring that in a synallagmatic or bilateral contract the obligations of the parties are interdependent. It also performs a function similar to that discharged by consideration in the doctrine of total failure of consideration.

As a matter of terminology it is important for an English lawyer to know that the French "unilateral contract" denotes an agreement which creates only rights in one party and duties in the other, as in the case of a gratuitous promise to pay money (by contrast with a synallagmatic or bilateral contract, which creates rights and duties in both). On the other hand, a unilateral contract in the English sense, i.e. a promise in return for an act, can be enforceable in French law only if it can be said, however artificially, to conform to the definition of a contract as an agreement, i.e. if the offer is accepted. And it will then be a bilateral, not a unilateral, contract.

* * *

PROBLEM 1–1:

1. Can you apply the concepts from these excerpts from Bell and from Nicholas to a fact situation? For example, can you determine whether a sales contract has been formed in a relatively common fact pattern? For example, suppose the following three communications were exchanged by Alpha and Santa Claus in attempting to establish a documentary sale contract. Would they have formed a contract: a) at Common Law? b) under the French Civil Law concepts described by Bell and by Nicholas?

2. At Common Law, Form 1 would probably be a request for an offer, Form 2 would be an offer, and Form 3 would be either the acceptance of that offer or a counter-offer. Form 2 gives two different price quotations, each dependent upon the type of delivery term the buyer wants. Form 3 is probably an acceptance, although it is arguable that "Delivery required prior to July 1," or the "request" for an order acknowledgment, are additional terms which make it a rejection and a counter-offer. [The reference to 110% insurance coverage is not a different term, under INCOTERMS.] Note that there is not even a need to analyze any "consideration" issues, or the Statute of Frauds. That is typical in any commercial contract.

3. Under French Civil Law, Nicholas states the requisites as "the consent of the party who places himself under an obligation," "capacity, an object, and a cause." Is there sufficient evidence of consent to their

obligations by both parties in Forms 1—3? Does Nicholas give you enough information to analyze this issue?

There seems to be no significant "capacity" issue, as long as that has its tradition meaning at Common Law, and does not mean "authority"—i.e., are the employees who sign the communications duly authorized by their employers to bind the employers to such contracts. What is the "object" of this contract? What is its "cause?"

If a contract is formed, is it "nominate" or "innominate?" (See ¶ 15.) How would you determine whether Santa Claus has undertaken an obligation de moyens, an obligation de résultat, or an obligation de garantie? (See ¶ 16.)

FORM 1. LETTER FROM BUYER REQUESTING
PROFORMA INVOICE

ALPHA COMPANY

ATHENS

GREECE

April 1, 2000

Santa Claus Company
Main Street
East Aurora, New York 14052

Gentlemen:

We have visited your booth at the Nürnburg Toy Fair and now wish to give you our order. We require a Proforma Invoice, four copies, for the following:

Item 930—Play Family Garage	252 Pieces
Item 942—Play Family Lift & Load	252 Pieces
Item 300—Scoop Loader	360 Pieces
Item 313—Roller Grader	360 Pieces
Item 307—Adventure People & Their Wilderness Patrol	360 Pieces
Item 936—Medical Kit	360 Pieces
Item 993—Play Family Castle	225 Pieces

Please indicate your best price and delivery, including export packing, C.I.F. Athens, Greece. Prices and terms should be quoted firm for a period of 90 days.

Yours very truly,
ALPHA COMPANY

Alexandros Pappas

FORM 2. PROFORMA INVOICE

SANTA CLAUS COMPANY

EAST AURORA, NEW YORK

Alpha Company
Athens, Greece

April 13, 2000

PROFORMA INVOICE NO. G-12

Your Ref. No.:   Your letter of April 1, 2000
Price: Net, including export packing, CIF Athens, Greece
Payment Terms: Confirmed Irrevocable Letter of Credit confirmed by U.S. bank and calling for payment against documents in New York City in U.S. funds.
Shipment: Approximately 15 days after receipt of your order and Confirmed Irrevocable Letter of Credit.
Estimated Total Weight: 9,633 Lbs.   4369.576 Kgs.
Estimated Measurement: 2102.4 Cu. Ft.   59.53 M3

QUANTITY	DESCRIPTION	UNIT PRICE U.S. $	AMOUNT U.S. $
252 Pcs.	930 Play Family Garage	$10.95	$ 2,759.40
252 Pcs.	942 Play Family Lift & Load	10.95	2,759.40
360 Pcs.	300 Scoop Loader	5.25	1,890.00
360 Pcs.	313 Roller Grader	4.25	1,530.00
360 Pcs.	307 Adventure People & Their Wilderness Patrol	8.75	3,150.00
360 Pcs.	936 Medical Kit	6.65	2,394.00
225 Pcs.	993 Play Family Castle	12.95	2,913.75

TOTAL PRICE F.O.B. EAST AURORA, NEW YORK $17,396.55
INLAND FREIGHT TO NEW YORK CITY $ 500.00

OCEAN FREIGHT N.Y.C. TO ATHENS, GREECE $ 2,044.00
FORWARDING FEES $ 45.00

INSURANCE $ 87.00

TOTAL PRICE C.I.F. ATHENS, GREECE $20,072.55

THE PRICES QUOTED ABOVE ARE FIRM FOR 90 DAYS AFTER THE DATE OF THIS PROFORMA INVOICE

SANTA CLAUS COMPANY

RACHEL SMITH
EXPORT MANAGER

FORM 3.   PURCHASE ORDER
ALPHA COMPANY

ATHENS, GREECE

April 26, 2000

Santa Claus Company

East Aurora

New York

Re: Our Purchase Order 1234

Your G-12

Gentlemen:

Please supply in accordance with your Proforma Invoice No. G-12 the following:

252 Pcs.	930	Play Family Garage	@ $10.95 each
252 Pcs.	942	Play Family Lift & Load	@ $10.95 each
360 Pcs.	300	Scoop Loader	@ $ 5.25 each
360 Pcs.	313	Roller Grader	@ $ 4.25 each
360 Pcs.	307	Adventure People & Wilderness Patrol	@ $ 8.75 each
360 Pcs.	936	Medical Kit	@ $ 6.65 each
225 Pcs.	993	Play Family Castle	@ $12.95 each

Total Price

C.I.F. Athens, Greece $20,072.55

Delivery required prior to July 1, 1995

Insurance to be covered by yourselves at 110% C.I.F. value.

Import License No. 143210

MARKS:

ALPHA CO.

ATHENS, GREECE

ORDER NO. 1234

MADE IN U.S.A.

NOS. 1/UP

We have instructed our bank, COMMERCIAL BANK OF GREECE, in Athens to open the Letter of Credit per your Proforma Invoice through the Marine Midland Bank Western in Buffalo.

We would appreciate receiving your order acknowledgement by early mail.

Very truly yours,

Alpha Company

_____

Alexandria Pappas

SPANOGLE, THE ARRIVAL OF INTERNATIONAL PRIVATE LAW

25 Geo. Wash. J. Int'l I. & Econ. 477 [1991].*

* * * [There is a] difference between the use of language in the drafting styles of statutes in common law and civil law jurisdictions. The difference is easily perceived by comparing a statute enacted in a common law state with one enacted in a civil law state. An overdramatized, but illustrative, comparison would be: the civil law product will be shorter and contain fewer definitions, more ambiguities that have been left for solution by judicial construction, and statements of general application which overlap and contain conflicts that have no formal resolution. The common law product will begin with a multitude of formal definitions and then state a great number of long and detailed specific provisions including rules that are restricted so that there is no intentional conflict, although unintentional conflicts may remain.

There are at least two underlying reasons for these differences: one conceptual and one arising out of the typical drafting process. Conceptually, the twentieth century statutes in both common law and civil law jurisdictions rest on a foundation of nineteenth century law. But the foundations are different, common law being composed of case law and civil law of a very general civil code. The civil code covers, from a modern perspective, very limited subject matter, and supplementation is expected. Case law, however, grows by analogy and is infinitely expansive as to subject matter.

When a twentieth century, or any other, statute is used to supplement common law case law, this addition is an alien growth on the foundation, and its "differentness" is expected to be emphasized. Thus, most statutes in a common law jurisdiction are drafted to stand alone. Such statutes can restate existing decisions, as far as the drafters understand them, or contradict them and even preempt future decisions; there is no need for them to "fit" the current case law doctrines. However, if statutes do contradict or even preempt case law doctrines, they must do so with exquisite clarity. In the past, any statute considered "in derogation of the common law" was construed "strictly." Thus, the statute drafters must specify those provisions that may contradict or modify case law concepts with so much clarity that the common law courts *cannot* "misconstrue" the intended result. Such a drafting technique requires concreteness of expression and great precision—which, in turn, requires great detail. On the other hand, the drafter has great flexibility, can easily use totally new concepts, and may seek the precise result desired.

The civil law statute, whether arising out of the French or German tradition, is expected to fit harmoniously with the foundation civil code and the other more basic codes. To be successful, it must not be alien to its foundation but must look like a new branch of the same tree— venturing into new areas, but utilizing the same methodology, and attempting to avoid any contradiction of well-settled rules.[106] Thus, it is always preferable to take a known concept from other subject matter areas and modify it to furnish basic provisions than to create a new concept that might conflict with prior accepted doctrine. Further, the style of the new statute will replicate that of the civil code, with concentration on general statements that overlap and with no formal resolution of the resulting conflicts. This system of drafting, using general statements of basic doctrines, allows courts to use the whole body of civil law to resolve clashes of competing interests.

This conceptual basis for different drafting styles is buttressed by the differences in the typical processes of drafting statutes practiced in the different types of jurisdictions. The common law "ideal"[107] is to sit two dozen attorneys around a table, each one representing a different set of interests, and have them negotiate until all conflicts are resolved. They are expected to do this on an issue-by-issue basis and to concentrate on what result is desired in practical problem situations which are likely to arise. All resulting compromise decisions should be spelled out in complete detail, leaving as little as possible to discretionary decision by the court.

In contrast, the civil law ideal, again overdramatized, is for one most acclaimed professor of law to draft a set of general legal principles to govern the development of the law of the new subject matter. This should be done without receiving briefs or drafts from advocates representing any of the private interests that will be affected by the new statute. The primary concern is to ensure that the provisions of the statute are extensions of the doctrine of prior codes and that the statute provides general guidance to courts and laymen, not that it foresees and forestalls the machinations that might be practiced by the devious in actual commerce. Skillful interpretation by the courts, not always literal, of the entire body of codified law is expected to deal with such machinations.

The substantive international private law conventions produced by the international organizations are a compromise between these two drafting styles. The first draft, usually produced by the Secretariat, will often resemble the civil law drafting style, but with one significant difference. Such drafts are usually drafted with a concentration on what result is desired in practical problem situations that are likely to arise;

---

106. Such avoidance can be a major undertaking especially when, as in the French civil code, there are pocket parts to the code provisions that include case reports.

107. These common law and civil law "ideals" have been deliberately overdrama-

tized and are not necessarily accomplished in practice for either system, but they should help to illustrate the differences as to how drafters perceive that statutes should be drafted.

that difference from civil law drafting practice will never be lost. Because the proposed convention will be expected to fit into the context of many, widely-varying legal regimes, extensions of current doctrines cannot be its primary concern. In fact, drafts of such conventions are more likely to adopt totally new doctrines and language to signify that their concepts are not derived from the doctrines of any particular legal system.[108] These conventions adopt new legal concepts, and the common law drafting style is initially more suited to handling the introduction of new doctrines.

The drafting process itself has the impact of pushing the drafting style of the conventions even further toward the common law standard of drafting. As the delegates debate the specific issues raised by a provision, they will reach a series of compromises concerning them, each with a set of details. These issues are normally debated in the context of developing a preferred result to a series of practical problem situations, so the details are set forth with clarity to reflect accurately the distinctions recognized in striking the compromises. The addition of such details reflects the common law approach to drafting, setting forth determinations issue by issue and assuming that the statute must stand alone. Thus, the longer a convention is in the drafting process, the more its drafting style is likely to reflect common law techniques.[111]

B. WHAT DOES AN INTERNATIONAL SALE OF GOODS TRANSACTION LOOK LIKE?

These course materials focus on the 1980 United Nations Convention on Contracts for the International Sale of Goods. During the course of the semester you will consider difficult questions of legal interpretation and construction. Before considering these *legal* questions, however, you should have some familiarity with how the transnational sale works in practice. The following excerpt illustrates both what is done and why it is done in a particular way in the transaction (described in Problem 1—1), when it is completed without any legal dispute arising.

* * *

If the sale in Problem 1—1 took place, how would each of the parties perform the obligations they have undertaken? In particular, what does

---

108. For example, in article 79 of the CISG, the drafters deliberately used the requirement of "impediment beyond his control" for excuse of a failure to perform, rather than any of the known terminology, such as "frustration," *imprevision* "failure of presupposed conditions," or "impracticable," in common usage in different domestic law provisions.

111. * * *
It should be noted that the drafting style of many *modern* civil law statutes—especially in the fields of taxation and environmental law—more closely resembles its common law counterparts. However, these are not private law statutes, but public law, and therefore are drafted, at some point in the process, by representatives of different interests negotiating specific issues and striking compromises. These compromises, in turn, are presented through concrete and detailed language. This public law process indicates that statutes in civil law jurisdictions can and will be drafted with the detailed style of common law statutes if they are drafted by a group that acknowledges that it includes representatives of different competing interests.

it mean to have payment by a "Confirmed Irrevocable Letter of Credit," and what steps do buyer and seller have to take to establish such a "letter"?

R. FOLSOM, M. GORDON & J.A. SPANOGLE, INTERNATIONAL BUSINESS TRANSACTIONS

35–60 (4th ed., 1999).*

The international trading community * * * has sought to avoid large and uncertain risks by creating devices which break them down into many small and measurable risks. That is what the documentary transaction is all about. For example, the letter of credit is a device to assure that seller will be paid upon shipment of the goods. However, there are interrelationships which must be understood. Thus, use of a documentary transaction to assure payment upon shipment may deprive the buyer of its ability to inspect the goods before payment—but a third-party Inspection Certificate may re-establish buyer's position.

How is a documentary sale set up by the parties? To explain this process, the remainder of this introduction will trace such a sale of toys between the Santa Claus Company of East Aurora, New York, and Alpha Company of Athens, Greece.* * *

PART B. *THE SALES CONTRACT*

* * * The initial contact is Form 1, a letter sent by Alpha, the buyer, to Santa Claus, the seller, requesting a price quotation. Alpha could send a simple letter asking for quotations from Santa Claus' price catalog; but, since this is a specialized sale, it will request a proforma invoice which should state the cost of each of the components of the international sale. In addition, Alpha's request can indicate sale terms which it prefers—e.g., payment and shipping terms, including the preferred method of handling insurance during transit.

Santa Claus' response is a Proforma Invoice, * * *. The "C.I.F." Price is the price of the goods delivered in Athens, the destination point. This price includes all of the factors included in "F.O.B. Port of New York City," and in addition the cost of ocean freight, handling fees of various types, and insurance covering the goods during the ocean voyage. "C. & F." would be the price term used if Alpha did not want Santa Claus to purchase insurance coverage during that voyage. Under a contract using a C.I.F. or C. & F. price term, Santa Claus must bear the cost of the freight charges (and perhaps insurance as well). In addition, Santa Claus must also bear the risk of fluctuations in freight costs (and perhaps insurance also) until they arrive at their destination port. Thus, there are advantages to Santa Claus to quote prices "F.O.B. Santa Claus

Plant." However, a sales contract bearing a C.I.F. term requires buyer to pay when presented with documents—such as bills of lading—usually before the goods arrive, so there are also advantages to Santa Claus to sell on a C.I.F. basis.

After receipt of the Proforma Invoice, and comparison shopping, Alpha decides to purchase Santa Claus' toys. It therefore sends a Purchase Order (Form 3) which duplicates the pricing in the Proforma Invoice. The Purchase Order Form may or may not have a large amount of small print clauses set forth on the reverse side. If it does, a "Battle of the Forms" can arise. * * * Santa Claus' normal practice, in any event, is to acknowledge all purchase orders with an Order Acknowledgement Form, which repeats the terms of the Purchase Order. The Order Acknowledgement Form may or may not have large amounts of small print clauses on the reverse side. Again if it does, "Battle of the Forms" problems arise.

PART C. *LETTER OF CREDIT*

Both the Proforma Invoice and the Purchase Order state as the payment term "Letter of Credit." Payment through the letter of credit device assures Santa Claus of payment as long as it can demonstrate to a bank through appropriate documents that it has shipped the goods. Thus, Santa Claus will not risk rejection of the goods after they arrive in Greece, where it will be expensive and inconvenient either to reship or to resell.

A letter of credit is simply another contract—a promise by Buyer's Bank which runs directly to Seller that Buyer's Bank will pay the sales contract amount to Seller, if Seller produces the documents required by the sales contract which evidence that Seller has shipped the goods required by the sales contract (i.e., a negotiable bill of lading). Letters of credit may be revocable or irrevocable, but in a documentary sales transaction it is customarily understood that an irrevocable one is required. Letters of credit may also be either confirmed or not. A confirmed letter of credit includes a promise from Seller's Bank to Seller that Seller's Bank will pay the contract amount to Seller if Seller produces the required documents evidencing shipment of the goods. Thus, under a confirmed letter of credit, Seller has a promise from a local bank, before shipment of the goods, of payment if the goods are shipped.

To obtain a letter of credit, Alpha goes to its bank, The Commercial Bank of Greece, and requests it to issue a letter of credit in favor of Santa Claus. Alpha has done business with this bank for many years, and it knows Alpha's financial position, so no additional bank investigation is needed. However, if Alpha was a stranger to the issuing bank, the bank would investigate Alpha's credit standing, or even require it to provide sufficient funds to cover the amount of letter of credit. Alpha will also provide the Commercial Bank of Greece with a copy of its Purchase Order or the Proforma Invoice, so that the bank will know what documents are required by the contract. Commercial Bank of Greece then telexes its New York correspondent bank, Marine Midland Bank, advising the latter that it has opened a letter of credit in Santa Claus' favor, and stating all the details of the letter of credit contract.

Marine Midland Bank then contacts Santa Claus. If the letter of credit is not to be confirmed, then Marine Midland Bank will send Santa Claus an "Advice of Credit", notifying Santa Claus of the action taken by Commercial Bank of Greece. However, in this transaction Marine Midland Bank sends Santa Claus a Confirmed Irrevocable Letter of Credit. * * * Santa Claus' performance is specified in detail—the types of documents, originals or copies, the specific vessel, import license numbers, etc. However, if Santa Claus meets these detailed requirements it will be paid in dollars in the United States as soon as it ships the goods. * * * What has this letter of credit accomplished? Without this device, Santa Claus and Alpha, neither of which knows anything about the trustworthiness or credit standing of the other, are in a situation which seems to demand that one of them must trust or extend credit to the other. Either Santa Claus must ship, and then await payment; or Alpha must pay, and then await shipment and delivery of the goods.

After issuance of the letter of credit, Commercial Bank of Greece has promised to pay Santa Claus when presented with the required documents, and that bank has the risk of Alpha's financial failure or refusal to perform the contract. However, Commercial Bank of Greece has a unique ability to evaluate Alpha's credit standing, and can enforce contract obligations locally. Marine Midland Bank has also promised to pay Santa Claus against the required documents, and it has the risk of the financial failure, or refusal to perform, of Commercial Bank of Greece. However, Marine Midland Bank can obtain information on the financial standing of Commercial Bank of Greece with relative ease, and can enforce contract obligations through banking channels. Santa Claus now can ship the goods without having received any prior payment, but is at risk only if Marine Midland, Commercial Bank of Greece and Alpha fail financially or refuse to perform. Any refusal to perform by Marine Midland Bank is subject to enforcement through courts in the United States.

FORM 4.   LETTER OF CREDIT—CONFIRMED, IRREVOCABLE

Marine Midland Bank—Western   Letter of Credit # 34576
    Buffalo, New York   Issued on May 1, 1995
To: Santa Claus Company   From: Alpha Company
    East Aurora, New York   Athens, Greece

Gentlemen:

We are instructed by Commercial Bank of Greece, Athens, Greece, to inform you that they have opened their irrevocable credit in favor for account of Alpha Company, Athens, Greece, for the sum in U.S. dollars not exceeding a total of about $21,000.00 (Twenty One Thousand and $^{00}/_{100}$ Dollars), available by your drafts on the Commercial Bank of Greece, to be accompanied by:

1. Full Set On Board Negotiable Ocean Bills of Lading, stating: "Freight Prepaid," and made out to the order of Commercial Bank of Greece.

2. Insurance Policy or Certificate, covering Marine and War Risk.

3. Packing List.

4. Commercial Invoice in triplicate:

Covering 252 Pcs. 930 Play Family Garage
          252 Pcs. 942 Play Family Lift & Load
          360 Pcs. 300 Scoop Loader
          360 Pcs. 313 Roller Grader
          360 Pcs. 307 Adventure People & Their Wilderness Patrol
          360 Pcs. 839 Medical Kit
          225 Pcs. 993 Play Family Castle
Total Value $20,072.55 C.I.F. Athens, Greece
Import Lic. No. 143210, Expires July 13, 1995

5. Shipper's Export Declaration Partial Shipment Permitted. Transshipment Not Permitted. Merchandise must be shipped on SS Livorno.

All documents must indicate Letter of Credit No. 34576, Import License No. 143210, expires July 13, 1995.

All drafts must be marked "Drawn under Letter of Credit No. 34576, confirmed by Marine Midland Bank-Western". Drafts must be presented to this company not later than July 1, 1995.

This credit is subject to the Uniform Customs and Practices for Documentary Credits (1993 Revision) International Chamber of Commerce Publication No. 500.

We confirm the credit and thereby undertake to purchase all drafts drawn as above specified and accompanied by the required documents.

                    By:
                    International Credit Department

FORM 6.   COMMERCIAL INVOICE

SANTA CLAUS COMPANY
EAST AURORA, NEW YORK 14052

INVOICE

SANTA CLAUS COMPANY
EAST AURORA, NEW YORK 14052

D-U-N-S 00-210-1863

SOLD TO

ALPHA COMPANY
ATHENS
GREECE

Ship Date	Invoice No.
May 9, 2000	A-10

CONTAINER NO: XTRU #423890
LETTER OF CREDIT NO: 34576

SHIP TO

SAME

SHIPPING TERMS ARE C. I. F. FOREIGN
PORT OF ENTRY. TITLE TO THE GOODS
PASSES TO BUYER UPON DELIVERY OF
THE GOODS TO BUYER AT THE
PORT OF SHIPMENT.

Your Order No./Dept. No.	Store No.	Terms		Shipped Via	FRT. TO
1234		Conf Irrev L/C U.S. Funds		EXPORT MOTOR NEW YORK S.S. Livorno	NEW YORK to Athens

Our Order No.	Ship to Cust.	Bill to Cust.	Slsm
61245	0425	0426	

Item	Description	Pcs Ordered	Price Per Piece	Pieces Back Ord	Pcs Shipped	Amount	
930	Play Family Garage	252	10 95		252	$2,759	00
942	Play Family Lift & Load	252	10 95		252	2,759	00
300	Scoop Loader	360	5 25		360	1,890	00
313	Roller Grader	360	4 25		360	1,530	00
936	Medical Kit	360	6 25		360	2,394	00
993	Play Family Castle	225	12 95		225	2,913	75
307	Adventure People & their Wilderness Patrol	360	8 75		360	3,150	00

IMPORT LICENSE NO. 143210

TOTAL PRICE F.O.B. EAST AURORA, NY	17,396	55
INLAND FREIGHT TO N.Y.C.	500	00
TOTAL PRICE F.A.S. NEW YORK CITY	17,896	55
OCEAN FREIGHT - N.Y.C. TO ATHENS, GREECE	2,044	00
FORWARDING FEES	45	00
TOTAL PRICE C & F ATHENS, GREECE	19,985	55
INSURANCE	87	00
TOTAL C.I.F. ATHENS, GREECE	20,072	55

THESE COMMODITIES LICENSED BY
U.S.A. FOR ULTIMATE DESTINATION
GREECE. DIVERSION OR RE-EXPORT
CONTRARY TO U.S. LAW PROHIBITED.

CERTIFIED TRUE AND CORRECT AND
OF U.S. MANUFACTURE

SANTA CLAUS COMPANY
EAST AURORA, N.Y.

Rachel Smith
RACHEL SMITH
EXPORT MANAGER

	Cartons	Pounds			
File All Claims For Damage or Shortage with Delivering Carrier	513	9633	2102.4 CuFS	20,072	55

[D4663]

FORM 10. BILL OF LADING

INTERNATIONAL BILL OF LADING
NOT NEGOTIABLE UNLESS CONSIGNED "TO ORDER"

(2) SHIPPER/EXPORTER (COMPLETE NAME AND ADDRESS) SANTA CLAUS COMPANY EAST AURORA, NEW YORK 14052	(5) BOOKING NO (5A) BILL OF LADING NO A-10 (6) EXPORT REFERENCES
(3) CONSIGNEE (COMPLETE NAME AND ADDRESS) TO ORDER OF SHIPPER	(7) FORWARDING AGENT F M C NO F.W. MYERS (ATLANTIC) & CO., INC. One World Trade Center New York, New York 10048 (212) 432-0670 (8) POINT AND COUNTRY OF ORIGIN EAST AURORA, NEW YORK FMC 1397
(4) NOTIFY PARTY (COMPLETE NAME AND ADDRESS) ALPHA COMPANY ATHENS GREECE	(9) ALSO NOTIFY · ROUTING & INSTRUCTIONS notify on arrival in NYC Mr. J. Emma Phone 432-0670 for pier delivery instructions EXPORT MOTOR FREIGHT TO DELIVER TO PIER DOCK RECEIPTS LODGE AT PIER
(12) PRE-CARRIAGE BY ✱ EXPORT MOTOR FREIGHT (13) PLACE OF RECEIPT BY PRE-CARRIER ✱ EAST AURORA, NY	
(14) VESSEL VOY FLAG SS LIVORNO (15) PORT OF LOADING NEW YORK	(10) LOADING PIER/TERMINAL Pier 29, Black Ball Terminal (10A) ORIGINAL(S) TO BE RELEASED AT
(16) PORT OF DISCHARGE ATHENS (17) PLACE OF DELIVERY BY ON-CARRIER ✱	(11) TYPE OF MOVE (IF MIXED, USE BLOCK 20 AS APPROPRIATE)

PARTICULARS FURNISHED BY SHIPPER

MKS & NOS./CONTAINER NOS. (18)	NO OF PKGS (19)	HM	DESCRIPTION OF PACKAGES AND GOODS (20)	GROSS WEIGHT (21)	MEASUREMENT (22)
K ALPHA CO. ATHENS, GREECE ORDER NO. 1234 Made in U.S.A. NOS. 1-513			CONTAINER XTRU STC: 513 Cartons Childrens Toys IMPORT LICENSE #143210 Letter of Credit #34576 CLEAN ON BOARD G-DEST	9633 lbs.	2102.4 C.F.

These Commodities Licensed by the U.S. for Ultimate Destination   GREECE
Diversion Contrary to U.S. Law Prohibited.

23) Declared Value $ _____ If shipper enters a value, carriers package limitation of liability does not apply and the ad valorem rate will be charged.

(23A) RATE OF EXCHANGE   (24) FREIGHT PAYABLE AT/BY

TP	RATED AS	PER	RATE	PREPAID	COLLECT	LOCAL CURRENCY
	TOTAL CHARGES					

☐   If this box is checked, goods have been loaded, stowed and counted by Shipper. Carrier has NOT done so and is not responsible for accuracy of count, condition or nature of goods described in PARTICULARS FURNISHED BY SHIPPER

THE RECEIPT, CUSTODY, CARRIAGE AND DELIVERY OF THE GOODS ARE SUBJECT TO THE TERMS APPEARING ON THE FACE AND BACK HEREOF AND TO CARRIER'S APPLICABLE TARIFF

In witness whereof three (3) original bills of lading all of the same tenor and date, one of which being accomplished the others to stand void, have been issued by the originating carrier for and on behalf of itself other participating carriers, the vessel and her master and owners or charterers

Dated ....

At ....

.... Originating Carrier

By ....

BILL OF LADING NO   DATE   ✱ APPLICABLE ONLY WHEN USED FOR MULTIMODAL TRANSPORTATION

PART D. *SELLER SHIPS THE GOODS*

After receipt of the letter of credit, it is Santa Claus' duty to manufacture, crate, and ship the goods. The actual details of arranging the shipment will usually be handled by a "freight forwarder." However,

Santa Claus must give detailed instructions to the forwarder. It will send to the forwarder a Letter of Instructions, and some required documents, such as the Commercial Invoice (Form 6), the Packing List and the Shipper's Export Declaration. It will also provide the forwarder with documents required by the government, even if not specifically mentioned in the letter of credit, e.g., Certificate of Origin.

Once the forwarder has made arrangements, Santa Claus can have the goods transported to Carrier's pier. Carrier's clerk will then issue a Dock Receipt which covers the goods until the named vessel arrives. When the vessel arrives, the goods are loaded on board, and carrier then issues a "bill of lading" (Form 10) covering them. The forwarder prepares the bill of lading by filling in the blanks on a standard form created by Carrier. Forwarder fills out the form stating the description of the goods and the description, markings and weight of the crates or containers as directed by Shipper's Letter of Instructions, so that the bill of lading conforms to the requirements of the letter of credit. Carrier prepares the basic, printed language of the bill of lading, for it is also the contract between Carrier and Santa Claus.

Carrier promises to take the goods to a named destination, and Santa Claus promises that carrier's fee will be paid. If the freight is "prepaid," Santa Claus has paid it before shipment; if it is "collect," buyer is to pay it before receiving delivery. The bill of lading is to state which arrangement is made, and the sale contract should state which arrangement is to be made. If the bill of lading is "non-negotiable," Carrier promises to deliver the goods only to the person named as cosignee in the bill of lading, or to a person named by the consignee. If the bill of lading is "negotiable," Carrier promises to deliver the goods only to the person who is in possession of the bill of lading, properly indorsed. Thus, with a negotiable bill of lading, control of the bill itself is the equivalent of control of the goods—for the Carrier may not deliver the goods without first obtaining the surrender of the bill of lading. It should be understood that a letter of credit transaction requires a negotiable bill of lading.

Note that the bill of lading may be stamped "Clean On Board." Carriers can also issue "Received for Shipment" bills of lading, but they do not evidence that the named vessel has arrived at the time that the bill of lading is issued, or that the goods have survived the risk of being loaded on board the vessel. The sales contract or letter of credit will often call for "Clean on Board" bills of lading.

If the sales contract is C.I.F., Santa Claus must also procure, at its expense, insurance covering the goods during their transportation. In such a case, the letter of credit will require, as one of the necessary documents, an Insurance Certificate which states that all premiums are prepaid. The Insuror will limit its risks to a stated value, a named vessel, and transportation between designated places. Even if the sales contract is F.O.B. seller's plant, seller may still procure insurance to cover the goods during transportation (to protect buyer), but it is clear that seller may add the cost of any insurance to the price of the goods if it is prepaid. In any documentary transaction, the banks will usually insist on inclusion of any insurance certificate, to assure themselves that *their* security in the goods is protected from the perils during transportation.

Once Santa Claus has drawn a draft on Commercial Bank of Greece, how does it obtain payment? It uses the banking system as a collection agent. It takes the draft, together with all required documents (Forms 5, 6, 7, 11) to Marine Midland Bank. There it endorses both the draft and the negotiable bill of lading to the bank and presents all the documents to the bank. In the letter of credit, the bank said it would "purchase" such drafts, and it does so by paying Santa Claus—usually by crediting Santa Claus' bank account, either with Marine Midland Bank or with some other bank with which Santa Claus already has an account.

Marine Midland Bank will then endorse the draft and forward that draft, with the required documents attached, to Commercial Bank of Greece in Athens. This transaction is actually a "presentment for payment" of the draft to the Commercial Bank of Greece. Since there is already a correspondent bank relationship between the two banks, Commercial Bank of Greece will credit Marine Midland's account with the payment. Commercial Bank of Greece will then advise Alpha that the documents have arrived, and that payment is due under the letter of credit contract. Since Alpha and Commercial Bank of Greece have an established relationship, the usual course of events will be for the bank to be authorized to charge the amount of the draft to Alpha's bank account, and to forward the documents to Alpha. If Alpha has arranged for credit from Commercial Bank of Greece, the credit will be advanced when the draft and documents arrive. If there was not an established relationship between Buyer and its bank, Buyer would be required to pay (or to arrange sufficient credit for) the draft before the documents were released to it. As the draft and documents are forwarded from Santa Claus to Marine Midland to Commercial Bank of Greece, each of these parties will endorse the bill of lading (Form 10) to the next party. To better understand this transaction pattern, consult the diagram below.

When the goods arrive, Alpha uses the negotiable bill of lading, properly endorsed to it, to obtain the goods from Carrier. Note that Alpha has effectively paid for the goods while they were at sea, long before their arrival. In fact, Alpha was bound to pay for the goods as soon as the draft and required documents were presented to Marine Midland Bank. If the goods failed to arrive, Alpha must look to its Insurance Certificate for protection and reimbursement. When the goods arrive, Carrier may not release them to Alpha unless it is in possession of the negotiable bill of lading, properly endorsed *to* Alpha. Further, the terms of the bill of lading will prohibit Alpha from even inspecting the goods unless it has obtained physical possession of the bill of lading.

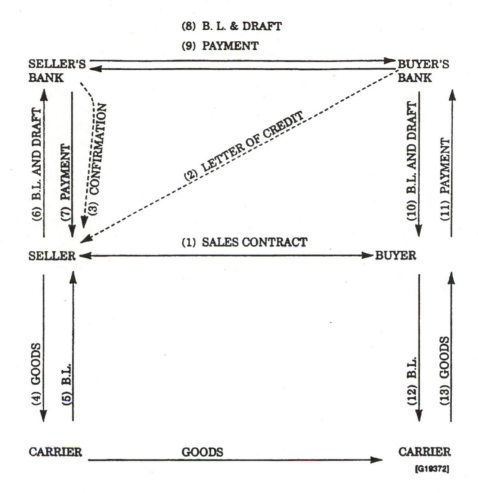

Thus, until Commercial Bank of Greece is satisfied that it will be paid by Alpha, it can control the goods by controlling the bill of lading.

Questions and Comments

* * *

3. An integral part of the Basic Transaction is the negotiable bill of lading (Form 10), for when Alpha pays "against the documents," and before inspection of the goods, this bill of lading is both its proof of shipment of the goods and the method of obtaining possession of the goods from the carrier after the arrival of the SS Livorno. The bill of lading must, therefore: (1) control ownership of the goods themselves, and (2) conform to the sales contract, especially in its description of the goods.

There are two different types of bills of lading—a "straight," or nonnegotiable, bill of lading, and an "order," or negotiable, bill of lading. (These are also known in the trade as "white" and "yellow" for the different colors of paper on which they are often printed.) Each usually represents the shipper's contract with the carrier, and expressly or implicitly will set forth the terms of that contract.

In the cash transaction, in theory, seller has control of the goods until payment is in hand, and buyer has control of the goods as soon as they are paid for. In reality, these measures of control are available only in the face-to-face exchange of goods between buyer and seller. In a documentary exchange, the only method available to seller to obtain equivalent control of the goods is first, for seller to maintain control of the bill of lading until the goods are paid for, and second, for possession of the bill of lading to control the goods themselves. If a straight bill of lading is used, the carrier must deliver the goods to the person named as consignee on the bill of lading, and possession of the straight bill of lading is irrelevant. Thus, straight bills of lading are not appropriate for a documentary transaction, and the case reporters are full of litigation where an attorney tried a short-cut using a straight bill of lading as the "easy" way to do this transaction—and sacrificed the client's interests.

On the other hand, the order, or negotiable, bill of lading requires the carrier to deliver the goods to the holder of the document. Thus, the seller can maintain control of the goods by obtaining a negotiable bill of lading to his own order, and then maintaining control over the document. By controlling the document, and thereby keeping control over the goods, seller can maintain an interest in the goods until buyer has "paid against the document."

There are other specific types of bills of lading which may be required by specific terms in the sale contract. For example, "F.O.B. vessel" in the sales contract requires, unless otherwise agreed, that seller obtain an "on board" bill of lading, stating that the goods have actually been loaded. On the other hand, "C.I.F." or "C. & F." in the sales contract is satisfied, unless otherwise agreed, by a "received for shipment" bill of lading, which does not state that the goods have been loaded.

4. To understand the collection transaction by the banking system, consult the flow chart on page 37. A confirming bank will purchase the documents, but an advising bank will usually take these documents "for collection", although it is also possible for the bank to "discount", or buy, the documents outright and become the owner. Seller's Bank is required to send the draft and its accompanying documents for presentment to the buyer which is usually done by sending them through "customary banking channels." Seller's Bank deals with "for collection" items individually, without assuming that they will be honored, and therefore without giving seller a provisional credit in the seller's account until the buyer pays the draft.

The draft, with its attached documents, will finally pass through "customary banking channels" to Buyer's Bank, which will notify the buyer of the arrival of the documents. Buyer's Bank will demand that the buyer pay the amount of draft. The buyer may require the bank to "exhibit" the documents to it to allow the buyer to determine whether they conform to the contract. The buyer has three banking days after the notice was sent to decide whether to pay, if mere notice is sent. However, if the documents are exhibited directly to the buyer, the buyer must decide whether to pay or not by the close of business on that same day, unless there are extenuating circumstances.

5.   Note the risks to each party. If the seller ships goods to a foreign buyer without setting up a full documentary transaction, including a letter of credit, he has shipped goods for which he has not yet been paid. Even if the contract provides for "payment against documents," and the seller obtains a bill of lading and forwards it to the buyer with a sight draft attached, the buyer might refuse to pay the sight draft, with documents attached, when it arrives. This would give the seller a cause of action, but often it is usable only in the buyer's jurisdiction, which means bringing a suit abroad with its extra expense, delay and uncertainty. In particular, a plaintiff could feel that it will be the target of discrimination in the courts of another nation.

The seller would still have control of the goods, because after dishonor of the draft the bill of lading will be returned to the seller. However, the goods would now be at a foreign destination—one at which the seller has no agents, and no particular prospects for resale. In addition, if the seller wished to bring the goods back to its base of operations (and normal sales territory), it would have to pay a second transportation charge, and this may be substantial in relation to the value of the goods.

Thus, the dishonor of the draft and rejection of the goods by the buyer can create economic circumstances where seller's only rational option is a distress sale in buyer's nation. It is to protect against that possibility that the letter of credit is used. Despite its fancy name, the letter of credit is just another contract—this time between Buyer's Bank and the seller. In this contract, Buyer's Bank promises to pay drafts accompanied by stated documents. The bank's promise is issued directly to the seller, and therefore is a direct obligation of that bank to the seller, regardless of what action the buyer may or may not take. Naturally, the bank will also have a contract with the buyer, to ensure that the buyer reimburses Buyer's Bank. The letter of credit can be revocable, but usually it is irrevocable (a "firm credit") because an irrevocable credit is more useful in calming the seller's fears concerning a wrongful rejection of the goods by the seller.

The requirement that the buyer provide a letter of credit is a term of the sales contract which must be separately bargained for and stated. If the sales of goods contract merely states "payment against documents," that does not establish a requirement for a letter of credit; that merely obligates buyer, not a bank, to honor the draft which accompanies the bill of lading. As pointed out above, the letter of credit term should specify not only the bank, but also precisely what documents are required for payment.

In many instances, the seller does not trust Buyer's Bank any more than the buyer. Buyer's Bank may be a foreign, state-owned bank, or a foreign, private bank, or simply a bank with which seller is not familiar. The seller wants the promise of a United States bank, preferably a known bank. In fact, the seller wants the promise of its bank that, if a presentation of certain documents is made, payment *will* be made. Seller can get such a promise by including a term in the sale of goods contract requiring a "confirmed" letter of credit, and specifying its bank as the "confirming bank." If Seller's Bank merely writes "confirmed" and its signature on

Buyer's Bank's letter of credit, that constitutes Seller's Bank direct obligation to the seller that it will pay the seller against the described documents. The seller will now have three independent promises to pay: (1) from buyer (sales contract), (2) from Buyer's Bank (letter of credit), and (3) from Seller's Bank (confirmation of letter of credit).

6.   Now, note how the risks of this international transaction between two people who know nothing about each other have been broken down and distributed to a party which has the ability to evaluate it with some degree of accuracy.

A.   If the buyer cannot pay (becomes insolvent) or will not pay (wrongfully rejects the goods), Buyer's Bank must still pay the seller against conforming documents. What protects Buyer's Bank? It has protection from the bill of lading and promises of other parties, including possible resale of the goods, but it is also in a particularly good position to investigate and to evaluate the risk of the buyer's insolvency, and to either obtain funds from the buyer when issuing the letter of credit or sue the buyer for breach of contract if there is a wrongful refusal to pay.

B.   If Buyer's Bank cannot or will not pay (in a confirmed letter of credit transaction), Seller's Bank has the credit risk concerning solvency of Buyer's Bank, which it can evaluate better than either the buyer or the seller, and concerning breach of contract, which, since it has multiple level relationships with Buyer's Bank, it is in a better position to induce compliance than the other parties. Thus, when the seller ships and procures conforming documents, there is a risk of nonpayment only if both Buyer's Bank and Seller's Bank fail.

C.   And, if Seller's Bank refuses to pay, the seller can deal with its personnel directly in resolving the dispute, or bring an action against it in United States courts.

One large risk has been reduced to several smaller ones, and each smaller risk placed on a party which can fairly evaluate it. The lack of substantial risk in the vast bulk of these transactions can best be seen by looking at the usual bank charges for this service.

7.   Under the foregoing analysis, the seller seems to have extensive protection: under a confirmed letter of credit, the seller has the separate promises of a local bank, a foreign bank, and the buyer that each will pay seller upon presentation of the required documents. The buyer has some protection, in that it need not pay until presentation of the documents—and the documents purport to evidence the shipment of the goods described in them. But, how well is the buyer protected? * * *

C. HOW CAN THE DIFFICULTIES CREATED BY DIFFERENT LEGAL SYSTEMS BE REDUCED?

If we go back to your potential client who wishes to sell 500 electronic notepads to a buyer in France, what difficulties can arise due to these differences between the U.S. and French legal systems?

Consider what happens when a dispute arises between the parties and the contract does not designate the law applicable to the contract. Because the parties did not choose the applicable law, the judge or arbitrator will have to do so. If the claim is brought before a French judge, he or she will use French choice-of-law rules—and these rules may be quite different from the choice-of-law rules that a U.S. judge would apply if the claim were brought before a U.S. court.[1] * * * Moreover, these non-uniform choice-of-law rules may point to domestic sales law. This sales law may not only be foreign in both substance and language, but may also be drafted without the transnational sales in mind.

It is with these possibilities in mind that you will analyze your client's claim. When you do so you will go through three steps. First, you will have to determine what forum will hear the claim. Only *after* the forum has been selected can you analyze the second step: whether U.S. law, French law, or some other country's law govern's the parties' rights and obligations. You must then construe the applicable law to predict how the dispute will be resolved by the judge or arbitrator. All three steps of the analysis are costly to carry out and subject to a greater possibility of error than if the transaction was a domestic sale governed by the Uniform Commercial Code.

Are these problems resolved if you have the parties designate U.S. law as the applicable law? A moment's reflection suggests that the answer is a qualified "no". Although the risk of non-enforcement is slight, you still must consider whether all possible fora will enforce the choice-of-law clause. Even if a French court would enforce the clause, would you feel comfortable having to prove the content (translated into French) of U.S. law to that court? Finally, consider your own professional responsibility. If French law gives greater protection to the seller than U.S. law does, have you necessarily advised a client properly if you have the parties designate U.S. law as applicable? Aren't you obliged, in other words, to know enough about the possible alternatives (e.g., U.S. law, French law) to advise a client on the best possible alternative? Given these considerations, of course, the practical problem is that the initial question assumes that you or the seller can persuade the French buyer to accept U.S. law as the applicable law. Remember that to the French buyer U.S. law and the Uniform Commercial Code will be unfamiliar and it will therefore probably prefer French law.

Your life, in other words, would be much simpler if U.C.C. Article 2—or some other uniform sales law—were the law in both the United States and France. Put another way, the non-uniformity of national sales laws creates "transaction costs" for international trade.

There are several possible ways to reduce, if not eliminate, these transactions costs.

---

1. These choice-of-law rules are part of national law. Indeed, in the United States a federal court will defer to the choice-of-law rules of the state in which the court sits. Choice-of-law rules themselves are subsets of conflict of law rules; jurisdiction and the enforcement of foreign judgments being the other subsets. In many other parts of the world, conflict of law rules are known as "private international law." This latter designation is misleading in that it suggests that these rules are a part of "international" law rather than domestic law. *See generally* E. Scoles & P. Hay, CONFLICT OF LAWS 1–3 (2d ed. 1992).

First, as just suggested, all the world's States might adopt a uniform sales law for transnational sales, or, more ambitiously, for both domestic and transnational sales.

Second, but more modestly, these same States might unify choice-of-law rules, thereby assuring parties that the same national sales law will govern no matter what forum considers the dispute.

Third, courts and arbitral tribunals might recognize and enforce a supranational "law merchant" (sometimes referred to as *lex mercatoria*) incorporating principles and rules of contract law tailored for international trade.

Finally, international traders themselves might develop standard form contracts or general conditions incorporated into their agreements.

These techniques, of course, are not incompatible with each other. International organizations concerned with elimination of these transaction costs, however, have tended to specialize in one or more of these techniques. The following paragraphs summarize some of the results.

1. *UNIFORM SUBSTANTIVE SALES LAW*

The International Institute for the Unification of Private Law (UNIDROIT) began work in 1929 on preparation of uniform substantive legal rules to govern international sales. Although the issue was hotly debated, the Institute decided for political reasons to limit the proposed unification to legal rules governing *international* sales rather than to sales law governing both national and international sales. A diplomatic conference meeting at The Hague in 1964 ultimately incorporated the Institute's work in two uniform sales laws appended to international conventions and usually known by the acronyms *ULIS* and *ULF*. These uniform laws dealt respectively with the formation of international sales contracts and the substantive rights and obligations of parties to such contracts. The United Nations Commission on International Trade Law (UNCITRAL), in turn, redrafted these 1964 texts and proposed a 1978 draft incorporating the substance of the two earlier uniform laws. This UNCITRAL text was the basis of the U.N. Convention on Contracts for the International Sale of Goods adopted at a 1980 diplomatic conference meeting in Vienna.[2]

Regional efforts to unify sales law have also been successful. Early in the 20th century, for example, the Scandanavian countries agreed to adopt a uniform sales law. More recently, they have amended this uniform law to conform with the 1980 Sales Convention. Prior to the events of 1989, Socialist States that were members of the Council for Mutual Economic Assistance had adopted "General Conditions of Delivery of Goods between Organizations of the Member Countries of the [CMEA]."

---

2. United Nations Convention on Contracts for the International Sale of Goods, *opened for signature* April 11, 1980, 19 I.L.M. 668 (entered into force January 1, 1988).

2. *UNIFORM CHOICE–OF–LAW RULES*

The Hague Conference on Private International Law also began work in the late 1920s on a proposal to unify choice-of-law rules for international sales, a project that led to a 1955 convention[3] and the 1986 Convention on the Law Applicable to Contracts for the International Sale of Goods. Although the former convention is in force it has had limited success; the latter convention is not yet in force. More successful has been the regional European Economic Communities Convention on the Law Applicable to Contractual Obligations, which came into force on January 1, 1991.[4]

3. *RULES OF THE "LAW MERCHANT"*

In the last 30 years legal writers in Europe have expressed great interest in the development of what they describe as a new "law merchant" or *lex mercatoria*. Relying especially on evidence in arbitral awards that arbitrators look to general principles of law for the resolution of contract disputes, these authors argue that there is now a body of supranational legal principles and rules that govern transnational contracts. Working against this background, UNIDROIT adopted *Principles of International Commercial Contracts*[5] in 1994. Although not in the form of an international convention, the UNIDROIT Principles might serve as the basis of a supranational "Restatement" of the *lex mercatoria*.

4. *STANDARD CONTRACTS AND GENERAL CONDITIONS*

Several trades actively engaged in international sales have developed standard contracts which are then adopted in whole or in part by traders who enter into these sales. The Grain and Feed Trade Association, for example, have developed such standard contracts widely used in the sale abroad of North American grain. Other trades have developed usages of trade that may not be codified or expressly incorporated in sales contracts although recognized by the parties.

States need not have any role in the development and enforcement of these standard contracts other than making available their courts for the enforcement of contracts or arbitral awards. In the 1950s, however, the United Nations Economic Commission for Europe prepared widely-used standard form contracts and general conditions for particular types of sale or for particular industries. After its creation in 1966, UNCITRAL also studied ways to encourage general conditions of sale and standard contracts.

---

3. Convention on the Law Applicable to International Sales of Goods, 510 U.N.T.S. 149 (1964).

4. Convention on the Law Applicable to Contractual Obligations, 1980, 23 *Official Journal of the European Communities*

L.266 (1980) entered into force on April 1, 1991.

5. UNIDROIT, *Principles of International Commercial Contracts* (1994).

NOTE, OVERVIEW OF THE U.N. SALES CONVENTION

The U.N. Sales Convention is a multilateral treaty to which the United States and 55[6] other countries are parties. The Convention entered into force on January 1, 1988. Being a treaty ratified by the United States on the advice and consent of the Senate, the Convention is the supreme law of the United States. U.S. Const. Art. VI. However, the Convention will rarely conflict with state law because the Convention only applies to *international* sales contracts. State law, including Article 2 of the Uniform Commercial Code, would not necessarily govern these international transactions because the Code is applicable only if choice-of-law analysis leads to U.S. state law.

The Convention covers (1) the formation of contracts for the international sale of goods, and (2) the rights and obligations of parties to these sales contracts. It expressly excludes from its coverage such important issues as contractual validity, the property consequences of a sales contract, and liability for death caused by a defect in the good sold. Moreover, the Convention only covers sales contracts. It therefore does not govern a number of contracts that are ancillary to an international sales contract: *e.g.*, distribution agreements, contracts of carriage and insurance, letters of credit, and dispute resolution clauses.

Like the legal rules in most domestic sales laws, the Convention's rules are "suppletory" rather than mandatory. Thus, even if a sales contract falls within the Convention's scope, the parties to the contract may agree to exclude the application of all or part of it. CISG art. 6. If, for example, the parties expressly agree on when the risk of loss shall pass, then the parties' agreement will displace ("derogate from") the Convention's provisions on this issue.

Uniform implementation is encouraged by the Convention's directive that regard is to be had to "the need to promote uniformity in ... application" when interpreting the Convention. CISG art. 7(1). This directive is particularly important because the official text is equally authentic in each of the six U.N. languages: Arabic, Chinese, English, French, Russian, Spanish.

To assist in the uniform application of the Convention, UNCITRAL has established a clearinghouse at its office in Vienna, Austria that publishes abstracts of cases under the acronym "CLOUT". A network of National Correspondents prepare the abstracts and submit copies of the cases to UNCITRAL. These abstracts are available in both a paper and an electronic form (http://www.un.or.at/uncitral/index.html). Several unofficial sources also make available these opinions. Transnational Pub-

---

6. As of May 18, 1999, the following 56 countries were parties to the Convention: Argentina, Australia, Austria, Belarus, Belgium, Bosnia & Herzegovina, Bulgaria, Burundi, Canada, Chile, China, Croatia, Cuba, Czech Republic, Denmark, Ecuador, Egypt, Estonia, Finland, France, Georgia, Germany, Greece, Guinea, Hungary, Iraq, Italy, Kyrgyzstan, Latvia, Lesotho, Lithuania, Luxembourg, Mexico, Moldova, Mongolia, Netherlands, New Zealand, Norway, Peru, Poland, Romania, Russia, Singapore, Slovakia, Slovenia, Spain, Sweden, Switzerland, Syria, Uganda, Ukraine, U.S.A., Uruguay, Uzbekistan, Yugoslavia, and Zambia.

lishers, Inc. publishes abstracts and opinions edited in English by UNI-LEX. The *Journal of Law & Commerce* publishes translations and comments annually. Opinions may also be found on the internet.[7]

NOTE: RESOURCE MATERIALS

The best longer introductions to the Convention are John O. Honnold, *Uniform Law for International Sales Under the 1980 United Nations Convention* (Deventer/Boston: Kluwer, 3d ed. 1999) and Peter Schlechtriem, *Commentary on the UN Convention on the International Sale of Goods (CISG)* (Oxford: Clarendon Press, 1998). A good short introduction is Joseph Lookofsky, *Understanding the CISG in the USA* (Deventer/Boston: Kluwer, 1995). Among the relevant internet sites, the CISG database of the Pace Law School International Institute of Commercial Law (http://cisgw3.law.pace.edu) is of particular importance.

The official proceedings of the 1980 diplomatic conference at which the Convention was adopted are published in *United Nations Conference on Contracts for the International Sale of Goods—Official Records* (1981) (Sales No. E.82.V.5). For an annotated collection of the documents that make up the drafting history, see John Honnold, *Documentary History of the Uniform Law for International Sales* (Deventer/Boston: Kluwer, 1989).

NOTE: WHY SHOULD YOU KNOW ABOUT
THE SALES CONVENTION?

There are several "professional responsibility" reasons for learning more about the Sales Convention.

Because parties may agree to exclude the Convention altogether, it has occasionally been suggested that attorneys should automatically advise clients to exclude the Convention. CISG art. 6. A moment's reflection upon your professional responsibility to your clients should suggest that this advice is simplistic. Even if your client has the market power to insist on having U.S. law govern the sales contract you should know enough about the Convention to determine whether state law (e.g., the Uniform Commercial Code) or the Convention better protects your client's interests. If your client is unable to dictate the choice-of-law term, you should, *a fortiori*, have a command of the Convention's advantages and disadvantages

To say that the Convention should not be excluded without study does not mean either that you should always select the Convention or that you should ignore the uncertainties inherent in a new law. Even proponents of the Convention concede that there will be uncertainties and these uncertainties will persist at least until there is a large body of both case law and doctrinal commentaries.

This fear of uncertainty, however, is often exaggerated. As more and more countries become parties to the Convention, for example, clients trading in numerous foreign countries may discover that it is more efficient

---

7. Pace Law School International Institute of Commercial Law–CISG Database: http://cisgw3.law.pace.edu; French cases: http://www.jura.uni-sb.de/ FB/LS/Witz/cisg.htm; German cases: http://www.jura.uni-freiburg.de/ipr1/cisg/; Italian cases: http://www.cnr.it/CRDCS/case_law.htm.

to have a single contract form governed by the Convention than several different contract forms governed by different national sales laws. Moreover, there will be times when neither trading partner is willing to have the law of the other party govern their contract. This may be the case especially with state enterprises from Third World countries or with enterprises in eastern Europe. The Convention may provide a suitable compromise because it is the domestic national law of neither party.

A second "professional responsibility" concern is more threatening: what is the responsibility of an attorney to his or her client when the attorney fails to recognize that the Convention may apply to a contract? Consider, for example, the following recent case

> *GPL Treatment, Ltd. v. Louisiana–Pacific Corp.,* 133 Or. App. 633, 894 P.2d 470, 26 UCC Rep. Serv. 2d 316 (1995), *aff'd,* 323 Or. 116, 914 P.2d 682 (1996) [CLOUT Case 137]

> Plaintiffs, three Canadian manufacturers and sellers of raw shakes (long wooden shingles), sued a U.S. corporation to recover damages for breach of alleged contracts for the sale and purchase of truckloads of cedar shakes. Defendant denied entering into these contracts. Defendant moved *in limine* for dismissal on the ground that plaintiffs failed to satisfy the writing requirement of the "statute of frauds" of the Uniform Commercial Code as enacted in Oregon. The trial court denied the motion. During the trial, the plaintiffs attempted to raise the issue of whether the CISG, rather than the UCC, governed, but the trial court ruled that plaintiffs' attempt was untimely and that they had waived reliance on that theory. The jury returned a verdict awarding lost profits to the plaintiffs and the trial court entered judgment on the verdict.

> Defendant appealed to an intermediate appellate court on the ground, *inter alia,* that the trial court had erred when it denied defendant's motion *in limine*. A majority of the three-judge appellate court found that plaintiffs had satisfied the UCC statute of frauds. The dissenting judge disagreed with the majority's analysis of the UCC as applied to the facts in the case. In a final footnote, the dissenting judge also stated that he would have addressed the issue of whether the trial court abused its discretion in its ruling on the applicability of the CISG.

> On appeal to the Oregon Supreme Court, the decision of the trial and intermediate courts were affirmed. The majority, concurring, and dissenting opinions do not address the issue of whether the CISG governed or whether the trial court abused its discretion.

Assuming that the purported sellers were Canadian companies and that the purported buyer was a U.S. corporation, there is little doubt that the Convention applied to the transaction. Article 11 of the Convention states expressly that "[a] contract of sale need not be concluded in or evidenced by writing. . . . It may be proved by any means, including witnesses." While it is possible to argue that the sellers implicitly excluded the Convention by filing a complaint with a reference to the Uniform Commercial Code (to which the buyer concurred by raising the statute of frauds defense), it is not clear that the attorney proceeded knowingly. Should such an attorney responsible ultimately for the costs of his or her clients' appeals on points of law that could have been avoided?

* * *

BRAND, PROFESSIONAL RESPONSIBILITY IN A TRANSNATIONAL TRANSACTIONS PRACTICE

17 J. Law & Com. 301, 335–36 (1998).*

A.   MUST A LAWYER INVOLVED IN NEGOTIATION OR LITIGATION OF A CONTRACT MATTER BE AWARE OF THE SALES CONVENTION?

This question is not a difficult one. The duty of competence set forth in Model Rule 1.1 clearly requires of a lawyer "the legal knowledge, skill, thoroughness and preparation reasonably necessary for the representation." Any lawyer involved in the negotiation or litigation of a contract for which the parties have their places of business in different countries has a duty to determine (1) whether two or more countries involved are contracting states to the Sales Convention, and (2) if one country is a party to the Sales Convention, whether that country has filed an Article 95 reservation to Article I(1)(b). If, as a result of either of these inquiries, the lawyer determines that the Sales Convention applies to the transaction, he or she then has a duty to understand fully the rules of the Convention and the application of those rules to the transaction in question. If the representation is in the context of negotiations, the lawyer is also responsible for determining and advising the client whether exercising the Article 6 possibility of "opting out" of the Convention rules would be to the benefit of the client. If the representation is in the context of litigation, the lawyer clearly has an obligation to know (1) whether the Convention applies to the transaction in question, and (2) if it does, the impact on his or her client of application of the Convention rules. The failure to understand and properly apply the Convention in regard to any of these obligations clearly constitutes a violation of Rule 1.1.

NOTE ON THE UNIDROIT "PRINCIPLES"

"UNIDROIT" is the short name used by the International Institute for the Unification of Private Law in Rome. The Institute is an inter-governmental body reestablished after World War II. Its mission is "to examine ways of harmonizing and co-ordinating the private law of States and groups of States, and to prepare gradually for the adoption by the various States of uniform legislation in the field of private law." The United States has been a member of the Institute since 1964.

The "Principles of International Commercial Contracts" are a restatement of the general principles governing transnational commercial contracts. The closest domestic analogy is the Restatement (Second) of the Law of

Contracts. Although inspired in part by the U.N. Sales Convention, the Principles are far more comprehensive. Drafted over a period of 20 years, the UNIDROIT Governing Council approved the Principles at its May 1994 meeting. The principal commentary may be found in M.J. Bonell, *An International Restatement of Contract Law* (2d ed. 1997).

The preamble to the UNIDROIT Principles sets out the purposes of the Principles and in doing so suggests when they may be relevant:

- [The Principles] shall be applied when the parties have agreed that their contract be governed by them.

- They may be applied when the parties have agreed that their contract be governed by general principles of law, the *lex mercatoria* or the like.

- They may provide a solution to an issue raised when it proves impossible to establish the relevant rule of the applicable law.

- They may be used to interpret or supplement international uniform law instruments.

The Principles are considered an outstanding success. Attorneys reportedly use the Principles as a guide in their contract negotiations and some even choose the Principles as the "applicable law." A growing number of arbitral awards refer to the Principles, while an impressive list of countries are taking the Principles into account as these countries revise their law of contracts. References in law school courses to the Principles have also proliferated—as have the number of scholarly studies analyzing the text.

The Governing Council of UNIDROIT has convened a working group to extend the Principles, *inter alia,* to agency, limitation periods, assignment, and contracts for the benefit of third parties. This working group met for the first time in March 1998.

M. J. BONELL, AN INTERNATIONAL RESTATEMENT OF CONTRACT LAW
65, 70–84 (2d ed. 1977).*

It was both the merits and the shortcomings of CISG which prompted UNIDROIT to embark upon a project as ambitious as the Principles. * * * [T]he decisive criterion in the preparation of the UNIDROIT Principles was not just which rule was adopted by the majority of countries ("common core-approach"), but rather which of the rules under consideration had the most persuasive value and/or appeared to be particularly well-suited for cross-border transactions ("better rule-approach").

* * *

Since the UNIDROIT Principles were not intended to become a binding instrument aimed at unifying national laws relating to international contracts, they were much less conditioned by the differences existing between the various legal systems. As a result, it was possible

---

* Copyright © 1977 and reproduced by permission from M.J. Bonell.

for them to address a number of matters which are either completely excluded or not sufficiently regulated by CISG.

Thus, in the chapter on formation, new provisions were included on the manner in which a contract may be concluded, on writings in confirmation, on the case where the parties make the conclusion of their contract dependent upon reaching an agreement on specific matters or in a specific form, on contracts with terms deliberately left open, on negotiations in bad faith, on the duty of confidentiality, on merger clauses, on contracting on the basis of standard terms, on surprising provisions in standard terms, on the conflict between standard terms and individually negotiated terms and on the battle of forms.

Further, a whole chapter on validity was added which moreover is not restricted to the classical cases of invalidity, *i.e.* the three defects of consent such as mistake, fraud and threat, but also addresses the much more controversial issue of "gross disparity".

Equally new are, among others, the *contra proferentem* rule, the provision on linguistic discrepancies and that on supplying an omitted term in the chapter on interpretation, the provision on implied obligations in the chapter on content; those on payment by cheque or other instruments, on payment by funds transfer, on currency of payment, on the determination of the currency of payment where it is not indicated in the contract, on the costs of performance, on the imputation of payments, on public permission requirements and on hardship in the chapter on performance; the provisions on the right to performance, on exemption clauses, on the case where the aggrieved party contributes to the harm, on interest rates and on agreed payment for non-performance in the chapter on non-performance.

Yet it was not only because the UNIDROIT Principles were less hampered by the differences between the various domestic laws that they were able to deal with additional matters not covered by CISG. Another reason for the addition of new provisions was that the scope of the UNIDROIT Principles is not limited to sales contracts but also encompasses other kinds of transactions, above all service contracts.

* * *

(a) *CISG and the UNIDROIT Principles: no real competition*

Since CISG only deals with contracts for the sale of goods, and the scope of the UNIDROIT Principles is much wider, no overlap can occur where contracts other than sales contracts are concerned.

Yet even in respect of sales contracts, the two texts are not necessarily incompatible and indeed can even usefully support one another.

To begin with, notwithstanding the worldwide acceptance of CISG it might still occur that a sales contract is entered into between two parties not situated in Contracting States, thereby escaping the scope of application of CISG. In such cases there could be room for applying the UNIDROIT Principles as an alternative set of internationally uniform rules, either because of an express choice to this effect by the parties themselves or because a reference in the contract to "general principles of law" or the *"lex mercatoria"* or the like as the governing law is considered to be equivalent to a reference to the UNIDROIT Principles.

* * *

(b) UNIDROIT Principles as a means of interpreting and supplementing CISG

Yet even in cases where the international sales contract is governed by CISG, the UNIDROIT Principles may serve an important purpose.

According to paragraph 1 of Art. 7 CISG,

> "[i]n the interpretation of this Convention regard is to be had to its international character and to the need to promote uniformity in its application [. . .]."

So far, the principles and criteria for the proper interpretation of CISG have had to be found each time by the judges and arbitrators themselves. The UNIDROIT Principles could considerably facilitate their task in this respect.

* * *

(c) UNIDROIT Principles and CISG side by side

In view of the more comprehensive nature of the UNIDROIT Principles, parties may well wish to apply them in addition to CISG in respect of matters not covered therein. To this effect, they may include a clause in the contract which might read as follows:

> "This contract shall be governed by CISG, and with respect to matters not governed by this Convention, by the UNIDROIT Principles of International Commercial Contracts."

* * *

State courts will tend to consider the parties' reference to the UNIDROIT Principles as a mere agreement to incorporate them into the contract and to determine the law governing that contract on the basis of their own conflict-of-law rules. As a result, they will apply the UNIDROIT Principles only to the extent that the latter do not affect the provisions of the proper law from which the parties may not derogate. This may be the case, for instance, with the rules on contracting on the basis of standard terms or on public permission requirements. On the other hand, the rules relating to validity or to the court's intervention in cases of hardship will only be applied to the extent that they do not run counter to the corresponding provisions of the applicable domestic law.

The situation is different if the parties agree to submit their disputes arising from the contract to arbitration. Arbitrators are not necessarily bound to base their decision on a particular domestic law. Hence they may well apply the UNIDROIT Principles not merely as terms incorporated in the contract, but as "rules of law" governing the contract together with CISG irrespective of whether or not they are consistent with the particular domestic law otherwise applicable. The only mandatory rules arbitrators may take into account, also in view of their task of rendering to the largest possible extent an effective decision capable of enforcement, are those which claim to be applicable irrespective of the law otherwise governing the contract ("*loi d'application nécessaire*"). Yet the application, along with the UNIDROIT Principles, of the mandatory rules in question will as a rule not give rise to any true conflict, given their different subject-matter.

* * *

D. SPHERE OF APPLICATION OF THE U.N. SALES CONVENTION

The first six articles of the U.N. Sales Convention define its sphere of application. It governs *contracts for the sale* of *goods* when the transaction is *international*. The Convention defines only the third of these elements. As to the first two elements, the Convention provides some guidance by its articles that exclude certain issues and types of transaction from the Convention's coverage. This part of the chapter first explores what it means for a transaction to be international and what relation to the transaction must have to a State party to the Convention. We then turn to what contracts for the sale of goods are covered. Read articles 1–6 carefully and then analyze the following problems and cases.

Article 1(1) is the key provision. For the purposes of paragraph (1)(a) of Article 1, a contract is international when the seller and buyer have their places of business in different States when those States are Contracting States.

> *Illustration 1.* Seller has its place of business in Texas; Buyer has its place of business in Mexico. (Both Mexico and the United States are parties to the Convention.) If the parties have not excluded the Convention and they bring a dispute before a Texas court, the court will apply the Convention by virtue of paragraph (1)(a) of Article 1.

If the Convention is applicable by virtue of paragraph (1)(a) then it is unnecessary to refer to choice-of-law rules. Thus, the Convention governs in Illustration 1 without regard to paragraph (1)(b).

Paragraph (1)(b) provides an additional ground for application of the Convention. If only one party—or if neither party—has its place of business in a Contracting State, the Convention may still govern by virtue of paragraph (1)(b). Under this subparagraph, the Convention applies if choice-of-law rules make the law of a Contracting State the applicable law.

> *Illustration 2.* Seller has its place of business in France; Buyer has its place of business in the United Kingdom. (France is a party to the Convention, but the United Kingdom has not yet ratified.) If the

parties have not excluded the Convention and they bring a dispute before a French court, the court will first apply French choice-of-law rules. These rules will point to French substantive law as the governing law. By virtue of paragraph (1)(b) of Article 1, the relevant French substantive law will be the Convention.

Article 95 authorizes Contracting States to declare that they will not be bound by paragraph (1)(b). The United States has made such a declaration. As a result, a court sitting in the United States is required to apply the Convention only if the parties before it have their places of business in different Contracting States.

Illustration 3. Seller has its place of business in New York; Buyer has its place of business in England. If the parties do not mention the Convention and they bring a dispute before a New York court, the court is not required to apply the Convention.

Several other articles supplement the basic test of Article 1(1). To avoid surprise, Article 1(2) makes an exception when a party is unaware that the other party has its place of business in a different country. Thus, if either the seller or the buyer in Illustration 1 did not know that the other party came from a different country, then the Convention will not apply because the fact that the parties have their places of business in different States is to be disregarded.

* * *

1. *WHEN PARTIES FAIL TO DESIGNATE THE AP-PLICABLE LAW*

Assume you represent Universal Pipe Inc., a Kansas manufacturer of pipe insulation. If Universal enters into a domestic sales contract that does not have a choice-of-law clause, how do you determine what law governs? You would begin your research by consulting § 1–105(1) of Uniform Commercial Code. That section provides:

§ 1–105. *Territorial Application of the Act; Parties' Power to Choose Applicable Law*.

(1) ... *Failing such agreement [by the parties] this Act applies to transactions bearing an appropriate relation to this state.*

Literally, this text again requires you to determine in what forum the dispute will be brought because the version of the Code ("this Act") of the state in which the forum sits ("this state") will govern. The text was adopted in 1951 when it was unclear how many states would enact the Code. The drafters hoped to make the Code applicable to as many transactions as possible. Wide-spread enactment of the Code in the 1960s makes this initial policy obsolete. Many courts have recently ignored the literal language and have read the phrase "appropriate relation" to mean "most appropriate relation"—a reading that is consistent with the choice-of-law approach of section 188 the Restatement (Second) of the Conflict of Laws. Read this way, the text encourages application of the same version of the Code no matter which forum hears the dispute.

Given, of course, that all the states except Louisiana have enacted Article 2 (Sales) of the Uniform Commercial Code, the choice-of-law analysis is much less significant. Unless a state has enacted relevant non-uniform amendments or unless its courts have developed non-uniform interpretations of relevant Code provisions, you will be able to consult Article 2 directly.

QUINN, UCC COMMENTARY AND LAW DIGEST
1–16 (2d ed. 1991).*

[In *Boudreau v. Baughman*, 368 S.E.2d 849 (N.C. 1988) the] Supreme Court of North Carolina was faced with the problem of applying 1–105 when a Massachusetts resident injured his foot on the metal surface of a chair in Florida. Suit for breach of warranty was brought in North Carolina against the North Carolina manufacturer of the chair. Should the law of Florida, North Carolina, or Massachusetts apply?

Since suit had been brought in North Carolina, North Carolina was directed by 1–1015 to apply its version of the Code if there was an "appropriate relation" between the transaction and that state. Was there?

If, as the Supreme Court of North Carolina analyzed the matter, this required only some "significant contact" as had been suggested, the required linkage is minimal. The resulting ruling becomes forum-oriented. It would allow a state, in the early days of the Code, to prefer its Code law over the non-Code law of some other states as long as some minimal linkage could be found. With the code now the law of virtually all the states, however, such a rule opens the way to forum shopping. The rule was rejected by North Carolina as "outmoded."

A second solution was to read the language as requiring the forum state simply to apply its usual choice-of-law rules. The pre-Code rules in these matters, if rigid, would remain as rigid and inflexible under the Code. Section 1–105 would introduce little change. North Carolina rejected this as well.

Still a third approach required a balancing of the respective interests of the various states in the transaction with a view to determine "which state has the most significant relationship" to the case. So understood, the "appropriate relationship" would mean the "most significant relationship."

North Carolina opted for the third, "grouping of interests," approach. That decided, it applied the law of Florida to the case as the state with the most "significant relationship," since Florida had been "the place of sale, distribution, and use of the products, as well as the place of injury."

Consider now the complications that arise when the transaction is transnational.

* * *

PROBLEM 1–2.

The president of Universal Pipe Inc., a Kansas manufacturer of pipe insulation, attends an international trade fair in New York where he meets with the manager of EuroBuilders S.A. of Rouen, France. Euro-Builders has a contract to build an oil refinery in France and is interested in Universal Pipe's insulation for use in the refinery. The president and manager agree that Universal Pipe will sell a specified quantity of pipe insulation at an agreed price to EuroBuilders, the goods to be shipped from Chicago to Calais, France "C.I.F. Calais." They do not agree on what law governs their contract or what forum will hear any dispute arising in the course of its performance. They immediately draw up and sign a contract document.

(a) As attorney for Universal Pipe you anticipate that legal disputes between the parties will be heard in Kansas courts. Assuming for the purposes of this problem that the U.N. Sales Convention is not yet in force, what law do you anticipate will govern the validity and interpretation of the contract? Please read U.C.C. § 1–105(1)(2d sent.) in the Documents Supplement and discussed above. Does section 1–105 distinguish between contracts for domestic and international sales?

(b) EuroBuilders may, however, bring a claim before a French court, and France has not enacted the Uniform Commercial Code. Thus, the French courts will use different choice-of-law concepts than U.C.C. § 1–105. What substantive law would a French court apply? For international sales contracts, France is a party to the 1955 Convention on the Law Applicable to International Sales of Goods and French courts will apply Article 3 of that Convention. That article is set forth in the Documents Supplement and must be consulted in order to analyze this part of Problem 1–2.

LANDO, THE 1955 AND 1985 HAGUE CONVENTIONS ON THE LAW APPLICABLE TO THE INTERNATIONAL SALE OF GOODS
Rabels Zeitschrift 155, 167–69 (1993).*

States concluding conventions on the law applicable to contracts do it mainly to obtain predictability for the parties to an international contract.

Parties need to know the rules of which country will apply to their agreement. Knowing which law will apply allows the parties to calculate the risks and costs and arrange matters. When the Convention of 1955 was signed there were great divergences between the substantive contract laws and the choice-of-law rules of the world, and there was a need for predictability.

Predictability can best be obtained by rules which are clear and simple. * * * "The aim of a convention on sales is to facilitate commercial exchanges. It can only fulfil its role if it is easily understood, not only for the lawyers, but also and notably, for the businessmen. They must be able to understand the text, and from this text clearly see the consequences of their agreements. Otherwise, the whole undertaking must fail. Practitioners will mistrust a text if its meaning is unclear and if its content appears to hide pitfalls. This will result in a general refusal to comply with a text which in itself is too complicated and whose provisions are cryptic."

* * *

An aim which was not expressed in the Report but which clearly carried the rules proposed by the Special Commission was to abolish the lex forism "homeward trend" which, as will be shown, had been so abundantly resorted to by the courts of the European countries. Lex forism excludes predictability. It makes the applicable law depend upon in which country the suit is brought. It thereby encourages the plaintiff to go to the court of the country whose laws will give him the most favourable judgment (forum shopping).

In line with its aims, the Special Commission made hard and fast rules and gave preference to the law of the habitual residence of the seller; see on this IV below.

* * *

IV.   Law Applicable Absent a Choice of Law by the Parties

1.   The Background

A survey of the Member States' choice of law rules governing sales shows the following picture:

The sales contract was in principle governed by the choice of law rules respecting contracts in general. Until the nineteenth century the contract was governed by the law of the country in which it was made. This, it is believed, was due to the manner in which contracts at that time were concluded and performed. The sale of goods, for example, was generally concluded inter praesentes and was performed at the time and place where it had been made. When the first codifications of Private International Law took place in the eighteenth century and the beginning of the nineteenth century, the rule that the law of the place of contracting applies was reaffirmed; the early Continental law reports also show that the lex loci contractus was preferred throughout the first half of the nineteenth century. Many authors and many courts based their reliance on the law of the place of contracting, and—when used in a few cases—on the law of the place of performance, upon the presumed intention of the parties.

In the nineteenth century the place of contracting lost its paramount importance both in large parts of the European Continent and in England. This was partly due to a change in the habits and the techniques of international trade.

Until the beginning of that century merchants had owned the ships carrying their goods and they themselves or their agents had bought and sold their cargoes in the ports. When around 1840 international trade began to increase rapidly, shipping had already become a separate trade; the merchants and their agents accompanied the ships less often, and contracts of sale were no longer concluded primarily at the place where the goods were loaded and unloaded. From 1850 onwards postal and telegraph services were developed for the convenience of international trade, and the activities of banks also increased through the use of a new form of credit. All this broke up the unity of place and time in the making and performance of contracts. Now both these acts were done by each party at different places and at different times.

* * *

In England, France and Germany the proper law of the contract was the law by which the parties intended or might fairly be presumed to have intended the contract to be governed. This standard gave the courts freedom from the tyranny of fixed tests. International contracts which cover a multitude of often unpredictable combinations of facts and which show a surprising tendency of shifting connecting factors could not be fitted into the straitjacket of a fixed rule. By relying on the test of the presumed intention of the parties, the courts were able to weigh the connecting factors of each contract. They were also able to follow the homeward trend. In almost every country it was, as Beale said in his comment on English case law, remarkable to notice the great regularity with which the courts found by various methods that it was the law of England which was intended by the parties. The law of the forum, however, was not applied in every case, and in most of the countries no rules and not even presumptions were established.

* * *

2. The Convention of 1955

For the sales contract the Special Commission in 1931 followed the approach adopted by the International Law Association at its conference in Vienna. It discarded the flexible methods. The application of the law presumably intended by the parties was abandoned. The possibility of providing instead for the application of the law most closely connected with the contract does not seem to have been considered. This idea was not unknown in 1931. In 1908 the Institut de Droit International advocated the application of the law "which was most suitable for a reasonable regulation of the legal relationship"—a concept which is similar to the closest connection. Nor was the possibility of supporting the flexible methods with presumptions, as proposed by the Institut in 1908, considered. Rigid rules were provided.

The 1955 Convention lays down the following main rules:

Article 3(1) provides that in the absence of a choice of law by the parties a sale is governed by the substantive law of the country where the seller has his habitual residence at the time he received the order. If the order is received by a branch office of the seller, the law of the country governs where the branch is located.

There are, however, two important exceptions from this rule.

First, Art. 3(2) provides that the substantive law of the country in which the buyer has his habitual residence, or in which the branch of his business that has placed the order is situated, governs if the order has been received in that country either by the seller or by his agent. If, for instance, the agent of the French seller has received the Italian buyer's order in Italy, Italian substantive law will apply.

Second, according to Art. 3(3) a sale effected at a commodity exchange or at a public auction is governed by the substantive law of the country in which that exchange is located or in which the auction takes place.

The law of the habitual residence was chosen because it could be determined easily, safely and uniformly in most cases—qualities, which the laws of the place of contracting and of the place of performance did not have.

The rules chosen were in line with the general approach of the Special Commission. They were clear and simple rules which would not allow the lex forism to creep in.

JUENGER, THE E.E.C. CONVENTION ON THE LAW APPLICABLE TO CONTRACTUAL OBLIGATIONS: AN AMERICAN ASSESSMENT
Contract Conflicts, 299–300 (P. North, ed. 1982).*

Let us now discuss the problem of the law applicable in the absence of a contractual choice. * * *

How well have American and European conflicts experts coped with the difficult and frustrating problem of selecting a law for the parties? Not too well, I am afraid. The Second Restatement imposes a formidable task on the judiciary. The first paragraph of its section 188 requires a separate choice-of-law analysis for each contracts issue presented. The key term of this provision, the "most significant relationship", has an appealing ring. But what sounds simple and straightforward becomes quite complex if one attempts to apply the qualifying proviso, which requires recourse to the choice-influencing considerations the Restatement enumerates in section 6. That section contains a shopping list of desiderata, all of which are very plausible, except that they conflict with one another. How, for instance, is it possible to pursue, at the same time, the goals of certainty, predictability and uniformity of result mentioned in letter (f) of Section 6, second paragraph, and the protection of forum policies specified in letter (b)? Nor does it simplify matters if paragraph 2 of section 188 lists numerous contacts, and then ordains that they should be evaluated in the light of their relative importance to the particular issue presented. The permutations of any number of issues, six choice-of-law factors and five contacts, combined with the need to evaluate the contacts in the light of each particular issue, would stymie a computer.

Everyone might agree that the search for the proper law should not be a mechanical process of counting contacts. But even a juggler, not to mention a trial judge, can only cope with a finite number of balls in the air. The Second Restatement, of course, recognizes this difficulty. To alleviate it the last paragraph of section 188 diffidently offers a near-rule, which provides that if the place of negotiation coincides with the place of performance, the law of that jurisdiction should "usually" be applied, whatever that may mean. Sections 189–197 try to offer some further guidance by stating tentative rules for a number of specific contracts. However, these rules in turn are subject to an escape clause that permits application of whatever law has a more significant relationship to the specific issue. Nor are the black-letter statements of sections 198–207 (which deal with various specific contract issues, such as form requirements and capacity) of much help, for most of them simply refer back to the general provisions of sections 187–188.

* * *

NOTE ON PRIVATE INTERNATIONAL LAW CONVENTIONS

The 1955 Convention on the Law Applicable to International Sales of Goods is just one of several conventions which attempt to harmonize and unify the different choice-of-law rules for contracts. That convention was drafted specifically for problems arising under international sales contracts. Only nine States have become a party to the 1955 Convention and all but one of these States is in Western Europe.[8] Following adoption of the U.N. Sales Convention in 1980, the Hague Conference on Private International Law undertook the redrafting of the 1955 Convention to coordinate the provisions of the two texts. The result was a 1986 Convention which has not yet come into force.

Still another approach is represented by the 1980 Convention on the Law Applicable to Contractual Obligations, also known as the "Rome Convention,"[9] negotiated among members of the European Economic Community. The Rome text provides general choice-of-law rules for contracts, including contracts for sale. France is a party to both the Rome and the 1955

8. As of January 1, 1999 the following States were parties to the 1955 Convention: Belgium, Denmark, Finland, France, Italy, Niger, Norway, Sweden, and Switzerland.

9. The following States are parties to the Rome Convention: Belgium, Denmark, France, Germany, Greece, Ireland, Italy, Luxembourg, the Netherlands, and the United Kingdom.

Convention, but as between the two conventions, France will apply the 1955 text because Article 21 of the Rome Convention gives way to the earlier text. There will, however, be other European states, such as Germany, that will be a party to the Rome Convention but not the 1955 Convention.

The Rome Convention would apply different concepts to identify the law applicable in the absence of a choice between the parties. Article 4 of the Rome Convention example, provides rules which depend upon the determination of the "characteristic performance" of a sales contract. There are at least four actions which concern performance of the contract: Seller ships the goods, buyer receives and accepts the goods, buyer sends payment for the goods, and seller receives and accepts the payment. Which of these is *the* "characteristic performance"? Most commentators have argued that the seller's act of shipping the goods is the most characteristic performance of a sale contract.

A more recent regional attempt is found in the 1994 Inter–American Convention on the Law Applicable to Contracts[10]. The draft is closely modeled on the Rome Convention. Instead, however, of a reference to the "characteristic" performance when the parties have not designated the applicable law, Article 9 if the Inter–American Convention refers instead to the law of the State with which the contract has "the closest ties." Does this test provide greater certainty than the "characteristic" performance test?

* * *

PROBLEM 1–3

In Problem 1–2 we assumed that the Sales Convention was not in force. As you know, however, the Convention came into force on January 1, 1988. Both France and the United States have ratified the Convention. Reconsider the facts of the previous problem in the light of the Convention.

If the contract does not include a choice-of-law term or a term excluding application of the U.N. Sales Convention, does the U.N. Sales Convention govern the contract? Read Article 1(1). Does this situation fall under subparagraph (1)(a) or subparagraph (1)(b)? If the answer is "both," then note that the Convention becomes applicable under "either" subparagraph (1)(a) or (1)(b).

Now read Article 95. The United States, but not France, has made a declaration pursuant to Article 95. Note that Article 95 mentions only Article 1(1)(b). Is Article 95 relevant to the scope, substance or interpretation of Article 1(1)(a)? If not, then the U.S. declaration has no impact upon any transaction governed by Article 1(1)(a) where the seller and the buyer each has its place of business in a different Contracting State.

* * *

10. As of May 1, 1999, Mexico and Venezuela were the only parties to the Inter–American Convention. Bolivia, Brazil, and Uruguay have signed but not yet ratified the Convention.

NOTE ON THE ARTICLE 95 DECLARATION BY THE U.S.

U.S. State Department, Legal Analysis of the United Nations
Convention on Contracts for the International Sale of
Goods (1980), Appendix B

APPENDIX B

Proposed United States Declaration Under Article 95 Excluding
Applicability of the Convention Based on Article 1(1)(b)

Under Article 1 the Convention will apply only if two basic requirements are met: (1) The sale must be international—i.e., the seller and the buyer must have their "places of business in different states," and (2) the sale must have a prescribed relationship with one or more States that have adhered to the Convention. This statement is concerned with the second requirement—the relationship between the Convention and one or more Contracting States.

The Convention, in subparagraphs (1)(a) and (1)(b) of Article 1, states two such relationships, either of which will suffice.

(a) *First*, under subparagraph (1)(a) the Convention applies when the places of business of the seller and the buyer are in different Contracting States.

(b) *Second*, under subparagraph (1)(b) the Convention would also apply:

> (b) when the rules of private international law lead to the application of the law of a Contracting State.

At the 1980 Diplomatic Conference, delegates of the United States and several other countries proposed the deletion of the second of these grounds for applicability—subparagraphs (1)(b) of Article 1. This proposal was defeated; as a compromise, the Convention's Final Provisions (Part IV) provide in Article 95 that a Contracting State may, by reservation, declare "that it will not be bound by subparagraph (1)(b) or article 1".

The United States, in signing the Convention, stated that ratification subject to the Article 95 reservation was contemplated. This position, recommended by the American Bar Association, will promote maximum clarity in the rules governing the applicability of the Convention. The rules of private international law, on which applicability under subparagraph (1)(b) depends, are subject to uncertainty and international disharmony. On the other hand, applicability based on subparagraph (1)(a) is determined by a clear-cut test: whether the seller and buyer have their places of business in different Contracting States.

A further reason for excluding applicability based on subparagraph (1)(b) is that this provision would displace our own domestic law more frequently than foreign law. By its terms, subparagraph (1)(b) would be relevant only in sales between parties in the United States (a Contracting State) and a *non*-Contracting State. (Transactions that run between the United States and another contracting State are subject to the

Convention by virtue of subparagraph (1)(a).) Under subparagraph (1)(b), when private international law points to the law of a foreign *non*-Contracting State the Convention will not displace that foreign law, since subparagraph (1)(b) makes the Convention applicable only when "the rules of private international law lead to the application of the law of a *Contracting* State." Consequently, when those rules point to United States law, subparagraph (1)(b) would normally operate to displace United States law (the Uniform Commercial Code) and would not displace the law of foreign *non*-Contracting States.

If United States law were seriously unsuited to international transactions, there might be an advantage in displacing our law in favor of the uniform international rules provided by the Convention. However, the sales law provided by the Uniform Commercial Code is relatively modern and includes provisions that address the special problems that arise in international trade.

For these reasons it seems advisable for the United States to exclude applicability of the Convention under sub-paragraph (1)(b) by the declaration (reservation) permitted by Article 95. Fortunately, this position will not interfere with broad application of the Convention to international sales. Widespread adoption of the Convention can be anticipated; hence it is expected that eventually a substantial portion of United States international trade will involve other Contracting States and will receive the benefits of the Convention by virtue of subparagraph (1)(a) of Article 1. Moreover, parties who wish to apply the Convention to international sales contracts not covered by Article 1(1)(a) may provide by their contract that the Convention will apply.

INTERNATIONAL CHAMBER OF COMMERCE:
CASE NO. 8182 (1995)
123 J. du Droit Int'l 1024 (1996) (Peter Winship trans.)

The parties' contract does not contain a clause designating the applicable law ...

* * *

The different possibilities are Austrian law, which is where the Defendant (the seller) has its place of business, and Swiss law, which is where the Claimant (the buyer) has its place of business. Swiss law might also be applicable because the I.C.C. has designated Basel, Switzerland as the place of the arbitration. In addition, because the I.C.C. Court of Arbitration has appointed a German arbitrator, German law could also be applied as a neutral law. One must likewise mention the possibility of applying Ukrainian law because the Claimant was required to send to the Ukraine the sacks which the Defendant wished to use to satisfy its obligation to deliver with the help of its Ukrainian supplier.

Switzerland, Austria, Germany, and the Ukraine are all signatories of the Convention on Contracts for the International Sale of Goods. In each of these countries the Convention had entered into force before the date the parties signed this contract.

. . . This contract is a sales contract because the parties have clearly designated themselves as buyer (the Claimant) and seller (the Defendant). Moreover, the preamble of the contract is unequivocal: "the seller sells and the buyer buys the following product subject to the following terms."

The contract signed by the parties satisfies the conditions of article 1(1)(a) of the Vienna Convention according to which the Convention applies to contracts of sale if the parties have their places of business in different States and these States are Contracting States. Accordingly, the Convention's provisions apply to the litigation subject to the present arbitral proceeding. . . .

* * *

UNCITRAL CLOUT Case 104

International Chamber of Commerce, International Court of Arbitration, 1993.*

The dispute concerned the failure of the Bulgarian buyer to pay the Austrian seller within the time period agreed in the sales contract.

The arbitral tribunal found that, while the parties did not specify any applicable law, the application of Austrian and Bulgarian rules of private international law led to the application of Austrian law. In view of the fact that CISG had been incorporated into the Austrian legal system, the tribunal decided to apply CISG, in accordance with article 1(1)(b) of the Convention.

The tribunal also noted that, as the applicable rules of private international law led to the application of the law of Austria, where the seller had its place of business, it was immaterial that Bulgaria, where the buyer had its place of business, was not a party to the Convention at the time the contract was concluded. . . .

* * *

UNCITRAL CLOUT Case 152

France: Court of Appeal of Grenoble (Commercial Division), 1995.

A company with its place of business in France sold to an individual resident in Portugal a used warehouse for the price of 500,000 French francs, including the cost of dismantling and delivery, . . .

The Court of Appeal . . . stressed that the contract had been concluded between a seller with its place of business in France and a buyer resident in Portugal, that France was a State Party to CISG whereas Portugal had neither signed nor ratified it, and that it was therefore necessary to ascertain whether CISG was applicable through the provisions of private international law (art. 1(1)(b)).

Having invoked the Hague Convention of 15 June 1955 on the Law applicable to International Sales of Goods, the court arrived at French law, this being the law of the country where the seller had its habitual residence at the time when it received the order (art. 3, first paragraph, Hague Convention). The court accordingly applied CISG because "since 1 January 1988, the French domestic law applicable to international sales was the Vienna Convention of 11 April 1980"....

* * *

INTERNATIONAL CHAMBER OF COMMERCE: CASE NO. 5713 (1989)
15 Y.B. Comm. Arb. 70–73 (1990).

In 1979, the parties concluded three contracts for the sale of a product according to certain contract specifications. The buyer paid 90% of the price payable under each of the contracts upon presentation of the shipping documents, as contractually agreed.

The product delivered pursuant to the first and third contracts met the contract specifications. The conformity of the second consignment was disputed prior to its shipment. When the product was again inspected upon arrival, it was found that it did not meet the contract specifications. The product was eventually sold by the buyer to third parties at considerable loss, after having undergone a certain treatment to make it more saleable.

The seller initiated arbitration proceedings to recover the 10% balance remaining due under the contracts. The buyer filed a counterclaim alleging that the seller's claim should be set off against the amounts which the buyer estimates to be payable to the buyer by the seller, i.e., the direct losses, financing costs, lost profits and interest.

Excerpt

I. Applicable Law

[1] "The contract contains no provisions regarding the substantive law. Accordingly that law has to be determined by the Arbitrators in accordance with Art. 13(3) of the ICC rules. Under that article, the Arbitrators will 'apply the law designated as the proper law by the rule of conflicts which they deem appropriate'.

[2] "The contract is between a Seller and a Buyer [of different nationalities] for delivery [in a third country]. The sale was f.o.b. so that the transfer of risks to the Buyer took place in [the country of the Seller]. [The country of the Seller] accordingly appears as being the jurisdiction to which the sale is most closely related.

[3] "The Hague Convention on the law applicable to international sales of goods dated 15 June 1955 (Art. 3) regarding sales contracts, refers as governing law to the law of the Seller's current residence.... [The country of the Buyer] has adhered to the Hague Convention, not [the country of the Seller]. However, the general trend in conflicts of law is to apply the domestic law of the current residence of the debtor of the essential undertaking arising under the contract. That debtor in a sales contract is the Seller. Based on those combined findings, [the law of the country of the Seller] appears to be the proper law governing the Contract between the Seller and the Buyer.

[4] "As regards the applicable rules of [the law of the country of the Seller], the Arbitrators have relied on the Parties' respective statements on the subject and on the information obtained by the Arbitrators from an independent consultant.... The Arbitrators, in accordance with the last paragraph of Art. 13 of the ICC rules, will also take into account the 'relevant trade usages'."

II. Admissibility of the Counterclaim

(a). Under [the law of the country of the Seller]

(. . . .)

(b). Under the international trade usages prevailing in the international sale of goods

[5] "The Tribunal finds that there is no better source to determine the prevailing trade usages than the terms of the United Nations Convention on the International Sale of Goods of 11 April 1980, usually called 'the Vienna Convention'. This is so even though neither [the country of the Buyer] nor [the country of the Seller] are parties to that Convention. If they were, the Convention might be applicable to this case as a matter of law and not only as reflecting the trade usages.

[6] "The Vienna Convention, which has been given effect to in 17 countries, may be fairly taken to reflect the generally recognized usages regarding the matter of the non-conformity of goods in international sales.   * * *"

* * *

PROBLEM 1–4

Universal Pipe, Inc., agrees in writing with Commonwealth Construction, Ltd., of London that Universal Pipe to sell a specified quantity of pipe insulation to Commonwealth, the goods to be shipped from Chicago to London. The agreement contains no choice-of-law provision and does not exclude application of the U.N. Sales Convention. Given that the United Kingdom is not a party to the Convention, what substantive law will apply to a dispute arising from the sales contract?

This problem presents a transaction between an enterprise in the United States and one in a non-Contracting State. Article 1(1)(a) clearly does not make the Convention applicable: the parties do not have their places of business in two different Contracting States. Moreover, because the U.S. declaration pursuant to Article 95 states that U.S. courts are "not bound" by Article 1(1)(b), that provision does not make the Convention applicable. The applicable law will therefore be determined by traditional choice-of-law analysis.

(a) If the dispute is before a Kansas court, the court will probably look to Kansas law as the governing law. But is the relevant law the Convention or the UCC? Reread the U.S. State Department's explanation of why the United States made the Article 95 declaration. Does the declaration prohibit a U.S. court from deciding that the Convention applies to a transaction like that set out in Problem 1–3?

(b) If the dispute is before a court in the United Kingdom, the court will begin its analysis by looking to Article 4 of the Rome Convention on the Law Applicable to Contractual Obligations. Under that article, the seller's performance is usually assumed to be the characteristic performance. The U.K. court will probably apply the substantive law of Kansas. Is the relevant law the Sales Convention or the UCC?

* * *

R. FOLSOM, M. GORDON & J. SPANOGLE, INTERNATIONAL BUSINESS TRANSACTIONS IN A NUTSHELL
47–48 (6th ed., 2000).*

THE SPHERE OF APPLICATION OF CISG

* * *

This "place of business" criterion will cause difficulty whenever one or both parties have more than one place of business. However, CISG Article 10(a) provides some help in such situations by specifying which "place of business" is to be considered. Unfortunately, Article 10(a) does not define what a "place of business" is, although the drafting history of the Convention suggests that a permanent establishment is required and that neither a warehouse nor the office of a seller's agent qualifies as a "place of business." Article 10(a) does specify which one of multiple offices is to be used in determining the internationality of a transaction, but even this is subject to ambiguity—"the place of business is that which has the closest relationship to the contract *and* its performance" (emphasis added). Thus, where one office is more closely associated with the formation of the contract and a second office is more closely associated with a party's performance of its contractual obligations, there is an unresolved issue concerning which of those offices is the relevant "place of business." However, Article 10(a) does limit the usable facts in making a choice between multiple offices to those circumstances known to "the parties" before a binding contract is formed. This should permit well-advised parties to resolve possible ambiguities by stating in the contract which office of each party they believe to have "the closest relationship to the contract."

* * *

PROBLEM 1–5

In the previous problems we assumed that neither the seller nor the buyer had more than one place of business and that both parties knew they were dealing with an enterprise from another country. Consider, however, the following modifications to these assumptions.

(a) Assume that EuroBuilder is building the refinery in a Persian Gulf nation and under the EuroBuilder–Universal contract Universal agrees to ship the insulation to Araby, but no other information is given to Universal. Araby is not a party to CISG. Does the Convention govern the contract? CISG arts. 1, 10. Does the fact that EuroBuilder is doing some construction in Araby automatically imply that it has "a place of business" there? Note that neither Article 1 nor Article 10 defines "place of business."

(b) Assume that EuroBuilders maintains an office in New York with one sales representative and several secretaries. EuroBuilders' manager visits this office at least once every three months. The manager was on a visit to this New York office when he executed the contract with Universal Pipe. Does the Convention govern the contract? Is this a contract between two parties with their relevant "places of business" in the United States? Does EuroBuilders' New York office have the closest relationship *to the contract*? Certainly it has the closest relationship to the execution of the contract, but what if the Rouen office issued the original EuroBuilders purchase order and stored the executed contract documents? Does the New York office have the closest relationship *to the performance* of the contract?

(c) Assume that Universal Pipe's president meets with EuroBuilders' manager at EuroBuilders' office in New York. The manager reveals that he is acting for EuroBuilders, but Universal Pipe's president wrongly assumes that EuroBuilders in New York is a wholly-owned subsidiary incorporated in New York and not a branch of the European company. He therefore assumes that U.S. law would therefore govern the EuroBuilders–Universal Pipe contract. Is the Convention nevertheless applicable? CISG art. 1(2), (3). Does EuroBuilders' French connection "appear" from either the contract or the parties' dealings? Consider the information likely to be part of any written contract: the name and address of each party, the place of delivery, the necessity for export licenses to be procured, and certificates of origin, etc. Is there any realistic likelihood that the parties will not know where their trading partner's place of business is?

* * *

UNCITRAL CLOUT Case 158
France: Paris Court of Appeal (15th Division), 1992.

The plaintiff, a French buyer, had ordered on 22 March 1990 several batches of electronic components from the defendant, a German seller, through the defendant's liaison office in France. The buyer had accepted the price previously stated by the supplier but had requested its reduction in accordance with the drop in prices on the market. In its acceptance of the order, the seller had replied that the prices could be adjusted upwards or downwards, as agreed, in accordance with the market, but that various specific items could not be delivered. A telephone conversation took place between the parties on 26 March, and the German seller sent his partner a telex on the same day recording the latter's agreement to amend one item of the order. By telex of 13 April, the French buyer changed his order once again, a change which the German seller stated that it could not accept for short-term deliveries. . . .

The Court of Appeal held that the seller's liaison office based in France did not have due legal personality and that the contract was therefore an international sales contract concluded between a French company and a German company. It found that CISG (art. 1(1)(b)) was applicable in the case in point. . . .

* * *

ATTORNEYS TRUST v. VIDEOTAPE COMPUTER PRODUCTS, INC.
United States Court of Appeals, Ninth Circuit, 1996.
94 F.3d 650.

MEMORANDUM[11]

Attorneys Trust, assignee for collection, commenced this action against Videotape Products, Inc. (VTP) to collect a debt allegedly owed to CMC. [Eds.: Attorneys Trust and VTP have their places of business in the United States; CMC has its place of business in Taiwan.] VTP, in turn, cross-complained against CMC for breach of warranty in the sale of certain videotape housings. After the district court found in favor of VTP and entered judgment against AT and CMC, they appealed. They claim that the district court had no subject matter jurisdiction and that it made a number of errors in deciding the merits of this case. We affirm.

* * *

(5) CMC's final attempt to avoid the district court's judgment consists of its assertion that the district court erred because it should have applied the United Nations Convention on Contracts for the International Sale of Goods. That would have led to the application of the law

---

11. This disposition is not appropriate for publication and may not be cited to or by the courts of this circuit except as provided by 9th Cir. R. 36–3.

of Taiwan to this case, says CMC. However, this claim is too little too late. Assuming that Taiwan is a party to the Convention, "[a] party who intends to raise an issue concerning the law of a foreign country shall give notice by pleadings or other reasonable written notice." Fed. R. Civ. P. 44.1. The failure to raise the issue results in application of the law of the forum, here California.[12] See Interpool Ltd. v. Char Yigh Marine (Panama) S.A., 890 F.2d 1453, 1458 (9th Cir.1989); . . . The parties cited only California law to the district court. Indeed, they cite only California law to us. The district court did not err.

AFFIRMED.

Notes & Questions

1.   If the Sales Convention governed, would its provisions lead to application of the domestic law of Taiwan? Had the parties implicitly chosen to exclude application of the Convention? Does it make any difference that the assignee of the right to payment has its place of business in the same country as the buyer who owes payment?

2.   Knowledge of public international law and current events is sometimes desirable even for parties to private transactions. For example, public international law rules on state succession became relevant to exporters and importers of goods to and from the former Soviet Union, Yugoslavia, and Czechoslovakia following the break up of these countries into independent states. In the *Attorneys Trust* case, it might have been helpful to know that Taiwan could not have been a party to the Sales Convention because the United Nations does not recognize Taiwan as independent state with the power to become a party to international conventions. As the designated depositary for the Sales Convention (CISG art. 89), the U.N. Secretary–General would therefore not have accepted an attempt by Taiwan to deposit an instrument of accession.

* * *

2.   *WHEN PARTIES CHOOSE THE APPLICABLE LAW*

In the preceding section we examined the consequences when a seller and buyer do not choose the applicable law. We turn now to the problems raised when parties to the sales contract agree on the applicable law. What if the parties choose the law of a state that is a party to the Sales Convention? Must the transaction or the parties to the contract have some relation to the jurisdiction chosen? What if the jurisdiction chosen is not a party to the Convention? The following materials explore these and other issues.

* * *

---

12. Under California's choice of law rules, a California court "will apply its own rule of decision unless a party litigant timely invokes the law of a foreign state." *Hur-* *tado v. Superior Court*, 11 Cal. 3d 574, 581, 522 P.2d 666, 670, 114 Cal. Rptr. 106, 110 (1974) (emphasis added).

PROBLEM 1–6

The president of Universal Pipe meets with the manager of Tempomex S.A. of Monterey, Mexico at an international trade fair in New York. They agree that Universal Pipe will sell a specified quantity of pipe insulation to Tempomex to be shipped by truck to Mexico from Kansas. They immediately draw up and sign a contract document. The contract expressly states that "the law of Kansas, including the Uniform Commercial Code as enacted in Kansas, will govern this contract."

(a) Assume for the purposes of this problem that the U.N. Sales Convention is not in force, would a Kansas court enforce this contractual choice-of-law term? Please read again U.C.C. § 1–105(1) set forth in the Documents Supplement, concentrating this time on the first sentence and the Official Comment.

(b) Would Mexican court enforce the term? The 1955 Inter–American Convention, on the Law applicable to International Contracts is in force in Mexico. Article 7(1) of that Convention provides: "The contract shall be governed by the law chosen by the parties." Is this provision ambiguous?

(c) If, instead of a Mexican buyer, the buyer is from Germany, would a German court enforce the term? Germany is a party to the Rome Convention and has incorporated its provisions into its Civil Code. Is article 3 of the Rome Convention (see Documentary Supplement) ambiguous? The major difference between choice-of-law principles set forth in the UCC and in the Rome Convention is that the Convention requires only that the parties' choice be expressed "with reasonable certainty" and therefore does not require a "reasonable relationship" as required by U.C.C. § 1–105. Thus, one need not wrestle with abstract "relationship" concepts, and may instead concentrate on clarity of expression in drafting. Did Universal and EuroBuilders express their choice clearly?

(d) If the buyer was from France, would a French court enforce the term? Is Article 2 of the 1955 Hague Convention (see Documentary Supplement) ambiguous?

* * *

JUENGER, THE INTER–AMERICAN CONVENTION ON THE LAW APPLICABLE TO INTERNATIONAL CONTRACTS: SOME HIGHLIGHTS AND COMPARISONS
42 Am. J. Comp. L. 381 (1994).*

II.   THE EUROPEAN MODEL

The new regional choice-of-law convention is not the first of its kind. The European Union's member states are parties to the 1980 Rome

Convention on the Law Applicable to Contractual Obligations, which was inspired by the exigencies of European integration. Quite naturally, from the very beginning this European effort served as a model for our hemisphere's drafters who, like their European counterparts, worked in the context of regional integration ranging from the NAFTA over the ANCOM to the MERCOSUR, with NAFTA, like the European Union, including both common law and civil law jurisdictions. In addition, the Rome Convention commended itself as the work product of eminent scholars. Its reporters, the late Italian professor Giuliano and his French colleague Lagarde, as well as a number of the member state delegates, were academicians of considerable distinction and international repute.

1. *Party Autonomy*

(a) The freedom to choose the applicable law

Before sketching the Mexico City Convention's highlights it seems appropriate to comment on its European antecedent. Since much has been written about the Rome Convention, it will suffice briefly to touch upon some of its essential features. The Convention's lodestar is party autonomy. Its article 3 provides the parties with ample freedom to select the law they wish to govern their agreement. Specifically, the chosen law need not have any connection with the transaction or the parties. The choice need not be express; article 3(1) permits judges and arbitrators to infer the parties' intent to select a particular law from the agreement's terms or the circumstances of the case, e.g., from the use of a particular language or concepts peculiar to a legal system, or from a forum-selection clause. The parties may opt for a consensual *dépeçage* by submitting different aspects of a single contract to different laws. According to article 3(2) they may even change their minds after the fact and decide at a later time, e.g., at trial, to submit their contract to a law different from that which governed it at the outset.

(b) Restrictions on the freedom to choose

The freedom to stipulate the applicable law is limited by the public policy reservation of article 16 and by article 7(2), which provides that the forum may apply those of its own "rules ... [that] are mandatory irrespective of the law otherwise applicable" (the so-called *lois de police* or "rules of immediate application".) According to article 7(1), a court or arbitral tribunal may even take into account the mandatory rules of a third country with which the transaction has a close connection. With respect to parties of unequal bargaining power article 5 provides that a contractual choice of law may not, as a rule, deprive a consumer of the protection of mandatory rules of his country of habitual residence. Similarly, article 6(1) protects employees by precluding the parties from stipulating out of the mandatory rules of the otherwise applicable law.

(c) Laws that cannot be chosen

In addition to these commonsensical and unobjectionable restrictions on party autonomy there is one of dubious wisdom, which may escape the attention of all but the most careful readers. Pursuant to article 1(1) the Rome Convention's rules govern the "choice between the laws of different countries." As one of the Reporters explains, this wording reflects a deliberate decision to limit the parties' choice to the positive laws of particular states and nations. In other words, the freedom to choose authorized by the Rome Convention does not include a choice of, for instance, either such model laws as the recently adopted UNIDROIT Principles or the *lex mercatoria*. This strange positivistic feature, a throwback to an earlier age, is at odds with current commercial and judicial practice. Since the highest courts of several countries have begun to recognize, directly or indirectly, the parties' power to select rules that are not part of any state or national legal system, such as the general principles of commercial law, the Rome Convention's restrictive feature has become an anachronism.

* * *

III.   THE MEXICO CITY CONVENTION

1.   *Party Autonomy*

For all the flaws that mar the Rome Convention, in light of the peculiar evolution of contracts choice of law in this hemisphere even a mere carbon copy of the European original would have nevertheless spelled progress. The laudable and long-standing cooperation of Latin American nations in the field of conflict of laws, which dates back to the last century, paradoxically served to retard the development of their contract choice of law principles. The 1889 Montevideo Conference on Private International Law yielded, *inter alia*, a convention that implicitly outlawed party autonomy, a decision that was explicitly reiterated in the 1940 Montevideo Tratado de Derecho Civil Internacional. The reasons for rejecting a principle of proven usefulness in international practice were entirely of a conceptualistic and positivistic nature.

This early misstep had the consequence of impeding the evolution of contract choice of law in Latin America until our days. The anti-autonomy stance not only tied the hands of judges, it lead academics astray. As eminent a conflicts scholar as Uruguay's Quintín Alfonsín maintained that party autonomy amounts to an alien element in the conflict of laws and, in spite of its venerable history, merits censure rather than approbation. * * *

* * *

* * * Nor, regrettably, is this conceptualistic rejection of a key feature of international trade and commerce a mere relic of a long discredited choice-of-law approach. Disregarding the principle's worldwide acceptance, modern American unilateralists continue to express doubts about party autonomy. To be sure, both the Uniform Commercial Code and the Second Conflicts Restatement expressly recognize the power of private parties to choose the law governing their contract. Yet U.C.C. section 1–105(1) still provides that the law chosen must have some link with the agreement. Even the more liberal Second Restatement requires, with respect to issues of essential validity, the parties to show "some other reasonable basis" in the absence of a "substantial relationship" of the chosen law to the parties or the transaction, even though in the real world a capricious choice should be rare. Such spurious restrictions on party autonomy make little sense as long as the parties are of equal bargaining power. In fact, the U.S. Supreme Court has gone as far as to force a consumer, in a much criticized decision, to litigate far away from home on the strength of a forum-selection clause contained in a contract of adhesion.

In light of the uneven evolution of party autonomy on our Continent, the Mexico City Convention performs the important function of conferring upon that principle the status of an inter-American tenet. In terse and unambiguous terms, article 7(1), first sentence, states that "The contract shall be governed by the law chosen by the parties." Paralleling article 3(1), second sentence, of the Rome Convention, the third sentence of article 7(1) permits contractual *dépeçage*. Similarly, article 8 follows the European model by permitting the parties to change the applicable law at any time, allowing them either to amend an earlier choice, or to contract away from the otherwise applicable law. Party autonomy is limited only by the public policy reservation of article 18 and the "mandatory rules" referred to in article 11.

By providing—in line with article 3(1) of the Rome Convention— that the parties' choice need not be express but can be implied, article 7(1), second sentence, of the Mexico City Convention in effect grants courts and arbitrators a considerable leeway of discretion. The reference to "the parties' behavior and ... the clauses of the contract" is broad enough to allow the decisionmaker to rely on an implied intent for the purpose of reaching a desirable result, especially to validate an agreement. As far as the bases for implying a choice are concerned, article 7(2) states that the selection "of a certain forum by the parties does not necessarily entail selection of the applicable law." Though phrased negatively, this provision in effect incorporates the English presumption *qui elegit judicem elegit ius*, which allows the forum to apply its own law, thus helpfully obviating the expense and delay that an inquiry into foreign law inevitably entails.

* * *

PROBLEM 1–7

In the previous problem we assumed that the Sales Convention was not in force. Reconsider the facts of the previous problem now that the Convention is in force. Both Germany and the United States are parties to the Sales Convention.

(a) Does the U.N. Sales Convention govern the contract if the contract contains a clause stating: "This contract shall be governed by the law of Kansas, including its Uniform Commercial Code, and not by the U.N. Convention on Contracts for the International Sale of Goods"? CISG art. 6. Note that CISG is not "mandatory law," so the parties have the "autonomy" to opt out of its application. Unless the parties have opted out pursuant to Article 6, however, the Convention governs. Thus, CISG is an "opt-out" legislative system, not one that requires parties to "opt in."

(b) Would your answer be different if the parties had agreed that the "law of Kansas" is to govern their contract? CISG arts. 1(1), 6.

(c) Would your answer be different if the parties had agreed that the "law of Germany" is to govern their contract? Does this term choose German domestic sales law or the Convention?

When answering these questions consider the following comment:

* * *

WINSHIP, INTERNATIONAL SALES CONTRACTS UNDER THE 1980 VIENNA CONVENTION
17 U.C.C.L.J. 55 (1984).*

Whether application of the convention may be excluded by implication is a question on which the commentators are divided. Several authors point to the omission in the convention of a provision in the 1964 uniform sales law that states that exclusion may be either express or implied and these authors conclude that exclusion of the 1980 convention must therefore be express. Professor John Honnold, on the other hand, argues that the drafting history of the U.N. convention shows that the draftsmen omitted the 1964 clause merely to prevent a forum from excluding the convention on insubstantial evidence of the parties' intent. He suggests that a forum should determine whether parties agreed to exclude the convention by using the rules of interpretation set out in Articles 8 and 9, which do not require an agreement to be express. On balance, Professor Honnold appears to have the more persuasive argument given the drafting history. The obvious lesson is that parties should *both* exclude the convention expressly *and* specify the law that they want to govern their agreement.

This debate about implied exclusions is important when considering the effect of several clauses commonly found in international sales contracts. The most important of these clauses is a choice-of-law clause which specifies that "this agreement shall be governed by the law of [New York]." If the United States ratifies the convention, it could be argued that the relevant law in [New York] is the convention. On the other hand, it is quite possible that the parties chose [New York] law on the assumption that the UCC as enacted in [New York] would govern their sales contract. As suggested above, it should be open to the parties to proffer evidence of their actual intent on exclusion. The same principle should apply if the parties agree on a forum-selection clause (e.g., arbitration in New York), although it is more difficult to infer from this clause an intent to exclude the convention.

NOTE: THE U.N. SALES CONVENTION AND CHOICE–OF–LAW RULES

Choice-of-law rules will remain relevant even if all States become parties to the U.N. Sales Convention. The Convention itself refers to these rules in the following three contexts.

(1) *Determining the Convention's sphere of application.* As the previous problem illustrates, article 1(1)(b) uses choice-of-law rules to determine whether or not the Convention applies to a transaction.

(2) *Filling "gaps" in the Convention.* Article 7(2) states that gaps are to be filled by consulting, first, "the general principles on which [the Convention] is based" and then, if there are no relevant general principles, "in conformity with the law applicable by virtue of the rules of private international law."

(3) *Determining precedence between conflicting Conventions.* Article 90 of the Convention states that the Convention "does not prevail over" any international agreement "which contains provisions concerning the matters governed by this Convention, provided that the parties have their places of business in States parties to such agreement." Theoretically, there might be such conflict between the U.N. Sales Convention and the 1955 or 1986 Hague Sales Conventions.

UNCITRAL CLOUT Case 48

Germany: Oberlandesgericht Düsseldorf; 1993.

The German buyer of fresh cucumbers appealed against the decision of the court of first instance, which ordered the German buyer to pay to the Turkish seller the balance of the price due under the contract....

The appellate court found that the parties, during the oral hearings before the court of first instance, had agreed to submit their dispute to German law and held that CISG was applicable as part of German law....

* * *

UNCITRAL CLOUT Case 103

International Chamber of Commerce, International Court of Arbitration, 1993.

The parties concluded a contract for the sale of goods. The buyer contested the conformity of the goods to the contract specifications.

The arbitral tribunal applied the CISG on the grounds that: the parties had chosen French law as applicable law and the Convention was in force in France at the time the contract was concluded; the contract concerned international trade interests because its performance assumed a movement of goods and payments across frontiers; and the goods concerned fell within the scope of application of the CISG. The tribunal also noted that the buyer was located in Syria, which was a party to the Convention at the time the contract was concluded and that the seller was located in Germany which became a party to the Convention after the time of the conclusion of the contract. . . .

* * *

UNCITRAL CLOUT Case 92
Italy: Ad hoc Arbitral Tribunal—Florence, 1994.

A contract concluded by an Italian seller and a Japanese buyer for the supply of leather and/or textile wear contained a clause under which the contract was to be "governed exclusively by Italian law."

By majority, the arbitral tribunal decided that CISG did not apply to the contract, either because Japan had not yet ratified CISG or because the contract itself had been made subject exclusively to Italian law. In the view of the tribunal, the choice of Italian law by the parties amounted to an implicit exclusion of CISG (art. 6 CISG).

One of the arbitrators, dissenting, held that CISG did apply since the choice of Italian law confirmed that the parties intended to apply CISG pursuant to article 1(1)(b) CISG and was not a declaration pursuant to art. 6 CISG.

* * *

R. FOLSOM, M. GORDON, & J. SPANOGLE, INTERNATIONAL BUSINESS TRANS- ACTIONS IN A NUTSHELL
50–52 (6th ed. 2000).*

If the parties can "opt out" of CISG, can they also "opt in" in circumstances not covered by Article 1? For example, can a sales contract between a United States party and another party in N, a non-Contracting State, be made subject to CISG by including a clause stating: "This contract shall be governed by the United Nations Convention on Contracts for the International Sale of Goods, 1980"?

First, it should be noted that, although CISG Article 6 gives wide recognition to "party autonomy" (the ability of the parties to determine the terms of their deal), it only recognizes the ability of the parties *to exclude* the Convention. CISG itself has no provisions allowing adoption of the Convention through "party autonomy." Usually the United States courts try to recognize "party autonomy," and follow any express statement of applicable law. However, difficulty arises under current United States law. The Convention does not apply through its own terms. The contract does not involve parties in two Contracting States, and the United States reservation makes choice-of-law rules (including "party autonomy" rules) irrelevant as to whether CISG applies.

Under the *Erie* doctrine, the relevant choice of law rules should be furnished by state law—the UCC. And, the UCC does limit "party autonomy". Under UCC 1–105 choice of law provisions, parties may choose the applicable law from among those jurisdictions "having a reasonable relation to the transaction." Yet, the whole purpose of the United States reservation was to limit the influence of CISG to transactions with Contracting States only. The authorities are unanimous in believing that CISG will be applied in such a case, but provide no consistent rationale. * * * Thus, courts should be expected to fulfill the parties' directions, but analytical difficulties remain.

* * *

PROBLEM 1–8

Universal Pipes, Inc. agrees in writing with Commonwealth Construction, Ltd., of London that Universal will sell a specified quantity of pipe insulation to Commonwealth, to be shipped from Chicago to London. The written agreement states: "The laws of Kansas, including the U.N. Convention on Contracts for the International Sale of Goods, will govern this contract." Is this choice-of-law provision enforceable?

Note that CISG Article 6 expressly allows "exclusion" (opting out) of CISG, but is silent on "opting in." Is that issue controlled by CISG or by "the laws of Kansas"? If the latter, then we must consider U.C.C. § 1–105 once again. That section restricts the ability of the parties to choose the applicable law, and requires that the law chosen be that of a state or nation "bearing a reasonable relation" to the transaction. Does CISG (as federal law) bear such a reasonable relation to the transaction? Or, since the transaction is not between businesses in two different Contracting States, has the United States through its Article 95 declaration determined that no such relationship can exist for such a transaction? Reread the explanation for the U.S. declaration set out above. Does it state that the Uniform Commercial Code is the only appropriate U.S. law unless the transaction is between enterprises in different Contracting States?

Consider also the Official Comment to U.C.C. § 1–105. Does it suggest that the choice-of-law term agreed upon by Universal and Commonwealth has incorporated the provisions of CISG into their sales contract?

* * *

Note

The United Kingdom has ratified the EC Convention on the Law Applicable to Contractual Obligations. Article 3 of that Convention grants the parties nearly unfettered discretion to choose whatever law they wish. (See Problem 1–8.) Does this mean that Universal and Commonwealth can agree to use non-U.S. choice of law principles and require a U.S. court of follow those principles? To prevent application of the UCC? Despite UCC § 1–105.

For example, suppose the written agreement states: "The Parties agree that United Kingdom choice-of-law principles shall govern the contract." That would refer to the EC Convention, and under art. 3 of that convention, the parties have an unlimited ability to choose any substantive laws to govern the contract. Would that include the U.N. Convention on Contracts for the International Sale of Goods; and, if so, would such a choice-of-law provision be enforceable?

3. WHAT SALE CONTRACTS AND WHAT ISSUES ARE NOT COVERED?

The U.N. Sales Convention itself removes a number of transactions and issues from its coverage. Articles 2 and 3 exclude consumer and service transactions, while Articles 4 and 5 exclude most products liability issues, issues of validity, and questions of what effect the contract for sale has on property claims to the goods sold. The most important of these exclusions are of consumer and service transactions. Of necessity there will be difficult borderline transactions just as there are in domestic sales transactions. Attorneys whose clients engage in these transactions will, however, usually recognize that there is a potential problem and should include in the contracts they draw up for these clients an explicit statement about whether or not the Convention is to apply.

* * *

a. Goods

PROBLEM 1–9

Farmer in Washington State sells her entire crop of apples to Merchant in Singapore, while the crop is still growing and before it is harvested. Does the Sales Convention govern this sales transaction? See CISG art. 2. Does it matter whether the crop will be picked by Farmer or by Merchant?

If it is doubtful whether the Convention governs the contract but the parties want the Convention to apply, can the parties make it applicable by expressly agreeing that the Convention applies? In other words, can the parties "opt in"? See CISG art. 6. Compare your answer to your analysis in Problem 1–7.

* * *

NOTE ON TIMBER AND AGRICULTURAL PRODUCTS AS "GOODS"

RICHARDS, CONTRACTS FOR THE INTERNATIONAL SALE OF GOODS: APPLICABILITY OF THE UNITED NATIONS CONVENTION

69 Iowa L. Rev. 209 (1983).*

Interpretation of the CISG requires an understanding of the early ULIS clarifications and ambiguities. Like article 5 of the ULIS, article 2 of the CISG gives no clear definition of a good. The Philippine delegation to the UNCITRAL Conference argued that an affirmative definition ought to be included. Ambiguity exists because the CISG definition merely lists items that are not considered goods for the purposes of the Convention. This negative phrasing might pose interpretation problems for the attorney accustomed to applying the definitions of U.C.C. sections 2–105 and 2–107.

If an item is not excluded by the CISG definition, interpretation problems arise. For example, timber is not an excluded item; thus, . . . [the] contract providing for the shipment of wood products clearly could be a sale of goods within the CISG. Difficulties arise, however, when, . . . , the timber is uncut at the time that the agreement is made. Nevertheless, most jurisdictions in the United States would classify this type of contract as a sale of goods within U.C.C. section 2–107.

As noted earlier, universality is the primary policy concern in problems dealing with Convention applicability. Universality is furthered if the Convention text is widely applied and contracts for all but excluded materials are considered sales of goods. In addition, the Draft Commentary notes that one purpose of the CISG is to reduce the necessity of resorting to private international law rules. Thus, the more transactions to which the Convention applies, the less the parties will need to resort to conflict-of-laws rules.

An argument favoring application of the CISG to the uncut timber issue . . . thus would be based on several factors. First, timber is severable from real estate, and the agreement anticipates severance. Second, nothing in article 2 of the CISG would exclude uncut timber. Finally, a clear policy exists that favors applying the Convention broadly to effectuate its purpose of promoting international trade through uniform law. Therefore, the CISG should be applied.

UNCITRAL CLOUT Case 131
Germany: Landgericht München I; 1995.

The German defendant ordered a computer programme from the French plaintiff. The programme was delivered and installed. The parties also intended to conclude a second contract concerning the use of the programme, but the negotiations on that contract failed. The defendant then refused to pay the purchase price of the programme, which was delivered and installed.

The court held that the CISG was applicable as the parties had their place of business in different CISG Contracting States and as the CISG applies to standard software. The court further found also that the parties had agreed on all particulars of the sale of the programme and therefore had concluded a sales contract.

It was held that the defendant could not rely on a possible lack of conformity of the software programme, since it had not effectively given notice of the defect but had only asked for assistance in addressing the problems identified. As a result, the court ordered the defendant to pay the purchase price and interest at the rate of 5%.

* * *

UNCITRAL CLOUT Case 122
Germany: Oberlandesgericht Köln; 1994.

The plaintiff, a Swiss market research institute, had elaborated and delivered a market analysis, which had been ordered by the defendant, a German company. The defendant refused to pay the price alleging that the report did not comply with the conditions agreed upon by the parties.

The court held that the CISG was not applicable, since the underlying contract was neither a contract for the sale of goods (article 1(1) CISG) nor contract for the production of goods (article 3(1) CISG). Noting that the sale of goods is characterized by the transfer of property in an object, the court found that, although a report is fixed on a piece of paper, the main concern of the parties is not the handing over of the paper but the transfer of the right to use the ideas written down on such paper. Therefore, the court held that the agreement to prepare a market analysis is not a sale of goods within the meaning of articles 1 or 3 CISG.

* * *

b. Service Contracts

Article 3(a) excludes contracts by which the "buyer" supplies "a substantial part" of the materials necessary for production. Article 3(b) excludes contracts by which the "preponderant part" of the "seller's" obligations are to supply services. The terms "substantial" and "preponderant" are not defined.

* * *

PROBLEM 1–10

Illinois wholesaler agrees to purchase assembled electronic notepads from a Chinese enterprise. China is a Contracting State. The wholesaler supplies one of the five necessary components but this one component is worth 50% in value of all the components. The Chinese enterprise supplies the other four components and the unskilled labor. Expenses for the unskilled labor constitute 20% in value of the assembled notepads. Does CISG govern the contract? CISG art. 3. Which paragraph of Article 3 is applicable? If it is doubtful that the contract is governed by CISG but the parties want CISG to govern it, can they make CISG applicable by expressly agreeing that the CISG governs?

* * *

UNCITRAL CLOUT Case 152
France: Court of Appeal of Grenoble (Commercial Division), 1995.

A company with its place of business in France sold to an individual resident in Portugal a used warehouse for the price of 500,000 French francs, including the cost of dismantling and delivery, the price of the warehouse being 381,200 francs and the dismantling and delivery costs amounting to 118,800 francs. Following the buyer's refusal to pay the last part of the price on the grounds that the dismantled metal elements were defective, the Court of Appeal of Grenoble found that the disputed contract covered the sale of a used warehouse together with its dismantling and that it was apparent from the invoices submitted that the supply of services did not constitute the preponderant part [of the contractual obligations]. The court concluded that the contract therefore fell within the scope of application of CISG (art. 3(2)). . . .

* * *

c. *Consumer Goods and Consumer Transactions*

Sales to a person who buys goods for personal, family, or household use are not covered by the Convention unless the seller did not know that the sale is to such a person. Please read CISG Article 2(a), set forth in the Documents Supplement, which makes CISG inapplicable to certain consumer sales.

The definition of consumer transactions is similar to that found in the Uniform Commercial Code, although the latter does not provide for the exception where the seller is unaware that the sale is to a consumer. U.C.C. § 9–109(1).

Suppose Seller, an Italian manufacturer of bicycles, sells a bicycle to a visiting housewife from New York, who plans to use the bicycle in Italy during her one month tour of the country. Is this sale governed by CISG? CISG Article 1(1) requires that the seller and buyer have their "places of business" in different countries. If the New York tourist does not have a place of business, Article 10(b) directs the reader to substitute the buyer's "habitual residence"—i.e., New York in this case. Because both Italy and the United States are Contracting States, Article 1(1)(a) is satisfied. Moreover, Article 1 does not require that the goods sold move across national boundaries so the sale can be international whether or not the buyer plans to take the bicycle back with her to New York after her Italian tour.

Before concluding that CISG applies, however, you must also consult Article 2. Subparagraph (a) of that article expressly exclude "goods bought for personal, family or household use." Thus, if the buyer plans to use the bicycle only for Sunday rides in Central Park, the Convention would be inapplicable by its own terms. If, however, the buyer plans to use the bicycle to run messages in midtown Manhattan, her principal occupation, then the exclusion in Article 2(a) is inapplicable and the Convention applies.

What if nothing is said about the intended or potential use of the bicycle at the time of sale? First, would the transaction be an "international" one if the parties said nothing? One of your authors believes that any Italian shopkeeper would recognize a New Yorker, even if Italian-speaking, as a *straniero* and probably as an American. Thus, one could not rely on Article 1(2) to exclude application of the Convention.

Second, would the transaction be considered a "consumer good" transaction if no statement of intended use were requested or made? Note the construction of CISG Article 2(a). How you classify the bicycle initially depends upon the "purpose" for which the goods are bought—which, in turn, would seem to depend upon the *buyer's* subjective intent, declared or not. The "unless" clause declares an exception for the unknowing seller, but *only* if the seller "neither knew nor ought to have known" of such intended use. Non-disclosure alone does not protect the seller, if it "ought" to know of that the buyer would use the bicycle for personal, family or household purposes. Is there any argument that, if nothing is said, seller "ought" not to know that a bicycle is bought for personal use? This analysis applies to a whole range of items usually labeled "consumer goods."

Why would CISG exclude sales of "consumer goods" from its coverage? Consider the range of special domestic "consumer" legislation in many countries. This legislation sets standards for performance and safety, regulate what kinds of clauses may be included or must be excluded in consumer contracts, and provide additional remedies to aggrieved consumer buyers. It was never contemplated that CISG would displace such domestic legislation. It was not even contemplated that the application of such legislation would depend upon analysis of "validity" issues under CISG Article 4(a). At the retail level, inclusion of "business" transactions only was an underlying assumption very early in the drafting process.

If retail sales of "consumer goods" are excluded from CISG, what about sales of the same goods by the manufacturer to a wholesaler, or by the wholesaler to a retailer?

* * *

PROBLEM 1–11

Manufacturer of bicycles has its place of business in Italy. Manufacturer sells 100 bicycles to a Retailer of bicycles with its place of business in New York. The New York Retailer plans to sell the bicycles to consumers who use them to ride in Central Park on Sundays.

(a) Assume that the New York Retailer informs Manufacturer of this plan to sell the bicycles to consumers. Does the Convention govern the contract? Would you change your answer if Manufacturer could show that it did not know of the intended use? CISG arts. 1(2), 2(a).

(b) If, in answer to the previous questions, you conclude that the Convention does apply to the Manufacturer–Retailer contract, what law governs the sales by Retailer to consumers in New York? Will having different laws govern the Manufacturer–Retailer and Retailer–Consumer contracts create potential difficulties? What if, for example, the scope of the warranties given by the sellers differ?

If you conclude that having different laws governing the contracts may create difficulties, what steps should Retailer take to minimize the difficulties?

(c) If Retailer included a term in the Retailer–Consumer contract document that purported to make the Convention the applicable law, would a New York court enforce this term? What if Retailer sells the bikes "as is" but provides each consumer buyer with a "warranty in a box" from Manufacturer, which claims to be governed by the Sales Convention? Would a New York court accept that claim? Compare your answer on this "opt in" issue to your analysis of Problem 1–7. Should there be any difference? Why?

d. *Excluded issues.*

Articles 2 and 3 exclude certain transactions and certain types of property from the Convention's coverage. Article 4 and 5 exclude from the Convention's coverage most products liability issues, issues of validity, and questions of what effect the contract for sale has on property claims to the goods sold.

Products liability. Products liability issues are dealt with by several different Convention provisions. The Convention governs only the rights and obligations of the seller and buyer to a sales contract. CISG art. 4 states that the Convention governs only the formation of the contract of sale and the rights and obligations of the seller and the buyer arising from such a contract. See the Documents Supplement. By necessary implication, the Convention does not cover claims against other parties in the manufacturing or distribution chain. The Convention also expressly excludes claims for death or personal injury caused by the defects in the goods sold. CISG art. 5 states that the Convention does not apply to the liability of the seller for death or personal injury caused by the goods to any person.

Illustration 1. Seller has its place of business in Germany; buyer has its place of business in Connecticut. Buyer purchases heavy equipment from seller. A defect in a component of the equipment causes a fire at buyer's Connecticut plant. The fire injures an employee of the buyer, destroys the heavy equipment purchased, and damages other equipment owned by the buyer. The Convention does not govern liability for injury to the employee, but will govern damages to the equipment and to the other personal property of the buyer.

Validity. Issues of "validity"—e.g., fraud, duress, illegality, and unconscionability—are left to non-uniform national law under CISG Article 4(a), set forth in the Documents Supplement. What issues may be called ones of validity is a matter of some concern because if this exclusion is read broadly courts would undermine the uniformity that the Convention is designed to enhance.

Illustration 2. Seller has its place of business in France; Buyer has its place of business in New Jersey. The parties agree that if Seller fails to perform as agreed it will pay the sum of $100,000. Assume that French law would uphold this term but New Jersey law would not enforce this term because the sum is unreasonably large "in the light of anticipated or actual harm." U.C.C. § 2–718(2). Whether this term is enforceable is not resolved by the Convention, which leaves the issue to the domestic law chosen by application of traditional choice-of-law analysis.

Property in the goods sold. The property aspects of sales contracts are also left to national law. CISG Article 4(b) states that the Convention is not concerned with "the effect which the contract may have on the property in the goods sold."

Illustration 3. Seller is an enterprise in Germany; Buyer is an Illinois corporation. In their sales agreement, Seller reserves title to secure payment of the purchase price. If the enforceability of this retention of title term is called into question, the Convention will not resolve the issue and it will be resolved under the domestic law made applicable through a choice-of-laws analysis.

The seller must, however, deliver goods "which are free from any right or claim of a third party, unless the buyer agreed to take the goods subject to that right or claim." CISG art. 41. There is also special treatment for intellectual property claims. CISG arts. 42–43.

Chapter 2

FORMATION OF THE SALES CONTRACT

A. INTRODUCTION

If you were to analyze the basic fact patterns of conduct that lead to the formation of legally-enforceable contracts, you would find that they fall along a spectrum running from the casual to the formal. At one end of the spectrum you find the most casual interaction between buyer and seller. Further along the spectrum of formality is the point where one or both parties use pre-prepared standard forms. At the other end of the spectrum is the fully-negotiated "deal." As we shall see, legal issues will differ depending on where a particular fact pattern falls on the "formality" spectrum.

What role the lawyer plays will also differ. Parties to an informal agreement will rarely consult a lawyer until a dispute arises that cannot be resolved informally. For these parties, the lawyer takes on the role of litigator. When a seller or buyer wishes to draw up a standard form contract the lawyer will be called upon to act as "draftsman" but will rarely be consulted in connection with the formation of a particular contract. When the stakes are high, as in a "big deal," the parties may ask lawyers not only to act as "draftsmen" but also to assist as "negotiators" or "planners."

* * *

WINSHIP, FORMATION OF INTERNATIONAL SALES CONTRACTS UNDER THE 1980 VIENNA CONVENTION
17 Int'l Law. 1, 3–5, 7 (1983).*

Part II of the CISG (Arts. 14–24) sets out the rules regulating the formation of an international sales contract. The first four articles of Part II govern the offer. These articles provide for the prerequisites of an

* Copyright © 1983 and reproduced by permission from the International Lawyer.

offer (Art. 14) and the withdrawal, revocation, and termination of an offer (Arts. 15–17). The following five articles set out the corresponding rules on acceptance. They provide for the form an acceptance may take (Art. 18), the effect of an acceptance that varies the terms of an offer (Art. 19), the time allowed for acceptance (Arts. 20–21), and withdrawal of an acceptance (Art. 22). Article 23 states that a contract is concluded when an acceptance becomes effective, which normally will be when a notice of acceptance reaches the offeror. A final provision, Article 24, defines when a communication "reaches" a party.

A reader trained in the common law and the Uniform Commercial Code will find some surprises in both the style and the scope of these provisions. In style the articles in Part II follow the civilian model of a comprehensive collection of brief, general rules rather than the more detailed and convoluted statements found in common law legislation. In scope Part II omits several matters the common lawyer would expect to find among formation rules. There is no statute of frauds; there is no reference to modification of a contract; and there is no requirement that there be consideration in order to have an enforceable contract. Several of these omissions are filled by provisions found elsewhere in the CISG. An article in Part I provides that an enforceable sales contract may be concluded without a writing (CISG art. 11) and a provision in Part III states that a contract may be modified by agreement of the parties in any form unless the original contract requires the modification to be in writing (CISG art. 29). The CISG, however, contains no provision for consideration. Of course this will rarely be a problem in the context of sale where exchange of goods for money is the object of the transaction.

Notwithstanding these differences in style and scope the CISG provisions constitute a comprehensive codification which provides many of the same answers found in the common law and the Uniform Commercial Code. [The author goes on to illustrate this point with several simple hypothetical cases.]

* * *

P. SCHLECHTRIEM, COMMENTARY ON THE U.N. CONVENTION ON CONTRACTS FOR THE INTERNATIONAL SALE OF GOODS
99–102 (G. Thomas translator) (2d ed., 1998).*

2. Other forms of concluding the contract. Articles 14 to 24 lay down contract formation rules which accord with "traditional theory", using "offer" and "acceptance" as the elements through which agreement between the parties is created. As is shown by the research led and published by Schlesinger on the formation of contracts, Ernst Rabel's work and the conclusions of von Mehren, that is in conformity with ideas common to all legal systems. Nevertheless, as already shown by Schlesinger and by work on ULF and the CISG, there are other forms of reaching agreement (e.g. agreement reached in point-by-point negotiations or by lengthy exchange of correspondence), where the "dissection" of individual statements into "offer" and "acceptance" would constitute an arbitrary legal operation. The dispatch of offers which cross, or a failure to object to a commercial letter of confirmation are also methods of reaching binding agreement which do not automatically fit within the scheme of offer/acceptance. At the Hague Conference there was even a proposal from the American delegate Mentschikoff that a rule be included which would have permitted agreement of the parties to be deduced from their contract, as in §§ 2–204 and 207(3) of the UCC; there was no approval for that proposal, since it would have altered the overall scheme of the CISG. There were also proposals that the CISG should lay down rules for the conclusion of a contract by proof of agreement (instead of by offer and acceptance) and also by cross-offers; the proposals were eventually withdrawn, again because of the "extreme difficulty of formulating an acceptable text".

It must be established whether the CISG's rules for establishing the formation of a contract by offer and acceptance are intended to be conclusive only to that extent, so that the domestic law invoked under conflicts of law rules is still applicable with respect to other forms of reaching agreement, or whether Article 7(2) permits or even requires a solution first to be found on the basis of the principles underlying the Convention. In that respect, the majority view is that there is a gap in the Convention which must be filled using the principles of the Convention. In the present author's opinion, two aspects must be distinguished when appraising non-regulated events relating to agreement. First, it must be asked whether a "question concerning matters governed by this Convention" is involved (Article 7(2)) and then must be examined whether the CISG contains adequate principles for solving the actual problem.

a. Conclusion of a contract by silence. The conclusion of a contract as a result of failure to respond to a commercial letter of confirmation is, in a broad sense, one means of establishing contractual agreement. It was a matter on which there were negotiations and provisions at The Hague. Since, as the German representatives wished, trade usage was regarded as having normative effect, this was also considered to be a matter which fell within the notion of "conclusion of the contract". The question of the commercial letter of confirmation was also raised in Vienna, although one of the grounds for a proposal to widen the scope for gap-filling on the basis of the Convention's principles was that German rules on commercial letters of confirmation, as domestic law invoked under conflict of law rules, could thereby be prevented from applying (!). From this and other references to the commercial letter of confirmation, it must be concluded that such a letter was regarded as an instrument capable of indicating the conclusion of a contract and was to be appraised under the CISG. In addition, it was decided that the German rules should in any event be taken into account as a trade usage, if and in so far as a trade usage could apply under Article 9(1) or (2). The requirement for its applicability under Article 9(1) or (2) are most likely to exist where the parties have their place of business in states which—at least in the relevant trade sector—have rules similar to those on the commercial letter of confirmation and on the effect of the addressee's silence under German law. In the case of a sales contract between parties with a place of business in Austria and in Switzerland respectively, the Zivilgericht Basel held that a commercial letter of confirmation from the Austrian supplier gave rise to a contract, because a commercial letter of confirmation could have such an effect both in Austria and in Switzerland and, therefore, it had to be assumed that both parties must have recognized its legal effects; in addition, on the basis of a previous letter of confirmation, the existence of a practice established between the parties within the meaning of Article 9(1) had to be presumed. Consequently, in such cases, despite the clear inclination of those participating in the UN Conference at Vienna not to favour the commercial letter of confirmation or its contractual effect, such a letter should be significant also in the international sale of goods. Moreover, its evidential significance under domestic procedural law is unaffected. That means, however, that there is generally no room for recourse via conflicts of law rules to domestic law and its rules on commercial letters of confirmation.

b. Agreement without clear offer and acceptance. Agreements reached without clearly identifiable elements of offer and acceptance also fall within the scope of the CISG's rules on objective agreement, as is shown by their treatment in ULF and CISG and the attempts to lay down rules for them in those conventions. A contrary conclusion cannot be drawn from the fact that those attempts were abandoned, since there was no decision to exclude the application of uniform law on contract formation to such ways of reaching agreement; the attempts were abandoned above all on account of difficulties encountered in formulating an appropriate rule. It is therefore necessary to find a solution which is in conformity with the principles of the CISG. It will still often be possible to discern an offer and an acceptance in the events leading to the reaching of an agreement. By virtue of Article 9(1), practices of the parties which depart from the traditional model for contract formation are not only significant but also to be regarded as establishing the conclusion of a contract under the CISG, which excludes recourse to conflicts of law rules and domestic law, even, and in particular, where an agreement of that type is unknown under that law.

The appropriate principles to be applied in order to deal with the remaining cases are the principle of consensus and the principle that it must be possible to discern the minimum content required for a contract (as defined by the requirements for an offer (Article 14)). If a state has entered a reservation concerning requirements as to form (Articles 12 and 96), such consensus and minimum contractual content must be documented in accordance with its formal requirements. If an agreement reached by the parties satisfies these basic requirement, either where they have reached agreement on successive, point-for-point basis, simultaneously signed a document, or where identical, irrevocable offers have crossed, then the formation of a contract under Articles 7(2) and 14 *et seq.* can be presumed, so that recourse to conflict of law rules and domestic law is not only unnecessary, but even excluded.

H. DE VRIES, CIVIL LAW AND THE ANGLO–AMERICAN LAWYER
378–88 (1976).*

C. *Formation*

The modern Anglo-American law of contract is based upon a commercial approach, the idea of a bargain as an indispensable element, the doctrine of consideration reflecting the notion of *quid pro quo*. In contrast, civil law systems start with the assumption of valid consent as the essential element.

In French legal theory, the contract is formed when free and untrammeled consent of the parties has resulted in "a meeting of the minds" with respect to a determined subject matter. Mistake, duress, fraud and misrepresentation, all defects in consent (*vices de consentement*), are problem areas in determining whether consent is affected by improper pressures. The requirement of lawful *cause*, the prohibition against a *condition potestative* (illusory promise) in Articles 1170 and 1174, the devices for setting aside manifestly unfair arrangements (Article 1855, invalidating the "lion's share" distribution of profits—the *clause léonine*; Articles 1674 *et seq.*, on *lésion*), all affect the validity rather than the existence of the contract. Governmental economic regulations also have raised issues of validity of loan agreements and price clauses expressed in foreign currency on grounds of internal and international public policy.

Anglo-American law still tends to regard the formation of contract (other than standardized or form contracts) as consisting of two fairly separate phases: that of negotiation of pre-contractual, defined by offer and acceptance, and that of formation of a "signed, sealed, and delivered" instrument, detailed, self-sufficient, and immutable within the terms of the intent expressed.

In Continental law a broad spectrum of unilateral oral or written declarations may range from the simple invitation to deal through the unilateral right of first refusal, the promise to sell, and the bilateral agreement to contract, to the completed private agreement and the contract in notarial form. In the absence of the doctrine of consideration and without a parole evidence rule assuring integration of the entire transaction, Continental legal systems favor binding intermediate commitments provided the essential conditions of the type-contract involved are expressed.

1. *Preliminary Agreements*

In the process of formation of international contracts a preliminary agreement is often signed terminating a stage of negotiation. The binding effect of such preliminary agreements, depends on a legal system's minimum requirement of form and language, verbal expression of an intent to be bound and the terms considered essential to the transaction involved.

In continental systems, for example, a promise to grant a loan is enforceable if there is agreement on the maximum amount of the loan and the date of repayment. An agreement to form a *société* is enforceable if the *avant contrat* sets forth the purpose, the amount of each member's contribution, its duration and the mode of sharing profits and losses.

* * *

D. *Requirements of Form*

In matters of form French law distinguishes sharply between civil and commercial matters. With few exceptions as in express statutory provisions setting forth government economic regulations, in commercial dealings the requirement of form seldom affects validity. Further, as a general rule, all modes of proof are admissible to establish the existence of an agreement and the intent of the parties. Thus the rule of Article 1341 of the Civil Code barring testimonial evidence to establish the existence and intent of actes juridiques involving more than a minor sum is not applicable to business arrangements.

In civil matters the requirement of the *acte* authentique or notarial instrument may impose a higher degree of formality, often affecting validity. Thus a mortgage and or a promise to make a gift are void if not in the notarial form. When a Frenchman marries, invests or borrows, settles a decedent's estate, draws a will or organizes a company, he visualizes the notarial form. Essentially, however in most contracts not governed by commercial law, the notion of pre-constituted proof is the keystone of the requirement of writing, seldom affecting validity but generally barring testimonial proof in the absence of a minimum of written evidence.

In addition to the requirement of writing, French law contains formal requirements in civil contracts as to counterparts, registration and handwritten insertions which present a useful precautionary list for the Anglo-American lawyer accustomed only to the Statute of Frauds and the parol evidence rule.

* * *

B. FORMATION OF THE CASUAL CONTRACT

In this part of the chapter we explore the casual interaction between buyer and seller. The buyer and seller talk with each other face to face, over the phone, by telex, telegram, letters or other simple written orders. The "conversation" may be brief and the seller and buyer may only discuss basic terms, such as quantity and price. The archetype of this fact pattern is the telephone conversation: "Send me 100 electronic notepads for $1,000"; and "They're on their way." Despite the informality, the seller and buyer will perform "the contract" in a high proportion of cases. Frequently they will have dealt with each other before or be part of an established trade conducted without time-consuming formalities. When disputes arise, the parties will often resolve them without going to lawyers or using legal process. This is not to say that legal rules are irrelevant: they may affect the negotiating position of the parties as they settle their differences. These legal issues rarely involve whether the parties have "agreed." Instead, the legal issues involve answering questions such as (1) whether the agreement satisfies evidentiary or cautionary problems concerning informal contracts, or (2) how "gaps" in the contract terms are to be filled.

Below we explore how well the U.N. Sales Convention deals with the first of the fact patterns outlined above. We divide the materials in this part into three distinct parts. The first part explores the Convention's "offer-acceptance" paradigm, with special attention to how the Convention deals with the "firm" offer. In the second part we consider the extent to which the Convention does away with "consideration" and the formality of a required writing. We turn in the third part to how the Convention fills in the details of the contract when the seller and buyer themselves have expressly agreed on only basic terms, such as quantity and price. This last part concludes with a study of how specific the price term must be for there to be an enforceable offer under the Convention.

1. OFFER AND ACCEPTANCE

PROBLEM 2–1.

Able Co., a French manufacturer of transistors, receives an e-mail from Baker Co., a Virginia-based manufacturer of electronic equipment, stating: "We wish to buy 1,000 A7S transistors. How much are they?" Able replies by e-mail: "We can let you have them for U.S. $6 apiece." Baker's e-mail responds: "Good. Done."

(a) Did Able make an "offer"? If so, is it sufficiently definite to satisfy the Sales Convention? Does it indicate the intention of the offeror to be bound? Must it do each of these? CISG art. 14(1).

(b) Is Baker's response an acceptance or an offer. Does it indicate the intention to be bound? CISG art. 14, 18(1), (2).

(c) Assuming that eventually there was an offer and an acceptance, what event occurred to conclude the contract? CISG art. 18 (2), 23. Compare the result to the "mail box" rule in Adams v. Lindsell, 106 Eng. Rep. 250 (K.B. 1818).

(d) Assuming that there was an offer and an acceptance, *where* did the event occur which concluded the contract? Is this question relevant if the Convention governs the contract? Where the contract was concluded might be relevant for other purposes (*e.g.*, court jurisdiction). Should the Convention have addressed the issue?

* * *

UNCITRAL CLOUT CASE 135
Oberlandesgericht Frankfurt a.M., 1995.

The plaintiff, a German glass manufacturer, agreed to manufacture and deliver 220,000 test-tubes to the Italian defendant. During the course of negotiations, the appropriate glass type was the point of discussion as different types were mentioned. The plaintiff finally delivered test-tubes in Fiolax quality and demanded payment. The defendant refused to pay and alleged to have ordered the better Duran quality.

The court found that the CISG was applicable (art. 1(1)(a) CISG). According to articles 62 and 59 CISG, the seller can claim the price, if a contract has been concluded, i.e., if there is a valid offer and acceptance. The court found that the acceptance of the plaintiff's offer was missing as the seller and the buyer did not reach an agreement towards a specific glass quality (art. 18(1), 19(1), 19(3) CISG). It was held therefore that the plaintiff could not demand payment. . . .

EORSI, "ARTICLE 16"
Commentary on the International Sales Law: The 1980 Vienna
Convention, 155–160 (C. Bianca & M. Bonell eds. 1987).*

2.1.1.   There are three basic approaches to the problem of revocability. In the common law an offer is revocable and, as a historical remnant of the consideration doctrine, its revocability is affected neither by a promise not to revoke it nor by a provision that it will not be revoked before a stated date (*but see* the different rule adopted by § 2–205 of the United States Uniform Commercial Code). In romanistic systems (*e.g.*, French law), although revocation of an offer is permitted—particularly if it states a fixed time for acceptance—the offeror is bound to indemnify the offeree or to pay damages in case of revocation. In German law and in some other civil law systems an offer is binding unless the offeror stated that the offer was revocable At the 1964 Hague Conference and at the Vienna Conference the romanistic pattern was not discussed and the debate centred on the common law and the German pattern.

These two patterns contradict each other at a crucial point of contract formation. The situation is further aggravated when contracts are concluded by traders, who have particular difficulty in knowing which doctrine applies to their contract. At most, unification efforts can choose one of the doctrines, or try to compromise. Even in the latter case there is no possibility of a "fifty-fifty" compromise because the two doctrines are irreconcilable. There seems to be no choice but to select one doctrine as the main rule and the other as an exception to it. This is precisely what was done. The Convention follows the common law pattern but permits exceptions.

2.1.2. The time span for revocation in civil law countries last until the contract is concluded. But, here again, the two legal systems diverge. The common law applies the mailbox theory, which means that revocation is not effective if the offeree dispatches an acceptance before the revocation has reached him. * * * It might perhaps be added that by virtue of Article 18 (1), conduct of the offeree indicating assent (*e.g.,* shipping the goods or paying the price) amounts to acceptance. Therefore, conduct to the effect of an acceptance might be regarded as equivalent to dispatch.

The purpose of the mailbox rule is to shorten the time of uncertainty for the offeree by permitting him to cut short the time available for revocation. The disadvantage of this rule is that it involves an element of surprise for the offeror. He loses the right to revoke his offer at the moment of dispatch of the acceptance although at that time he is not yet aware that an acceptance is on the way, and therefore that he may no longer revoke his offer. In contrast, in civil law systems the time span for revocation lasts until the acceptance reaches the offeror. Therefore, uncertainty on the part of the offeree lasts longer since the offeror may revoke his offer up to the time when the acceptance reaches him. On the other hand, there is no element of surprise in the course of making the contract. Here again the common law pattern was narrowly adopted (*see* Article 16 (1)).

2.1.3. To sum up, an effective offer (*see* Article 15) may be revoked if the contract is not yet concluded (*see* Article 23) and the acceptance was not yet dispatched. If, for instance, the acceptance is dispatched on May 10 and reaches the offeror on May 15, the contract is concluded on May 15 but the right to revoke lapses on May 10. It might be added that, due to the rapidity of contemporary communication, the above-mentioned element of surprise will, in most cases, not materialize. When this is not the case it is up to the offeree to prove at what time the acceptance was dispatched.

2.2. Article 16 (2) provides for an exception to the main rule of revocability. Although it might seem that sub-paragraphs (a) and (b) provide for two different exceptions, they express the same exception. Sub-paragraph (a) does it with civil law language, and sub-paragraph (b) with common law language. The question presented is, when is it reasonable for the offeree to rely on the offer as being irrevocable? The answer is when the offer indicates that it is irrevocable. It seems impossible that where the offer indicates that it is irrevocable reliance on the offer could at the same time be unreasonable; and, correspondingly, for it to be reasonable to rely on an offer as irrevocable, there must be an indication that it is irrevocable.

Seemingly, sub-paragraph (a) offers the civil law systems their own law and sub-paragraph (b) does the same for the common law jurisdictions. This reasoning, however, was not followed in discussions of the

Working Group. A number of delegations did not understand the reliance doctrine well, and common law delegations interpreted sub-paragraph (a) in their own way. The common law delegations maintained that even if the offer states a fixed period of time for acceptance, this, in itself, does not necessarily mean that the offer is irrevocable; after all, revocability and irrevocability do not necessarily depend on whether a fixed time for acceptance was stated in the offer. Thus, common law delegations were inclined to read the civil law languages in the common law way. The Secretariat's Commentary states only:

The offer may also indicate that it is irrevocable by stating a fixed time for acceptance.

This seems to indicate that stating a fixed time for acceptance is not in itself sufficient to make the offer irrevocable.

2.2.1.   Sub-paragraph (a) would be unambiguous if it provided the following: "If (the offer) indicates a fixed time for acceptance or otherwise indicates that it is irrevocable". As a matter of fact sub-paragraph (a) as adopted by the Working Group at its eighth session stated that an offer cannot be revoked "if it expressly or impliedly indicates that it is firm or irrevocable; or (b) if the offer states a fixed period of time for [acceptance] [irrevocability]..." This would mean that an offer which stated a fixed time for acceptance would always be irrevocable. Such a wording could not meet the approval of common law delegations. Therefore, the "compromise" solution reads: "if it indicates, whether by stating that a fixed time...". For a civil law jurist this wording would lead to the same result, namely that the offer is irrevocable during the time fixed for acceptance. On the other hand, for a common law jurist the text would mean that the offer is irrevocable only if the manner of "stating a fixed time for acceptance" indicated that the offer was irrevocable. Stating a fixed time for acceptance may not by itself mean irrevocability. Many of the delegations were fully aware of this ambiguity, but it seemed that this was the only way to achieve unification. The unification achieved is probably strictly formal except for parties coming from legal systems which resemble each other. What the common law or the civil law parties should do under such circumstances is employ Article 8 (1), and interpret their contract accordingly.

If the offer states, "Our offer is at any rate good till May 13", then the offer is irrevocable. But, if it states merely, "Our offer is not good after May 13", then common law jurists might conclude that the offer is a revocable one that lapses on May 13. "I stand by my offer till I get your answer" is an indication to the effect that the offer is irrevocable during that time.

The indication required in sub-paragraph (a) may be a statement, a declaration, conduct of the offeror or simply a situation or circumstances known by the offeree or which ought to have been known by him.

2.2.2.   Sub-paragraph (b) incorporates the reliance doctrine into the mechanism of making a contract. This doctrine may be compared with the famous general clause *"Treu und Glauben"* ("good faith") of the

Federal Republic of Germany Civil Code and the Swiss Code, although its scope is not so wide as that of this general clause. The common purpose of the civil law and common law doctrine is to prevent a fair and fully competent party from being unexpectedly deceived in his lawful expectations. This is "soft law" (in contrast with "harsh law"), a product of what is termed "social law" which provides, among other things, increased protection for those who deserve it. In other words, it protects those whose frustrated expectations were not only lawful but also reasonable in the given situation.

Sub-paragraph (b) applies when two conditions are satisfied: first, it was reasonable for the offeree to rely on the offer as being irrevocable, and second, he has already acted in reliance on the offer. Thus, reliance on the offer is in itself irrelevant: for the purpose of resorting to sub-paragraph (b) an act or a conduct in reliance of the offer is needed. Such an act or conduct may consist of preparation for production, buying or hiring materials or equipment, incurring expenses, provided that such an act or conduct was regarded as normal in the trade concerned, or was supported by preliminary negotiations, or should otherwise have been foreseen by or known to the offeror. Such an act or conduct would in such cases also serve as an "indication" under sub-paragraph (a). * * *

* * *

PROBLEM 2–2

Dietrich, a German paper manufacturer telephones Charlie, a Maine manufacturer of rollers for pulp mills. He asks Charlie: "I need four replacement rollers for one of my mills. Can you help me out?" Charlie replies: "Of course I can let you have them in 30 days, but you'll have to let me know by the end of next week whether you want them." Dietrich responds: "Let me get back to you," and then hangs up.

(a) Three days after this conversation (*i.e.*, before "the end of next week") Charlie telephones Dietrich and says that he is taking back the offer. Is this "taking back" an attempted withdrawal, or a revocation, of the offer? No matter what it is called, is the taking back effective? CISG arts. 15, 16.

(b) Assume that Dietrich, rather than Charlie, makes the "firm" offer (*e.g.*, "I'll purchase four replacement rollers, for delivery in 30 days, but you'll have to accept my offer by the end of next week"). If Dietrich calls three days later to take back his offer, will this be effective? Is there "consideration" for the firm offer? If not, does this matter? CISG art. 8.

(c) Assume that the "firm" offer is made by Dietrich, but that Dietrich is Australian rather than German. Australia is a party to the Convention, but the Australian legal system is part of the Anglo–American legal family and a firm offer is enforceable only if there is consideration. Could it be argued successfully that when two parties come from common law countries their "intent" is informed by the domestic legal system with which they are familiar? CISG art. 8. If so, reconsider your answers to the scenarios with Charlie and Dietrich from the U.S. and Germany, respectively. Is it relevant that German law does not permit the revocation of a "firm offer" or that U.C.C. § 2–205 also limits the revocation of a firm offer that complies with that section?

* * *

FILANTO, S.P.A., v. CHILEWICH INTERNATIONAL CORP.

United States District Court, Southern District of New York, 1992.
789 F. Supp. 1229.

BRIEANT, CHIEF JUDGE.

By motion fully submitted on December 11, 1991, defendant Chilewich International Corp. moves to stay this action pending arbitration in Moscow. Plaintiff Filanto has moved to enjoin arbitration or to order arbitration in this federal district.

This case is a striking example of how a lawsuit involving a relatively straightforward international commercial transaction can raise an array of complex questions. Accordingly, the Court will recount the factual background of the case, derived from both parties' memoranda of law and supporting affidavits, in some detail.

Plaintiff Filanto is an Italian corporation engaged in the manufacture and sale of footwear. Defendant Chilewich is an export-import firm incorporated in the state of New York with its principal place of business in White Plains. On February 28, 1989, Chilewich's agent in the United Kingdom, Byerly Johnson, Ltd., signed a contract with Raznoexport, the Soviet Foreign Economic Association, which obligated Byerly Johnson to supply footwear to Raznoexport. Section 10 of this contract—the "Russian Contract"—is an arbitration clause, which reads in pertinent part as follows:

> "All disputes or differences which may arise out of or in connection with the present Contract are to be settled, jurisdiction of ordinary courts being excluded, by the Arbitration at the USSR Chamber of Commerce and Industry, Moscow, in accordance with the Regulations of the said Arbitration." [sic]

* * *

The first exchange of correspondence between the parties to this lawsuit is a letter dated July 27, 1989 from Mr. Melvin Chilewich of Chilewich International to Mr. Antonio Filograna, chief executive officer of Filanto. This letter refers to a recent visit by Chilewich and Byerly Johnson personnel to Filanto's factories in Italy, presumably to negotiate a purchase to fulfill the Russian Contract, and then states as follows:

> "Attached please find our contract to cover our purchase from you. Same is governed by the conditions which are enumerated in the standard contract in effect with the Soviet buyers [the Russian contract], copy of which is also enclosed."

* * *

The last paragraph of the September 2, 1989 letter from Filanto to Chilewich states as follows:

"Returning back the enclosed contracts n 10001–10002–10003 signed for acceptance, we communicate, if we do not misunderstood, the Soviet's contract that you sent us together with your above mentioned contract, that of this contract we have to respect only the following points of it:

–n 5 Packing and marking

–n 6 Way of Shipment

–n 7 Delivery—Acceptance of Goods

We ask for your acceptance by return of post." [sic]

* * *

The next document in this case, and the focal point of the parties' dispute regarding whether an arbitration agreement exists, is a Memorandum Agreement dated March 13, 1990. This Memorandum Agreement, number 9003002, is a standard merchant's memo prepared by Chilewich for signature by both parties confirming that Filanto will deliver 100,000 pairs of boots to Chilewich at the Italian/Yugoslav border on September 15, 1990, with the balance of 150,000 pairs to be delivered on November 1, 1990. Chilewich's obligations were to open a Letter of Credit in Filanto's favor prior to the September 15 delivery, and another letter prior to the November delivery. This Memorandum includes the following provision:

"It is understood between Buyer and Seller that USSR Contract No. 32–03/93085 [the Russian Contract] is hereby incorporated in this contract as far as practicable, and specifically that any arbitration shall be in accordance with that Contract."

... Chilewich signed this Memorandum Agreement, and sent it to Filanto. Filanto at that time did not sign or return the document. Nevertheless, on May 7, 1990, Chilewich opened a Letter of Credit in Filanto's favor in the sum of $2,595,600.00. The Letter of Credit itself mentions the Russian Contract, but only insofar as concerns packing and labelling. . . .

* * *

Then, on August 7, 1990, Filanto returned the Memorandum Agreement, sued on here, that Chilewich had signed and sent to it in March; though Filanto had signed the Memorandum Agreement, it once again appended a covering letter, purporting to exclude all but three sections of the Russian Contract.

* * *

According to the Complaint, what ultimately happened was that Chilewich bought and paid for 60,000 pairs of boots in January 1991, but never purchased the 90,000 pairs of boots that comprise the balance of Chilewich's original order. Complaint at PP 9–11. It is Chilewich's failure to do so that forms the basis of this lawsuit, commenced by Filanto on May 14, 1991.

* * *

Against this background based almost entirely on documents, defendant Chilewich on July 24, 1991 moved to stay this action pending arbitration, while plaintiff Filanto on August 22, 1992 moved to enjoin arbitration, or, alternatively, for an order directing that arbitration be held in the Southern District of New York rather than Moscow, because of unsettled political conditions in Russia.

Jurisdiction/Applicable Law

* * * This Court ... finds another overriding basis for subject matter jurisdiction which will affect our choice of law: chapter 2 of the Federal Arbitration Act, which comprises the Convention on the Recognition and Enforcement of Foreign Arbitral Awards and its implementing legislation, codified at 9 U.S.C. § 201 et seq. The United States, Italy and the USSR are all signatories to this Convention, and its implementing legislation makes clear that the Arbitration Convention governs disputes regarding arbitration agreements between parties to international commercial transactions:

> "An arbitration agreement or arbitral award arising out of a legal relationship, whether contractual or not, which is considered as commercial, including a transaction, contract, or agreement described in section 2 of this title, falls under the Convention. An agreement or award arising out of such a relationship which is entirely between citizens of the United States should be deemed not to fall under the Convention ..." 9 U.S.C. § 202.

The Arbitration Convention specifically requires courts to recognize any "agreement in writing under which the parties undertake to submit to arbitration...." Convention on the Recognition and Enforcement of Foreign Arbitral Awards Article II(1). The term "agreement in writing" is defined as "an arbitral clause in a contract or an arbitration agreement, signed by the parties or contained in an exchange of letters or telegrams". Convention on the Recognition and Enforcement Of Foreign Arbitral Awards Article II(2).

* * *

This Court concludes that the question of whether these parties agreed to arbitrate their disputes is governed by the Arbitration Convention and its implementing legislation....

* * *

Courts confronted by cases governed by the Arbitration Convention must conduct a limited, four-part inquiry:

> "1) Is there an agreement in writing to arbitrate the subject of the dispute. Convention, Articles II(1), II(2).

2) Does the agreement provide for arbitration in the territory of a signatory country? Convention, Articles I(1), I(3); 9 U.S.C. § 206; Declaration of the United States Upon Accession, reprinted at 9 U.S.C.A. § 201, Note 43.

3) Does the agreement arise out of a legal relationship, whether contractual or not, which is considered as commercial? Convention, Article I(3); 9 U.S.C. § 202.

4) Is a party to the contract not an American citizen, or does the commercial relationship have some reasonable relation with one or more foreign states? 9 U.S.C. § 202."

... In this case, the second, third and fourth criteria are clearly satisfied, as the purported agreement provides for arbitration in Moscow, the Chilewich–Filanto relationship is a "commercial" relationship, and Filanto is an Italian corporation. The central disputed issue, therefore, is whether the correspondence between the parties, viewed in light of their business relationship, constitutes an "agreement in writing".

Courts interpreting this "agreement in writing" requirement have generally started their analysis with the plain language of the Convention, which requires "an arbitral clause in a contract or an arbitration agreement, signed by the parties or contained in an exchange of letters or telegrams", Article I(1), and have then applied that language in light of federal law, which consists of generally accepted principles of contract law, including the Uniform Commercial Code....

However, as plaintiff correctly notes, the "general principles of contract law" relevant to this action, do not include the Uniform Commercial Code; rather, the "federal law of contracts" to be applied in this case is found in the United Nations Convention on Contracts for the International Sale of Goods (the "Sale of Goods Convention"), codified at 15 U.S.C. Appendix. * * * Since the contract alleged in this case most certainly was formed, if at all, after January 1, 1988, and since both the United States and Italy are signatories to the Convention, the Court will interpret the "agreement in writing" requirement of the Arbitration Convention in light of, and with reference to, the substantive international law of contracts embodied in the Sale of Goods Convention.

Not surprisingly, the parties offer varying interpretations of the numerous letters and documents exchanged between them. The Court will briefly summarize their respective contentions.

Defendant Chilewich contends that the Memorandum Agreement dated March 13 which it signed and sent to Filanto was an offer. It then argues that Filanto's retention of the letter, along with its subsequent acceptance of Chilewich's performance under the Agreement—the furnishing of the May 11 letter of credit—estops it from denying its acceptance of the contract. Although phrased as an estoppel argument, this contention is better viewed as an acceptance by conduct argument, e.g., that in light of the parties' course of dealing, Filanto had a duty timely to inform Chilewich that it objected to the incorporation by reference of all the terms of the Russian contract. Under this view, the return of the Memorandum Agreement, signed by Filanto, on August 7, 1990, along with the covering letter purporting to exclude parts of the Russian Contract, was ineffective as a matter of law as a rejection of the March 13 offer, because this occurred some five months after Filanto received the Memorandum Agreement and two months after Chilewich furnished the Letter of Credit. Instead, in Chilewich's view, this action was a proposal for modification of the March 13 Agreement. Chilewich rejected this proposal, by its letter of August 7 to Byerly Johnson, and the August 29 fax by Johnson to Italian Trading SRL, which communication Filanto acknowledges receiving. Accordingly, Filanto under this interpretation is bound by the written terms of the March 13 Memorandum Agreement; since that agreement incorporates by reference the Russian Contract containing the arbitration provision, Filanto is bound to arbitrate.

Plaintiff Filanto's interpretation of the evidence is rather different. While Filanto apparently agrees that the March 13 Memorandum Agreement was indeed an offer, it characterizes its August 7 return of the signed Memorandum Agreement with the covering letter as a counteroffer. While defendant contends that under Uniform Commercial Code § 2–207 this action would be viewed as an acceptance with a proposal for a material modification, the Uniform Commercial Code, as previously noted does not apply to this case, because the State Department undertook to fix something that was not broken by helping to create the Sale of Goods Convention which varies from the Uniform Commercial Code in many significant ways. Instead, under this analysis, Article 19(1) of the Sale of Goods Convention would apply. That section, as the Commentary to the Sale of Goods Convention notes, reverses the rule of Uniform Commercial Code § 2–207, and reverts to the common law rule that "A reply to an offer which purports to be an acceptance but contains additions, limitations or other modifications is a rejection of the offer and constitutes a counter-offer". Sale of Goods Convention Article 19(1). Although the Convention, like the Uniform Commercial Code, does state that non-material terms do become part of the contract unless objected to, Sale of Goods Convention Article 19(2), the Convention treats inclusion (or deletion) of an arbitration provision as "material", Sale of Goods Convention Article 19(3). The August 7 letter, therefore, was a counteroffer which, according to Filanto, Chilewich accepted by its letter dated September 27, 1990. Though that letter refers to and acknowledges the "contractual obligations" between the parties, it is doubtful whether it can be characterized as an acceptance.

More generally, both parties seem to have lost sight of the narrow scope of the inquiry required by the Arbitration Convention.... All that this Court need do is to determine if a sufficient "agreement in writing" to arbitrate disputes exists between these parties....

* * *

Since the issue of whether and how a contract between these parties was formed is obviously related to the issue of whether Chilewich breached any contractual obligations, the Court will direct its analysis to whether there was objective conduct evidencing an intent to be bound with respect to the arbitration provision. . . .

The Court is satisfied on this record that there was indeed an agreement to arbitrate between these parties.

There is simply no satisfactory explanation as to why Filanto failed to object to the incorporation by reference of the Russian Contract in a timely fashion. As noted above, Chilewich had in the meantime commenced its performance under the Agreement, and the Letter of Credit it furnished Filanto on May 11 itself mentioned the Russian Contract. An offeree who, knowing that the offeror has commenced performance, fails to notify the offeror of its objection to the terms of the contract within a reasonable time will, under certain circumstances, be deemed to have assented to those terms. . . . The Sale of Goods Convention itself recognizes this rule: Article 18(1), provides that "A statement made by or other conduct of the offeree indicating assent to an offer is an acceptance". Although mere "silence or inactivity" does not constitute acceptance, Sale of Goods Convention Article 18(1), the Court may consider previous relations between the parties in assessing whether a party's conduct constituted acceptance, Sale of Goods Convention Article 8(3). In this case, in light of the extensive course of prior dealing between these parties, Filanto was certainly under a duty to alert Chilewich in timely fashion to its objections to the terms of the March 13 Memorandum Agreement—particularly since Chilewich had repeatedly referred it to the Russian Contract and Filanto had had a copy of that document for some time.

* * *

In light of these factors, and heeding the presumption in favor of arbitration, which is even stronger in the context of international commercial transactions, the Court holds that Filanto is bound by the terms of the March 13 Memorandum Agreement, and so must arbitrate its dispute in Moscow.

Remedy

Having determined that the parties should arbitrate their disputes in accordance with their agreement, the Court must address the question of remedy. As this action is governed by the Convention and its implementing legislation, the Court has specific authority to order the parties to proceed to arbitration in Moscow. Defendant has not sought this remedy, since it would likewise be the defendant in the arbitration. However, it would be clearly inequitable to permit the party contending that there is an arbitration agreement to avoid arbitration. In the interests of justice, the Court will compel the parties to arbitrate in Moscow. . . .

WINSHIP, THE U.N. SALES CONVENTION AND THE EMERGING CASELAW
Emptio-Venditio Inter Nationes, 227–237 (1997).*

* * * [I]n the *Filanto* case, * * *, the judge does not identify the relevant past conduct that would give rise to the parties' expectation that Filanto's silence constituted acceptance. None appears in the recital of facts at the beginning of the opinion. Indeed, all the prior communications cited clearly state that Filanto did not agree to arbitrate. The language used by the judge suggests, however, that he had in mind the general long-term relationship between the parties rather than any specific acts: *"in light of the extensive course of dealing between these parties,* Filanto was certainly under a duty to alert Chilewich in timely fashion to its objections" (emphasis supplied). If so, the opinion may have much broader significance than generally recognized. It may be read as saying that parties in a long-term relationship owe to each other a duty to communicate, a duty which ultimately may be derived from a duty to act in good faith. This reading would, in turn, support those commentators who find a duty to act in good faith in Article 7 (1) of the Sales Convention.

Whether or not the reader accepts this broader reading of the *Filanto* opinion, there is a second disturbing aspect to the judge's reliance on acceptance by silence: it may not satisfy Article II (2) of the New York Convention. The English-language version of Article II (2) provides:

> The term "agreement in writing" shall include an arbitral clause in a contract or an arbitration agreement, signed by the parties or contained in an exchange of letters or telegrams.

This text is ambiguous. If, for example, the contract is created by an exchange of letters or telegrams, must each party sign a letter or telegram setting out the arbitral clause? In his 1981 review of decision under the New York Convention, ALBERT JAN VAN DEN BERG finds that there are diverging views about when an exchange of letters or telegrams satisfies the subsection's requirements. Although he supports a ?broad? interpretation of Article II (2) as more consistent with the drafting history, even Dr. VAN DEN BERG concludes that "where the text requires an exchange of letters, there must have been a mutual transfer of documents; the mere transmission of one document by a party to the other cannot linguistically fulfil the word 'exchange'." Yet the *Filanto* opinion ignores this very point. Filanto had agreed to arbitrate, reasons the judge, by its silence—not by its written communications. So much for an analysis of the "plain language" of the Convention.

* * *

PROBLEM 2–3

Radical Student Bookstore in Chicago has established a site on the World Wide Web. Books listed in the bookstore's inventory may be

---

* Copyright © 1997 and reproduced by permission from the author.

ordered by filling a form on the bookstore's webpage. The University of Toronto Bookstore in Canada fills out a form to order specified books from the Chicago bookstore.

(a) Does the Sales Convention govern the transaction? If so, is there an enforceable contract?

(b) Would your answers be different if the Toronto bookstore had a computer program that controlled inventory by automatically placing orders by electronic data interchange (EDI) to replace books sold to customers? (EDI is computer-to-computer communication by use of standardized message form.)

(c) If the Chicago bookstore's computer automatically processed the EDI message, including acknowledgment of the order, would there be an offer and acceptance?

* * *

2. FORMAL REQUIREMENTS

P. SCHLECHTRIEM, UNIFORM SALES LAW: THE UNCONVENTION ON CONTRACTS FOR THE INTERNATIONAL SALE OF GOODS
45 (1986).*

According to Article 11 sentence 1, the lack of form requirements means that "consideration" is not required. Otherwise there could be difficulties in contract modifications which favour one side. Sentence 2 also overrides domestic rules of procedure which exclude parole evidence and thereby indirectly pressure the parties into using a written form. This rule applies to all legally relevant statements and communications which are or will be required for the formation of a sales contract, its modification or termination.

Even when contracting states make use of the reservation in Article 96, domestic requirements on form are only to be regarded, despite the broad wording in Articles 12 and 96 ("or other indication or intention"), as far as they relate to the formation of the contract, its modification or consensual termination. In particular, the more precise formulation, "Its modification or termination by agreement" makes clear that a one-sided declaration to terminate a contract does not fall within the scope of the reservation and the corresponding domestic regulations on form,) nor does a declaration to reduce the price according to Article 50 sentence 1. In my opinion, notification of defects, the fixing of time limits, and other communications are, therefore, not subject to form requirements, even when, on the basis of the Article 96 reservation, the contract, in principle, is subject to domestic form regulations which require that such communications adhere to formal writing requirements. The Conference

* Copyright © 1986 and reproduced by permission from Manzsche Verlag und Universitatsbuchhandlung, Wien.

also passed a proposal by the Federal Republic of Germany, whereby the Article 96 reservation may also be invoked after signing the Convention. Thus, the Convention can be signed even if, at the time of the signing, it is not clear whether there are any applicable domestic requirements on form. Later withdrawal of that reservation is possible (Article 97(4) sentence 1).)

* * *

PROBLEM 2–4

Brendan, who has his place of business in Virginia, telephones his friend Sergei, who has his place of business in Russia, and states: "Sergei, I need 1,000 A7S transistors. How much are they?" Sergei replies: "I can let you have them for 10 Deutch Marks apiece." Brendan responds: "Good. Done." Brendan then hangs up.

(a) Does the absence of a written contract document mean that the agreement is unenforceable? CISG art. 11. Russia has made a declaration pursuant to Article 96 saying that Article 11 does not apply where a seller or a buyer has its place of business in the declaring state. If the Convention does not govern this issue, what law does? Assume that Russian law would require that the entire contract be in a signed writing, while U.S. law has a statute of frauds for sales contracts (U.C.C. § 2–201). Can you answer whether the agreement is enforceable without knowing whether choice-of-law rules would make Russian or U.S. law the applicable law? Choice-of-law rules pointing to the applicable law governing contract formalities are not uniform. *See* UCC § 1–105 and the Rome Convention on the Law Applicable to Contractual Obligations, art. 9, both set forth in the Documents Supplement.

(b) If the parties used e-mail, rather than the telephone, would your analysis be different?

* * *

RAJSKI, ARTICLE 11
Commentary on the International Sales Law: The 1980 Vienna Sales
Convention, 122–123 (C.M. Bianca & M.J. Bonell eds., 1987).*

* * *

2.1   Article 11 establishes as one of the basic rules of the Convention a concept well-known in continental European law: the theory of consensualism. According to this theory contracts are not subject to any specific formal requirements. The parties are entirely free to determine the form of their contract of sale. The majority of States accept this principle, although sometimes it is modified to a certain degree by the introduction of formal requirements provided for certain purpose.

The theory of consensualism has been widely adopted in international commercial practice, and by various international interstate or professional organizations and associations in their formulations of general conditions for sales contracts. * * *

2.2.   According to Article 11, the contract of sale is not subject to any requirement as to form. This means that any such requirement prescribed by the domestic law of the Contracting State does not apply, except as pursuant to Article 12, to contracts subject to the Convention, irrespective of the nature of the requirement and of the purposes it is supposed to serve.

* * *

3.1.   The provision of Article 11 is of a non-mandatory nature. The parties may agree on other requirements concerning the form of the contract, or of any declaration connected with it. They may depart from the provision of Article 11 either wholly or partially, expressly or implicitly (*see* Article 6). Article 11 may also be excluded by usages to which the parties have agreed or from any practices which they have established between themselves (*see* Article 9).

In fact, the situations envisaged above occur frequently in international commercial practice. Some offers contain stipulations that an acceptance must be in writing. Sometimes the offeree conditions conclusion of the contract on written confirmation by the offeror. * * *

NOTE ON CONSIDERATION

In problems 2–1 through 2–4, the promises of the buyers and sellers easily satisfy the doctrine of "consideration". However, the Convention does not seem to require that there be "consideration". Is the Convention silent on whether consideration is required or does article 23 eliminate the requirement by negative implication? CISG art. 23.

Also, if buyer and seller later agree to modify their contract and increase the unit price of the goods, there seems to be no requirement in the Convention for consideration for the modification of the initial agreement. CISG art. 29(1). Is it clearer than art. 23? Compare the Convention language to U.C.C. § 2–209(1) ("An agreement modifying a contract within this Article needs no consideration to be binding").

Note that French law (and most other legal systems) does not require consideration. How difficult do you believe it was for negotiators from Common Law legal systems to decide not to insist upon the inclusion of a consideration requirement for the commercial contracts covered by the Convention?

3.   TERMS OF THE CONTRACT

PROBLEM 2–5

As in Problem 2–1, Baker Co. sends an e-mail to Able Co. which states : "We wish to buy 1,000 A7S transistors. How much are they?" Able replies: "We can let you have them for U.S. $6 apiece." Baker's e-mail responds: "Good. Done." Assume for the moment that Able and Baker have not done business with each other before and that there is no relevant usage of trade. What are the terms of the contract? Obviously Able and Baker have not covered many potential issues in their brief conversations: *e.g.*, the time, place, and manner of delivery of the goods or payment of the price. The first problem in the next chapter considers most of these issues. At this point consider only two questions:

(1) When must the transistors be ready for delivery or shipment? CISG art. 33.

(2) When must payment be made? Is this a "cash sale" or a sale on credit? CISG art. 58(1).

* * *

UNCITRAL CLOUT CASE 52
Hungary: Municipal Court Budapest, 1992.

The plaintiff, a German company demanded payment of the price and interest for goods sold and delivered to the defendant, a Hungarian company. At first the defendant disputed the existence of a contract and delivery of goods. However, the court found that delivery had taken place on the basis of documents obtained from the Hungarian Customs Authority and the forwarding agent had delivered the goods upon receipt signed by an employee of the defendant.

The court relied upon a sales contract that had previously been concluded between the parties, in order to determine the price of the goods and the other elements of the contract and ordered the defendant to pay (art. 9(1) and 53 CISG).

J. HONNOLD, UNIFORM LAW FOR INTERNATIONAL SALES UNDER THE 1980 UNITED NATIONS CONVENTION
125–131 (3d ed. 1999).*

(1) *Usages to which the Parties have Agreed*

* * * When a contract uses a technical term drawn from chemistry tribunals scarcely need statutory authorization to consult standard works that give the generally understood meaning of the term. The same approach is appropriate for the technical terms of commerce. The basic definition of a trade term in a standard work like *Incoterms* is a better guide to international understanding than language in a domestic judicial opinion. Giving weight to the basic provisions of widely-accepted commercial definitions could be supported simply as an intelligent approach to interpretation of the contract without invoking the rules on "usage" in Article 9.

However, some "definitions" of trade terms include details regarding the performance of the parties that may not be "widely known to, and regularly observed by, parties to contracts of the type involved *in the particular trade concerned.*" Art. 9(2). These details become binding under Art. 9(1) by express incorporation or in trades where the parties regularly use and rely on this set of trade definitions (Art. 9(2)). On the other hand, proposals to give effect to trade definitions that did not meet the above standard set forth in Article 9(2) were rejected.

* * *

(2) *Practices Established between Two Parties*

Expectations that have the force of contract can be established by patterns of conduct established by the seller and the buyer. Under Article 9(1) the parties are bound by the "practices which they have established between themselves."

"Practices" are established by a course of conduct that creates an expectation that this conduct will be continued. Article 8(2) provides that the "conduct of a party" (Party A) is to be "interpreted according to the understanding that a reasonable person of the same kind as the other party (Party B) would have had in the same circumstances." Under Article 9(1) a course of conduct by A in past transactions may create an expectation by B that will bind A in a future contract. Of course A will not be bound if he notifies B of a change before B enters into a new contract; further reliance by B may also become unreasonable when circumstances change. * * *

(3) *Binding Trade Usages: Article 9(2)*

(a) Inapplicable Concept of Usage. "Usage" and similar legal ideas have been used in settings that are fundamentally different from the trade usages to which Article 9 refers. "Custom" or "customary law" has sometimes been invoked as a source of law without regard to the intent of the parties. In those settings, "custom" is strictly confined; to bind "a plurality of persons" the custom must be "long established," or even "ancient."

Even more remote from our current problem is "custom" as a source of public international law that binds States. Governments have sometimes viewed such "custom" as inconsistent with their sovereignty and with principles on which their regimes were based. Echoes of these fears were heard in UNCITRAL in early discussions of trade usage but it became evident that construing sales contracts in the light of the expectations current in international trade does not impair the sovereignty of States.

(b) Trade Term Definitions and Usage Standards.

* * *

In sum, definitions of trade terms can bind the parties even though they have not been incorporated into the agreement under Article 9(1), but only when their regularity of observance meets the standards of Article 9(2). World-wide legal effect from some details in definitions of trade terms and forms of contract must await the wider homogenization of international practice than has yet been achieved.

(c) *Trade Usage Under the Convention.* As we have seen, Article 9(2) applies only to a trade usage "of which the parties knew or ought to have known" and which "in international trade is widely known to, and regularly observed by, parties to contracts of the type involved in the particular trade concerned." This language invokes a pattern of conduct only if it is so "widely known" and "regularly observed" that it can be assumed to be a part of the expectations of the parties.

(d) *Usage of Trade in Domestic Law.* Similar principles of contract interpretation have been widely accepted in domestic law. The approach of modern case law has been articulated in the (U.S.A.) Uniform Commercial Code (§ 1–205(2)), which defines "usage of trade" as "any practice or method of dealing having such regularity of observance in a place, vocation or trade as to justify an expectation that it will be observed with respect to the transaction in question." * * *

(e) *Standards for Usage: Time and Place.*

* * *

Must the usage be "international"? This question can lead to confusion but the Convention clarifies the issue. Under Article 9(2) the usage must be one which "in international trade is widely *known to,* and regularly *observed by,* parties to "such transactions. A usage that is of local origin (the local practices for packing copra or jute, or the delivery dates imposed by arctic climate) may be applicable if it is "widely known to, and regularly observed by" parties to international transactions involving these situations.

Requirement of Internationality (1) GER. OLG Frankfurt a M., 9U81/94, 05–07–1995; German usage (France contra) held that a letter of confirmation was binding if the recipient did not object. This usage could not be given effect since the usage was not international. UNILEX D. 1995–17.4. * * *

Trade Usage Applied. NETH. GH Hartogenbusch, 456/95, 24–04–96; standard terms of Assn of Yarn Traders binding although not included in contract; both the seller (German) and the buyer (Netherlands) were familiar with the above Association practices. UNILEX D. 1996–5.2.

* * *

(5) *Practice and Usage and the Convention*

Suppose that a usage specifies a time or place for delivery or a time for the transfer of risk that differs from the rules of Articles 31, 33 or 67. Which is applicable? Under Article 6, "The parties may ... derogate from or vary the effect" of the provisions of the Convention. An applicable practice or usage has the same effect as a contract. Under Article 9(1) practices established by the parties become part of the contract and under Article 9(2) the parties "are considered, unless otherwise agreed, to have *impliedly made applicable to their contract*" those usages that meet the specified criteria. There is one limitation: A practice or usage is invalid if a contract term to the same effect would be invalid under applicable domestic law. Article 4 states that the Convention "is not concerned with: 1(a) the *validity* of the contract or of any of its provisions or of any *usage.*" This provision, of course, does not give effect to domestic rules on the circumstances that make a usage applicable; this question is governed by Article 9 of the Convention.

Occasionally domestic legislation or case-law jurisprudence declares that a commercial usage is so firmly established that it has the force of law and is binding on the parties without proof that the usage meets the standards of Article 9(2). If such a rule is inconsistent with a provision of the Convention does it, like customs established in accordance with Article 9(2), prevail over the Convention? The answer must be No. CISG 9(2) governs the circumstances in which a usage may be part of the contract and thereby prevail over provisions of the Convention; the crucial point is that factual compliance with these international standards must be established for each case. Many of the rules of domestic law may be thought to be supported by commercial usage; giving effect to domestic law on this ground would be inconsistent with the standards established by Article 9(2) and would undermine the Convention's central goal to establish uniform law for international trade.

* * *

John Honnold's measured, diplomatic phrases do not come close to revealing the depth of developing countries' hostility to the concepts of "custom" and "usage." With some reason, they regard the concepts as exclusively Western, since they have had little input into their design or drafting, and their usual application as extensions of "colonialism."

* * *

PROBLEM 2–6

Assume that Easy Co., an Egyptian seller of cotton, and Fox Fashions, a New Jersey producer of cloth have done business with each other for three years. On prior occasions, Easy has sold Egyptian long-staple cotton to Fox on open account (credit) and allowed Fox to deduct two percent of the purchase price if it was paid within 30 days after shipment of the goods.

(a) May Easy condition the next delivery of the cotton on immediate payment by Fox? In other words, does the prior course of dealing between the parties create obligations in the present transaction? If the course of dealing differs from the Sales Convention's provisions, which prevails? CISG arts. 6, 9, 58(1).

(b) Instead, suppose Easy and Fax had not done business together before but, to the knowledge of both, it is the custom in the transnational trade in Egyptian long-staple cotton to sell the cotton on open account and to deduct two percent from the purchase price for prompt payment.

If Easy conditions delivery on immediate payment of the full price, how much is Fox obligated to pay, and when, under the contract? CISG art. 9(2). If the custom was a custom in domestic Egyptian trade in cotton and not in transnational trade, would you answer be different?

(c) Assume that only Fox knows of the transnational usage of trade with respect to payment terms, and that Easy and Fox have not done business together before. Easy does not demand payment before delivering the cotton and accepts Fox's tender of the price, less two percent, within 30 days of delivery. Two months later Easy demands payment of the two percent. Fox responds that his performance is evidence of the parties' actual agreement and that he is therefore not responsible for the additional payment. Who should prevail? CISG arts. 8, 9(1).

EÖRSI, ARTICLE 14
Commentary on the International Sales Law: The 1980 Vienna Sales
Convention, 136–144 (C.M. Bianca & M.J. Bonell eds., 1987).*

2.   Meaning and purpose of the provision.

.   .   .

2.2.2.   . . . [I]ndications of the goods to be bought or sold, and the quantity and price thereof seem to be the *essentialia negotii* under this article. These indications must be present, and are sufficient (*but see* § 2.2.4., *infra*). . . .

.   .   .

2.2.4.3.   . . . Where there is no indication of the price whatsoever, the proposal does not in itself amount to an offer. Still, if an acceptance reaches the alleged offeror and he does not object promptly, then the contract is concluded. In such cases it becomes evident that the proposal indicated the intention to be bound in case of acceptance and the proposal was regarded by the parties as an offer. In such cases Article 55 applies.

3.   Problems concerning the provision.

.   .   .

3.4.   Article 14 provides that an offer should also either include the price or make provision for determining it. At the same time Article 55 provides for a situation in which a contract has been "validly concluded but does not expressly or implicitly fix or make provision for determining the price". As there is no offer without an indication of the price, a contract without such an indication seems to be a manifest contradiction (*but see* § 2.2.2., *supra* and contrary on Article 55 2.3.2.).

J. HONNOLD, UNIFORM LAW FOR INTERNATIONAL SALES UNDER THE 1980 UNITED NATIONS CONVENTION
150–52 (3d ed. 1999).*

The Price

(a) Scope of the Problem. In UNCITRAL and at the 1980 Vienna Conference this question arose: Do the parties have the power to make a binding sales contract that does not (Art. 14) "expressly or implicitly" fix or make "provision for determining" the price? As we shall see, the answer calls for close attention to both Articles 14 and 55.

Usually sales contracts specify the price; long-term contracts may make elaborate provision for adjusting the initial price on the basis of changes in cost. Smaller transactions may make no specific reference to price but the least likely possibility is that the parties have no understanding concerning the price. A common situation in which the price is not expressly stated but (Art. 14) is "implicitly fixed" in the course of a series of communications may be illustrated as follows:

Example 14A. Seller distributed catalogues describing various types of goods and listing prices. Buyer sent Seller a telex requesting Seller to ship goods, designated by a model number in Seller's catalogue, to which the telex referred. Buyer's telex did not specify the price.

Buyer's order in response to Seller's catalogue did not close a binding contract. Under Article 14(1) Seller's catalogue was not addressed to "specific persons" and is not to be construed as an offer but as an invitation to submit offers. (The catalogue will probably state that the listed prices are subject to change; even in the absence of such a statement Seller may modify the price since the catalogue did not make a binding offer.) Buyer's order was, however, an offer that implicitly referred to the price stated in the catalogue.

Seller will usually respond to Buyer's order by an "Order Acknowledgement form" that will state the price. If the price is the same as that stated in Seller's catalogue a contract will be closed. If Seller's prices have changed Seller may phone or telex Buyer informing Buyer of a modification in the catalogue price and asking for confirmation of the order at the new price. If Buyer confirms the order, the price has then been fixed and the Order Acknowledgement closes a contract.

If Seller's catalogue prices have not changed Seller may immediately ship the goods and notify Buyer of the shipment by an invoice that states the catalogue price. Under Article 18(3) Seller's shipping, followed by appropriate notification, accepted Buyer's offer "by performing an act, such as one relating to the dispatch of the goods". (Buyer's offer (Art. 14(2)) had "implicitly fixed" the price as that stated in the catalogue to which Buyer referred in its order.)

Let us suppose that Seller had announced higher prices than those in the catalogue to which Buyer referred but, in haste or carelessness, shipped without securing Buyer's agreement to the new prices. This placed Seller at risk. If Buyer accepts the goods without knowledge of

Seller's price change the parties are bound by contract at the lower price in Seller's catalogue: Buyer had reason to expect this price, and Seller's shipment without notification would reasonably be understood by Buyer as accepting Buyer's offer at the catalogue's price. Art. 8(2), § 108, Example 8B, *supra*. If Seller notified Buyer of the price change before Buyer accepted the goods Buyer could either (1) reject the goods or (2) accept the goods at the modified price. If Buyer objects to the higher price he would normally phone or telex Seller and an agreement would be reached on the price. (Seller may find it difficult to redispose of the goods in Buyer's country and may be amenable to a compromise.)

Because of the importance of price to economic success, only rarely will the parties enter into a binding contract without at least (Art. 14(1)) an "implicit" understanding on the price or a means "for determining" the price. Situations that approach the edge involve emergency orders for the manufacture of minor replacement parts or requests to rush a shipment of goods for which the seller has not listed a price. Even here, as the examples suggest, the buyer will seldom accept the goods before he receives an invoice or other notification of the seller's price. In other cases a method for determining the price will be established by trade usage or by a practice the parties have established. Hence, rarely will it be necessary to face the question whether the Convention bars the parties from making a contract that neither "expressly" nor "implicitly" fixes or *makes provision for determining* . . . the price".

. . .

UNCITRAL CLOUT CASE 106
Austria: Supreme Court, 1994.

The Austrian buyer ordered in Germany a large quantity of chinchilla pelts of middle or better quality at a price between 35 and 65 German Marks per piece. The German seller delivered 249 pelts. The Austrian buyer, without opening the packaged goods, sold them further to an Italian pelt dealer at the same price. The Italian dealer returned 13 pelts arguing that they were of inferior quality to that agreed. The Austrian buyer sent to the German seller an inventory list setting out the rejected pelts and refused to pay their price arguing that it had sold the pelts further on behalf of the German seller as its agent.

The first instance court ordered the Austrian buyer to pay the price of the rejected pelts, since the pelts were as specified in the contract. Having found that pelts of middle quality were sold in the market at a price up to 60 German Marks, the court considered that a price of 50 German Marks per pelt was a reasonable one.

The Court of Appeal confirmed that decision. It found that CISG was applicable since the parties had their places of business in States parties to the Convention and the subject matter of the dispute fell within the scope of application of the Convention. The Court of Appeal further found that a valid contract had been concluded on the basis of the order, which was sufficiently definite both as to the quantity and the quality of the goods.

The Court of Appeal further found that the agreement as to the price range (35 to 65 German Marks) did not preclude the valid conclusion of a contract since under article 55 of the Convention, if the price is not explicit or implicit in the contract, the parties are considered to have agreed on the usual market price. The Court of Appeal noted that the price of 50 German Marks per pelt, which had been established by the court of first instance based on the market price, had not been questioned by the parties. As to the currency of payment, the court found that payment was due in German Marks, since payment should be made at the place of business of the German seller (article 57 CISG).

The Supreme Court confirmed the decision of the Court of Appeal. It found that the Convention was applicable since an international sales contract in the sense of article 1(1)(a) CISG was involved. It also found that the order was sufficiently definite to constitute an offer under article 14 CISG, since it could be perceived as such by a reasonable person in the same circumstances as the seller (article 8(2) and (3) CISG). In determining that the order was sufficiently definite, the Supreme Court took into consideration the behaviour of the Austrian buyer who accepted the delivered goods and sold them further without questioning their price, quality or quantity. In particular, the price was found to be sufficiently definite, so as to make the application of article 55 CISG unnecessary. As to the place of payment, the Supreme Court found that it was the place of business of the seller since the goods were sent by post and no their party had been appointed to receive payment in Austria on behalf of the German seller.

* * *

UNCITRAL CLOUT CASE 158
France: Paris Court of Appeal (15th Division), 1992.

The plaintiff, a French buyer, had ordered on 22 March 1990 several batches of electronic components from the defendant, a German seller, through the defendant's liaison office in France. The buyer had accepted the price previously stated by the supplier but had requested its reduction in accordance with the drop in prices on the market. In its acceptance of the order, the seller had replied that the prices could be adjusted upwards or downwards, as agreed, in accordance with the market, but that various specific items could not be delivered. A telephone conversation took place between the parties on 26 March, and the German seller sent his partner a telex on the same day recording the latter's agreement to amend one item of the order. By telex of 13 April, the French buyer changed his order once again, a change which the German seller stated that it could not accept for short-term deliveries.

Before the Paris Court of Appeal, the plaintiff maintained that the contract had not been formed because of alteration of the initial order which had led to disagreement between the parties, and invoked for that purpose article 19 CISG. The plaintiff further ruled that, under article 4 of that instrument, there were grounds for taking account of French common law with regard to the purchase price. . . .

Regarding the formation of the contract, the Court of Appeal held that the contract had been validly formed by virtue of the consent of the parties to the object at issue and the price and that it had become effective on receipt by the buyer of the seller's acceptance of the order in accordance with article 23 CISG. In addition, since the buyer had argued that the seller had delivered surplus goods, the Court of Appeal held that if the quantity of goods delivered did not correspond to the quantity specified in the order, it was the responsibility of the buyer to return the surplus goods immediately. Finally, regarding the price, the court held that the parties' agreement regarding the adjustment of the price in accordance with the market had not rendered the price indeterminable; it did not, however, state the legal principles whereby it considered the price to be determinable.

* * *

UNCITRAL CLOUT CASE 139
Russia: Tribunal of International Commercial Arbitration at the Russian Federation Chamber of Commerce, 1995.

An Austrian firm (claimant) brought a claim against a Ukrainian firm (respondent) for damages resulting from the latter's refusal to deliver a certain quantity of goods. The respondent denied liability on the grounds that no such agreement had been reached between itself and the claimant.

In settling this dispute, the tribunal noted that, under article 14 CISG, a proposal for concluding a contract should be sufficiently definite. It was considered to be such if it indicated the goods and expressly or implicitly fixed or made provision for determining their quantity and price. A telex communication from the respondent regarding the delivery of the goods within a specified period indicated the nature of the goods and their quantity. However, it omitted to indicate the price of the goods or any means of determining their price. The indication in the telex that the price of the goods in question would be agreed ten days prior to the beginning of the new year could not be interpreted as making provision for determining the price of the goods, but was merely an expression of consent to determine the price of the goods at a future date by agreement between the parties. The claimant, who confirmed the contents of the telex communication, thus expressed its consent to the price of the goods being made subject to further agreement between the parties.

The tribunal also noted that in this particular instance article 55 CISG, allowing the price of goods to be determined where it was not expressly or implicitly fixed in a contract or where a contract made no provision for determining it, was not applicable since the parties had implicitly indicated the need to reach agreement on the price in future.

Agreement on the price had not subsequently been reached by the parties. The respondent indicated to the claimant that it was not possible to conclude a contract for the specified quantity of goods. Finding that no contract had been concluded between the parties, the tribunal dismissed the claim.

* * *

PROBLEM 2–7

L'Oiseau, a French newspaper, telephones the St. Vitus Co, an Estonian paper manufacturer and states: "We are running out of paper. We need 25 tons for the Sunday edition. Can you deliver that by Saturday?" St. Vitus replies: "We can, if you'll pay the express charge." L'Oiseau responds: "Bien sur. Just make sure the invoice refers to the express charges." Both parties then hang up.

(a) St. Vitus now consults you as to whether it is obliged to ship the 25 tons of newsprint paper. Has either party made a sufficiently definite offer? CISG art. 14(1).

Does Article 55 provide any guidance? How do you reconcile Articles 14 and 55? There are further materials and discussion of these issues in Section D of this chapter.

(b) If L'Oiseau's offer is sufficiently definite and St. Vitus has accepted the offer, what is the price that L'Oiseau must pay? Would it be relevant if there is a large market with a relatively standard price for such paper? What if there was a published standard market price?

(c) If the offer is not sufficiently definite, can here be an *acceptance*? CISG art. 55. If not, is there a contract? Does Part II of the Sales Convention provide the exclusive rules for determining whether the parties have formed a contract? If there is "a gap" in the Convention here, it is to be filled in accordance with article 7(2). Where would you seek "general principles on which [the Sales Convention] is based" to aid your interpretation?

C. CONTRACT FORMATION WITH THE USE OF FORMS

Use of pre-prepared standard forms fall into two distinct fact patterns. In the first, each party has a form with "boiler-plate" terms which it sends to the other party. Only terms, such as quantity or price terms, that vary from transaction to transaction will be inserted in or added to the pre-prepared form. Neither party reads the other's form, yet each performs as if there is an enforceable agreement. As with informal contracts, few of these transactions will lead to disputes. When they do, the legal issues involve (1) whether the parties have an enforceable agreement and, if so, (2) which terms prevail (seller's, buyer's, or "gap-fillers" provided by law). You will recognize this fact pattern as *the battle of the forms*.

The common feature of the second fact pattern is that only one of the parties has a prepared standard form contract or a set of general terms. The form may be used in several factual variations. In one variation one of the parties has—at least in theory—a simple choice: either accept the first party's standard terms or refuse to deal (the contract of adhesion). In another variation, one of the parties signs the other's form without reading the fine print. A third variation has the parties agreeing orally, but only one of the parties follows up with a letter of confirmation setting out or incorporating standard terms. A subsequent dispute will rarely question whether there is a contract. Instead, the legal issue will be whether the standard terms are enforceable. Courts wrestle with the question off how, if at all, the Convention regulates letters of confirmation. In common law courts, this legal issue may raise the question of whether the Convention limits a domestic parol evidence rule which excludes evidence of nonwritten prior or contemporaneous agreements. In both civil and common law courts, the legal issue may be whether the standard terms are invalid because they are surprising or unconscionable—issues excluded from the coverage of the Convention by Article 4(a), and what relief is available.

1. EXCHANGE OF FORMS: "BATTLE OF THE FORMS"

J. HONNOLD, UNIFORM LAW FOR INTERNATIONAL SALES UNDER THE 1980 UNITED NATIONS CONVENTION
189–92 (3d ed., 1999.)*

[*Example 190. On June 1 Buyer delivered to Seller a Purchase Order that offered to purchase specified production machinery. The Order, in addition to identifying the machinery, stated the price at $20,000, to be paid one month after receipt of the machinery, and called for shipment by August 1. The reverse side of the Order set forth the following terms: Clause #1: Seller will be responsible for damages resulting from defects in the machinery; Clause #2: Any dispute will be settled by arbitration.*

On June 15 Seller delivered to Buyer an Order Acknowledgment stating that Seller would ship the machine ordered by Buyer by August 1 and that the price was $20,000 to be paid one month after receipt, as has been set forth in Buyer's Order. The reverse side of Seller's form included the following terms: Clause #1: Seller will replace or repair any defective part of the machinery but will not be responsible for shut-down costs or other consequential damages; Clause #2: An arbitration clause like the one in Seller's Order.

*Neither party mentioned the terms on the reverse of the other's forms. Seller shipped the goods on July 15 and they were received and put into use on August 1.] * * * Shortly after Buyer placed the machinery in* *operation, defects in the machinery led to shutdown in Buyer's assembly plant with serious consequential damages. Seller offered to repair or replace the defective machinery pursuant to Clause #1 on the back of Seller's Acknowledgment. Buyer contended that, in addition, Seller must pay for shutdown and other consequential damages pursuant to Clause #1 on the back of Buyer's Order.*

* * *

(4) *Conduct Showing Agreement: "Last Shot Theories"*

One approach seeks a way to choose between the terms of the two conflicting communications. One application of this approach gives effect to the *last* form in the sequence on the ground that further performance indicates agreement to its terms. (This is often called the "Last Shot" approach, invoking the metaphor that the parties have been engaged in a "Battle of the Forms" and the aphorism that battles are won by the side that "fires the last shot".)

Let us examine the "last shot" theory in the setting of Example 19D. One will recall that under Article 19 Seller's reply purported to accept Buyer's offer but contained a material modification and therefore was "a rejection of the offer" and constituted a "counter-offer". Seller then shipped the goods to Buyer. Since no contract was formed, Buyer would have been free to reject the goods but, instead, accepted them. Acceptance of the goods was an acceptance of Seller's "counter-offer"; Buyer is bound by the provision in Seller's Sales Order that limited liability to repair or replacement of the defective goods.

Again, the precise facts become important. Suppose the Seller had sent its Order Acknowledgment with a covering letter that drew attention to Clause #1 on the back of the form and asked Buyer to reply before the agreed time for shipment. In this setting Buyer's silence could be construed as assent. However, when there is merely an exchange of forms with a conflict between clauses on the reverse side, it is difficult to conclude that the Buyer gave (or was bound to give) closer attention to the Seller's form than the Seller apparently gave to Buyer's form.

It is especially troubling to place this burden on one who received a reply that purported to be an acceptance and thereby created an ambiguity between the purported acceptance on the front of the Acknowledgment and one of the form clauses on the back. When both parties proceed with performance in the face of this ambiguity, if it were necessary to choose between competing forms, Article 8(2) would be relevant: statements or conduct of one party "are to be interpreted according to the understanding that a reasonable person of the same kind as the *other party* would have had in the same circumstances"—the generally accepted principle that doubt is to be resolved against the party who created the ambiguity. This approach also might discourage ambiguity by denying benefit to the party who created the ambiguity by sending an ambiguous "acceptance". However, even this approach for choosing between conflicting forms seems artificial. (There may be a better way. See part (5).)

We can test the reality (as well as the practicality and fairness) of the "last shot" approach by the following case: Suppose that after arrival of the goods Buyer rejected the shipment. The "last shot" theory that there was no contract until buyer accepted the goods would support Buyer's rejection. It is difficult to conclude that such a rejection, in view of the transportation and redisposal costs typical in international sales, would be consistent with commercial expectations or with standards of good faith and fair dealing.

"Last shot" theories have been rightly criticized as casuistic and unfair. They do not reflect international consensus that justifies importing them into the Convention.

(5) *Gap–Filling by the Convention*

Analysis of Example 19D led to the following conclusions: (1) Performance by the parties showed that they made a contract of sale; (2) The question that led to dispute was not resolved by contract.

If these conclusions are sound we are dealing with the commonest problem in commercial law: a contract fails to solve a problem that leads to dispute. Indeed, providing solutions to gaps left in contracts is the most basic function of laws applicable to commercial sales. For the gap in the contract in Example 19D, the Convention, of course, supplies an answer—a body of rules on remedies for breach (Arts. 45–52, 61–65) and especially the general rule on measurement of damages in Article 74. The rule of Article 74 (and of many domestic systems) that a party in breach is liable for foreseeable consequential damages is not popular with sellers. Under Article 6 the parties can exclude or modify this and other provisions of the Convention but this must be done by agreement; fictitious theories for finding agreement should not suffice.

P. SCHLECHTRIEM, UNIFORM SALES LAW: THE UN-CONVENTION ON CONTRACTS FOR THE INTERNATIONAL SALE OF GOODS
56–57 (1986).*

At the Vienna Conference, Belgium suggested that the issues involved in the *battle of the forms* also be resolved. Unfortunately, the proposal did not arouse much interest. Even those who recognized the importance of the practical problem believed that the issue was not ripe for resolution, both because UNCITRAL had not discussed the problem and because there was still uncertainty about the proper solution in domestic law.) An argument from the German discussions was raised, namely that one could not force the parties to accept the provisions of a law which both had rejected in their standard contract terms. In my opinion, the reluctance is regrettable, and the assertion that the problem could not be resolved because of the uncertainties in domestic law is not convincing. Since the Convention does not address the problem of conflicting standard contract terms, the solution will depend on whether the deviations in the terms are material or immaterial, according to Article 19(2), which corresponds to the proposals submitted in connection with Article 7 of ULF.

The fact that certain provisions are proposed only in standard contract terms or fine print is not enough to characterize them in every case as immaterial. Since standard contract terms normally (also) affect the points mentioned in Article 19(3), where they do, they must be considered material modifications. Most of the time the party who last made reference to his conditions will prevail if the other party indicates assent—or is supposed to—under Article 18(3).

* * *

PROBLEM 2–8

Representatives of Universal Pipe Inc., a small Kansas manufacturer of pipe insulation, attend an international trade fair in New York where they meet with the manager of EuroBuilders S.A. ("Euro"), a builder of industrial facilities from Rouen, France. Euro's manager explains that Euro is interested in Universal's insulation for use in a refinery in France. Universal's representatives give Euro's manager a price list which states that Universal's "Standard Pipe Insulation Product A" is priced at $200 per 100 lb., F.O.B. Plant, Kansas City.

One month later Euro sends Universal a Purchase Order form which states "We order 5,000 lb. Universal Standard Pipe Insulation Product A for 57,000 FF (U.S. $10,000) F.O.B. Kansas City for delivery within 30 days to Rouen, France." On the front of the form, in French, are several printed, numbered paragraphs. One paragraph states that all sales are subject to the EC Product Codes and that all goods sold must conform to the quality specifications of those Codes. On the day Euro mails the order, the 57,000 French Francs is worth U.S. $10,000.

The same day it received the Purchase Order, Universal responded by sending one of its Order Acknowledgment Forms to Euro's Rouen office. That form states: "We accept your order to buy 5,000 lb. Universal Standard Pipe Insulation Product A for $10,000 F.O.B. Kansas City." On the front of the form, in English, are several printed paragraphs. One paragraph states: "All goods sold AS IS and with all faults (see U.C.C. § 2–316)." Another paragraph states: "This contract is governed by the laws of Kansas." A third paragraph reads: "All prices payable in dollars in Kansas City." An authorized agent of Universal signs the form. Seven days later Euro receives the Order Acknowledgment Form. Euro does not reply.

Universal fails to ship the insulation within 30 days, or even within 60 days, thus delaying the refinery construction project. Euro wants to know whether it has a cause of action against Universal.

(a) Assuming that the Sales Convention is applicable, is there an enforceable contract? CISG arts. 18(1), 19.

(b) If the Uniform Commercial Code were applicable, would there be an enforceable contract? At one time application of common-law principles to this fact pattern would have meant use of the "mirror-image rule": a purported acceptance that varied the offer in any respect would be a counter-offer. The Uniform Commercial Code sought to ameliorate the common-law rule. U.C.C. § 2–207. Is the Order Acknowledgment Form a "definite and seasonable expression of acceptance" or do the printed paragraphs on its front create an express condition?

(c) If French law were applicable, would there be an enforceable contract? If so, what are the terms of the contract?

VERGNE, THE "BATTLE OF THE FORMS" UNDER THE 1980 UNITED NATIONS CONVENTION ON CONTRACTS FOR THE INTERNATIONAL SALE OF GOODS

33 Am. J. Comp. L. 233, 250–251 (1985).*

. . . [P]ractically no typical cases of battle of the forms have been decided by French courts. In his study of this question, Bonassies gives two examples decided by the Cour d'Appel de Paris, but a more detailed study of these cases shows that they are not very relevant to his thesis and do not lead to the conclusion that offer and acceptance must "in any case" conform totally. In both cases, the difference considered "very slight" related to an element of the contract which is statutorily essential according to Article 1593 of the Civil Code.

In the absence of relevant precedent, one can turn to the scholarly analyses and treatises of civil law. A review of the main authors indicates that none of them addresses the specific question of the battle of the forms and most of them (while declaring that in principle the formation of a contract requires a complete agreement of the parties on all the conditions) admit the distinction between substantial and secondary elements of the contract and emphasize the importance of the intention of the parties.

In sum, to form a contract of sale under French law the offer and the acceptance must coincide. If the acceptance includes new terms regarding the essential points of the agreement (the main obligations of the parties) there can be a new offer but a contract is never formed. When an agreement is reached on the main points but disagreement persists on subsidiary elements, the contract is formed unless the intention of the parties was to subject their consent to these points. When the disagreement on secondary points is expressed in the contract, the parties' intentions must be scrutinized to ascertain whether they considered these points substantial.

* * *

PROBLEM 2–9

Assume the same facts as in the preceding problem except that this time Universal ships the insulation within 30 days and Euro uses the insulation in the refinery. Six months later, however, Euro discovers that the insulation corrodes the metal of the refinery piping, which piping is governmentally mandated and customarily used in all such facilities in Europe. Euro incurs a million dollars of loss.

Euro sues Universal in Kansas City on the theory that the goods were not fit for Euro's particular purposes (known to Universal) and were not merchantable. Universal has sold its product in the U.S. and Canada and has never had a similar problem, but the type of piping used in North America contains different critical alloys.

(a) Assuming that the Sales Convention is applicable, is there an enforceable contract? CISG arts. 18(1), 19. If so, does the contract include Universal's terms excluding all warranties and choosing Kansas law as the applicable law?

(b) If the Uniform Commercial Code were applicable, would there be an enforceable contract? U.C.C. § 2–207. If so, what are the terms of the contract?

(c) If French law were applicable, would there be an enforceable contract? If so, what are the terms of the contract?

(d) Now aware of the Sales Convention, Universal Pipe asks you to draft an *Acknowledgment Form* that will maximize the likelihood that its standard terms, including its warranty disclaimer, will prevail. Advise Universal Pipe.

Note

The following analysis of the problem was presented to the U.S. Senate Committee during CISG hearings. It analyzes the Euro–Universal hypothetical. Do you find it persuasive or even coherent?

Testimony of Frank A. Orban III, in *International Sale of Goods: Hearing Before the Committee on Foreign Relations*, U.S. Senate Treaty Doc. 98–9 at 47–48 (S.Hrg. 98–837) (April 4, 1984)

Under American law (*e.g.*, the Uniform Commercial Code of Kansas), which Universal knew well, Universal defends itself by saying that it, in full conformity with UCC 2–316, excluded any implied or express warranty of fitness for a particular purpose and merchantability. Such a defense being fully applicable to such a situation had it occurred in the U.S. Euro informs Universal that the sale is not governed by the Kansas Uniform Commercial Code, but by the U.N. Convention on Contracts for the International Sale of Goods, in particular Art. 19, 35, 36 and 74 among others. CISG has no counterpart to UCC 2–316. Furthermore, CISG Art. 19 states that if an acceptance of an offer contains different or new material terms to those in the offer, such terms do not become part of the contract. Art. 19(3) specifically states that terms altering the extent of one party's liability to the other are "material." Therefore, the exclusion of the implied warranty liability that Universal thought he had achieved does not exist; and Universal is liable to Euro for massive damages far exceeding the cost of the goods and probably not covered by insurance, since standard commercial insurance does not usually cover breach of contract damages (as opposed to product liability or tort damages—here the product was not defective but merely unsuitable).

[The facts in this problem are set out in Mr. Orban's testimony and he concludes: "This is only one example of the type of very common but disastrous pitfalls that can face a U.S. businessman unfamiliar with CISG's implications." Mr. Orban took the problem from a Heritage Foundation *Backgrounder*.]

* * *

PROBLEM 2–10

If Universal had consulted you immediately after returning from the international trade fair in New York and before receiving any Purchase Order forms from Euro, how would you advise Universal to handle foreign sales so as to minimize misunderstandings and potential litigation?

* * *

As already noted (see Schlechtriem at pages 117–18 *supra*). The diplomatic conference reviewing the draft Sales Convention declined to adopt a special provision to deal with the battle of the forums. The drafters of the UNIDROIT Principles were not so reticent. Does article 2.22 of the UNIDROIT Principles resolve the questions in the preceding problems more equitably and efficiently?

UNIDROIT PRINCIPLES FOR INTERNATIONAL COMMERCIAL CONTRACTS*
Article 2.22
(Battle of forms)

Where both parties use standard terms and reach agreement except on those terms, a contract is concluded on the basis of the agreed terms and of any standard terms which are common in substance unless one party clearly indicates in advance, or later without undue delay informs the other party, that it does not intend to be bound by such a contract.

COMMENT

1. *Parties using different standard terms*

It is quite frequent in commercial transactions for both the offeror when making the offer, and the offeree when accepting it, each to refer to its own standard terms. In the absence of express acceptance by the offeror of the offeree's standard terms, the problem arises as to whether a contract is concluded at all and if so, which, if either, of the two conflicting sets of standard terms should prevail.

2. *"Battle of forms" and general rules on offer and acceptance*

If the general rules on offer and acceptance were to be applied, there would either be no contract at all since the purported acceptance by the offeree would, subject to the exception provided for in Art. 2.11(2), amount to a counter-offer, or if the two parties have started to perform without objecting to each other's standard terms, a contract would be considered to have been concluded on the basis of those terms which were the last to be sent or to be referred to (the "last shot").

3. *The "knock-out" doctrine*

The "last shot" doctrine may be appropriate if the parties clearly indicate that the adoption of their standard terms is an essential condition for the conclusion of the contract. Where, on the other hand, the parties, as is very often the case in practice, refer to their standard terms more or less automatically, for example by exchanging printed order and acknowledgement of order forms with the respective terms on the reverse side, they will normally not even be aware of the conflict between their respective standard terms. There is in such cases no reason to allow the parties subsequently to question the very existence of the contract or, if performance has commenced, to insist on the application of the terms last sent or referred to.

It is for this reason that the present article provides, notwithstanding the general rules on offer and acceptance, that if the parties reach an agreement except on their standard terms, a contract is concluded on the basis of the agreed terms and of any standard terms which are common in substance ("knock-out" doctrine).

> 1. A orders a machine from B indicating the type of machine, the price and terms of payment, and the date and place of delivery. A uses an order form with its "General Conditions for Purchase" printed on the reverse side. B accepts by sending an acknowledgement of order form on the reverse side of which appear its own "General Conditions for Sale". When A subsequently seeks to withdraw from the deal it claims that no contract was ever concluded as there was no agreement as to which set of standard terms should apply. Since, however, the parties have agreed on the essential terms of the contract, a contract has been concluded on those terms and on any standard terms which are common in substance.

A party may, however, always exclude the operation of the "knock-out" doctrine by clearly indicating in advance, or by later and without undue delay informing the other, that it does not intend to be bound by a contract which is not based on its own standard terms. What will in practice amount to such a "clear" indication cannot be stated in absolute terms but the inclusion of a clause of this kind in the standard terms themselves will not normally be sufficient since what is necessary is a specific declaration by the party concerned in its offer or acceptance.

Illustrations

2. The facts are the same as in Illustration 1, the difference being that A claims that the contract was concluded on the basis of its standard terms since they contain a clause which states that "Deviating standard terms of the party accepting the order are not valid if they have not been confirmed in writing by us". The result will be the same as in Illustration 1, since merely by including such a clause in its standard terms A does not indicate with sufficient clarity its determination to conclude the contract only on its own terms.

3. The facts are the same as in Illustration 1, the difference being that the non-standard terms of A's offer contain a statement to the effect that A intends to contract only on its own standard terms. The mere fact that B attaches its own standard terms to its acceptance does not prevent the contract from being concluded on the basis of A's standard terms.

* * *

2. USE OF ONE FORM: PAROL EVIDENCE AND CONFIRMATION LETTERS

UNCITRAL CLOUT CASE 124
Germany: Oberlandesgericht München, 1995.

A Finnish company sold 3000 tonnes of electrolyte nickel/copper cathodes to the German defendant for about 17 million US dollars. Only the defendant signed the written contract form. The metal was delivered but not paid for. The Finnish company then assigned the payment claim to the plaintiff who demanded payment. The defendant denied the jurisdiction of the German court because of an arbitration clause and the valid conclusion of a sales contract.

Concerning the arbitration clause, the court found that the form requirements of the applicable article 2(2) of the United Nations Convention on the Recognition and Enforcement of Foreign Arbitral Awards of 1958 had not been satisfied, since the parties had not signed the agreement containing the arbitration clause and the Finnish company had not received the standard form which contained the clause.

Concerning the payment claim, the court applied the CISG since both parties to the sales contract had their places of business in different

Contracting States, namely in Finland and in Germany. It was held that a contract had been effectively concluded between the defendant and the Finnish company and that the plaintiff's claim for payment was justified under articles 53 and 62 CISG.

Even though Finland had declared that it would not be bound by Part II of the CISG concerning the "Formation of the Contract", an effective contract could still be concluded. According to the CISG other forms of consent are possible as long as they can be regarded as a mutual binding arrangement and the subject-matter of the contract is comparable to articles 14–24 CISG. In an *obiter dictum*, the court explicitly excluded recourse to the governing contract law. The defendant signed a contractual document thus showing its approval of the contract and also accepted the goods upon arrival. The Finnish company indicated assent to the contract by its conduct, namely through the delivery of the goods. A written contractual agreement is not necessary to evidence the parties' consent (art. 11 CISG).

* * *

MCC–MARBLE CERAMIC CENTER, INC. v. CERAMICA NUOVA D'AGOSTINO, S.P.A.

United States Court of Appeals, Eleventh Circuit, 1998.
144 F.3d 1384.

BIRCH, CIRCUIT JUDGE:

This case requires us to determine whether a court must consider parol evidence in a contract dispute governed by the United Nations Convention on Contracts for the International Sale of Goods ("CISG"). [FN1] The district court granted summary judgment on behalf of the defendant-appellee, relying on certain terms and provisions that appeared on the reverse of a pre-printed form contract for the sale of ceramic tiles. The plaintiff-appellant sought to rely on a number of affidavits that tended to show both that the parties had arrived at an oral contract before memorializing their agreement in writing and that they subjectively intended not to apply the terms on the reverse of the contract to their agreements. The magistrate judge held that the affidavits did not raise an issue of material fact and recommended that the district court grant summary judgment based on the terms of the contract. The district court agreed with the magistrate judge's reasoning and entered summary judgment in the defendant-appellee's favor. We REVERSE.

BACKGROUND

The plaintiff-appellant, MCC–Marble Ceramic, Inc. ("MCC"), is a Florida corporation engaged in the retail sale of tiles, and the defendant-appellee, Ceramica Nuova d'Agostino S.p.A. ("D'Agostino") is an Italian corporation engaged in the manufacture of ceramic tiles. In October

1990, MCC's president, Juan Carlos Mozon, met representatives of D'Agostino at a trade fair in Bologna, Italy and negotiated an agreement to purchase ceramic tiles from D'Agostino based on samples he examined at the trade fair. Monzon, who spoke no Italian, communicated with Gianni Silingardi, then D'Agostino's commercial director, through a translator, Gianfranco Copelli, who was himself an agent of D'Agostino. The parties apparently arrived at an oral agreement on the crucial terms of price, quality, quantity, delivery and payment. The parties then recorded these terms on one of D'Agostino's standard, pre-printed order forms and Monzon signed the contract on MCC's behalf. According to MCC, the parties also entered into a requirements contract in February 1991, subject to which D'Agostino agreed to supply MCC with high grade ceramic tile at specific discounts as long as MCC purchased sufficient quantities of tile. MCC completed a number of additional order forms requesting tile deliveries pursuant to that agreement.

MCC brought suit against D'Agostino claiming a breach of the February 1991 requirements contract when D'Agostino failed to satisfy orders in April, May, and August of 1991. In addition to other defenses, D'Agostino responded that it was under no obligation to fill MCC's orders because MCC had defaulted on payment for previous shipments. In support of its position, D'Agostino relied on the pre-printed terms of the contracts that MCC had executed. The executed forms were printed in Italian and contained terms and conditions on both the front and reverse. According to an English translation of the October 1990 contract, the front of the order form contained the following language directly beneath Monzon's signature:

[T]he buyer hereby states that he is aware of the sales conditions stated on the reverse and that he expressly approves of them with special reference to those numbered 1–2–3–4–5–6–7–8. Clause 6(b), printed on the back of the form states:

> [D]efault or delay in payment within the time agreed upon gives D'Agostino the right to ... suspend or cancel the contract itself and to cancel possible other pending contracts and the buyer does not have the right to indemnification or damages.

D'Agostino also brought a number of counterclaims against MCC, seeking damages for MCC's alleged nonpayment for deliveries of tile that D'Agostino had made between February 28, 1991 and July 4, 1991. MCC responded that the tile it had received was of a lower quality than contracted for, and that, pursuant to the CISG, MCC was entitled to reduce payment in proportion to the defects. D'Agostino, however, noted that clause 4 on the reverse of the contract states, in pertinent part:

> Possible complaints for defects of the merchandise must be made in writing by means of a certified letter within and not later than 10 days after receipt of the merchandise. . . .

Although there is evidence to support MCC's claims that it complained about the quality of the deliveries it received, MCC never submitted any written complaints.

MCC did not dispute these underlying facts before the district court, but argued that the parties never intended the terms and conditions printed on the reverse of the order form to apply to their agreements. As evidence for this assertion, MCC submitted Monzon's affidavit, which claims that MCC had no subjective intent to be bound by those terms and that D'Agostino was aware of this intent. MCC also filed affidavits from Silingardi and Copelli, D'Agostino's representatives at the trade fair, which support Monzon's claim that the parties subjectively intended not to be bound by the terms on the reverse of the order form. The magistrate judge held that the affidavits, even if true, did not raise an issue of material fact regarding the interpretation or applicability of the terms of the written contracts and the district court accepted his recommendation to award summary judgment in D'Agostino's favor. MCC then filed this timely appeal.

* * *

The parties to this case agree that the CISG governs their dispute because the United States, where MCC has its place of business, and Italy, where D'Agostino has its place of business, are both States Party to the Convention. Article 8 of the CISG governs the interpretation of international contracts for the sale of goods and forms the basis of MCC's appeal from the district court's grant of summary judgment in D'Agostino's favor. MCC argues that the magistrate judge and the district court improperly ignored evidence that MCC submitted regarding the parties' subjective intent when they memorialized the terms of their agreement on D'Agostino's pre-printed form contract, and that the magistrate judge erred by applying the parol evidence rule in derogation of the CISG.

I. Subjective Intent Under the CISG

Contrary to what is familiar practice in United States courts, the CISG appears to permit a substantial inquiry into the parties' subjective intent, even if the parties did not engage in any objectively ascertainable means of registering this intent. Article 8(1) of the CISG instructs courts to interpret the "statements ... and other conduct of a party ... according to his intent" as long as the other party "knew or could not have been unaware" of that intent. The plain language of the Convention, therefore, requires an inquiry into a party's subjective intent as long as the other party to the contract was aware of that intent.

In this case, MCC has submitted three affidavits that discuss the purported subjective intent of the parties to the initial agreement concluded between MCC and D'Agostino in October 1990. All three affidavits discuss the preliminary negotiations and report that the parties arrived at an oral agreement for D'Agostino to supply quantities of a specific grade of ceramic tile to MCC at an agreed upon price. The affidavits state that the "oral agreement established the essential terms of quality, quantity, description of goods, delivery, price and payment." The affidavits also note that the parties memorialized the terms of their oral agreement on a standard D'Agostino order form, but all three affiants contend that the parties subjectively intended not to be bound by the terms on the reverse of that form despite a provision directly below the signature line that expressly and specifically incorporated those terms.

* * *

Article 8(1) of the CISG requires a court to consider this evidence of the parties' subjective intent. Contrary to the magistrate judge's report, which the district court endorsed and adopted, article 8(1) does not focus on interpreting the parties' statements alone. Although we agree with the magistrate judge's conclusion that no "interpretation" of the contract's terms could support MCC's position, article 8(1) also requires a court to consider subjective intent while interpreting the conduct of the parties. The CISG's language, therefore, requires courts to consider evidence of a party's subjective intent when signing a contract if the other party to the contract was aware of that intent at the time. This is precisely the type of evidence that MCC has provided through the Silingardi, Copelli, and Monzon affidavits, which discuss not only Monzon's intent as MCC's representative but also discuss the intent of D'Agostino's representatives and their knowledge that Monzon did not intend to agree to the terms on the reverse of the form contract. This acknowledgment that D'Agostino's representatives were aware of Monzon's subjective intent puts this case squarely within article 8(1) of the CISG, and therefore requires the court to consider MCC's evidence as it interprets the parties' conduct.

II.   Parol Evidence and the CISG

Given our determination that the magistrate judge and the district court should have considered MCC's affidavits regarding the parties' subjective intentions, we must address a question of first impression in this circuit: whether the parol evidence rule, which bars evidence of an earlier oral contract that contradicts or varies the terms of a subsequent or contemporaneous written contract, plays any role in cases involving the CISG. We begin by observing that the parol evidence rule, contrary to its title, is a substantive rule of law, not a rule of evidence. The rule does not purport to exclude a particular type of evidence as an "untrustworthy or undesirable" way of proving a fact, but prevents a litigant from attempting to show "the fact itself—the fact that the terms of the agreement are other than those in the writing." As such, a federal district court cannot simply apply the parol evidence rule as a procedural matter—as it might if excluding a particular type of evidence under the Federal Rules of Evidence, which apply in federal court regardless of the source of the substantive rule of decision.

The CISG itself contains no express statement on the role of parol evidence. It is clear, however, that the drafters of the CISG were comfortable with the concept of permitting parties to rely on oral contracts because they eschewed any statutes of fraud provision and expressly provided for the enforcement of oral contracts. Compare CISG, art. 11 (a contract of sale need not be concluded or evidenced in writing) with U.C.C. § 2–201 (precluding the enforcement of oral contracts for the sale of goods involving more than $500). Moreover, article 8(3) of the CISG expressly directs courts to give "due consideration ... to all relevant circumstances of the case including the negotiations ..." to determine the intent of the parties. Given article 8(1)'s directive to use the intent of the parties to interpret their statements and conduct, article 8(3) is a clear instruction to admit and consider parol evidence regarding the negotiations to the extent they reveal the parties' subjective intent.

* * *

* * * [A]lthough jurisdictions in the United States have found the parol evidence rule helpful to promote good faith and uniformity in contract, as well as an appropriate answer to the question of how much consideration to give parol evidence, a wide number of other States Party to the CISG have rejected the rule in their domestic jurisdictions. One of the primary factors motivating the negotiation and adoption of the CISG was to provide parties to international contracts for the sale of goods with some degree of certainty as to the principles of law that would govern potential disputes and remove the previous doubt regarding which party's legal system might otherwise apply. See Letter of Transmittal from Ronald Reagan, President of the United States, to the United States Senate, reprinted at 15 U.S.C. app. 70, 71 (1997). Courts applying the CISG cannot, therefore, upset the parties' reliance on the Convention by substituting familiar principles of domestic law when the Convention requires a different result. We may only achieve the directives of good faith and uniformity in contracts under the CISG by interpreting and applying the plain language of article 8(3) as written and obeying its directive to consider this type of parol evidence.

This is not to say that parties to an international contract for the sale of goods cannot depend on written contracts or that parol evidence regarding subjective contractual intent need always prevent a party relying on a written agreement from securing summary judgment. To the contrary, most cases will not present a situation (as exists in this case) in which both parties to the contract acknowledge a subjective intent not to be bound by the terms of a pre-printed writing. In most cases, therefore, article 8(2) of the CISG will apply, and objective evidence will provide the basis for the court's decision. Consequently, a party to a contract governed by the CISG will not be able to avoid the terms of a contract and force a jury trial simply by submitting an affidavit which states that he or she did not have the subjective intent to be bound by the contract's terms. Moreover, to the extent parties wish to avoid parol evidence problems they can do so by including a merger clause in their agreement that extinguishes any and all prior agreements and understandings not expressed in the writing.

Considering MCC's affidavits in this case, however, we conclude that the magistrate judge and the district court improperly granted summary judgment in favor of D'Agostino. * * *

MCC asks us to reverse the district court's grant of summary judgment in favor of D'Agostino. The district court's decision rests on pre-printed contractual terms and conditions incorporated on the reverse of a standard order form that MCC's president signed on the company's behalf. Nevertheless, we conclude that the CISG, which governs international contracts for the sale of goods, precludes summary judgment in this case because MCC has raised an issue of material fact concerning the parties' subjective intent to be bound by the terms on the reverse of the pre-printed contract. The CISG also precludes the application of the parol evidence rule, which would otherwise bar the consideration of evidence concerning a prior or contemporaneously negotiated oral agreement. Accordingly, we REVERSE the district court's grant of summary judgment and REMAND this case for further proceedings consistent with this opinion.

P. SCHLECHTRIEM, UNIFORM SALES LAW: THE UN–CONVENTION ON CONTACTS FOR THE INTERNATIONAL SALE OF GOODS
56–57 (1986).*

It is not certain, whether and to what extent *commercial letters of confirmation* will have effect under the Convention. The issue was addressed several times, but unlike Hague Conference, it was not possible, during the discussions on the recognition of trade usages, to reach an agreement on whether the German rules commercial letters of confirmation were applicable as usages. On the contrary, from the wording of Article 9, it must be assumed that the letter of confirmation will be effective only if the relevant business customs exist between the parties of that particular branch of trade in international transactions. On the other hand, it cannot be assumed that the Uniform Law for International Sales, by limiting the formation of contracts to those created by an offer followed by an acceptance, has left other possibilities, such as the German laws on letters of confirmation, to the discretion of domestic laws applicable by virtue of conflict rules. Otherwise domestic formation provisions, unrelated to offer and acceptance would also be applicable, and the desired unification and legal certainty would be endangered. In my opinion, Article 7(1) forbids such a "fragmentation" of the law governing the formation of the contract. The entire process of contract formation is governed by CISG.

* * *

UNCITRAL CLOUT CASE 95
Switzerland: Civil Court of Basel–Stadt, 1992.

The Austrian seller sued the Swiss buyer for the purchase price of fibre. In support of its suit, the seller argued that a sales contract had been concluded between the parties on the basis of an order sent by the Swiss buyer and a written confirmation sent by the seller.

The court found that the letter of confirmation sent by the seller and the subsequent omission of any reaction by the buyer reflected a usage as to the formation of contracts in the sense of article 9(1) CISG; that the parties had impliedly made that usage applicable to their contract since they knew or ought to have known the binding nature of such confirmations under both Austrian and Swiss law; and that there was no evidence of any other particular rules or usages prevailing in the trade of fibre. Furthermore, the court found that the exchange of confirmations was consistent with the practice which the parties had established between themselves and which was binding pursuant to article 9(2) CISG. . . .

* * *

3. USE OF FORMS: ISSUES OF "VALIDITY"

UNCITRAL CLOUT CASE 232
Germany: Oberlandesgericht München, 1998.

A German buyer, defendant, ordered cashmere sweaters from an Italian seller, plaintiff. The seller sued the buyer for the outstanding purchase price. The buyer sought set-off, claiming that it had notified the seller that the sweaters were defective.

The court held that the CISG was applicable and that the seller was entitled to the purchase price under the CISG (articles 1(1)(a) and 53 CISG). The buyer's set-off claim was not granted as set-off claims are prohibited under the Standard Conditions of the German Textile and Clothing Industry, which the parties had made applicable to their contract (article 18 CISG). The set-off issue was to be determined in accordance with German law (article 4(a) CISG).

* * *

WINSHIP, COMMENTARY ON PROFESSOR KASTELY'S RHETORICAL ANALYSIS
8 Nw. J. Int'l L. & Bus. 623, 636–38 (1988).*

[Article 4 of the Convention] states that "except as otherwise expressly provided in this Convention, it is not concerned with: (a) the validity of the contract or of any of its provisions or of any usage." My concern is that a judge so disposed may find issues of validity much more readily than anticipated by the drafters and thereby turn to national law solutions. The issue of validity is a potential "black hole" removing issues from the Convention's universe, ...

. . . There was a similar exclusion in the 1964 uniform sales law. Article 8 of the [Uniform Law on the Formation of Contracts for the International Sale of Goods] provided that "the present Law shall not, except as otherwise expressly provided therein, be concerned with . . . the validity of the contract or of any of its provisions or of any usage." The unofficial commentary to the Uniform Law prepared by Professor Tunc states that issues of validity are difficult matters which the differing national traditions made difficult to unify in the Uniform Law. Although the Bulgarian delegate suggested that the Uniform Law should include references to validity, there was no protest to the exclusion of the issue of validity and virtually no discussion of the provision at the 1964 Hague conference.

The records of the 1964 uniform laws provides some guidance as to what is meant by "validity." In his commentary Professor Tunc suggests that the issues of validity included questions of "the capacity of the parties or the exchange of their consents or in regard to vitiating factors," as well as "[municipal] regulations of a police character or for the protection of persons." A French comment on a draft text gives the examples of rulemaking agreements enforceable for lack of a writing or for lack of a specified price.

Deliberations within UNCITRAL did not consider the exclusion of issues of validity controversial. Indeed, governments and international organizations made virtually no comments on Article 8 of the 1964 Uniform Law on the International Sale of Goods. When the text was placed before the Commission at its 1977 session, it was suggested that the provision be deleted because it was merely declaratory. The argument ultimately prevailed that such a provision was useful in preventing the "overruling [of] domestic law on validity of contracts." In the meantime, the Commission's Working Group on International Sales studied whether to include provisions on validity at its eighth and ninth sessions, and ultimately concluded that there should not be any rules on validity. The 1980 conference approved the final draft text of Article 4 with very little debate.

Despite this lack of controversy, Article 4(a) has the potential for mischief. The very reason for excluding issues of validity—the differing and strongly felt national traditions—suggests that judges and arbitrators will be tempted to enforce domestic rules of validity: either of the forum, or of the state whose laws would apply by virtue of the rules of private international law.

Professor Kastely's analysis of related problems suggests some of the steps to be taken to guard against this temptation. Article 7(1) directs that Article 4(a) is to be read in a way so as to maintain uniform application of the Convention. Interpretation of "validity" is not, therefore, initially a question of domestic law. As Professor Honnold has written, "the substance rather than the label of characterization of the competing rule of domestic law determines whether it is displaced by the Convention; the crucial question is whether the domestic rule is invoked by the same operative facts that invoke a rule of the Convention." If the same operative facts are involved, then the Sales Convention does expressly provide otherwise and there is no exclusion of issues of validity. This will be the case, for example, with some aspects of the civilian concept of "error."

It is possible that a common core of meaning can be given to "validity" as used in the Convention. Most (if not all) countries will not enforce agreements on the grounds of illegality, capacity, fraud, mistake, and duress. Even within the "catch-all" category of illegality, there are generally accepted "police" regulations for the safeguard of persons or vital national interests.

It is with the less definite concepts such as unconscionability, that the possibility of abuse appears. As to these latter concepts, Professor Schlechtriem suggests that the contractual clause should be governed by the Convention rather than by domestic law. Thus, he suggests, a contract clause that limits recoverable damages to foreseeable losses should be valid because of the damage principles of the Convention (Articles 74 and 76) even if domestic law would declare such clauses unconscionable. It is not clear, however, that the Convention will always provide guidance. Consider, for example, the closely related contract clause that purports to liquidate damages, but which would be unenforceable in an Anglo–American jurisdiction as a penalty clause. The Convention does not address this issue in its damage provisions. While it recognizes the principle of freedom of contract (Article 6 on freedom of the parties to exclude or derogate from the Convention), that principle is subject to the express exclusion of validity issues.

* * *

PROBLEM 2–11

A German manufacturer has recently developed a machine that harvests nuts from trees and shells the nuts in one continuous process. After reading a story about the machine in a trade journal, an Alabama agricultural enterprise writes the manufacturer a letter inquiring about the machine. In response, the German manufacturer described the machine and offered to sell it for a price of $35,000 CIF Mobile payable by a confirmed letter of credit. The manufacturer's letter also stated that the sale would be sold subject to its "General Conditions" and that "the validity, interpretation, and enforcement of the sales contract will be governed by German law." The Alabama enterprise responded with a purchase order form ordering one machine.

When the Alabama enterprise received the machine it discovered that the machine did not process the quantity of nuts per hour that the enterprise expected. It consulted its lawyers about its right to reject the machine and get its money back. A junior member of the law firm has raised the following possible grounds for "getting out of the contract." Evaluate whether these grounds would be effective.

(a) There was mutual mistake because the manufacturer's statement that the machine would process "76,0 nuts/hour" was understood by the Alabama enterprise to mean 760 pounds per hour, not 76 kilograms as understood by the manufacturer.

(b) The contract is unconscionable because a copy of the General Conditions were not given to the Alabama enterprise, because the Conditions were in the German language only, and because one of the conditions required the buyer to give notice of any defect within six months of delivery or be barred from any remedy.

(c) The choice of German law to govern issues of validity is contrary to Alabama public policy.

* * *

Would your analysis of Problem 2–11 be easier if you applied articles 2.19–2.21 of the UNIDROIT Principles (set out below)? Would you conclude the transaction was not enforceable? When is an Alabama (or German) court going to look to the Principles as the applicable legal rules?

UNIDROIT PRINCIPLES FOR INTERNATIONAL COMMERCIAL CONTRACTS*
Article 2.19
(Contracting under standard terms)

(1) Where one party or both parties use standard terms in concluding a contract, the general rules on formation apply, subject to Articles 2.20–2.22.

(2) Standard terms are provisions which are prepared in advance for general and repeated use by one party and which are actually used without negotiation with the other party.

COMMENT

1. Contracting under standard terms

This article is the first of four articles (Arts. 2.19–2.22) which deal with the special situation where one or both parties use standard terms in concluding a contract.

2. *Notion of "standard terms"*

"Standard terms" are to be understood as those contract provisions which are prepared in advance for general and repeated use by one party and which are actually used without negotiation with the other party (para. (2)). What is decisive is not their formal presentation (e.g. whether they are contained in a separate document or in the contract document itself; whether they have been issued on pre-printed forms or whether they are only on computer, etc.), nor who prepared them (the party itself, a trade or professional association, etc.), nor their volume (whether they consist of a comprehensive set of provisions covering almost all the relevant aspects of the contract, or of only one or two provisions regarding, for instance, exclusion of liability and arbitration). What is decisive is the fact that they are drafted in advance for general and repeated use and that they are actually used in a given case by one of the parties without negotiation with the other party. This latter requirement obviously relates only to the standard terms as such, which the other party must accept as a whole, while the other terms of the same contract may well be the subject of negotiation between the parties.

3. *General rules on formation apply*

Usually, the general rules on formation apply irrespective of whether or not one or both parties use standard terms (para. (1)). It follows that standard terms proposed by one party bind the other party only on acceptance, and that it depends upon the circumstances of the case whether the two parties must refer to the standard terms expressly or whether the incorporation of such terms may be implied. Thus, standard terms contained in the contract document itself will normally be binding upon the mere signature of the contract document as a whole, at least as long as they are reproduced above that signature and not, for instance, on the reverse side of the document. On the other hand, standard terms contained in a separate document will normally have to be referred to expressly by the party intending to use them. Implied incorporation may be admitted only if there exists a practice established between the parties or usage to that effect.

Illustrations

1. A intends to conclude an insurance contract with B covering the risk of liability for accidents of A's employees at work. The parties sign a model contract form presented by B after filling in the blank spaces relating, among other matters, to the premium and to the maximum amount insured. By virtue of its signature, A is bound not only by the terms which it has individually negotiated with B, but also by the General Conditions of the National Insurers' Association, which are printed on the form.

2. A normally concludes contracts with its customers on the basis of its own standard terms which are printed as a separate document. When making an offer to B, a new customer, A fails to make an express reference to the standard terms. B accepts the offer. The

standard terms are not incorporated in the contract unless A can prove that B knew or ought to have known of A's intention to conclude the contract only on the basis of its own standard terms, e.g. because the same standard terms had regularly been adopted in previous transactions.

3.   A intends to buy grain on the commodity exchange in London. In the contract concluded between A and B, a broker on that exchange, no express reference is made to the standard terms which normally govern brokerage contracts concluded at the exchange in question. The standard terms are nevertheless incorporated in the contract because their application to the kind of contract in question amounts to a usage.

ARTICLE 2.20

(Surprising terms)

(1) No term contained in standard terms which is of such a character that the other party could not reasonably have expected it, is effective unless it has been expressly accepted by that party.

(2) In determining whether a term is of such a character regard shall be had to its content, language and presentation.

COMMENT

1.   Surprising terms in standard terms not effective

A party which accepts the other party's standard terms is in principle bound by them irrespective of whether or not it actually knows their content in detail or fully understands their implications. An important exception to this rule is, however, laid down in this article which states that, notwithstanding its acceptance of the standard terms as a whole, the adhering party is not bound by those terms which by virtue of their content, language or presentation are of such a character that it could not reasonably have expected them. The reason for this exception is the desire to avoid a party which uses standard terms taking undue advantage of its position by surreptitiously attempting to impose terms on the other party which that party would scarcely have accepted had it been aware of them. For other articles intended to protect the economically weaker or less experienced party, see Arts. 3. 10 and 4.6.

2.   Terms "surprising" by virtue of their content

A particular term contained in standard terms may come as a surprise to the adhering party first by reason of its content. This is the case whenever the content of the term in question is such that a reasonable person of the same kind as the adhering party would not have expected it in the type of standard terms involved. In determining whether or not a term is unusual, regard must be had on the one hand to the terms which are commonly to be found in standard terms generally used in the trade sector concerned, and on the other to the individual negotiations between the parties. Thus, for example, a term excluding or limiting the contractual liability of the proponent may or may not be considered to be "surprising", and in consequence ineffective in a particular case, its effectiveness depending on whether or not terms of that kind are common in the trade sector concerned, and are consistent with the way in which the parties conducted their negotiations.

Illustration

1. A, a travel agency, offers package tours for business trips. The terms of the advertisement give the impression that A is acting as a tour operator who undertakes full responsibility for the various services comprising the package. B books a tour on the basis of A's standard terms. Notwithstanding B's acceptance of the terms as a whole, A may not rely on a term stating that, with respect to the hotel accommodation, it is acting merely as an agent for the hotel-keeper, and therefore declines any liability.

3. Terms "surprising" by virtue of their language or presentation

Other reasons for a particular term contained in standard terms being surprising to the adhering party may be the language in which it is couched, which may be obscure, or the way in which it is presented "typographically, for instance in minute print. In order to determine whether or not this is the case, regard is to be had not so much to the formulation and presentation commonly used in the type of standard terms involved, but more to the professional skill and experience of persons of the same kind as the adhering party. Thus, a particular wording may be both obscure and clear at the same time, depending on whether or not the adhering party belongs to the same professional category as the party using the standard terms.

The language factor may also play an important role in the context of international transactions. If the standard terms are drafted in a foreign language it cannot be excluded that some of its terms, although fairly clear in themselves, will turn out to be surprising for the "adhering party who could not reasonably have been expected fully to a appreciate all their implications.

Illustrations

2. A, an insurance company operating in country X, is an affiliate of B, a company incorporated in country Y. A's standard terms comprise some 50 terms printed in small type. One of the terms designates the law of country Y as the applicable law. Unless this term is presented in bold letters or in any other way apt to attract the attention of the adhering party, it will be without effect since customers in country X would not reasonably expect to find a choice-of-law clause designating a foreign law as the law governing their contracts in the standard terms of a company operating in their own country.

3.   A, a commodity dealer operating in Hamburg, uses in its contracts with its customers standard terms containing, among others, a provision stating "Hamburg–Freundschaftliche Arbitrage". In local business circles this clause is normally understood as meaning that possible disputes are to be submitted to a special arbitration governed by particular rules of procedure of local origin. In contracts with foreign customers this clause may be held to be ineffective, notwithstanding the acceptance of the standard terms as a whole, since a foreign customer cannot reasonably be expected to understand its exact implications, and this irrespective of whether or not the clause has been translated into its own language.

4.   Express acceptance of "surprising" terms

The risk of the adhering party being taken by surprise by the kind of terms so far discussed clearly no longer exists if in a given case the other party draws the adhering party's attention to them and the adhering party accepts them. The present article therefore provides that a party may no longer rely on the "surprising" nature of a term in order to challenge its effectiveness, once it has expressly accepted the term.

ARTICLE 2.21

(Conflict between standard terms and non-standard terms)

In case of conflict between a standard term and a term which is not a standard term the latter prevails.

COMMENT

Standard terms are by definition prepared in advance by one party or a third person and incorporated in all individual contract without their content being discussed by the parties. It is therefore logical that whenever the parties specifically negotiate and agree on particular provisions of their contract, such provisions will prevail over conflicting provisions contained in the standard terms since they are more likely to reflect the intention of tile parties in the given case.

The individually agreed provisions may appear in the same document as the standard terms, but may also be contained in a separate document. In the first case they may easily be recognised on account of their being written in characters different from those of the standard terms. In the second case it may be more difficult to distinguish between the provisions which are standard terms and those which are not, and to determine their exact position in the hierarchy of the different documents. To this effect the parties often include a contract provision expressly indicating the documents which form part of their contract and their respective weight.

Special problems may however arise when the modifications to the standard terms have only been agreed upon orally, without the conflicting provisions contained in the standard terms being struck out, and those standard terms contain a provision stating the exclusive character of the writing signed by tile parties, or that any addition to or modification of their content must be in writing. For these cases see Arts. 2.17 and 2.18.

D. THE "DEAL"—THE LONG–TERM CONTRACT FORMED THROUGH NEGOTIATION

In this final section we examine the fully-negotiated "big deal." In this transaction type the parties negotiate with each other over each term, with special attention paid to the price and quantity terms. Usually they will want to be bound, but bound to a continuing relationship and to a formal format for future dealing, rather than to specific prices and quantities. Because negotiation of the terms take so much effort they will also want the terms to be sufficiently flexible that they will not have to renegotiate soon. Each party may have to compromise on one or more terms to arrive at an agreement that satisfies both parties. When they arrive at this agreement, the parties reduce its terms to a formal, written document that they then sign. In subsequent disputes between the parties, the legal issues usually concern construction of the written text, especially the price and quantity terms. Legal questions may also be raised about the relevance of representations that preceded the signing of the formal contract documents.

1. PROVIDING FLEXIBILITY FOR LONG-TERM CONTRACTS

UNITED TECHNOLOGIES INT'L PRATT & WHITNEY COMMERCIAL ENGINE BUSINESS v. MALEV HUNGARIAN AIRLINES
(Supreme Court, Hungary, 1992).
13 J.Law & Com. 31 (1993).* 2

IN THE NAME OF THE REPUBLIC OF HUNGARY

The Supreme Court of the Republic of Hungary has passed the following judgment against the partial judgment No.3.G.50. 289/1991/32 brought by the City Court of Budapest in the lawsuit initiated by the Plaintiff, United Technologies International Inc. Pratt & Whitney Commercial Engine Business * * * against the Defendant, MALEV Hungarian Airlines * * * in respect of validity of contract due to the appeal submitted by the Defendant during the trial, held on the 25th day of September 1992:

The Supreme Court changes the partial judgment of the City Court of Budapest, the court of first instance, by revising the partial judgment as a judgment, and rejects the Plaintiff's claim.

---

* Copyright © 1992 and reproduced by permission from the Journal of Law and Commerce.

2. This Journal of Law & Commerce case translation was prepared by Dr. and Mrs. Laszlo Szlavnits. Dr. Szlavnits was the attorney for the Plaintiff. Any reader who intends to rely on this case must consult the original text, a copy of which can be obtained from the Journal of Law and Commerce.

The Supreme Court obligates the Plaintiff to pay HUF 15,150,000, i.e. fifteen million one hundred and fifty thousand forints, the cost of the original lawsuit and of the appeal, into the account of the Defendant's legal representative.

Plaintiff is to bear its costs itself.

Reasons adduced:

From the fall of 1990 negotiations had been conducted by the parties to the suit and the American VALSAN Co., on the one hand, about the conditions given which the Plaintiff would replace the ineffective engines on the Defendant's Soviet made Tupolyev TU–154 aircrafts with PRATT JT 8D–219 engines, manufactured by the Plaintiff (engine replacement), and on the other hand, about the Plaintiff supplying the PW 4000 series engines for the wide bodied aircrafts, to be purchased by the Defendant. On December 4, 1990 the parties signed a Letter of Intention about their negotiations on the replacement of the engines on the Defendant's already existing Soviet made aircrafts. They expressed their intention- without undertaking any obligations whatsoever-to sign a final agreement in the future in accordance with those contained in the declaration. In the above-mentioned Letter of Intention the Plaintiff stipulated a condition, among others, according to which the signing of the final agreement depended on Defendant's acceptance of Plaintiff's support offer for the purchase of PW 4000 series engines from Plaintiff by Defendant for the wide bodied aircrafts to be purchased.

Plaintiff submitted two purchase-support offers, dated December 14, 1990, to Defendant with the aim of aiding the purchase of two aircrafts, supplied with Plaintiff's engines, whose order was finalized, another one with an option to buy, furthermore, the purchase of one spare engine with a finalized order, and another one with an option to buy. These support offers replaced the one dated November 9, 1990, making that null and void. Both offers made a reference to the Appendix containing the PW 4000 series engines' Guarantee Plan. One of the offers was made in case the Defendant decided to purchase a 767–200 ER aircraft assembled with PW 4056 engines, the other in case Defendant purchased a 310–300 aircraft equipped with the new PW 4152 or 4156 jet engine systems. At this time Defendant was negotiating with two aircraft manufacturers and had not yet come to a decision about the type of the aircraft to be bought and the company to purchase from. The support offers involved financial assistance (lending), engine warranties, product maintenance and repair services in order to select the engines or jet engine systems produced by Plaintiff.

The offers were kept open by Plaintiff until December 21, 1990 on condition that the validity of Defendant's declaration of acceptance depends on the appropriate provisions to be made by the Government of Hungary and that of the United States. Point Y of both support offers contained the purchase agreements. The place where the Defendant was to sign the support offers in case of acceptance was clearly marked on the document. Defendant did not sign either support offers, but in the presence of Plaintiff's proxy, who at this time extended the offer to include the PW 4060 engine, as well, and on the basis of the discussions carried out with him/her, composed a letter together with him/her, which was sent to the Vice–President of Plaintiff's company by telex, notifying him/her that-based on the evaluation of technical data and efficiency, furthermore taking the financial assistance also into consideration-they had selected the PW 4000 engine for the new wide bodied fleet of aircrafts. Defendant also informed Plaintiff that it is looking forward to the cooperation with PW, especially with respect to the replacement of the TU–154 aircraft engines, furthermore that the present declaration of acceptance is wholly based on the conditions included in the PW engine offer, dated December 14, 1990. In the meantime Defendant asked Plaintiff to keep this information strictly confidential until they were ready to make a joint public announcement.

Later, in the beginning of February, 1991, the Parties had a verbal discussion, with reference to which Plaintiff addressed a letter to Defendant on February 11, 1991. In this letter Plaintiff declared that an advertising budget of USD 65,000.00 "will be added" to the premium for signing, and offered assistance in selecting a partner for engine maintenance and cooperation in the creation of a spare-parts pool for the maintenance of the line. It was also said that Plaintiff would come to Budapest to continue the discussions on the replacement of the TU–154 aircrafts' engines and to finalize the PW 4000 contract.

Following that Defendant notified Plaintiff in writing that Defendant would not choose PW 4000 series engines for the Boeing 767 aircraft. In response to that, still on the same day Plaintiff stated its standpoint, according to which Defendant had definitely and irrevocably committed itself to purchase the new 767 aircraft with PW 4000 engines, asked Defendant to meet its obligations without delay, notify Boeing about its selection of PW 4000 engines and make a public announcement about it. Defendant, on account of its different standpoint, refused to do so.

Plaintiff initiated a suit on July 23, 1991 asking the court to declare that the contract between the Parties legally came to force on December 21, 1990, that its provisions were violated by Defendant, that Defendant was to meet its contractual obligations, and also asked for the allowance of the legal costs. Plaintiff claimed that Defendant, with its declaration, dated on December 21, 1990, accepted Plaintiff's contractual offer, dated on December 14, 1990, thus a valid, and legally binding contract was made for the sale and purchase of PW 4056 engines and spare engines. According to Plaintiff's position, the December 14, 1990 offer fully complies with the content of Paragraph 1, Section 14 of the United Nations Agreement [Convention] on International Sales Contracts, dated in Vienna on April 11, 1980 (hereinafter the "Agreement"), and therefore with the acceptance of the offer the contract had legally come to force. For the offer clearly states the product, its quantity and contains data on the basis of which the price can be determined precisely. The circumstance that Defendant talked about PW 4000 series engines in its declaration of acceptance is insignificant, since the engines listed in the offer all belong to this series, furthermore, the offer indicated the engines' number within the series, as well. The extension of the December 14, 1990 offer to include the PW 4060 engine and the modification of the engine's maintenance and cost warranty plans by the Plaintiff's business representative were precisely in response to Defendant's request. The offer provided an opportunity for Defendant to choose the type of the aircraft from the two alternatives and, accordingly, that offer should be deemed accepted, which corresponded to the type of the selected aircraft. The quantity could also be defined on the basis of the offer, since it depended upon the Defendant purchasing two or three planes. The price was also defined, since it could be arrived at by calculating the costs. Defendant knew the technical characteristics of the engines involved in the suit, had received the engine's specifications and additional necessary documentation to which Defendant referred in its declaration of acceptance. Later in the course of the lawsuit, Plaintiff requested Defendant to be ordered to reimburse Plaintiff for costs incurred by the discovery proceedings, in relation to the present lawsuit, that had been initiated by Defendant, and indicated the amount to be USD 64,816.20.

Defendant asked for the dismissal of the suit. Defendant did not acknowledge entering into a contract with Plaintiff about the engines involved in the suit. According to Defendant's position, Plaintiff's December 14, 1990 offers could not be regarded as a contractual offer, for they did not contain the data stipulated by Paragraph 1, Section 14 of the Agreement. The support offers, dated December 14, 1990, did not properly identify the goods, i.e. any one of the actual engines, that could be the subject of the contract and should be delivered by the Plaintiff. Neither did the definition of quantity comply with the provisions of Paragraph 1, Section 14 of the Agreement and the document did not indicate the price of the engines to be installed at all. For the price of the PW 4056 series spare engine is not identical with the price of the PW 4056 engine, neither is the price of the PW 4056 series engine identical with the price of the PW 4000. The so called pricing formula could only be applied if the base price of the given engines would have been defined at the time of making the contract. According to the data supplied by Plaintiff the base price would also have to be calculated, however, the data were not even sufficient for that, since Plaintiff did not indicate its own price index. Engines do not have general market prices, therefore, general market prices cannot be used for guidelines. Since the aircraft manufacturer would be paid by Defendant, while Plaintiff would be paid by the aircraft manufacturer for the engines, the precise knowledge of the price is absolutely necessary, for it is to be harmonized with the financial conditions and the terms of payment given by the aircraft manufacturer. According to Defendant's position the debated offer involved in the lawsuit does not qualify as an offer, if the cited Section of the Agreement is interpreted correctly, for it does not express Plaintiff's intention to regard itself to be under contractual obligation in case of acceptance. This is also proven by the fact that in its letter of February 11, 1991, Plaintiff still writes about the finalization of the contract and did not transfer the 1 million US dollar premium for signing either. This is the buyer's contractual premium, in case the offer is accepted within its deadline.

* * *

The court of first instance * * * stated that, based on the Plaintiff's December 14, 1990 offers, the Defendant's December 21, 1990 declaration of acceptance, and on the negotiations conducted between December 16 and December 21, 1990, furthermore on the attached documents, the contract was established.

In case of legal disputes, based on the agreeing declarations of the Parties, the provisions of the United Nations Agreement on international sales contracts, dated in Vienna, on April 11, 1980, was applied. Considering Paragraph 1, Section 14 of this Agreement the Court stated that Plaintiff's December 14, 1990 offers are defined, for they have indicated the product and essentially determined the quantity and the price, as well. In respect of defining the product, the court of first instance refers to the fact that with the decision being made about the type of the aircraft (December 29, 1990) the type, that forms the subject of the contract, became unambiguously identified from the ones listed. The quantity of the product can also be determined knowing how many planes will be bought by the Defendant. Prices are stated for all the types in the offer. The circumstance that Defendant could select the engine based on the offer itself, depending on the selection of the aircraft, meant a 'unilateral power' for Defendant.

Defendant's December 21, 1990 declaration was regarded as the offer's acceptance by the court of first instance. The reasoning was that the declaration was entirely based upon the December 21, 1990 P & W engine offer. * * *

According to the reasons adduced the court of first instance brought a partial judgment in the lawsuit initiated by the Plaintiff, because Plaintiff also submitted a claim for compensation-pertaining to the Plaintiff's legal fees emerging in the course of the discovery procedure-thus, the Court continues the proceedings in respect of the claim for compensation and legal costs.

Defendant appealed against the above partial judgment and primarily asked for the reversal of the partial judgment of the court of first instance and the nonsuit of the Plaintiff. Secondly, in case the evidences were to be supplemented, asked the court of the second instance to annul the partial judgment of the first instance and to order the court of first instance to retrial the suit and to pass a new judgment.

* * *

Further in its appeal Defendant protested that the court of first instance regarded Plaintiff's December 14, 1990 declarations as an offer aiming at the closing of a contract that in content fully satisfies all requirements stipulated in Paragraph 1, Section 14 of the Agreement. In this respect, apart from reiterating its defense, presented during the legal proceedings of the first instance, Defendant also referred to Paragraph 1, Section 8 of the Agreement. According to Defendant's position, the debated offers of the Plaintiff, when their content is properly interpreted, do not express intentions toward final commitments, rather they assume that later a final contract can be drawn up at the Defendant's initiative. This follows from the fact that in the debated offers Plaintiff talks about providing various kinds of loans after a general introduction. The provision of loans, however, was tied to the condition, according to which loans can be granted only if Plaintiff had received a notification in writing about the Defendant having sent a final and irrevocable order for the aircraft and the spare engine. Therefore, the debated offers referred to the establishment of a preliminary agreement at the most.

This interpretation is also supported, according to the Defendant, by Plaintiff's letter of February 11, 1991 in which Plaintiff writes about the finalization of the PW 4000 contract and the continuation of the discussions on the replacement of the TU–154 aircrafts' engines. Based on these support offers, as they were not proposals for entering into a contract, the sales contract for the engines involved in the suit would not have been closed even if Defendant had accepted them. However, Defendant made no declaration of acceptance, did not sign the debated proposals, it was not Defendant's intention to do so-at that time Defendant had not yet made a decision about the type of the planes to be purchased and was still continuing discussions with Plaintiff about certain technical-economic issues. They had not yet reached an agreement in the question of the supply of spare parts and the setting up of an engine maintenance network. Without these, however, no airline would purchase aircrafts. It is precisely for that reason that the Defendant's letter was put together-on Plaintiff's request. To explore the creation and signing of this letter, and of Defendant's intention with signing the letter, Defendant requested to call the participants of the suit to the witness' stand. Defendant also attached a declaration from the participants on the Defendant's side, which was to prove the circumstances of the writing of the latter, and Defendant's intention with it.

According to Defendant's position, the court of first instance misinterpreted the conditions on which the validity of the Defendants legal declaration depended. Pertaining to this, Defendant argued that in order to close the contract (1) a type-suitability certificate is to be obtained according to Paragraph 1, Section 8 of the 17/1981 (VI.9.) Council of Ministers [Cabinet] Decree, issued for the implementation of Act 8 of 1981, and (2) according to the Paragraph no international trade contract can be closed until that. Neither did the Plaintiff possess an actual export license, and such a license would have been necessary also because the engines manufactured by Plaintiff were still on the COCOM list in December, 1990. Thus Defendant's declaration would not be legally binding even if it could be qualified as acceptance. Defendant also claimed that Plaintiff's offer violates competition laws for the replacement of the TU–154 aircrafts' engines were tied to the acceptance of the present offer.

* * *

Plaintiff submitted a counter-appeal aiming at the confirmation of the judgment of the first instance. In this counter-appeal Plaintiff essentially repeated its position, presented during the proceedings of the suit of the first instance, according to which on December 14, 1990 Plaintiff gave Defendant a proposal for the closing of the contract, the content of which was in full compliance with the stipulations of the Agreement and bore with all further documents with which it met all requirements of the Agreement. These documents were handed over to Defendant during their discussions and the content of these remained unchanged in spite of the modifications of the proposal in the meantime. Plaintiff also referred to the fact that it did not need to obtain a license to close the contract involved in the suit, the license from the American authorities was to be applied for the actual export of the engines, however, there was plenty of time to do so in view of the performance deadline. On the other hand Plaintiff had the license to hand over to Defendant the technical data concerning the engine series.

Plaintiff also claimed, against the Defendant's attached "testimonials" and with reference to Mr. Hajek, who negotiated on behalf of Plaintiff, that it did not request a declaration of intention from the Defendant. Defendant signed the declaration of acceptance being aware of its intention to close the contract. Plaintiff attached a sample price calculation of the engine to be delivered to the counterappeal.

Plaintiff's position concerning the issue of the proposal involved in the suit and the replacement of the TU–154 aircrafts' engines was that Defendant's intention to purchase engines was independent from the replacement program.

Plaintiff declared, in reply to the judge's question, during the hearing of the appeal, that concepts of "jet engine system" and "engine" are not identical. The jet engine system includes other parts, as well, for instance the so called nacelle. In case Defendant had purchased Boeing planes, Plaintiff would have sold the engines only, since the aircraft manufacturer manufactured the nacelle itself, but in the case of the Airbus, Plaintiff would have delivered the gondola together with the engine. The price of the jet engine system and of the engine are not identical because of the technical differences. Plaintiff did not debate that its offer bid not include the base price of the jet engine system. Plaintiff, however, alleged that Defendant was aware of the prices.

The appeal was well founded.

* * *

* * * On December 4, 1990 [the parties] signed a letter of intention (memorandum) about their negotiations concerning the replacement of the engines. In this document, the Parties stated (Point 8.b) that, among other things, the contract depends on whether Defendant accepts one of the Plaintiff's two support offers, dated November 9, 1990, i.e. whether Defendant selects the PW 4000 series engine for the new wide bodied aircrafts. In case Defendant would not accept this offer, Plaintiff reserved the right to revise its declaration of intention in respect of the TUPOLYEV engine replacement program, which-by the way-was signed without undertaking any sort of obligations. Apart from the above, the strong connection between the replacement program and the sale of aircraft engines is also proven by Defendant's December 21, 1990 declaration and Plaintiff's letter, dated on January 11, 1991.

On December 14, 1990 plaintiff made two different offers in case Defendant selects Boeing or in case it selects Airbus. These offers annulled the November 9, 1990 offers and replaced them. In the December 14, 1990 purchase-support offer for the Boeing scenario Plaintiff indicated two engines, taking the modification also into consideration, the PW 4056 and the PW 4060, from which, according to Point Y.1 of the offer Defendant was to choose and to notify the aircraft manufacturer about its choice. In Point Y.2 Plaintiff undertook to sell the engines to Defendant on the basis of a separate agreement with the manufacturer. In this offer Plaintiff indicated the price of the new PW 4056 engine to be USD 5,847,675, which could increase according to the stability of value calculations from December, 1989. The modified offer does not contain the base price of the PW 4060 engine and spare engine.

The other offer, dated on the same day and intended for the Airbus scenario, among the PW 4000 series engines indicated two engines, PW 4152 or PW 4156, a jet engine system and a spare engine, from which Defendant was to make its selection according to Point Y.1 and Y.2 of the offer, and upon acceptance of the offer to notify the aircraft manufacturer immediately. According to Point Y.2 Plaintiff undertook to sell the jet engine systems, the number of which was indicated, on the basis of a separate contract made with the aircraft manufacturer. In this offer Plaintiff indicated the price of the new PW 4152 spare engine base unit to be USD 5,552,675, and the price of the new PW 4156/A spare engine to be USD 5,847,675, with stabilizing their values starting from December, 1989.

According to Point Y.4 of both offers, with the acceptance of the offer Defendant was to send a finalized and unconditional order for the spare engines indicated in the offers.

In case of the offer for the Airbus scenario, the indicated jet engine system includes the engine, other parts and the gondola as well, while 'engine' means the motor only, therefore the price of the jet engine system is not identical with the price of the engine (motor). The offer contained the price of neither jet engine systems.

In the appeal proceedings, based on the Defendant's appeal, a declaration was to be made also about whether, interpreting the Parties' declarations on the basis of Paragraph 1, Section 8 of the Agreement, Plaintiff's December 14, 1990 offers comply with the conditions stipulated in Paragraph 1, section 14 of the Agreement and whether Defendant's December 21, 1990 declaration qualifies as an acceptance.

According to Paragraph 1, Section 14 of the Agreement a proposal to enter into a contract, addressed to one or more persons, qualifies as a bid if it is properly defined and indicates the bidder's intention to regard itself to be under obligation in case of acceptance. A bid is properly defined if it indicates the product, expressly or in essence defines the quantity and the price, or contains directions as to how they can be defined. This means that the Agreement regards the definition of the subject of the service (product), its quantity and its price to be an essential element of a bid.

It can be determined on the basis of the given evidences and the Parties' declarations, that Plaintiff made two parallel offers for the same deal on December 14, 1990, depending on Defendant's choice of the Boeing or the Airbus aircraft. In case Boeing was selected, within the respective offer two separate engines (PW 4056 and PW 4060) were indicated. This offer did not contain the base price of the PW 4060 engine.

In case Airbus was selected, within the respective offer two different jet engine systems (PW 4152 and PW 4156), belonging to the same series, and two different spare engines (PW 4152 and PW 4156/A) were indicated. The base price of the jet engine systems is not included in the offer, only that of the spare engines, in spite of the fact that these two elements are not identical either technically or in respect of price. In case there is no base price, value stability calculations have no importance. The price cannot be determined according to Section 55 of the Agreement either, as jet engine systems have no market prices.

The court of appeals did not accept Plaintiff's position, according to which it did not have to make an offer in respect of the jet engine systems' price, for these would have been billed to the aircraft manufacturer, who includes it in the price of the airplane. For according to the offers (Point Y.2) the engines, the jet engine systems and the spare engines would have been purchased by Defendant from Plaintiff, therefore Plaintiff would have established a contractual relationship with Defendant, as the buyer. That is, the two offers, involved in the suit, related not only to the sales of the spare engines, but also to the engines to be built in and the jet engine systems. Therefore, according to Section 14 of the Agreement, Plaintiff would have had to provide the price of all the products, engines and jet engine systems in its parallel or alternative offer involved in the suit, or the directions for the determination of the price thereof, to the Defendant.

It clearly follows from the above, that none of Plaintiff's offer, neither the one for the Boeing aircraft's engines, nor the one for the

Airbus aircraft's jet engine systems, complied with the requirements stipulated in Paragraph 1, Section 14 of the Agreement, for it did not indicate the price of the services or it could not have been determined.

Plaintiff's parallel and alternative contractual offers should be interpreted, according to the noticeable intention of the offer's wording and following common sense, so, that Plaintiff wished to provide an opportunity to Defendant to select one of the engine types defined in the offer at the time of the acceptance of the offer.

For according to the wording of Section Y of the offers:

– Defendant, following the acceptance of the proposal, immediately notifies the aircraft manufacturer about the selection of one of the numerically defined engines (jet engine systems) for use on the wide bodied aircrafts;

– Plaintiff sells the selected engine (jet engine system) to Defendant according to a separate agreement made with the aircraft manufacturer;

– Thereby (that is, with the acceptance of the proposal) Defendant sends a final and unconditional purchase order to Plaintiff for the delivery of the spare engines of the determined type.

In addition to grammatical interpretation, the assumption of Plaintiff granting "power" to Defendant, made by the court of first instance, essentially entitling Defendant to make its selection until some undetermined point of time or even during performance from the services offered alternatively, goes against economic reasoning as well. For the legal consequences of this would be that Plaintiff should manufacture the quantity, stipulated in the contract, of all four types-two engines and two jet engine systems-and prepared with its services wait for Defendant to exercise its right to make its selection with no deadline.

It follows from this all that Plaintiff provided an opportunity to choose a certain type of engine or jet engine system at the time of the acceptance of its offer.

Plaintiff's offers were alternative, therefore Defendant should have determined which engine or jet engine system, listed in the offers, it chose. There was no declaration made, on behalf of Defendant, in which Defendant would have indicated the subject of the service, the concrete type of the engine or jet engine system, listed in the offers, as an essential condition of the contract. Defendant's declaration, that it had chosen the PW 4000 series engine, expresses merely Defendant's intention to close the contract, which is insufficient for the establishment of the contract.

Therefore, the court of first instance was mistaken when it found that with Defendant's December 21, 1990 declaration the contract was established with the "power"-or, more precisely stipulation-according to which Defendant was entitled to select from the indicated four types (PW 4056 or PW 4060 engine and spare engine, PW 4152 or PW 4156 jet engine system and spare engine) with a unilateral declaration later, after the contract had been closed. The opportunity to choose after closing the contract does not follow from the offer. If perhaps such a further condition would have been intended by Defendant, then this should have been regarded as a new offer on its behalf.

Lacking an appropriately explicit offer from Plaintiff and not having a clear indication as to the subject of the service in Defendant's declaration of acceptance, no sales contract has been established between the Parties.

It is a different issue, whether the series of discussions and Defendant's declaration of acceptance created such a special atmosphere of confidence, where Plaintiff could seriously count on closing the contract and failing that Plaintiff suffered economic and other disadvantages. With this question and with its legal grounds, no suit being initiated, the court of appeals was not entitled to deal with.

* * *

Plaintiff has lost the case, therefore, according to Paragraph 1, Section 78 of the Civil Procedure, in addition to bearing its own costs, it is obligated to reimburse all costs that emerged during the first and the appeal procedure to Defendant. Defendant's costs consist of legal fees, determined on the basis of Point B, Paragraph 1 of the Decree of the Minister of Justice of 12/1991 (IX.29.), and a HUF 150,000 appeal duty. Plaintiff indicated more than 2 billion forints as the subject of the suit, the court has determined the court fee, which amounts to 0.5% of the above sum for the proceedings of the first instance, while in the appeal proceeding half of that amount.

Budapest, on the 25th day of September, 1992.

* * *

PROBLEM 2–12

You are an attorney for Pratt and Whitney. It does not want to change its usual transaction pattern for selling engines for wide-body jet passenger airplanes, which has been a success from a marketing perspective. However, the company is aware of the Hungarian Supreme Court decision, above, and wants you to ensure that this difficulty will not arise in any subsequent transaction. Please advise the company as to what changes in the transaction pattern it must make in order to avoid any such difficulty—and, whether such changes will guarantee protection from such rulings in future cases.

* * *

P. SCHLECHTRIEM, UNIFORM SALES LAW: THE UN–CONVENTION ON CONTRACTS FOR THE INTERNATIONAL SALE OF GOODS
50—52 (1986).*

The retention of the definite price requirement for a valid offer and, in many cases, for contract formation is regrettable. In special circumstances, such as urgency or trust in the seller's sincerity, when the parties have waived price negotiations, the definite price requirement can endanger the validity of a contract and provide a pretext for escaping a disadvantageous agreement. The Article also poses an unsatisfactory contradiction to Article 55, which presupposes the possibility of forming a contract without a fixed or determinable price. It can only be explained by the desire of the Scandanavian countries to introduce the Uniform Law for International Sales without Part III [*sic*], and to have a provision in Part II [*sic*] in case the price has not been determined. On the other hand, the position of those who wished to require a definite price is also understandable. Large organizations can be so limited by the comprehensive planning that the price they have agreed upon is an indispensable factor for the planning of the entire organization. Above all, the developing countries are also understandably concerned about using the shorthand of the seller's standard price or even allowing the seller discretion to set the price within the bounds of equity, as in §§ 316 and 315(1) of the German Civil Code. The more flexible system can be practicable or at least tolerable in countries or economic systems with comparatively homogeneous and well-known market structures. But in world trade, price transparency is a given at most for raw materials, *i.e.*, for the products of the developing countries, but not for the industrial goods imported by these countries. Finally the French position can perhaps be explained on the basis of the French experience with Article 1591 of the French Civil Code, which, since the beginning of the 1970's, has experienced a renaissance as an instrument of control of contracts that exploit the weaker party, such as contracts between a gas-station owner and his supplier.

The practicality of Article 14(1) sentence 2 probably cannot be determined until there is experience with its application. Unfortunately, there are likely to be divergent results. In particular, it is possible that domestic courts will make only limited use of the tacit price agreement or an implied reference to circumstances which make a determination of price possible. They may even employ Article 14(1) sentence 2 as an additional instrument to control validity in pursuing certain legal-political purposes. The wording of the law, however, permits—indeed encourages—a broader application. Where the "price generally charged" exists at the time the contract is concluded and can be determined by the other

---

party, an order that does not name a price must frequently be understood as an implied reference to these sales prices (list prices, catalogue prices, etc.). A price can also be determined expressly or implicitly be reference to a particular market at delivery or at some other time. Reference to price lists or catalogues which reserve the right to change prices can also be understood as a reference to the price valid at the time of delivery. In any case, the parties may generally exclude the application of Article 14(1) sentence 2 and agree to allow one side to set the price— as long as there are no domestic prohibitions applicable under Article 4(a).

Articles 9 and 8(3) indicate that due consideration must be given to trade usages, and above all to the intent of the parties, the negotiations, established practices between the parties, and usages, as well as to the parties' later conduct, whenever tacit agreement on price, an agreement on price determinability, or even the implicit exclusion of Article 14(1) sentence 2 is in question. Finally, a statement which is intended as an offer but lacks a definite price will be treated as an invitation to make an offer, while the addressee's reply may contain sufficient indication of the price or of its determination to be an offer; the addressee's conduct, such as the acceptance of delivered goods, can then be considered as an indication of assent in the sense of Article 18(1) sentence 1. On the whole, the Germans will, in practice, be able to live with Article 14(1) sentence 2, although it is advisable that offers and acceptances indicate as definitely as possible a price or a mechanism for fixing the price.

* * *

H. DE VRIES, CIVIL LAW AND THE ANGLO-AMERICAN LAWYER
378–88 (1976).*

2. *Essential Conditions*

To constitute a valid sale the price to be paid by the buyer must be expressed in money. The price must be determined or at least determinable. The courts have held that so long as the price clause refers to factors independent of the will of the parties, the price is determined and the sale is not void.

In a recent series of decisions involving the price clause in arrangements between petroleum companies and gasoline service stations French courts have passed on the issue of determinable price. In *Socomanut* v. *Esso Standard*, the plaintiff garage operator sued for declaration of termination of its agreement of exclusive purchase from the oil company. The agreement contained no price clause, but was subject to the governmental price control provision issued in 1952 defining permissible prices as between oil companies and the distributors. In 1963 the system of price control was changed so that only the price to the consumer was regulated. Prices charged to the station operators by the oil companies were fixed by the Professional Commission for Petroleum. This Commission representing all oil companies marketing these products in France, would inform the selling companies of the price to be charged.

The Court of Appeal of Paris in its decision of April 22, 1969 found that after change in the price fixing measure of 1952 there was no basis for assuming that the parties could have intended to maintain the prices in effect at that time. Further, there was no "market price" as between the oil companies and the retailers. It rejected the contention of Esso Standard that the Professional Commission's price determination was an industry wide standard on the ground that the Commission as representative, solely of the oil companies could not be considered a third party within the meaning of Article 1592 of the Civil Code. However the Court of Appeal upheld the continuing validity of the contracts on the finding that in the course of negotiations for new arrangements, a "sort of average trend" ("*une sorte de cours moyen*") had been established.

The Supreme Court reversed, holding that the rules of determined or determinable price applied to exclusive distributor arrangements. It found it error for the laws court to rely on "average trend" of price resulting from continuing negotiations, stressing the need for a market price or a price determined by objective factors.

STE. BRONZAVIA v. ANGOT
Cour de Cassation, Chambre Commerciale, March 24, 1965.
J.C.P. 1965.II.14378.

(In 1961 the Bronzavia Company appointed Angot exclusive distributor of its products for a period of 25 years. Relations between the parties having become strained, the distributor sues for rescission and damages for breach of contract by the manufacturer.

The *Cour d'Appel* in 1963 held for plaintiff, characterizing the 1961 contract as a sale. In passing on Bronzavia's contention that the contract, if one of sale, was void for lack of agreement on price that court found that the price would be determined by acceptance by the buyer of the preferential price list which the seller would grant him, which list would be established in good faith based on clearly defined factors including cost to and profit of Bronzavia.)

The Court:

In view of Article 1591 of the Civil Code, a contract of sale is not complete unless from its terms the price can be determined from elements no longer dependent on the will of one of the parties nor on the conclusion of later agreements. In this case it does not appear that the price is determinable from the factors indicated. Further, the definiteness of price is dependent on the later formulation in good faith of a preferential price list, to the offer of this list by the seller and its acceptance by the buyer, thus making the price depend on later agreements. The *Cour d'Appel* has violated Article 1591 of the Civil Code.

Judgment below quashed, case referred to *Cour d'Appel* of Amiens.

PRATI v. MAGER
Cour de Cassation, Chambre Civile, November 24, 1965.
J.C.P. 1966.II.14607.

(Prati agreed to sell Mager real estate for a price to be fixed by two experts chosen by the parties. Mage appointed his expert within the time indicated, Prati failed to do so. Mager sues to have the agreement declared void for lack of price and for damages. The *Cour d'Appel* held for plaintiff granting Prati damages of 5,000 Francs, stating that even if the sale did not take place for lack of price the perfectly lawful agreement for appointment of experts must be given effect).

The Court:

The lower court in holding that non-performance of the obligation to appoint an expert is compensable in damages correctly applied Art. 1142 of the Civil Code.

Petition for review denied.

* * *

J. HONNOLD, UNIFORM LAW FOR INTERNATIONAL SALES UNDER THE 1980 UNITED NATIONS CONVENTION
150–56 (3d ed. 1999).*

The Price

(a) Scope of the Problem. In UNCITRAL and at the 1980 Vienna Conference this question arose: Do the parties have the power to make a binding sales contract that does not (Art. 14) "expressly or implicitly" fix or make "provision for determining" the price? As we shall see, the answer calls for close attention to both Articles 14 and 55.

Usually sales contracts specify the price; long-term contracts may make elaborate provision for adjusting the initial price on the basis of changes in cost. * * *

* * *

(b) The Power of the Parties to Contract without Providing for the Price. The contested issue of theory can be exposed and tested in the setting of the following improbable case. (Improbable conduct is more useful to legal theory than to commerce.)

Example 14B. Following negotiations, Seller and Buyer signed a "Contract of Sale" that called for Seller to manufacture and ship goods according to specifications and quantity stated in the agreement. The agreement did not fix a price and instead stated: "We intend to be bound by this agreement, and hereby derogate from any implication of Article 14(1) of the 1980 U.N. Convention that we have not made a binding contract in the absence of fixing or otherwise determining the price". Seller manufactured and delivered the goods which Buyer accepted and used. Thereafter, the parties were unable to agree on the price.

Seller seeks to recover for the goods and invokes Article 55 of the Convention * * *.

Buyer defends on the ground that the agreement did not "expressly or implicitly fix ... or make provision for determining the ... price" as required by Article 14, and therefore there was no contract.

Buyer's argument has to face, at the outset, the fact that Article 14 states that the issue is whether a "proposal" is "sufficiently definite and indicates an intention to be bound" to be "an *offer*". Here the parties did not exchange an "offer" and "acceptance"; instead they signed a "Contract of Sale" that stated that they intended to be bound by contract even though the price had not been fixed. In addition (to lay bare the basic issue of validity) we assumed that the parties expressly stated that they derogated (Art. 6) from any provision of the Convention that would deny effect to their intent. (This intent would normally be evidenced merely by executing a contract of sale.)

In the Introduction to Part II, we noted that the Convention's definitions of "offer" and "acceptance" are useful and necessary for deciding whether a contract was made by an exchange of communications. We found, however, that the Convention recognizes that contracts can be made without following the two-step offer-acceptance pattern: Article 18(3) provides that a contract may be concluded "by performing an act", and Article 8(3) provides that statements (including terms of agreements) are to be interpreted to include trade usages and the parties' practices and also are to be construed in the light of "any subsequent *conduct of the parties*".

In the life of commerce, as in the above example, there is often no question as to whether a single communication should be construed as an "offer"; the parties' understanding will be disclosed by a series of communications, by their conduct (e.g. by delivering and accepting goods) or by executing a contract of sale.

Does Article 14 deal not only with whether a communication should be construed as an "offer" but also with the validity of a "Contract of Sale" that does not determine the price? This reading of Article 14 is difficult to sustain in the face of Article 4 which states that "except as otherwise *expressly* provided in this Convention, it is *not* concerned with: (a) *the validity of the contract or of any of its provisions* ...". Deference to the parties' agreement is also shown by Article 6: the parties may "derogate from or vary the effect of *any* of [the Convention's] provisions." In any event, further light is shed by the legislative history of Article 55.

(c) Article 55 and the Two-Point Compromise. The question whether Article 14 denies validity to the parties' clearly expressed intent to be bound is important for all States that adopt the Convention without excluding Part II on Formation. As we shall see in discussing Article 55, in developing this provision UNCITRAL in 1977 and the Diplomatic Conference in 1980 developed a two-part compromise between delegates that were opposed to and those that supported open-price contracts.

The Working Group draft that led to Article 55 provided: (1) "When a contract *has been concluded*" but does not make provision for the price, (2) the buyer must pay "the price generally charged *by the seller*" when the contract was concluded.

(1) In reviewing the above draft UNCITRAL in 1977 changed the opening clause, quoted at (1), to read "If a contract has been *validly* concluded . . .". The formal statement of the decision by the Commission (sitting as a Committee of the Whole) stated: "The Committee decided to introduce an express statement into the article to make it clear that it only applied to agreements which were considered *valid by the applicable law*". The discussion that led to this decision made clear that "applicable law" meant "the applicable *national* law". Indeed, discussion related to the Convention used the phrase "applicable law" to refer to *domestic* law "applicable by virtue of the rules of private international law" (Art. 7(2)), in contrast to the uniform international rules set forth in the Convention.

(2) The second part of the compromise was made in 1980 at the Diplomatic Conference. Some delegates objected that the reference to the price charged by the *seller* gave an unfair advantage to the seller; to meet this objection the reference to the seller's price was replaced by "the price *generally* charged at the time of the conclusion of the contract".

As a result of these two compromises, in the formal final votes by the Plenary of the Conference, Article 14 was adopted by 41 votes to none with 5 abstentions and Article 55 was adopted by 40 votes to 3 with 5 abstentions.

In view of this over-all compromise, including the concession to the *domestic* law of those States that make provision for the price an element of contract validity, it is quite impossible to conclude that Article 14 imposed such a rule of invalidity on all States that adopt Part II of the Convention.

* * *

Conclusion. Article 14(1) provides that a communication that does not state or make provision for the price is not an "offer" so that a reply "I accept" does not close a contract. However, Article 14(1) does not bar the parties from concluding a contract by express agreement or by conduct (*e.g.,* by shipping, receiving and using goods) that shows their "intention . . . to be bound" (Art. 14(1)). The only rule of "validity" with respect to agreement on price results from the opening phrase of Article 55 which defers to applicable domestic law.

(3) Decisions Relating to Definiteness and Price.

* * *

(3) GER. OLG Frankfurt a M., 10U80/93, 04–03–'94. B invited S to make an offer for lists of screws. S sent lists and prices; B disagreed as to prices for some items. S did not ship. B sued for either delivery or damages. B's claims were rejected: there was neither delivery nor contract. CLOUT 21, UNILEX D. 1994–7.1.

(4) ARB.ICC (Paris) 9324/1995. In sale of manganese, parties agreed on a provisional price (which B paid), subject to revision based on the price B received on resale. In view of prior usage of the parties, B was required to pay an additional sum. (French CISG law was applied.) UNILEX D. 1995–35.

* * *

PROBLEM 2–13

Glazium is a mineral used in the process of applying a glaze to very large pottery. The only existing mine presently producing glazium is near Roussillon, a small town in the south of France. Glazium Roussillon s.a.r.l., a French company owned by French citizens, owns the glazium mine. The company mines and markets throughout the world approximately 200,000 tons of glazium each year. The company markets the glazium through sole distributors in each importing country and these distributors sell to end-user manufacturers. Nevertheless, approximately 20,000 tons is available each year on a spot market through brokers of minerals. Each year for the last fifteen years Glazium Roussillon s.a.r.l. has exported approximately 80,000 tons to the United States through U.S. Mineral Import Inc., a Delaware corporation owned by U.S. citizens which has acted as the French company's sole distributor in the United States.

For the last ten years Pottery Warehouse Co., a general partnership established by U.S. citizens residing in California, have bought glazium on one-year supply contracts to use in its pottery manufacturing business from U.S. Mineral Import Inc. During this decade the partnership business has increased dramatically and its need for glazium for the next calendar year is projected to be 6,000 tons, more than four times its needs ten years ago. The partnership has had difficulty in its dealings with U.S. Mineral Import Inc., which will not guaranty the supply. The partners believe they can obtain a long-term guaranteed supply on better terms if they enter into a contract directly with the French supplier. The management of the French company is willing to meet in London with representatives of the partnership to discuss a possible contract.

You are legal adviser to the California partnership.

(a) The partners wish to conclude a long-term contract that will obligate the French supplier to supply the partnership's requirements. The partnership has projections of what these requirements will be but recognizes that these requirements will vary with the demand for its pottery. Assuming that the supplier is willing to agree to supply the partnership's requirements, will the Convention govern a "requirements" contract? Is article 14(1) relevant?

(b) The partners are willing to agree to a fixed price per ton for a short term (*e.g.*, one year) but wish to include in the final contract a flexible price formula that adjusts the price to reflect market conditions and changes in the partnership's requirements. Does the Convention pose any obstacle to including such a clause in the contract?

(c) The partners wish to conclude a contract for a fixed term (*e.g.*, five years) with the right in the partnership to extend this period. Does the Convention pose any obstacle to including such a clause in the contract?

(d) In the light of the points raised in the preceding questions, the partners ask you to draft quantity and price terms that could be used in the negotiations.

PROBLEM 2–14

PETRARG S.A. explores and develops oil fields in Argentina. It recently purchased oil rig equipment from Texas Petroleum Inc. ("TPI"), which operates in the United States. The agreed sales price of $1,180,000 was to be paid $100,000 in cash and the balance at $30,000 per month for 36 months. After making the first six monthly payments the manager of PETRARG informed the president of TPI that PETRARG needed to by some additional equipment if it was to stay in business, but could not buy the equipment unless TPI reduced the monthly payments to $10,000 per month. TPI's president orally agreed to the reduction in payments. TPI accepted the reduced payments for six months and then notified PETRARG that future payments must be $30,000 per month and that the cumulative shortage ($20,000 x 6= $120,000) must be made up within 60 days.

(a) Assuming the Sales Convention is applicable, may PETRARG show an oral modification to the original contract? CISG art. 29. If so, what are the contract terms? What additional facts, if any, do you need?

(b) Assuming the Uniform Commercial Code applies, may PETRARG show an oral modification? *See* U.C.C. § 2–209. If so, what are the contract terms? What additional facts, if any, do you need?

(c) Would your answers to the preceding questions change if the signed contract document included the following term?

This contract may only be modified or terminated by agreement of the parties expressed in a writing signed by both parties.

2. *THE LEGAL EFFECT OF "PRE-CONTRACTUAL"*
EVENTS

FARNSWORTH, PRECONTRACTUAL LIABILITY AND PRELIMINARY AGREEMENTS: FAIR DEALING AND FAILED NEGOTIATIONS
87 Colum. L. Rev. 217, 218–20 & 239–243 (1987).*

INTRODUCTION

Ours is an era of "deals"—for the long-term supply of energy, for the development of a shopping center, for the friendly takeover of a corporation, for the signing of a first-round draft choice. Much has been written on how to negotiate such deals. Little has been written on the law governing their negotiation. This Article discusses that law and the recent outpouring of cases that apply it.

The law governing the formation of contracts is usually analyzed in terms of the classic rules of offer and acceptance. They are seductive rules that proceed on a simple premise: two parties exchange proposals until an "offer" by one party is "accepted" by the other forming a contract. Their precise vocabulary of "offer" and "acceptance," of "revocation" and "lapse," of "rejection" and "counter-offer" dissects such tantalizing puzzles as those posed by the "battle of the forms" and contracts by correspondence. But however suited these rules may have been to the measured cadence of contracting in the nineteenth century, they have little to say about the complex processes that lead to major deals today.

Major contractual commitments are typically set out in a lengthy document, or in a set of documents, signed by the parties in multiple copies and exchanged more or less simultaneously at a closing. The terms are reached by negotiations, usually face-to-face over a considerable period of time and often involving corporate officers, bankers, engineers, accountants, lawyers, and others. The negotiations are a far cry from the simple bargaining envisioned by the classic rules of offer and acceptance, which evoke an image of single-issue, adversarial, zero-sum bargaining as opposed to multi-issue, problem-solving, gain-maximizing negotiation.

During the negotiation of such deals there is often no offer or counter-offer for either party to accept, but rather a gradual process in which agreements are reached piecemeal in several "rounds" with a succession of drafts. There may first be an exchange of information and an identification of the parties' interests and differences, then a series of compromises with tentative agreement on major points, and finally a refining of contract terms. The negotiations may begin with managers, who refrain from making offers because they want the terms of any binding commitment to be worked out by their lawyers. Once these original negotiators decide that they have settled those matters that they

---

regard as important, they turn things over to their lawyers. The drafts prepared by the lawyers are not offers because the lawyers lack authority to make offers. When the ultimate agreement is reached, it is often expected that it will be embodied in a document or documents that will be exchanged by the parties at a closing.

If the parties sign and exchange documents at the closing, there is no question that they have given their assent to a contract. There is little occasion to apply the classic rules of offer and acceptance. But if the negotiations fail and no documents are signed and exchanged, a number of questions may arise that the classic rules of offer and acceptance do not address: May a disappointed party have a claim against the other party for having failed to conform to a standard of fair dealing? If so, what is the meaning of fair dealing in this context? And may the disappointed party get restitution? Be reimbursed for out-of-pocket expenses? Recover for lost opportunities? As the paradigmatic deal has become larger and more complex, and the typical negotiation has become more complicated and prolonged, these questions have been reaching the courts in increasing numbers. Some observers have concluded that existing contract doctrines are not adequate to the task of protecting the parties. I argue that, on the contrary, those doctrines, imaginatively applied, are both all that are needed and all that are desirable.

The resolution of disputes occasioned by the failure of negotiations depends in any particular case on the legal "regime" under which the parties find themselves as they proceed through the negotiation process to ultimate agreement. In this Article, I identify and sketch the contours of four regimes and consider the requirement of fair dealing in each: the two polar regimes, negotiation and ultimate agreement, and the two intermediate regimes that may result from preliminary agreements, agreement with open terms and agreement to negotiate.

The two polar regimes, negotiation and ultimate agreement, are dealt with in Part I. Under the regime of negotiation, established bases of liability, if creatively used by litigants and liberally applied by courts, afford the parties sufficient protection. The stunted development of these bases in connection with negotiations is not due to any shortcomings in the bases themselves, but rather to the failure of litigants to exploit them fully, including a failure to seek damages for lost opportunities in appropriate cases. And if negotiating parties choose to move quickly to the regime of ultimate agreement in order to avoid the risks to which they are exposed under the regime of negotiation, existing contract law, with its tolerance of conditions, goes far in honoring their choice.

Parties who do not wish to rush to ultimate agreement are free instead to make a preliminary agreement to allocate the risks of their continuing negotiations. Such agreements, in particular agreements with open terms and agreements to negotiate, are the subject of Part II. I contend that existing contract law is fully capable of recognizing and enforcing such preliminary agreements, and that the refusal by some courts to enforce preliminary agreements to negotiate is not a justifiable restriction of party autonomy under existing contract law. Part III discusses the content of the duty of fair dealing when it is imposed under an agreement to negotiate.

* * *

6. *General Obligation as a Basis of Liability.*—Some scholarly writers have generalized from the cases decided on the grounds of misrepresentation and specific promise to argue that a general obligation of fair dealing may arise out of the negotiations themselves, at least if the disappointed party has been led to believe that success is in prospect. Thus Summers wrote that if courts follow *Red Owl*, "it will no longer be possible for one party to scuttle contract negotiations with impunity when the other has been induced to rely to his detriment on the prospect that the negotiations will succeed." American courts, however, have been unreceptive to these arguments and have declined to find a general obligation that would preclude a party from breaking off negotiations, even when success was in prospect. Their reluctance to do so is supported by the formulation of a general duty of good faith and fair dealing in both the Uniform Commercial Code and the Restatement (Second) of Contracts that, at least by negative implication, does not extend to negotiations.

European courts have been more willing than American ones to accept scholarly proposals for precontractual liability based on a general obligation of fair dealing. But even in Europe it is difficult to find cases that actually impose precontractual liability where an American court would clearly not do so on other grounds. In 1861, the German jurist Rudolf von Jhering advanced the thesis that parties to precontractual negotiations are contractually bound to observe the "necessary diligentia." A party who commits a breach of this contractual obligation—a *culpa in contrahendo* (fault in contractual negotiation)—is therefore liable for reliance damages. Jhering himself was concerned primarily with such problems as the effect of *culpa* on contracts concluded by mistake and never applied his thesis to situations involving failed negotiations. It was a French scholar, Raymond Saleilles, who in 1907 advanced the view that after parties have entered into negotiations, both must act in good faith and neither can break off the negotiations "arbitrarily" without compensating the other for reliance damages.

German courts have, however, relied on Jhering's thesis as a basis of precontractual liability. According to the *Bundesgerichtshof*, "a fault in contractual negotiations that renders one liable for damages can also exist in that one party awakes in the other confidence in the imminent coming into existence of a contract—subsequently not concluded—and thus causes the latter party to incur expenses." The court went on to say that

> the mere breaking off of negotiations by one party does not, without more, constitute a fault in contract negotiations.... [E]ither of the parties can create or strengthen in the other party, simply by the fact that he participates in such negotiations, the more or less

certain assumption that he is ready to contract. But this alone does not reduce his freedom of decision respecting the conclusion of the contract and does not yet render him ... liable, if he breaks off negotiations.

Such statements could be made by an American court speaking of misrepresentation as a basis of liability. A later decision of the *Bundesgerichtshof*, however, suggests that German courts are willing to go well beyond American courts and find liability where, after a party has "conducted himself in such a fashion that the other party could, and did, justifiably count on a contract with the negotiated content coming into existence" "he refuses to contract without an appropriate ground."

In France there has been a similar development, though precontractual liability is imposed not for breach of a contractual obligation but on a theory of tort (*délit*). The wrong is viewed as an abuse of right (*abus de droit*), for which bad faith without malice will suffice. Bad faith may be found not only where a party negotiates with no serious intention to contract, but also where a party breaks off negotiations abruptly and without justification. Thus in a well-known case, a French businessman was negotiating for the purchase of an American machine for the manufacture of cement pipes from the exclusive distribution in France. After the prospective buyer had made a trip to the United States to see the machine and the prolonged negotiations were far advanced, the distributor broke off negotiations "abruptly" ("entalement") and "without legitimate reason" and refused to sell to the prospective buyer. The lower court held the distributor liable for preparations made by the prospective buyer and the *Cour de Cassation* upheld this decision on the ground that there had been an "abusive rupture" of the negotiations. This is one of the few European cases that actually go beyond American precedents.

It is perhaps not surprising that American courts have rarely been asked to hold that a general obligation of fair dealing arises out of the negotiations themselves when they have reached a point where one of the parties has relied on a successful outcome. Often the reason may be that, as suggested earlier, the disappointed parties to negotiations are unaware of the possibility of a generous measure of precontractual liability. But it may also be that they are not greatly dissatisfied with the common law's aleatory view of negotiations and recognize that the few claims that arise are fairly treated under the existing grounds of restitution, misrepresentation, and specific promise. As long as these grounds are not often invoked and have not been pushed to their limits, there will be little pressure to add a general obligation of fair dealing.[95]

---

95. If our courts were to impose a general obligation of fair dealing, could the parties disclaim that obligation? Under Uniform Commercial Code §1–102(3), parties are powerless to disclaim the duty of good faith imposed by the Code under every contract, and it is hard to see why they should fare any better in the precontractual context. But a non-disclaimable duty would conflict with contemporary judicial tolerance of attempts to disclaim precontractual liability. In keeping with the common law's aleatory view of negotiation, courts have generally looked with favor on attempts to

There is ample justification for judicial reluctance to impose a general obligation of fair dealing on parties to precontractual negotiations. The common law's aleatory view of negotiations well suits a society that does not regard itself as having an interest in the outcome of the negotiations. The negotiation of an ordinary contract differs in this way from the negotiation of a collective bargaining agreement, in which society sees itself as having an interest in preventing labor strife. Although it is in society's interest to provide a regime under which the parties are free to negotiate ordinary contracts, the outcome of any particular negotiation is a matter of indifference.

There is no reason to believe that imposition of a general obligation of fair dealing would improve the regime under which such negotiations take place. The difficulty of determining a point in the negotiations at which the obligation of fair dealing arises would create uncertainty. An obligation of fair dealing might have an undesirable chilling effect, discouraging parties from entering into negotiations if chances of success were slight. The obligation might also have an undesirable accelerating effect, increasing the pressure on parties to bring negotiations to a final if hasty conclusion. With no clear advantages to counter these disadvantages there is little reason to abandon the present aleatory view.

* * *

PROBLEM 2–15

Over a three-month period a Pennsylvania food wholesaler negotiates with a French agricultural cooperative for a long-term contract to purchase camomile (Webster's Seventh New Collegiate Dictionary: "any of a genus of composite herbs with a strong-scented foliage and flower heads that contain a bitter medicinal principle"). At the end of three months, the Pennsylvania wholesaler breaks off negotiations on the ground that "negotiations are unlikely to be successful." The French cooperative sues the wholesaler in a U.S. court.

(a) Does the Convention govern the dispute? Are you persuaded, for example, by any of the following arguments made by attorneys for the French enterprise? Are the arguments from the Farnsworth excerpt relevant to this analysis?

— The wholesaler is in breach of an agreement to negotiate, which agreement had been entered into at the beginning of negotiations. Remedies for this breach are found in the Sales Convention because the parties agreed to negotiate a contract for sale.

— The two parties had agreed to a long-term supply contract at the beginning of the negotiations and their subsequent negotiations were merely to reach agreement on terms left open. Remedies for this breach

disclaim precontractual liability, except where misrepresentation is involved. They have been receptive to disclaimers of liability for restitution of benefits conferred during precontractual negotiations. Rutledge v. Housing Auth., 88 Ill. App. 3d 1064, 411 N.E.2d 82 (Ct. App. 1980). Courts have also been receptive to disclaimers of liability based on a specific promise.

are found in the Sales Convention because the long-term supply contract is for the sale of goods.

— The wholesaler has breached a general obligation of fair dealing imposed on the wholesaler by Article 7(1) of the Convention.

(b) During the course of negotiations, the representative of the French agricultural cooperative states that it processes the camomile in its own processing warehouse. Before executing contract documents, however, the wholesaler learns that the cooperative does not have a processing warehouse and must have the camomile dried and sorted by third parties. The wholesaler considers the cooperative's misstatement material because the wholesaler does not believe that there will be adequate assurance of quality control. Does the Convention provide a remedy for this misrepresentation?

(c) If you are consulted by the wholesaler before negotiations begin, what steps would you take to protect your client's interests from the risk that there may be "pre-contractual" liability?

Chapter 3

PERFORMANCE OF THE CONTRACT

Having entered into a binding agreement, the seller undertakes to deliver and transfer title to the goods sold, while the buyer undertakes to take delivery and pay for them. These general obligations inhere in the very definition of *contract of sale* and are found in all national sales laws as well as the U.N. Sales Convention.[1] But unless the sale is a cash sale concluded face-to-face with immediate delivery of the goods—a highly unlikely scenario in transnational trade—both the seller and the buyer will need further guidance on what they must do to deliver and pay for the goods sold. For these details the seller and buyer will look to the terms of their "dickered" agreement (terms actually negotiated) as supplemented by enforceable General Conditions, course of performance, course of dealing, usage of trade, and suppletory rules in the relevant sales law. This will be as true for contracts governed by the U.N. Sales Convention as it is for contracts governed by national sales laws.

Most legal disputes about a party's performance involve interpreting contract language or ascertaining and construing the parties' agreement from course of dealing or usage of trade. What steps a seller must take to deliver the goods, for example, will often require construction of "trade terms" that the parties incorporate into their sales contract—terms that codify the expectations of merchants who regularly buy and sell across national boundaries. The suppletory rules of the Convention or national sales laws play only a minor role. Because sales may range from the sale of eggs in a local market to the manufacture and sale of a hydro-electric turbine, these legal rules must necessarily be flexible, especially when it comes to defining the seller's performance.

* * *

---

1. *See* CISG arts. 30 & 53 (the seller must "deliver the goods, hand over any documents relating to them and transfer the property in the goods," while the buyer must "pay the price for the goods and take delivery of them"); *cf*. U.C.C. § 2–301 ("The obligation of the seller is to transfer and deliver and that of the buyer is to accept and pay in accordance with the contract").

163

A. SELLER'S OBLIGATIONS

1. DELIVERY

PROBLEM 3–1

Able Co., a French manufacturer of transistors, receives an e-mail from Baker Co., a Virginia-based manufacturer of electronic equipment, stating: "We wish to buy 1,000 A7S transistors. How much are they?" Able replies by e-mail: "We can let you have them for U.S. $6 apiece." Baker's e-mail responds: "Good. Done. Be sure to send them by air so that they arrive here by Friday."

(a) What must Able do to perform its obligation to "deliver" the transistors? CISG arts. 30, 31, 32.

(b) When must Able deliver the transistors? CISG art. 33.

(c) Can Able satisfy its obligation to deliver if it sends defective transistors or transistors other than the "A7S" model? CISG art. 35(1), (2).

(d) When does the risk of loss shift to Baker? CISG art. 67.

UNILEX CASE D. 1993–16

Germany: Landgericht Aachen, 1993.*

Abstract

A German seller had sent an invoice relating to ten acoustic prostheses to an Italian buyer who had previously expressed its intention to buy them. The buyer, by fax, stated it was able to take delivery of the goods, which it later did not do. After receiving a notice to perform the buyer notified the seller that it no longer intended to take the goods. Subsequently the parties came to a settlement agreement according to which the seller agreed to waive its contractual claims provided the buyer took delivery and paid part of the purchase price within a fixed term. As the buyer did not comply with the settlement agreement, the seller commenced action on the basis of the original agreement and claimed damages.

The Court applied Art. 5(1) of the EC Convention on Jurisdiction and the Enforcement of Decisions in Civil and Commercial Matters (Brussels 1968), pursuant to which a person domiciled in a Contracting State [i.e. the buyer] may be sued in the Court for the place of performance of the obligation in question (taking delivery of the goods). The Court applied CISG to determine the place of performance, as at the time of the conclusion of the contract the parties had their places of business in contracting States (Germany and Italy) (Art. 1(1)(a) CISG). As Art. 60(b) CISG does not specify the place of performance of the obligation to take delivery, the Court referred to Art. 31(b) and (c) CISG, which provides that the seller must make delivery at the seller's place of business, when there is no contrary agreement. The Court concluded that the buyer had to take delivery from the seller's place of business (Germany). The Court therefore affirmed its jurisdiction.

The Court found that the buyer was in breach of the obligation to take delivery of the goods and the seller, who had fixed an additional period of time for performance, was entitled to recover damages as per Arts. 61(1)(b) and 63 CISG.

NOTE: WHEN DOES CONTRACT INVOLVE THE CARRIAGE OF GOODS?

What if, in the preceding Problem, Baker had not said that it wanted Able to be sure to send the transistors by air so that they would arrive by Friday? Would the contract of sale involve the carriage of goods within the meaning of Article 31(a)? If so, Able performs its delivery obligation by handing over the transistors to the "first carrier" in Paris. But would Able be required to contact a carrier at all, or is that part of Baker's obligations? Note that, if the contract is interpreted not to "involve the carriage of goods," Baker must accept delivery of the goods at seller's place of business in France under CISG art. 31(c).

TRADE TERMS

The rules on the delivery of the goods and the handing over of documents set out in Articles 31–34 of the Sales Convention are "suppletory" rules. By their agreement parties are free to derogate from the rules or to vary their effect. Parties to transnational sales contracts will frequently agree on delivery terms by adopting the shorthand of a trade term that codifies an understanding on the delivery obligations of the parties. The most widely used of these codifications are the International Chamber of Commerce's *Incoterms*. Incorporation of an Incoterm, such as FOB, into a contract will effectively displace any contrary provisions of the Sales Convention. The following materials examine the status and content of these trade terms.

* * *

WINSHIP, INTRODUCTION
Basic Instruments of International Economic Law,
707–710 (S. Zamora & R. Brand eds., 1990).*

INTERNATIONAL CHAMBER OF COMMERCE, *INCOTERMS*

I. *Origin and Background*

"Incoterms" (an acronym for "*in*ternational *commercial terms*") are prepared by the Commission on International Commercial Practice of the International Chamber of Commerce. The International Chamber began study of the meaning of trade terms in 1921 and first adopted a uniform statement of the meaning of nine trade terms in 1936 under the title of *Incoterms: International Rules for the Interpretation of Trade Terms*. To adapt these terms more closely to British and American practice, the International Chamber published a revision in 1953. Subsequent publications of Incoterms in 1967, 1976, and 1980 added new terms but, with one exception, did not further revise the definitions set out in the 1953 publication. The latest revision of Incoterms in 1990 is a more thorough revision and reorganization. The 1990 revision is published as I.C.C. Publication No. 460 and entered into force on July 1, 1990.

Parties to a sales contract may use Incoterms as a short-hand form of stating their agreement with respect to delivery of the goods sold. Incoterms determine what the seller must do in order to deliver, what the buyer must do to make delivery possible, what costs the seller and buyer must bear, and when the risks of loss of goods sold are transferred from the seller to the buyer. Each of the Incoterms allocates these obligations, costs, and risks in a different pattern. If the seller, for example, wishes to minimize its delivery responsibilities it may ask the buyer to agree to delivery *ex works* [EXW], a term that requires the buyer to pick up the goods at seller's plant at the buyer's risk and expense. Some Incoterms are adapted to a particular mode of transport. The trade terms *FOB* and *CIF*, for example, have their origin in ocean carriage and are defined with this form of carriage in mind.

The post–1953 revisions reflect the changing practices in the transport industry. Containerization and combined modes of carriage, for example, have diluted the importance of the traditional emphasis on carriage of goods by sea. The changes have also forced a reevaluation of the responsibilities of the parties and the time when risk of loss is to pass to the buyer. New means of communication have likewise led to adjustments in the forms of documentation required in international trading transactions. This is apparent in the 1990 revision, which contemplates the use of electronic data interchange rather than the more traditional documentation.

Incoterms have enjoyed widespread success. In 1969 the U.N. Commission on International Trade Law concluded that "it would be desirable to give the widest possible dissemination to Incoterms 1953 in order to encourage their world-wide use in international trade." Following the 1980 revision, the leading international trade associations in the United States decided to recommend use of the Incoterms in place of the American Foreign Trade Definitions, which these same associations had adopted in 1919 and revised in 1941. The major Socialist trading countries, acting through the Council for Mutual Economic Assistance, have adopted trade terms which in content follow closely the Incoterms.

* * *

II. *Legal Status*

The International Chamber of Commerce is a non-governmental entity with its headquarters in Paris. The International Chamber was established in 1919 with the goal of promoting free competition and self-regulation by business. Given these goals, membership tends to be limited to representatives from capitalist countries. Participation by non-members in the International Chamber's work is indirect.

Incoterms are neither national legislation nor an international treaty. An Incoterm will be applicable to a sales contract if the contract incorporates the term expressly or implicitly. Express incorporation would include not only the trade term itself but also a reference to Incoterms. A statement that the delivery term is "CIF New York (Incoterms 1990 Revision)" would expressly incorporate the definition of the CIF delivery term found in the 1990 version of *Incoterms* (Publication No. 460).

Incoterms may also supply the content of a trade term used by parties to an international sales contract on the ground that Incoterms are codifications of international custom. Courts in France and Germany enforce Incoterms as part of international custom. In contrast to the Uniform Customs and Practice for Documentary Credits, also formulated by the International Chamber, the Incoterms are less subject to the charge that they are prescriptive rather than descriptive of actual practice. Because they provide a range of options for the contracting parties the terms cannot be said to favor either sellers or buyers. It does not matter what trade the parties are engaged in or what type of domestic economy adopted in the countries where they have their places of business.

Article 9(2) of the U.N. Convention on Contracts for the International Sale of Goods makes applicable to a sales contract "a[ny] usage of which the parties knew or ought to have known and which in international trade is widely known to, and regularly observed by, parties to contracts of the type involved in the particular trade concerned." With respect to Incoterms Professor Ramberg concludes that they qualify as such "usage." In its unofficial commentary to the 1978 draft sales convention, the UNCITRAL Secretariat mentions the Incoterms as such widely-observed trade terms in commentary to several of the articles.

Courts in the United States do not hesitate to enforce Incoterms when parties expressly agree upon their application.

If, however, U.S. law governs the contract and the parties have not expressly incorporated an Incoterm, it must be decided whether the Uniform Commercial Code's definitions of trade terms govern or whether Incoterms are applicable as a usage of trade. The Code defines some but not all the trade terms found in Incoterms and the common Code and Incoterm definitions vary somewhat in content. *See* Uniform Commercial Code Sections 2–319 (F.O.B.; F.A.S.); 2–320, 2–321 (C.I.F.; C. & F.); 2–322 (Ex-ship). These Code sections, however, are all expressly made subject to the contrary agreement of the parties. Since the Code deems usage of trade to be part of the parties' agreement it is possible to argue that Incoterms, as usage of trade, will be looked to rather than the Code. The Code defines a usage of trade as "any practice or method of dealing having such regularity of observance in a place, vocation or trade as to justify an expectation that it will be observed with respect to the transaction in question." For many international sales transactions a U.S. party should be able to show that Incoterms satisfy this definition. Interpretation of Incoterms then is a matter for the court rather than the jury.

INCOTERMS

6–17 (1990 ed.) (International Chamber of Commerce Pub. No. 460)*

INTRODUCTION

* * *

NEW METHOD OF PRESENTING INCOTERMS

5.   In connection with the revision work within the ICC Working Party, suggestions were made to present the trade terms in another manner for the purpose of easier reading and understanding. The terms have been grouped in four basically different categories; namely starting with the only term whereby the seller makes the goods available to the buyer at the seller's own premises (the "E"-term Ex works); followed by the second group whereby the seller is called upon to deliver the goods to a carrier appointed by the buyer (the "F"-terms FCA, FAS and FOB); continuing with the "C"-terms where the seller has to contract for carriage, but without assuming the risk of loss of or damage to the goods or additional costs due to events occurring after shipment and dispatch (CFR, CIF, CPT and CIP); and, finally, the "D"-terms whereby the seller has to bear all costs and risks needed to bring the goods to the country of destination (DAF, DES, DEQ, DDU and DDP). A chart setting out this new classification is given hereafter.

INCOTERMS 1990		
Group E Departure	**EXW**	Ex Works
Group F Main carriage unpaid	**FCA**	Free Carrier
	FAS	Free Alongside Ship
	FOB	Free On Board
Group C Main carriage paid	**CFR**	Cost and Freight
	CIF	Cost, Insurance and Freight
	CPT	Carriage Paid To
	CIP	Carriage and Insurance Paid To
Group D Arrival	**DAF**	Delivered At Frontier
	DES	Delivered Ex Ship

DEQ	Delivered Ex Quay
DDU	Delivered Duty Unpaid
DDP	Delivered Duty Paid

Further, under all terms, the respective obligations of the parties have been grouped under 10 headings where each heading on the seller's side "mirrors" the position of the buyer with respect to the same subject matter. Thus, if for instance according to A.3. the seller has to arrange and pay for the contract of carriage we find the words "No obligation" under the heading "Contract of carriage" in B.3. setting forth the buyer's position. Needless to say, this does not mean that the buyer would not in his own interest make such contracts as may be needed to bring the goods to the desired destination, but he has no "obligation" to the seller to do so. However, with respect to the division between the parties of duties, taxes and other official charges, as well as the costs of carrying out customs formalities, the terms explain for the sake of clarity how such costs are divided between the parties although, of course, the seller might not have any interest at all in the buyer's further disposal of the goods after they have been delivered to him. Conversely, under some terms such as the "D"-terms, the buyer is not interested in costs which the seller might incur in order to bring the goods all the way to the agreed destination point.

* * *

THE BUYER'S OPTIONS

7. In some situations, it may not be possible at the time when the contract of sale is entered into to decide precisely on the exact point or even the place where the goods should be delivered by the seller for carriage or at the final destination. For instance reference might have been made at this stage merely to a "range" or to a rather large place, e.g. seaport, and it is then usually stipulated that the buyer can have the right or duty to name later on the more precise point within the range or the place. If the buyer has a duty to name the precise point as aforesaid his failure to do so might result in liability to bear the risks and additional costs resulting from such failure. In addition, the buyer's failure to use his right to indicate the point may give the seller the right to select the point which best suits his purpose.

* * *

INSPECTION OF GOODS

10. In many cases, the buyer may be well advised to arrange for inspection of the goods before or at the time they are handed over by the seller for carriage (so-called pre-shipment inspection or PSI). Unless the contract stipulates otherwise, the buyer would himself have to pay the cost for such inspection which is arranged in his own interest. However, if the inspection has been made in order to enable the seller to comply with any mandatory rules applicable to the export of the goods in his own country he would have to pay for that inspection.

FREE CARRIER ... NAMED PLACE (FCA)

11. As has been said, the FCA-term could be used whenever the seller should fulfil his obligation by handing over the goods to a carrier named by the buyer. It is expected that this term will also be used for maritime transport in all cases where the cargo is not handed to the ship in the traditional method over the ship's rail. Needless to say, the traditional FOB-term is inappropriate where the seller is called upon to hand over the goods to a cargo terminal before the ship arrives, since he would then have to bear the risks and costs after the time when he has no possibility to control the goods or to give instructions with respect to their custody.

It should be stressed that under the "F"-terms, the seller should hand over the goods for carriage as instructed by the buyer, since the buyer would make the contract of carriage and name the carrier. Thus, it is not necessary to spell out in the trade term precisely how the goods should be handed over by the seller to the carrier. Nevertheless, in order to make it possible for traders to use FCA as an "overriding" "F"-term, explanations are given with respect to the customary modalities of delivery for the different modes of transport.

* * *

THE "C"-TERMS (CFR, CIF, CPT AND CIP)

12. Under the "C"-terms, the seller must contract for carriage on usual terms at his own expense. Therefore, a point up to which he would have to pay transportation costs must necessarily be indicated after the respective "C"-term. Under the CIF and CIP terms the seller also has to take out insurance and bear the insurance cost.

Since the point for the division of costs refers to the country of destination, the "C"-terms are frequently mistakenly believed to be arrival contracts, whereby the seller is not relieved from any risks or costs until the goods have actually arrived at the agreed point. However, it must be stressed over and over again that the "C"-terms are of the same nature as the "F"-terms in that the seller fulfils the contract in the country of shipment or dispatch. Thus, the contracts of sale under the "C"-terms, like the contracts under the "F"-terms, fall under the category of shipment contracts. While the seller would have to pay the normal transportation cost for the carriage of the goods by a usual route and in a customary manner to the agreed place of destination, the risk for loss of or damage to the goods, as well as additional costs resulting from events occurring after the goods having been handed over for carriage, fall upon the buyer. Hence, the "C"-terms as distinguished from all other terms contain two "critical" points, one for the division of costs and another one for the division of risks. For this reason, the greatest caution must be observed when adding obligations of the seller to the "C"-terms referring to a time after the aforementioned "critical" point for the division of risk. It is the very essence of the "C"-terms to relieve the seller from any further risk and cost after he has duly fulfilled his contract by contracting for carriage and handing over the goods to the carrier and by providing for insurance under the CIF- and CIP-terms.

It should also be possible for the seller to agree with the buyer to collect payment under a documentary credit by presenting the agreed shipping documents to the bank. It would be quite contrary to this common method of payment in international trade if the seller were to have to bear further risks and costs after the moment when payment had been made under documentary credits or otherwise upon shipment and dispatch of the goods. Needless to say, however, the seller would have to pay every cost which is due to the carrier irrespective of whether freight should be pre-paid upon shipment or is payable at destination (freight collect), except such additional costs which may result from events occurring subsequent to shipment and dispatch.

* * *

THE "ON BOARD REQUIREMENT" UNDER FOB, CFR AND CIF

16.   The contract of carriage would determine the obligations of the shipper or the sender with respect to handing over the goods for carriage to the carrier. It should be noted that FOB, CFR and CIF all retain the traditional practice to deliver the goods on board the vessel. While, traditionally, the point for delivery of the goods according to the contract of sale coincided with the point for handing over the goods for carriage, contemporary transportation techniques create a considerable problem of "synchronisation" between the contract of carriage and the contract of sale. Nowadays goods are usually delivered by the seller to the carrier before the goods are taken on board or sometimes even before the ship has arrived in the seaport. In such cases, merchants are advised to use such "F"- or "C"- terms which do not attach the handing over of the goods for carriage to shipment on board, namely FCA, CPT or CIP instead of FOB, CFR and CIF.

* * *

THE BILL OF LADING AND EDI PROCEDURES

18.   Traditionally, the on board bill of lading has been the only acceptable document to be presented by the seller under the terms CFR and CIF. The bill of lading fulfils three important functions, namely

  – proof of delivery of the goods on board the vessel

  – evidence of the contract of carriage

  – a means of transferring rights to the goods in transit by the transfer of the paper document to another party.

Transport documents other than the bill of lading would fulfil the two first-mentioned functions, but would not control the delivery of the goods at destination or enable a buyer to sell the goods in transit by surrendering the paper document to his buyer. Instead, other transport documents would name the party entitled to receive the goods at destination. The fact that the possession of the bill of lading is required in order to obtain the goods from the carrier at destination makes it particularly difficult to replace by EDI-procedures.

Further, it is customary to issue bills of lading in several originals but it is, of course, of vital importance for a buyer or a bank acting upon his instructions in paying the seller to ensure that all originals are surrendered by the seller (so-called "full set"). This is also a requirement under the ICC Rules for Documentary Credits (the so-called Uniform Customs and Practice, "UCP"; ICC Publication 400).

The transport document must evidence not only delivery of the goods to the carrier but also that the goods, as far as could be ascertained by the carrier, were received in good order and condition. Any notation on the transport document which would indicate that the goods had not been in such condition would make the document "unclean" and thus make it unacceptable under UCP (Art. 18; see also ICC Publication 473). In spite of the particular legal nature of the bill of lading it is expected that it will be replaced by EDI procedures in the near future. The 1990 version of Incoterms has taken this expected development into proper account.

NON-NEGOTIABLE TRANSPORT DOCUMENTS INSTEAD OF BILLS OF LADING

19.   In recent years, a considerable simplification of documentary practices has been achieved. Bills of lading are frequently replaced by non-negotiable documents similar to those which are used for other modes of transport than carriage by sea. These documents are called "sea way-bills", "liner waybills", "freight receipts", or variants of such expressions. These non-negotiable documents are quite satisfactory to use except where the buyer wishes to sell the goods in transit by surrendering a paper document to the new buyer. In order to make this possible, the obligation of the seller to provide a bill of lading under CFR and CIF must necessarily be retained. However, when the contracting parties know that the buyer does not contemplate selling the goods in transit, they may specifically agree to relieve the seller from the obligation to provide a bill of lading, or, alternatively, they may use CPT and CIP where there is no requirement to provide a bill of lading.

* * *

GARRO, THE U.N. SALES CONVENTION IN THE AMERICAS: RECENT DEVELOPMENTS
17 J. Law & Com. 219, 238–43 (1998).*

Bedial, Sociedad Anónima, v. Paul Müggenburg and Co., GmbH, 31 Oct. 1995, National Court of Appeals on Commercial Matters, Division C.

In this case, a different panel of the Commercial Court of Appeals affirmed a judgment of a commercial court of first instance (Juzgado Nacional de Primera Instancia en lo Comercial No. 11) dismissing a claim brought by an Argentine buyer (*Bedial*) against a seller based in Hamburg (*Müggenburg*).

On or about February 25, 1987, *Bedial* and *Müggenburg* concluded a contract for the sale of approximately one ton of dried mushrooms. The sale was concluded under the terms "C & F" (without insurance). The German seller, *Müggenburg*, had the goods shipped from the port of Hong Kong after the Argentine buyer, *Bedial*, obtained a letter of credit payable within 180 days from the date of shipment. Before shipping the goods, *Müggenburg* obtained three certificates from the Chinese authorities attesting as to the quality of the dried mushrooms and their fitness for human consumption. However, upon their arrival in Buenos Aires, a chemical analysis undertaken by customs authorities on one of the packages of the cargo indicated that the mushrooms were not fit for human consumption pursuant to the sanitary requirements imposed by Argentine law. *Bedial*'s reaction was to refuse payment under the letter of credit and send the mushrooms back to Hong Kong with a notice that the contract had been avoided.

Müggenburg commenced summary proceedings (*juicio ejecutivo*) before the Argentine courts and was able to collect the full amount due under the letter of credit. Immediately thereafter, *Bedial* sought to recover the money which it was compelled to pay to *Müggenburg* in the summary proceedings, also seeking damages for the alleged nonconformity of the goods. In essence, the court was asked to determine who should bear the risk of loss under this contract of sale. Both the trial and the appellate court found for the German seller, although the rationale followed by each court on the risk of loss was somewhat different. According to the trial court, the certificates obtained by the German seller attested that the goods were in satisfactory condition at the time of shipment, so that the causes for any eventual nonconformity must have originated during the transportation of the goods from Hamburg to Buenos Aires. Since the Argentine buyer had assumed the risk of loss in transit pursuant to the "C & F" term, it should follow that the buyer must bear the risk of loss. Moreover, the trial court noted that the buyer failed to object to the soundness of the inspection certificates, as well as to establish that the goods were in damaged condition before they passed the ship's rail. The court of first instance also placed the blame on the Argentine buyer for returning the whole shipment back to the port of dispatch despite the objections made by the German seller, and for failing to request a second inspection allowed under Argentine customs regulations. By shipping the goods back to the seller, the latter had missed the opportunity to verify whether the allegation of nonconformity was correct.

The rationale of the trial court for allocating the risk of loss was based on the C & F clause and Article 472 of the Argentine Commercial Code. As interpreted by courts and scholarly doctrine in Argentina, the risk of loss under Article 472 of the Commercial Code is shifted to the buyer upon delivery (*tradición*) of the goods to the carrier, the buyer being bound to pay the price unless he establishes that the goods were defective before the shipment. However, since the seller alleged the application of the CISG to the contract, the trial court referred to Article 31(a) of the Convention to indicate that whenever the sale involves the carriage of the goods, the issue of nonconformity must be settled at the time the goods are handed over by the seller to the first carrier. Since the risk of loss passed to the buyer at that point in time, under the CISG *Bedial* was bound to pay the price unless he could establish that the alleged loss or damage took place before the goods were handed over to the first carrier. The appellate court affirmed on the ground that *Bedial* had failed to establish, as required by Article 66 of the CISG, that the alleged damage to the goods was "due to an act or omission" of the seller.

* * *

Assuming, for the sake of argument, that the CISG were to apply to this case, the analysis of the transfer of risk made by the trial court appears to be correct. However, in a contract where the parties had expressly adopted trade terms such as "C & F," the rules of the CISG on transfer of risk add little, if anything, to a determination as to who should bear the risk of loss. According to a general understanding of those terms, the buyer bears "all risk of loss or damage to the goods from the time the goods have passed the ship's rail at the port of shipment." Under the "C & F" clause (without insurance) it was the buyer's obligation to procure marine insurance against the risk of loss of or damage to the goods during the transportation from Hong-Kong to Buenos Aires. The judgment of the trial court reveals that *Bedial* had contracted insurance, noting in passing that the fact of contracting such insurance provided an indication "that the insured (*Bedial*) was aware that the risk of loss during the carriage was his." This assumption is incorrect, because contracting insurance does not control who bears the risk of loss. Indeed, if the contract had been concluded "CIF" rather than "C & F," the fact that *Müggenburg* had contracted insurance would not have displaced the transfer of the risk to *Bedial* after the goods were shipped.

* * *

The decision in *Bedial* proceeded on the assumption that the goods did not conform to the contract specifications, focusing instead on who should bear the loss. It should be recalled that the German seller had entrusted the determination of the quantity and quality of the goods to an agency of the Chinese government, which issued an inspection certificate that became part of the documentary sales transaction. Unless agreed otherwise, the pre-shipment inspection arranged by the seller is not binding on the buyer, who retains the right—actually, the obligation—to examine the goods, or to "cause them to be examined," at the point of destination. Regardless of the condition of the goods at the time of loading, what is important for the buyer is to receive them in sound condition at destination, hence the buyer's insistence on inspection upon arrival. However, after the analysis of a sample of the goods undertaken by the customs authorities in Buenos Aires showed lack of conformity, the Argentine buyer proceeded to destroy that part of the cargo, rejected the goods by sending the whole shipment back to the seller, and communicated to the seller its intention to avoid the contract. A better way for the buyer to preserve his rights under the contract would have been to give prompt notice of the nonconformity revealed in the sample inspection, while enabling the seller or its representative to attend a "contradictory test" of the goods. Rather than destroying the sampled goods and incurring the uneconomical cost of shipping the remaining part of the cargo back to the seller, what the buyer should have done is to provide the seller with reasonable advance notice in order to allow him to be present at the "contradictory" inspection of the goods.

* * *

INTRODUCTORY NOTE: Before attempting to analyze this Problem, please read both the I.C.C. Incoterms "CIF" term which follows it and UCC § 2–320 in the Documents Supplement.

PROBLEM 3–2

Charlie, a Maine manufacturer of rollers for pulp mills, agrees to manufacture and sell to Dietrich, a German paper manufacturer, four replacement rollers for use in processing pulp into paper. Charlie is to manufacture the machine in Maine and Dietrich will use the machine in its paper mill in Germany. The written agreement does not include a choice-of-law clause and it does not exclude application of the U.N. Sales Convention. The delivery term is "CIF (Incoterms 1990) Hamburg" with shipment to be made from Portland, Maine by July 1.

(a) What must Charlie do to perform its obligation to deliver the rollers? Must Charlie obtain insurance for the rollers while they are in transit? Must Charlie deliver documents to the buyer? Must Charlie notify the buyer that it has arranged to deliver the rollers?

(b) Where must Charlie deliver the rollers? CISG art. 33. If so, when must it do so? CISG art. 34.

(c) Does the CIF term impose obligations on Charlie that the Convention does not impose?

(d) When does the risk of loss shift to Dietrich?

(e) May Dietrich inspect the rollers before accepting them?

* * *

PROBLEM 3–3

Assume, in the preceding problem, that the agreement between Charlie and Dietrich merely provides "CIF Hamburg" (i.e., it fails to refer expressly to Incoterms)? Are the Incoterms applicable in any event as "international usage"? CISG art. 9(1), (2). If the Incoterms are not applicable, are there "gaps" in the Convention to be filled? CISG art. 7(2). Are there general principles that underlie the Convention to fill the gap? If there are no relevant general principles, what national law is applicable? CISG art. 7(2). Would the Incoterms be applicable if U.S. law governs? When answering this last question, note that the Uniform Commercial Code both gives effect to "usages of trade" (U.C.C. § 1–205) and provides a statutory definition of "C.I.F." (U.C.C. § 2–320, set out in the Documents Supplement).

INCOTERMS

50–55 (1990 ed.)(International Chamber of Commerce Pub. No. 460)

COST, INSURANCE AND FREIGHT * * * (named port of destination)

"Cost, Insurance and Freight" means that the seller has the same obligations as under CFR but with the addition that he has to procure marine insurance against the buyer's risk of loss of or damage to the goods during the carriage. The seller contracts for insurance and pays the insurance premium.

The buyer should note that under the CIF term the seller is only required to obtain insurance on minimum coverage.

The CIF term requires the seller to clear the goods for export.

This term can only be used for sea and inland waterway transport.

When the ship's rail serves no practical purposes such as in the case of roll-on/roll-off or container traffic, the CIP term is more appropriate to use.

A. THE SELLER MUST:

1. Provide the goods and the commercial invoice, or its equivalent electronic message, in conformity with the contract of sale and any other evidence of conformity which may be required by the contract.

2. Obtain at his own risk and expense any export licence or other Official authorisation and carry out all customs formalities necessary for the exportation of the goods.

3.a) Contract on usual terms at his own expense for the carriage of the goods to the named port of destination by the usual route in a seagoing vessel (or inland waterway vessel as appropriate) of the type normally used for the transport of goods of the contract description.

b) Obtain at his own expense cargo insurance as agreed in the contract, that the buyer, or any other person having an insurable interest in the goods, shall be entitled to claim directly from the insurer and provide the buyer with the insurance policy or other evidence of insurance cover. The insurance shall be contracted with underwriters or an insurance company of good repute and, failing express agreement to the contrary, be in accordance with minimum cover of the Institute

Cargo Clauses (Institute of London Underwriters) or any similar set of clauses. The duration of insurance cover shall be in accordance with B.5. and B.4. When required by the buyer, the seller shall provide at the buyer's expense war, strikes, riots and civil commotion risk insurances if procurable. The minimum insurance shall cover the price provided in the contract plus ten per cent (i.e. 110%) and shall be provided in the currency of the contract.

4. Deliver the goods on board the vessel at the port of shipment on the date or within the period stipulated.

5. Subject to the provisions of B.5., bear all risks of loss of or damage to the goods until such time as they have passed the ship's rail at the port of shipment.

6. Subject to the provisions of B.6.

- pay all costs relating to the goods until they have been delivered in accordance with A.4. as well as the freight and all other costs resulting from A.3., including costs of loading the goods on board and any charges for unloading at the port of discharge which may be levied by regular shipping lines when contracting for carriage;

- pay the costs of customs formalities necessary for exportation as well as all duties, taxes and other official charges payable upon exportation.

7. Give the buyer sufficient notice that the goods have been delivered on board the vessel as well as any other notice required in order to allow the buyer to take measures which are normally necessary to enable him to take the goods.

8. Unless otherwise agreed, at his own expense provide the buyer without delay with the usual transport document for the agreed port of destination.

This document (for example, a negotiable bill of lading, a non-negotiable sea waybill or an inland waterway document) must cover the contract goods, be dated within the period agreed for shipment, enable the buyer to claim the goods from the carrier at destination and, unless otherwise agreed, enable the buyer to sell the goods in transit by the transfer of the document to a subsequent buyer (the negotiable bill of lading) or by notification to the carrier.

When such a transport document is issued in several originals, a full set of originals must be presented to the buyer. If the transport document contains a reference to a charter party, the seller must also provide a copy of this latter document. Where the seller and the buyer have agreed to communicate electronically, the document referred to in the preceding paragraphs may be replaced by an equivalent electronic date interchange (EDI) message.

9. Pay the costs of those checking operations (such as checking quality, measuring, weighing, counting) which are necessary for the purpose of delivering the goods in accordance with A.4.

Provide at his own expense packaging (unless it is usual for the particular trade to ship the goods of the contract description unpacked) which is required for the transport of the goods arranged by him. Packaging is to be marked appropriately.

10. Render the buyer at the latter's request, risk and expense, every assistance in obtaining any documents or equivalent electronic messages (other than those mentioned in A.8.) issued or transmitted in the country of shipment and/or of origin which the buyer may require for the importation of the goods and, where necessary, for their transit through another country.

B.   THE BUYER MUST:

1. Pay the price as provided in the contract of sale.

2. Obtain at his own risk and expense any import licence or other official authorisation and carry out all customs formalities for the importation of the goods and, where necessary, for their transit through another country.

3. Contract of carriage. No obligation.

4. Accept delivery of the goods when they have been delivered in accordance with A.4. and receive them from the carrier at the named port of destination.

5. Bear all risks of loss of or damage to the goods from the time they have passed the ship's rail at the port of shipment. Should he fail to give notice in accordance with B.7., bear all risks of loss of or damage to the goods from the agreed date or the expiry date of the period fixed for shipment provided, however, that the goods have been duly appropriated to the contract, that is to say, clearly set aside or otherwise identified as the contract goods.

6. Subject to the provisions of A.3., pay all costs relating to the goods from the time they have been delivered in accordance with A.4. and, unless such costs and charges have been levied by regular shipping lines when contracting for carriage, pay all costs and charges relating to the goods whilst in transit until their arrival at the port of destination, as well as unloading costs including lighterage and wharfage charges.

Should he fail to give notice in accordance with B.7., pay the additional costs thereby incurred for the goods from the agreed date or the expiry date of the period fixed for shipment provided, however, that the goods have been duly appropriated to the contract, that is to say, clearly set aside or otherwise identified as the contract goods.

Pay all duties, taxes and other official charges as well as the costs of carrying out customs formalities payable upon importation of the goods and, where necessary, for their transit through another country.

7. Whenever he is entitled to determine the time for shipping the goods and/or the port of destination, give the seller sufficient notice thereof.

8. Accept the transport document in accordance with A.8. if it is in conformity with the contract.

9. Pay, unless otherwise agreed, the costs of pre-shipment inspection except when mandated by the authorities of the country of exportation.

10. Pay all costs and charges incurred in obtaining the documents or equivalent electronic messages mentioned in A.10. and reimburse those incurred by the seller in rendering his assistance in accordance therewith.

Provide the seller, upon request, with the necessary information for procuring insurance.

* * *

SPANOGLE, INCOTERMS AND UCC ARTICLE 2—CONFLICTS AND CONFUSIONS
31 Int'l Lawyer 111, 119–21 (1997).*

Under the Incoterms Cost, Insurance, and Freight (CIF) commercial term, the seller is obligated to arrange for both transportation and insurance to a named destination port and then to deliver the goods on board the ship arranged for by the seller. Thus, the term is appropriate only for waterborne transportation. The seller must arrange the transportation and pay the freight costs to the *destination port*, but has completed its delivery obligations when the goods have "passed the ship's rail" at the *port of shipment*. The seller must arrange and pay for insurance during transportation to the *port of destination*, but the risk of loss transfers to the buyer at the time the goods pass the ship's rail at the *port of shipment*. The seller must notify the buyer "that the goods have been delivered on board" the ship to enable the buyer to receive the goods. The seller must provide a commercial invoice, or its equivalent electronic message, any necessary export license, and "the usual transport document" for the destination port.

The Incoterms definition has no provisions on either payment or post-shipment inspection terms under the contract. However, Incoterms does require that the transportation document "must … enable the buyer to sell the goods in transit by the transfer of the document to a subsequent buyer … or by notification to the carrier," unless otherwise agreed. The traditional method of enabling the buyer to do this, in either the "payment against documents" transaction or the letter of credit transaction, is for the seller to obtain a negotiable bill of lading from the carrier and to tender that negotiable document to the buyer through a series of banks. The banks allow the buyer to obtain possession of the document (and control of the goods) only after the buyer pays for the goods. Thus, the buyer "pays against documents," while the goods are at sea, and pays for them before any post-shipment inspection of the goods is possible. This transaction should still be regarded as the norm under Incoterms CIF, and the definition of the term in the 1990 version does refer to the use of a negotiable bill of lading.

The 1980 version of Incoterms was more precise on these payment obligations, requiring the buyer to "accept the documents when tendered by the seller ... and pay the price as provided in the contract." The implication of this provision was that the buyer had no right to inspect the goods before this payment against documents. The UCC also has a definition of "C.I.F." that requires the buyer to "make payment against tender of the required documents." The UCC "C.I.F." term is otherwise similar to Incoterms CIF in that it requires the seller to deliver to the carrier at a port of shipment and bear the risk of loss only to that port, but to pay freight costs and insurance to the port of destination.

Some ambiguity is introduced in the CIF definition, because it also refers to the use of nonnegotiable documents as well. However, the ICC's Introduction to the 1990 Incoterms recognizes that the use of nonnegotiable documents is inappropriate in a "payment against documents" situation and thus would not "enable the buyer to sell the goods in transit by surrendering the paper document" to the sub-buyer. The introduction then explains that sometimes the parties "may specifically agree to relieve the seller from" providing a negotiable document when they "know that the buyer does not contemplate selling the goods in transit." The 1990 Incoterms does not have any provisions on when title to the goods passes from the seller to the buyer. Thus, when title issues arise the courts must turn to the UCC for applicable provisions.

FRÉCON, PRACTICAL CONSIDERATIONS IN DRAFTING F.O.B. TERMS IN INTERNATIONAL SALES
3 Int'l Tax & Bus.Law. 346, 365–66 (1986).*

Securing insurance for international sales transactions can be a costly endeavor in itself. International traders minimize costs by securing insurance only for those events they consider most likely to occur. Standard insurance policies often exclude from coverage perils such as strikes, riots, and wars. Although coverage for these risks can be obtained, such insurance policies require special limited endorsements that are usually expensive. Even the most common "all risks" insurance coverage, despite its name, covers only theft, pilferage, nondelivery, damage or loss during handling, stowage, weather and water damage. Risks of war, strikes and riots are not covered, nor are risks inherent in the goods, losses caused by delays, or loss due to improper packing.

* * * Marine insurance policies, for example, contain terms not easily comprehensible to the layman or unsophisticated shipper. International shippers should familiarize themselves with words such as "barratry", which refers to willful and wrongful acts of the master or crew of the ship, and the "inchmare clause", which refers to damage caused to the cargo by faulty machinery or equipment of the boat.

Packaging, labelling, and other incidental costs can often prove burdensome. Air carriers, for example, impose special packaging requirements. Shipments by sea have packaging requirements and shipping rates which vary depending upon whether the goods are shipped "below deck" or "above deck". If a seller undertakes to ship goods to the country of final destination, she should be aware that certain countries assess customs duties on the gross weight of the goods. If packaging weight can be maintained at the lowest weight-to-safety ratio possible, the buyer can economize on customs duties. The savings in cost thus may result in lower selling prices in that country, thereby giving the buyer a competitive edge in the market.

Translation costs pose another potential burden. France, for example, requires the use of the French language in all documents pertaining to import transactions into that country. French officials have not hesitated in the past to detain goods for weeks, subject to the receipt of French translations, when shippers have failed to comply with French labeling requirements.

Proper marking of the goods for export also requires the use of international symbols and cautionary marks which may not necessarily meet the labeling requirements of a receiving country. Failure to comply with such requirements may result in costly delays or damages to the goods, which may not be, under the circumstances, recoverable from the insurance company.

Certain goods are subject to local health inspections, special licensing requirements, and export controls. Determining what these requirements are and how they are satisfied involves hidden costs in time and money. The U.S. Department of Commerce enforces regulations under the Export Administration Act of 1979, as amended, which lists those goods subject to special licensing and authorization requirements. Compliance with Commerce Department regulations, however, does not exempt a U.S. shipper from filing a U.S. Shipper's Export Declaration, nor from satisfying other U.S. statutory requirements, such as the Foreign Corrupt Practices Act and the U.S. Antiboycott Regulations. Filing the requisite registration and application forms is a complex process frequently requiring costly legal advice. Failure to comply with these statutes triggers civil penalties and sometimes criminal charges.

* * *

INTRODUCTORY NOTE: Before attempting to analyze this Problem, please read both the following excerpts and UCC §§ 2–319 and 2–504 in the Documents Supplement.

PROBLEM 3–4

Your client, Sam Silver, of Houston, Texas, wishes to consult with you about a contract for the sale of 10,000 electronic calculators that he has just negotiated with a buyer in Argentina, Señor Bolivar. Sam has never sold goods outside the United States before, but he, like many small businessmen, usually drafts his own contracts. Thus, when he comes to consult you, he has a piece of paper signed by both Señor Bolivar and himself. The paper is labeled "Contract" and contains all the necessary items for a contract, such as price, description, quantity, and quality of the electronic calculators to be delivered. The contract does not state whether the sale is for cash or on credit, but it does have a "price/delivery" clause that catches your eye: "U.S. $650,000.00—F.O.B. Houston." Sam says he wants you to advise him on "just a couple of things" about how to set up the transportation of the goods. In particular, he needs your advice on the following matters:

(a) Is Sam supposed to arrange for the transportation of the calculators to Argentina, or is that Señor Bolivar's responsibility?

(b) Is Sam to arrange for insurance on the calculators during transit, or is that Señor Bolivar's responsibility?

(c) If Señor Bolivar procures insurance, does Sam need any insurance coverage during transit?

(d) Sam also wants to know whether to get negotiable or non-negotiable bills of lading.

SPANOGLE, INCOTERMS AND UCC ARTICLE 2—CONFLICTS AND CONFUSIONS
31 Int'l Lawyer 111, 118–119 (1997).*

Under the Incoterms Free on Board (FOB) commercial term, the seller is obligated to deliver the goods on board a ship arranged for and named by the buyer at a named port of shipment. Thus, this term is also appropriate only for waterborne transportation, and the seller must bear the costs and risks of both inland transportation to the named port of shipment and loading the goods on the ship (until "they have passed the ship's rail"). The seller has no obligation to arrange transportation or insurance, but does have a duty to notify the buyer "that the goods *have been delivered* on board" the ship. The risk of loss will transfer to the buyer also at the time the goods have "passed the ship's rail." The seller must provide a commercial invoice, or its equivalent electronic message, any necessary export license, and usually a transport document that will allow the buyer to take delivery—or an equivalent electronic data interchange message.

The Incoterms definition has no provisions on either payment or post-shipment inspection terms under the contract. The UCC does define

---

*Copyright © 1997 and reproduced by permission from the author and the International Lawyer.

"F.O.B.," but it is not a term requiring waterborne transportation. Thus, as has been discussed above, the UCC "F.O.B." is more closely linked to the Incoterms FCA term. But the UCC also has a term "F.O.B. vessel," which does relate only to waterborne transportation and therefore is most closely linked to the Incoterms FOB term. Under the UCC, the term "F.O.B. vessel" requires the buyer to pay against a tender of documents, such as a negotiable bill of lading, before the goods arrive at their destination and before the buyer has any post-shipment opportunity to inspect the goods. Otherwise, the UCC "F.O.B. vessel" term is similar to the Incoterms "FOB" term, including obligating the seller only to deliver the goods to a named ship's rail and not obligating the seller to arrange transportation to a final destination.

However, in the 1980 version of Incoterms, the definition of FOB provided that payment against documents was not required for an FOB contract, while the 1980 Incoterms did not contain such payment provisions in its definitions of other commercial terms. Thus, it is more likely that the current version of Incoterms FOB is not intended to require payment against documents or to restrict inspection before payment, unless such a term is expressly added or there is a known custom in a particular trade. In addition, it is more likely that negotiable bills of lading are not intended to be used with Incoterms FOB shipments, unless the parties specify "payment against documents" or use of a letter of credit in the sale contract.

FRÉCON, PRACTICAL CONSIDERATIONS IN DRAFTING F.O.B. TERMS IN INTERNATIONAL SALES
3 Int'l Tax & Bus.Law. 346, 349–55 (1986).*

1. *The UCC*

The UCC provides three definitions from which the parties may choose to qualify the legal effect of the F.O.B. term. The parties' rights and obligations will differ depending on whether the sale is designated "F.O.B. Place of Shipment", "F.O.B. Place of Destination", or "F.O.B. Vessel, Car, or Other Vehicle".

Under an "F.O.B. Place of Shipment" term, the seller's liability for ensuring safe shipment and paying shipping fees terminates upon delivery of the goods to a named carrier. There is no further obligation of the seller to load the goods on board the carrier. Under an "F.O.B Place of Destination" term, the seller must bear these risks and expenses until the goods reach their stipulated destination. Where an "F.O.B. Vessel, Car, or Other Vehicle" term is used, in conjunction with an "F.O.B. Place of Shipment" or "F.O.B. Place of Destination" term, the seller is also responsible for the risks and costs of loading the goods on board the carrier. Whichever of the three alternative terms is chosen, the buyer must reasonably provide any instruction necessary for making delivery, including the location of the loading berth, the name of the vessel, and its sailing date. Failure to do so may be treated by the seller as a failure to cooperate.

* * *

3. *The Incoterms*

Under the "F.O.B. named port of shipment" term of the Incoterms, the risk of loss of the goods shifts to the seller upon passing of the rail of the vessel designated by the buyer. In this respect, the Incoterms definition is equivalent to the "F.O.B. Vessel, Car or Other Vehicle" term of the UCC and the "F.O.B. Vessel Named Point of Shipment" term of the RAFTD. Under the Incoterms definition, however, the seller must also obtain at his own risk any export license or other governmental authorization necessary for export of the goods. The seller must also pay any taxes or fees that may be levied by the country of exportation. These incidental costs are not automatically charged to the seller if the parties have adopted a UCC or RAFTD definition.

Technically, the Incoterms do not provide an "F.O.B. Place of Destination" or "named inland point in country of importation" term. If the parties wish to have the seller pay the costs and freight of transporting the goods to the place of destination, they should refer either to the RAFTD "F.O.B. (named inland carrier at named point of departure) Freight Prepaid To (named point of exportation)" term or to an Incoterm designation such as "Cost and Freight ('C & F') Named Port of Destination" which includes only cost and freight, or "Cost, Insurance and Freight (C.I.F.)". Under a "C & F" term, the seller is not obligated to procure marine insurance against risk of loss of, or damage to, the goods during carriage, because such risks are transferred to the buyer when the goods pass from the ship's rail at the port of shipment. If the seller is to bear all shipping obligations (marine insurance included) and risks of loss or damage, the term "C.I.F. Named Port of Destination" must be used.

In 1980 the Incoterms incorporated a "free carrier (named point)" term which permits the parties to designate the point at which the shipping obligations and risks of loss of, or damage to, the goods are transferred from the seller to the buyer. Under this term, "carrier" means any person with whom a contract of carriage by road, rail, air, sea, or any combination of modes has been made. The "free carrier" term offers the flexibility of allowing the parties to designate any point at which the seller can deliver the goods into the custody of the carrier.

The Incoterms' equivalent to an F.O.B. vessel shipment term under the UCC is the "Ex Ship Named Port of Destination" term. Under this term, the seller must load the goods on board the ship and bear the full cost and risks associated therewith until the arrival of the goods at their destination named in the sales contract.

Only the Incoterms provide specific terms for different modes of transport. For example, when goods are transported by rail, the term "F.O.R./F.O.T. (named departure point)" can be used. F.O.R. stands for "Free on Rail" while F.O.T. stands for "Free on Truck", which in fact refers to railway wagons and not to trucks. This term is most commonly used in Europe when goods are carried by rail. If the goods are transported by air carrier, the Incoterms provide an "F.O.B. Airport (named airport of departure)" term. Under this term, the seller's risks and obligations terminate upon delivery of the goods to the air carrier of the buyer's choice. The seller is not, however, responsible for loading the goods onto the aircraft. In this respect, this term is distinguishable from the Incoterms' "Named Port of Shipment" term, the UCC's "F.O.B. Vessel, Car, or Other Vehicles" term, and the RAFTD's "F.O.B. Vessel (named port of shipment)" term, all of which obligate the seller to load the goods on board the designated carrier.

C. Considerations in Application of the Terms

* * * [M]ost of the shipping definitions described above contain certain ambiguities. To avoid any potential misunderstandings, international traders should not hesitate to qualify and clarify their intent through additional contract provisions.

1. Use of the F.O.B. Term

The parties to an international contract should first avoid using an F.O.B. term without designating precisely the point at which the obligations and liabilities will pass from the seller to the buyer (e.g., port of importation, inland carrier, or place of seller's business). An F.O.B. destination term, for example, should designate the exact city of destination (e.g., Venice, Italy or Venice, California).

The parties should also clarify the scope of their obligations. For example, the use of an F.O.B. country or place of destination term which assigns the seller responsibility for securing transport of the goods in question to their final destination does not in itself imply that the seller is legally or contractually required to obtain marine and cargo war risk insurance. If the buyer expects the seller to insure the shipment against these risks, he should explicitly obligate the seller to do so on his behalf in a contractual provision (either in the contract for sale of goods or in the shipping documents) or through the use of another shipping term, such as the C.I.F. term of the Incoterms.

Some of the pre-established sets of definitions are also ambiguous as to which party is responsible for certain incidental expenses. For example, if a New York manufacturer agrees to an international sale under an "F.O.B." named place of shipment term under the UCC, it is unclear whether the manufacturer or the foreign buyer must bear the expenses of obtaining a certificate of origin and of paying the consular costs. Under the UCC, for example, the shipping obligations of the seller terminate upon delivery of the goods to the carrier in New York. Because the relevant documents are required upon delivery of the goods to the carrier in New York, however, the seller may be forced to secure them. The seller can argue that, since these documents are required by the buyer's country for his receipt of the goods, the buyer should bear the issuance costs. If the parties had established clearly their mutual contractual obligations, or if they had selected, for example, the "C.I.F" term of the Incoterms, the buyer would be justified in demanding that the seller bear not only the legal obligations, but also the expense of obtaining the documents, since all costs incurred are encompassed within the C.I.F. term. Regardless of which set of definitions is considered, the parties should negotiate in advance who will bear any incidental expenses and either qualify the F.O.B. term in the contract according to their agreement or choose another term.

* * *

PROBLEM 3–5

Assume that in the preceding problem Sam agrees to sell only 100 calculators to Señor Bolivar. Sam and Señor Bolivar agree orally that Sam will send the goods by airplane to Buenos Aires. When reducing the sales agreement to writing Sam drafts a contract term that provides "F.O.B. Houston." Is "F.O.B." an appropriate trade term when the calculators are to be sent by air? If not, is there a more appropriate term? If there is a more appropriate term, how do Sam's delivery obligations differ from his obligations when F.O.B. is appropriate?

SPANOGLE, INCOTERMS AND UCC ARTICLE 2—CONFLICTS AND CONFUSIONS
31 Int'l Lawyer 111, 116–17 (1997).*

Under the Incoterms Free Carrier (FCA) commercial term, the seller is obligated to deliver the goods into the custody of a carrier, usually the first carrier in a multimodal transportation scheme. The Incoterms definition of "carrier" includes freight forwarders. The seller has no obligation to pay for transportation costs or insurance. Usually the carrier will be named by, and arranged by, the buyer. However, the seller "may" arrange transportation at the buyer's expense if requested by the buyer, or if it is "commercial practice" for the seller to do so. But, even under such circumstances, the seller may refuse to make such arrangements as long as it so notifies the buyer. Even if the seller does arrange transportation, it has no obligation to arrange for insurance coverage during transportation and need only notify the buyer "that the goods *have been delivered* into the custody of the carrier." The risk of loss transfers to the buyer upon delivery to the carrier, but the buyer may not receive notice until after that time. The seller must provide a commercial invoice or its equivalent electronic message, any necessary export license, and usually a transport document that will allow the buyer to take delivery—or an equivalent electronic data interchange message. The Incoterms definition has no provisions on either payment or post-shipment inspection terms under the contract.

This FCA term is the Incoterms commercial term that is most comparable to the UCC's "F.O.B. place of shipment" term. However, there are two levels of confusion. One is that Incoterms has an "F.O.B." term that is different, and the UCC "F.O.B." term is more likely to be compared with the Incoterms "FOB" term. The other is that the obligations under FCA and the UCC "F.O.B. place of shipment" term are, in fact, different. The norm under the UCC's "F.O.B." is for the seller to arrange transportation, while the seller need do so under FCA only in special circumstances. Further, if the seller does ship, the seller usually must also arrange insurance coverage, unless instructed otherwise by the buyer. Under Incoterms FCA, the seller does not seem ever to have any obligation to arrange for insurance coverage. Traditionally, under both the 1980 version of Incoterms FAS and the UCC "F.O.B. place of shipment" term, there is no implied special payment or inspection terms, no implied requirement of payment against documents or payment before inspection. This would also seem to be a preferable interpretation of the current Incoterms FCA term.

* * *

2. *CONFORMITY OF THE GOODS*

Whether a buyer agrees to purchase grain, heavy equipment, or electronic toys the buyer will have expectations about the quality of the goods that the seller will deliver. At the very least, the buyer will expect to receive goods of the quality expressly promised by the seller. But even if the seller is silent the buyer may have reasonable expectations about the quality of the goods to be supplied. Both domestic law and the Sales Convention enforce the buyer's reasonable expectations.

Thus, the Uniform Commercial Code requires the seller to supply goods meeting the quality "expressly warranted" by the seller. The seller must also supply goods fit for the ordinary purposes for which such goods are used unless the seller and buyer have agreed otherwise. The goods must, in other words, be "merchantable." Similarly, when the buyer reasonably expects the seller to deliver goods fit for the buyer's particular purpose, the U.C.C. requires the seller to deliver goods fit for that purpose. The Uniform Commercial Code calls these statutory presumptions "implied warranties" and talks about "disclaimers" of these warranties when the parties agree to change the presumption. The Sales Convention uses different terminology but yields the same results. CISG art. 35.

Special mention should also be made about the seller's obligation with respect to "title" to the goods. The obligation to transfer good title goes to the quality not of the goods but of the buyer's rights to the goods. Nevertheless, one could approach this problem in much the same way as one approaches the warranties of quality described above. Even if the seller is silent, for example, the buyer will reasonably expect to receive good title to the goods sold. The risk that the seller will not transfer good title, in other words, should be placed on the seller as the party better able to identify and prevent the risk. Both the Uniform Commercial Code (U.C.C. § 2–312) and the Sales Convention (arts. 41–42) protect the buyer's expectations.

* * *

J. HONNOLD, UNIFORM LAW FOR INTERNATIONAL SALES UNDER THE 1980 UNITED NATIONS CONVENTION
252–55 (3d ed. 1999).*

A. *The Role of Rules about Quality*

Most sales controversies grow out of disputes over whether the goods conform to the contract. In many cases these disputes present only a question of fact: What was the condition of the goods? Disputes over quality, however, cannot always be resolved simply by measuring the goods against the specific terms of the contract. When an order is routine and calls for speedy shipment the parties may not even attempt to articulate the expectations that are associated with transactions in such goods. Even a carefully prepared contract will often fail to express the most basic expectations—that a machine will operate or that a steel girder will be structurally sound—because the parties assume that these points are so obvious that they "go without saying." Consequently, courts and codifiers have had to try to describe, in general terms, those understandings that would have been written into the contract if the parties had drafted a contract provision to deal specifically with the question that led to dispute.

Domestic legal systems address this problem in various ways. In United States law, the seller's obligations as to quality are referred to as "warranties", and are dealt with under three headings: (1) "express warranties", (UCC 2–313); (2) an implied warranty of merchantable quality (UCC 2–314); and (3) an implied warranty of fitness for a particular purpose (UCC 2–315). * * * Other legal systems use different concepts. Codes based on the French pattern tend to deal with questions of quality with a light touch that is directed to the distinction between latent defects *(vices cachés)* and apparent defects *(vices apparents)*. This brief approach has been supplemented by other doctrines such as *erreur;* students of the civil law report that the result is complex and unclear.

* * *

(1) *Quality Required by the Contract: Paragraph (1)*

Paragraph (1) emphasizes a point that could go without saying: the parties must comply with their contract. The Sales Article of the (U.S.A.) Uniform Commercial Code also emphasizes the importance of the contract. Section 2–313 (Express Warranties by Affirmation, Promise, Description, Sample) carried forward a provision, drafted by Professor Williston for the Uniform Sales Act (1906), that was designed to nullify decisions that had hesitated to give contractual effect to the seller's "representations" and "affirmations" (as contrasted with "promises") and also to overturn decisions that had insisted on evidence that the seller "intended to be bound" by statements concerning the quality of the goods.

The technical distinctions in these early cases have been softened by more recent case law. In any event, these distinctions are not useful in deciding what quality is "required by the contract" under Article 35(1). As we shall see, Article 35(2)(a) gives effect to the expectations latent in any "description" of the goods. And the basic rules on contract interpretation in Article 8 do not draw any technical distinction between different types of "statements" and emphasize the "understanding" that statements produce in a reasonable person.

(2) *Presumed Implications from the Contract: Paragraph (2)*

(a) *Description and Ordinary Purposes.* Paragraph (2)(a) embodies the clearest ideas that have been developed for defining the seller's responsibility for quality. These ideas are both subtle and fundamental. Commercial law does not impose standards of quality: it accommodates sales of cars for scrap as well as sales of new cars for resale to consumers. Often, detailed specifications in the contract will resolve any question as to quality but in routine transactions the parties would think it needless and a bit absurd to say things that "go without saying." In these situations interpretation of the contract, calls for finding the full meaning of the contract description in the light of the expectations that have developed for such sales.

The Convention builds on these assumptions and goes a step further. Things are bought for use—raw materials are bought for processing; machinery is bought for use in production; commodities are bought for resale and use. Legislators could not develop detailed, technical specifications for such goods; hence, paragraph (2)(a) asks whether the goods "are fit for the *purposes* for which goods of the same description would *ordinarily* be used." (Fitness for a *particular* purpose is dealt with in paragraph (2)(b).)

The basic standard in paragraph (2)(a) is similar to the warranty of "merchantable quality" developed in early English case law incorporated in the Sale of Goods Act (1893). However, the meaning of "merchantable quality" was left to case law. The basic ideas developed by the cases were used by the (U.S.A.) Uniform Commercial Code in defining "merchantable quality." Under Section 2–314(2), "goods to be merchantable" must "(a) pass without objection in the trade under the contract *description*" and "(c) are fit for the *ordinary* purposes for which *such* goods are used."

* * *

PROBLEM 3–6

The UVW GmbH, a German distributor of trucks, contracted to sell a new Volkswagon delivery truck to the Xerox Corp., an American company, through an exchange of e-mail messages. The messages did not mention German law, the UCC or CISG. The messages identified the make and model of the truck, but said nothing else about the quality of the goods or any warranties.

(a) What are UVW's obligations as to the quality of the truck? CISG art. 35. Is it sufficient if it looks, feels and smells like a new truck and has the right labels on it, or must the truck also propel itself from one place to another and carry a load?

(b) If the parties have not stated any terms labeled "quality obligations" in their contract, where do these obligations come from? Or, have the parties actually stated a quality obligation in their brief e-mails? Under the UCC (see below), the seller would have created a series of "warranties." Are the CISG art. 35 obligations of quality "warranties"? Why, or why not?

(c) If, UVW delivers a Mercedes delivery truck rather than the VW truck, but the Mercedes truck has a value equal to or greater than the value of the specified VW truck, has UVW fulfilled its obligations under the contract and CISG? CISG art. 35(1).

(d) If UVW delivers a VW truck, but U.S. Customs will not allow the truck off the dock because it does not have the emission controls required by U.S. law, has UVW fulfilled its obligations under the contract and CISG? CISG art. 35(2).

Legislation Note on UCC Provisions

As the excerpt from Honnold indicates, the UCC creates a series of "warranties" from seller to buyer. Some warranties are "express" under UCC § 2–313, others are "implied" under UCC §§ 2–314 and 2–315. The primary reason for the differentiation under UCC concepts is that "implied" warranties can be "disclaimed" under UCC § 2–316(2), while "express" warranties cannot.

* * *

J. HONNOLD, UNIFORM LAW FOR INTERNATIONAL SALES UNDER THE 1980 UNITED NATIONS CONVENTION
256–58 (3d ed. 1999).*

Some writers have felt that it is necessary to give a general answer to the following question: Does subparagraph (2)(a) refer to the understanding of the contract description of the goods that prevails at the seller's place of business or at the place where the buyer intends to use the goods? Writers have disagreed over the choice between these two places.

It should not be necessary to answer this question if one accepts the view, suggested above, that the role of Article 35(2) is to aid in *construing the agreement of the parties*. The question is this: What was the parties' understanding of the contract provision describing the goods? More precisely (in the language of Article 35(2)) what was their understanding of the "purposes for which goods of the same *description* would ordinarily be used"? Since the problem concerns fitness for the "ordinary" use of goods described in the contract, serious misunderstandings should be infrequent; in domestic law disputes under this test usually arise out of a question of fact: Were the goods subject to defects that were abnormal for goods sold under the description?

If the parties do have different understandings of the connotations of the agreed description, the problem needs to be resolved pursuant to the Convention's rules for interpreting sales contracts. These rules are set forth in Article 8, supplemented by the practices of the parties and trade usages Article 9. Under these rules the relevant facts are: Which party drafted the description? (This may be either the seller or buyer.) What, under Article 8(2), would be "the understanding that a reasonable person of the same kind as the other party would have had in the same circumstances"? To ascertain this understanding Article 8(3) directs attention to all relevant circumstances including "the negotiations, any practices which the parties have established between themselves, usages and any subsequent conduct of the parties."

In sum, under the Convention problems of contract interpretation are to be solved on the basis of the *facts of each transaction* and not under a general legal rule specifying that the seller's (or buyer's) region controls the parties' understanding.

Decisions; Conformity: Standards in Buyer's State; Compliance Required: (1) FR. CA Montpelier, 15–04–93. Excessive sugar basis for rejection; confirmed: C. de Cass. (Sup.Ct.) 173P. 23–01–1996. CLOUT 150, UNILEX D. 1996–2. (2) FR. CA Grenoble, 48992, 13–9–95, Ciato v. SFF. S knew that the cheese was to be resold in France; French standards were required. UNILEX D. 1994–24, CLOUT 202. (3) GER. LG Ellwangen, 1 KfH-O-32/95, 21–08–05. Paprica from Spain did not conform to German food standards; B avoided contract. UNILEX D. 1995–20. (4) FR. C. de Cass. (Sup.Ct.), Ceramique v. Musgrave, 2205D, 17–12–96. C. de Cass. reversed lower courts because, inter alia, French rules on *vice cache* were applied instead of CISG 35(2)(a). UNILEX D. 1996–11. * * *

Compliance with Standards Satisfied or not Required. GER. OLG Frankfurt a. M., 13U51/93, 20–04–1994, confirmed by BGH (Sup.Ct.). Claim that calcium of shellfish exceeded German standards; claim rejected. S can not be expected to observe standards or regulations in B's State unless they are the same as in S's State or B has informed S. CLOUT 84, UNILEX D. 1994–10, D. 1995–9 (BGH). * * *

(b) Fitness for Particular Purpose. The role of Article 35(2)(b) may be illustrated as follows:

Example 35A. Buyer wrote as follows to Seller, a manufacturer of drills. "Please ship me a set of drills [giving sizes] for drilling holes in plates of carbon steel." Seller shipped the Buyer a set of drills that were of the size designated by Buyer. The drills were satisfactory for drilling holes in ordinary steel, but were not sufficiently hard for carbon steel.

Relationship to Contract. In this example, as in most (perhaps all) of the sales that fall within paragraph (2)(b), it would be possible to conclude that the shipment of the drills created an "understanding" that the drills would meet the standards specified in Buyer's order; conformity of the goods with this understanding would be required by Article 35(1) although Seller had said nothing about whether the drills would cut through carbon steel. Thus, paragraph (2)(b) of Article 35 may not have been necessary, but may help to reduce uncertainty over whether a seller may be responsible for an understanding to which he was a party but which he did not articulate.

Reliance on Seller's Skill and Judgment. The structure of paragraph (2)(b) may lead tribunals to conclude that the buyer makes a *prima facie* case by showing that the seller knew of the buyer's particular purpose at the time of the conclusion of the contract and that the goods were unfit for that purpose; the seller then has the burden to show that "the buyer did not rely, or that it was unreasonable for him to rely, on the seller's skill and judgment."

In Example 35A, Seller would find it difficult to disprove reliance by Buyer. Seller, the manufacturer of the drills, would know more about their cutting qualities than Buyer, and Buyer relied on the Seller to select a drill that would cut through carbon steel, or inform Buyer that Seller had no such drill. Indeed, the crux of Article 35(2)(b) is the buyer's known reliance on the seller to select and furnish a commodity that will satisfy a stated purpose.

Decision; Fitness for Purpose. FR. CA Grenoble, RG93/4879, 26–04–95, M. Roque v. SARL. Purpose of hangar made known to S (Art. 31(b)); S was responsible for repairs.. UNILEX 1995–14, CLOUT 152.

MEDICAL MARKETING INTERNATIONAL, INC. V. INTERNAZIONALE MEDICO SCIENTIFICA, S.R.L.
United States District Court, E.D. Louisiana, 1999.
1999 WL 311945.

DUVAL, DISTRICT J.

Before the court is an Application for Order Conforming Arbitral Award and Entry of Judgment, filed by plaintiff, Medical Marketing International, Inc. ("MMI"). Having considered the memoranda of plaintiff, and the memorandum in opposition filed by defendant, Internazionale Medico Scientifica, S.r.l. ("IMS"), the court grants the motion.

FACTUAL BACKGROUND

Plaintiff MMI is a Louisiana marketing corporation with its principal place of business in Baton Rouge, Louisiana. Defendant IMS is an

Italian corporation that manufactures radiology materials with its principal place of business in Bologna, Italy. On January 25, 1993, MMI and IMS entered into a Business Licensing Agreement in which IMS granted exclusive sales rights for Giotto Mammography H.F. Units to MMI.

In 1996, the Food and Drug Administration ("FDA") seized the equipment for noncompliance with administrative procedures, and a dispute arose over who bore the obligation of ensuring that the Giotto equipment complied with the United States Governmental Safety Regulations, specifically the Good Manufacturing Practices (GMP) for Medical Device Regulations. MMI formally demanded mediation on October 28, 1996, pursuant to Article 13 of the agreement. Mediation was unsuccessful, and the parties entered into arbitration, also pursuant to Article 13, whereby each party chose one arbitrator and a third was agreed upon by both.

An arbitration hearing was held on July 13–15, July 28, and November 17, 1998. The hearing was formally closed on November 30, 1998. The arbitrators rendered their decision on December 21, 1998, awarding MMI damages in the amount of $357,009.00 and legal interest on that amount from October 28, 1996. * * *

* * *

At the arbitration, IMS argued that MMI was not entitled to avoid its contract with IMS based on non-conformity under Article 49, because IMS's breach was not "fundamental." IMS argued that CISG did not require that it furnish MMI with equipment that complied with the United States GMP regulations. To support this proposition, IMS cited a German Supreme Court case, which held that under CISG Article 35, a seller is generally not obligated to supply goods that conform to public laws and regulations enforced at the buyer's place of business. Entscheidungen des Bundersgerichtshofs in Zivilsachen (BGHZ) 129, 75 (1995). In that case, the court held that this general rule carries with it exceptions in three limited circumstances: (1) if the public laws and regulations of the buyer's state are identical to those enforced in the seller's state; (2) if the buyer informed the seller about those regulations; or (3) if due to "special circumstances," such as the existence of a seller's branch office in the buyer's state, the seller knew or should have known about the regulations at issue.

The arbitration panel decided that under the third exception, the general rule did not apply to this case. The arbitrators held that IMS was, or should have been, aware of the GMP regulations prior to entering into the 1993 agreement, and explained their reasoning at length. IMS now argues that the arbitration panel refused to apply CISG and the law as articulated by the German Supreme Court. It is clear from the arbitrators' written findings, however, that they carefully considered that decision and found that this case fit the exception and not the rule as articulated in that decision. The arbitrators' decision was neither contrary to public policy nor in manifest disregard of international sales law. This court therefore finds that the arbitration panel did not "exceed its powers" in violation of the FAA [Federal Arbitration Act].

* * *

PROBLEM 3–7

Société Ballard, a French company, agrees to manufacture and sell to Brooklyn Bottling Company in New York a bottle-capping machine. The written agreement includes an express term stating that the machine will cap 10,000 bottles per hour, but says nothing more about the quality of the machine.

(a) Assume it is customary in the bottling equipment trade for machinery to be allowed a tolerance of five percent plus or minus with respect to the number of bottles capped in an hour? Does Société Ballard satisfy its obligation with respect to the quality of the machine if it tenders a machine that caps 9,900 bottles per hour? CISG arts. 9(2), 35(1).

(b) At the time the sales contract was negotiated, Bottling Company informed Société Ballard that it would be capping bottles containing alcohol (*e.g.*, "Thunder Wines"). Société Ballard knows that the alcohol may corrode the bottling machine; Bottling Company is unaware of this possibility, although it knows that it must use special caps when capping bottles with alcohol. Société Ballard says nothing about the problem when Bottling Company orders the machine. Has Société Ballard made any "warranty"? CISG art. 35(2)(b), (3).

(c) Assume it is customary for machinery shipped from Cherbourg to New York to be crated in wooden crates. Must Société Ballard crate the machine? CISG art. 35(1), (2)(d). Who must bear the cost of crating the machine?

(d) Reviewing your answers to the previous questions, what would you recommend that your client, Bottling Company, include in its subsequent contracts with Société Ballard?

* * *

PROBLEM 3–8

Easy Co., an Egyptian seller of cotton, agreed to sell 22 tons of Egyptian long-staple cotton to Fox Fabrics, a New Jersey producer of cloth. The cotton is to be delivered "CIF New York (Inctoterms 1990)." When must the cotton conform to the promised quality: at the time it leaves Easy's warehouse in Cairo? When it is loaded on a ship in Alexandria? When it is unloaded on a New York pier? When it is received at Fox's plant in New Jersey? When it is being processed into cloth at Fox's plant? When the cloth is sold by Fox to clothing manufacturers? CISG arts. 36, 67.

* * *

PROBLEM 3–9

Assume that after your client, Fox Fashions, has agreed to purchase the cotton from Easy Co., your client calls you with the following questions:

(a) Does Fox have a right to inspect the cotton before accepting it? May Fox have a third party inspect the cotton while it is still in Easy's warehouse? May Fox wait until the cotton is delivered to its New Jersey plant before inspecting the cotton? CISG art. 38.

(b) Assume that upon promptly inspecting the cotton after delivery, Fox discovers that the cotton is not long-staple, and is probably not Egyptian. Must Fox inform Easy of the defect? CISG art. 39. Is there any penalty for failing to inform Easy? CISG art. 44. If you advise Fox to inform Easy, what, when and how should notice be given?

(c) In future contracts, what terms with respect to inspection would you recommend Fox include? What terms with respect to notice of defects would you recommend that Fox include?

* * *

Legislation Note on UCC Provisions

Under UCC § 2–513, buyer has a right to inspect the goods before it must either accept or pay for them. Even when shipment of the goods is involved, buyer may inspect after arrival at their destination before acceptance or payment, unless otherwise agreed. UCC § 2–513(1). However, buyer is not permitted to inspect before payment where the contract provides for delivery "C.O.D." or for payment against documents, UCC § 2–513(3). Under UCC § 2–320(4) (see the Documents Supplement), "CIF" is defined as requiring payment against documents. (Incoterms provides its own definition of "CIF," however).

Under UCC § 2–607, if buyer has accepted the goods and they are nonconforming, buyer must notify seller "of breach" within a reasonable time of discovery, or it is "barred from any remedy" under the UCC—unless the contract terms provide otherwise, UCC § 2–607(3)(a).

* * *

UNILEX CASE D. 1994–10
Germany: Oberlandesgericht Frankfurt am Main, 1994.

Abstract

A Swiss seller and a German buyer concluded a contract for the sale of New Zealand mussels. The buyer refused to pay the price after the mussels were declared "not completely safe" because of the quantity of cadmium they contained, which was significantly greater than the advised cadmium levels published by the German Federal Health Department. The buyer gave the seller notice of the non conformity and asked the seller to take back the goods. The lower Court decided in favor of the seller and the buyer appealed.

The Court held that the buyer's notice was an unmistakable declaration of its intention to avoid the contract (Art. 26 CISG).

The Court held, however, that the buyer was not entitled to avoid the contract under Arts. 25 and 49(1)(a) CISG, because the seller did not fundamentally breach the contract. First of all, in the opinion of the Court, the mussels were conforming to the contract, since they were "fit for the purposes for which goods of the same description would ordinarily be used" (Art. 35(2)(a) CISG). The Court observed that the directives issued by the Federal Health Department on fish products are non binding recommendations, and that the quantity of cadmium which makes food dangerous to the health varies according to the type of food (as a rule, mussels are eaten occasionally and in smaller quantities than other types of good). Moreover, the parties had not explicitly or implicitly agreed to the advised cadmium levels in the contract (Art. 35(2)(b) CISG).

In addition, the Court held that the goods would be "fit for the purposes for which goods of the same description would ordinarily be used" even if the directives issued by the Federal Health Department were binding public authority rules. According to the Court, the goods can be conforming even if the seller does not comply with the public law provisions concerning the merchantability of the goods in force in each of the countries where the goods might be exported. After all, only by disregarding these provisions can Art. 35 CISG be interpreted and applied uniformly in accordance with Art. 7(1) CISG.

The Court further held that, in the case at hand, there was no need to resolve the question whether the requirements of Art. 35(2)(a) CISG are met where the goods are of average quality (prevailing continental law rule), or where the goods are just merchantable (prevailing common law rule). Nevertheless, the Court observed that the latter seems correct, because during the negotiation of CISG a Canadian proposal concerning average quality was withdrawn.

According to the Court, the buyer was not entitled to avoid the contract because of non conformity of the packaging (Art. 35(2)(c) CISG). Under CISG the buyer must declare its intention to avoid the contract within a "reasonable time" after the discovery of the unsuitable packaging (Art. 49(2) CISG). Here, the buyer's declaration occurred over two months after the delivery, which the Court held was not within a reasonable time.

The seller was awarded payment of the price (Art. 53 CISG). As CISG does not determine the currency of payment, the Court enforced the parties' agreement concerning the currency.

UNILEX CASE D. 1995–9
Germany: Bundesgerichtshof, 1995.

Abstract

A Swiss seller and a German buyer concluded a contract for the sale of New Zealand mussels. The buyer refused to pay the purchase price after the mussels were declared "not completely safe" because of the quantity of cadmium they contained, which quantity was significantly greater than the advised cadmium levels published by the German Federal Health Department. The buyer gave notice to the seller of the contamination and asked it to take back the mussels. Six or eight weeks after the delivery of the mussels, the buyer complained about defects of the packaging. The seller commenced an action claiming payment and interest. At first instance the Court decided in favor of the seller, and the buyer's subsequent appeals were unsuccessful.

The Supreme Court confirmed the decisions of the lower Courts, stating that the contract between the parties was governed by CISG according to Art. 1(1)(a).

The Court held that the buyer had to pay the purchase price. It was not entitled to declare the contract avoided under Arts. 25 and 49(1)(a) CISG, since the seller did not commit a fundamental breach of the contract. The Court confirmed the findings of the lower Courts, according to which the mussels were conforming to the contract since they were fit for the purposes for which goods of the same description would ordinarily be used (Art. 35(2)(a) CISG). The Court did find that the fact that the mussels contained a greater quantity of cadmium than the advised cadmium levels could well affect the merchantability of the goods, provided that the corresponding public-law-requirements were relevant. However, like the lower Courts, the supreme Court excluded that the seller can generally be expected to observe special public-law-requirements of the buyer's state; it could only be expected to do so where the same rules also exist in the seller's country or where the buyer draws the seller's attention to their existence.

The Court equally confirmed that the buyer was not entitled to avoid the contract because of non-conformity of the packaging (Art. 35(2)(c) CISG). However, in the Court's opinion the decisive fact was that the buyer did not give notice of the alleged non-conformity of the packaging in time (notice was given approximately two months after delivery), rather than the fact it delayed in declaring the contract avoided.

* * *

PROBLEM 3–10

Dilbert's Donuts, a Buffalo bakery, sells "one dozen-dozen doughnuts" to Alice's Hideaway, a restaurant in Ft. Erie, Ontario, Canada. To carry out Alice's order, Dilbert delivers 144 (12x12) doughnuts to a trucker for shipment to Alice. Has Dilbert fulfilled its obligations under the contract and the Sales Convention? CISG art. 35(1); art. 37.

* * *

J. HONNOLD, UNIFORM LAW FOR INTERNATIONAL SALES UNDER THE 1980 UNITED NATIONS CONVENTION
310–13 (1982).*

Restrictions on warranty disclaimers of the UCC extend to commercial transactions. Section 2–316 includes the following: ... Under subsection (2) of the UCC provision just quoted, a provision of a contract that purports to exclude or modify the implied warranty of merchantability is ineffective unless it (1) "mentions merchantability" and (2) in a writing is "conspicuous." However, these restrictions do not apply if under paragraph (3), the contract uses "language which in common understanding calls the buyer's attention to the exclusion of warranties and makes plain that there is no implied warranty." The relationship between these rules of domestic law and the Convention raises two issues: (a) As a matter of domestic law, should the UCC be construed to make this aspect of Article 2 applicable to transactions that are subject to the Convention? (b) Does UCC 2–316 lay down rules of "validity" remitted to domestic law within the area governed by Article 4(2) of the Convention, as contrasted with rules of interpretation governed by Article 8 of the Convention? Unless the answer to both of these questions is Yes, these UCC disclaimer provisions will not apply.

(a) *Continued Applicability as a Question of Domestic Law*

Should the Code be construed so as to make provisions like UCC 2–316(2) applicable to sales subject to the Convention? The answer should be No. Section 2–316 was explicitly designed to fit with Section 2–314 that established the implied warranty of "merchantable quality," and with Section 2–315, that established the implied warranty of fitness for purpose. UCC 2–314 and 2–315 would of course be supplanted by Article 35(2) of the Convention. It would be awkward to require a contract to "mention merchantability" in order to disclaim an implied obligation under Article 35(2)(a) that is somewhat different from UCC 2–314 and does not itself refer to "merchantability."

(b) *Rules of "Validity" v. Rules of Interpretation*

As we have seen, the specific restrictions of paragraph (2) of UCC 2–316 are inapplicable when, under paragraph (3), the contract uses "language which in common understanding calls the buyer's attention to the exclusion of warranties and makes plain that there is no implied warranty." Do these rules govern "the validity of the contract or of any of its provisions ..." within the meaning of Article 4(a) of the Convention? The argument for concluding that these are rules of "validity" rests on the fact that, in some settings, general language disclaiming implied warranties is ineffective by virtue of UCC 2–316(2) and (3); a contractual provision that is denied legal effect might be described as "invalid."

The argument proves too much, for it leads to the conclusion that any domestic rule that denies full literal effect to a contract provision on the ground that it does not accurately represent the parties' understanding would constitute a rule of "validity." The reference to domestic rules of "validity" in Article 4(a) cannot be carried this far without intruding on the Convention's rules for interpreting international sales contracts. More specifically, Article 8 addresses a basic question of interpretation in a manner somewhat similar to the rules of domestic law in UCC 2–316. Under Article 8(2), the statements of a party (including contract terms he has drafted) "are to be interpreted according to *the understanding that a reasonable person of the same kind as the other party* would have had in the same circumstance"—language that is addressed to the same basic issue as the provision in UCC 2–316(3) giving effect to language which in "*common understanding* calls the *buyer's attention* to the exclusion of warranties and *makes plain* that there is no implied warranty." The point is not, of course, that Article 8 of the Convention and UCC 2–316 are identical but rather that both address the same issue. It follows that the reference to "validity" in Article 4(a) of the Convention may not be read so broadly as to import domestic rules that would supplant other articles of the Convention.

* * *

LONGOBARDI, DISCLAIMERS OF IMPLIED WARRANTIES: THE 1980 UNITED NATIONS CONVENTION ON CONTRACTS FOR THE INTERNATIONAL SALE OF GOODS

53 Fordham L. Rev. 863, 878–884 (1985).*

An examination of [section 2–316's] language, legislative history and public policy purposes demonstrates that its provisions set forth requirements for validity within the Convention's concept of that term.

A. *The language of Section 2–316*

Section 2–316(2) states that "to exclude . . . the implied warranty of merchantability . . . the language must mention merchantability and in case of a writing must be conspicuous." The implied warranty of fitness for a particular purpose may be disclaimed by general language, but such a disclaimer "must be by a writing and conspicuous." Such repeated use of the auxiliary verb "must" is a primary indication of section 2–316(2)'s mandatory character. "The effect of holding a statute mandatory is to require strict compliance with its letter in order . . . to enable persons to acquire rights under it." Section 2–316(2)'s mandatory nature indicates that its requirements are those of validity.

These requirements are, however, "subject to" section 2–316(3). A seller who has failed to comply with section 2–316(2) may still have made a valid disclaimer under section 2–316(3). Whereas section 2–316(2)'s requirements are quire specific, section 2–316(3) allows for generalities. The existence of such generalities may compel the conclusion that section 2–316 sets forth mere guidelines for interpretation of the parties' agreement rather than requirements for valid disclaimers. This argument is unpersuasive, however, because a disclaimer that fails to meet the requirements of either subdivision will be held to be invalid. Section 2–316(3)(a) enables a seller to exclude an implied warranty by using expressions such as "with all faults," "as is," "or other language which in the common understanding calls the buyer's attention to the exclusion of warranties and makes plain that there is no implied warranty." This is not an automatic disclaimer; the circumstances must be such as to give the buyer reason to know that there is no implied warranty.

Section 2–316(3)(b) authorizes disclaimers by examination. For such a disclaimer to be effective, the buyer must have either examined the goods before the contract was made or refused to examine them. It follows that the seller must demand that the buyer examine the goods, not merely make them available for inspection, in order for the buyer's refusal to examine to constitute a disclaimer.

Under section 2–316(3)(c), a course of dealing, course of performance or trade usage can also exclude an implied warranty. That section cannot be used, however, unless the facts indicate that such a practice was part of the parties' agreement.

It has been argued that section 2–316(3) does not set forth requirements for validity because it requires interpretation of circumstances. For example, "common understanding" under section 2–316(3)(a) seems to refer to a standard of a reasonable person under the circumstances. Similarly, section 2–316(3)(c) shows that a course of dealing, course of performance or usage of the trade can guide the interpretation of the parties' agreement. Merely because section 2–316 permits an interpretation of the disclaimer clause, however, does not give rise to an inference that the entire section is not language of validity. Interpretation is necessary only to determine whether the attempted disclaimer is valid. If the circumstances as contemplated in section 2–316(3) do not allow effect to be given to a disclaimer that has no effect under section 2–316(2), the disclaimer is invalid.

B. *Legislative History and Policy Considerations*

The official comments to section 2–316 state that it was designed "to protect a buyer from unexpected and unbargained language of disclaimer by . . . permitting the exclusion of implied warranties only by conspicuous language or other circumstances which protect the buyer from surprise." A disclaimer that does not meet section 2–316's requirements is contrary to the public policies expressed by the drafters: to prevent unfair surprise and harsh workings of a contract. The argument may be made, however, that if the drafters intended section 2–316 primarily to protect consumers, less concern need be given to transactions between merchants. Relative bargaining capacity suggests that merchants are in less need of protection from unbargained language of disclaimers and harsh results than are consumers. This argument would conclude that because the Convention's scope includes transactions between merchants, section 2–316 does not define requirements for validity as to them. The language of section 2–316, however, makes no distinction between consumers or merchants: Both are shielded from unexpected or harsh results. Furthermore, it is not always true that a merchant-buyer is in less need of protection than a consumer. Some merchants have less negotiating ability than others, and their bargaining power may not be great. Although they are not consumers, merchant-buyers ought still to be protected from unbargained language of disclaimers.

There is a further argument that because transactions between merchants allow for more interpretation than transactions involving a consumer, merchant-buyers should not be granted full protection under the Code. It is true that different standards exist in a transaction for a sale of goods between merchants. A merchant may be held to a higher duty to read, for example, and may be deemed to have noticed the term "merchantability" in a clause that would be held to be inconspicuous if sought to be enforced against a consumer. Yet it has already been shown that it is not the degree of interpretation permitted in a statute that determines whether that statute sets out requirements for effectiveness or mere guidelines for interpretation. In spite of the higher standards applicable to merchants, section 2–316 continues to set forth absolute mandates for valid disclaimers of implied warranties.

The public policy requirement of strict compliance with the language of section 2–316 effectively to disclaim implied warranties comports with the Convention's concept of validity as set out in Part I of this Note. Only those disclaimers that fulfill the requirements of section 2–316 are valid. "Public policy is necessarily variable [and] is evidenced by the expression of the will of the Legislature contained in statutory enactments.... [W]hen [the Legislature] has expressed its will and established a new policy, courts are required to give effect to such policy." It is well recognized in private international law that certain contractual matters, such as risk of loss clauses and Statute of Frauds, are sufficient public policy grounds for refusing to enforce a contract. A logical extension of this reasoning would include among such grounds disclaimers of implied warranties.

* * *

HARTNELL, ROUSING THE SLEEPING DOG: THE VALIDITY EXCEPTION TO THE CONVENTION ON CONTRACTS FOR THE INTERNATIONAL SALE OF GOODS

18 Yale J. Int'l L. 1, 85–86 (1993).*

The key question, therefore, is whether domestic laws regulating the manner of exclusion or modification of such obligations, such as U.C.C. § 2–316, are rules of validity that are preserved by CISG, article 4(a). Professor Honnold argues that U.C.C. § 2–316 is a law which "denies full effect to standard terms and form contracts prepared by one party on the ground that the other party may not grasp their full import." In his view, U.C.C. § 2–316 is a rule of *interpretation*, rather than a rule of validity, and is thus displaced by CISG, article 8(2) concerning interpretation of statements made by a party. He concludes that applying domestic rules "controlling contract clauses restricting responsibility for defective goods" without turning first to CISG, article 8(2) "would restrict the scope of the uniform law in violation of the rule of Article 7(1) that the Convention shall be interpreted with regard 'to the need to promote uniformity in its application. . . .' "

Professor Honnold's view has met with resistance. Those authors who contend that U.C.C. § 2–316 sets forth requirements for validity preserved to domestic law emphasize the mandatory nature of the provision and its public policy purpose. The connection between U.C.C. §§ 2–316 and 2–302 may help to resolve the debate over U.C.C. § 2–316. The gist of unconscionability is the "prevention of oppression and unfair surprise." U.C.C. § 2–316 also "seeks to protect a buyer from unexpected and unbargained language of disclaimer." Thus, the subsections of U.C.C. § 2–316 dealing with the exclusion or modification of implied warranties are primarily aimed at the prevention of unfair surprise, even though couched in interpretive terms. It is therefore difficult to sustain a neat distinction between U.C.C. § 2–302, which permits a court to invalidate exculpatory clauses because they are unconscionable, and the provisions of U.C.C. § 2–316 on implied warranties, which similarly permit a court to invalidate an attempted disclaimer. The conclusion that U.C.C. § 2–316 constitutes a rule of validity is warranted.

Therefore, the legal effect of most exculpatory clauses, if not all, will be left up to the domestic law that is otherwise applicable, and will not be evaluated under international standards developed within the framework of the CISG. This conclusion with regard to an important issue in international commerce would not appear to bode well for the goal of unification. However, the prospects are good that international standards to govern exculpatory clauses will evolve. Even in the absence of international unification, the rules governing exculpatory clauses lend themselves well to the balanced approach described in part III. This is an area in which much common ground can be found and in which adjudicators can accommodate the needs of international commerce by reading domestic public policy narrowly.

PROBLEM 3–11

DaimlerChrysler sells trucks from the U.S. to buyers in Mexico. The contracts all include the following term:

"Seller warrants this product to be free from defects in material and workmanship for 12 months. Seller makes NO other EXPRESS WARRANTY and NO IMPLIED WARRANTIES. Seller's obligation under this warranty is limited to repair or replacement of defective parts without charge to Buyer."

(a) Ignoring for the moment the question of whether this term would be valid under U.S. law, is this term effective to limit the provisions on seller's obligation of quality under CISG article 35? CISG art. 6.

(b) Issues of validity, as you no doubt remember, are not governed by the Sales Convention. CISG art. 4(a). The contract term set out above might not be effective to disclaim the "warranty of merchantability" under the Uniform Commercial Code because the disclaimer does not use the word "merchantability." U.C.C. §§ 2–316(2), (3); 1–201(10). Is the contract term invalid?

(c) Is the following disclaimer term preferable to the language set out in this problem? What modifications to this language would you make?

"DISCLAIMER OF OBLIGATION AS TO CONFORMITY OF THE GOODS. The parties agree that the seller undertakes no obligation with respect to the conformity of the goods to the contract except as otherwise provided in this contract document. In particular, the parties agree to EXCLUDE ALL IMPLIED WARRANTIES OF MERCHANTABILITY OR FITNESS FOR A PARTICULAR PURPOSE."

* * *

SHINN, LIABILITIES UNDER ARTICLE 42 OF THE U.N. CONVENTION ON THE INTERNATIONAL SALE OF GOODS
2 Minn. J.Global Trade 115, 124–35 (1993).*

The requirement of Article 42 that the seller deliver goods free of third-party intellectual property claims appears to be new in international commercial law. The essence of the obligation is that the seller must deliver goods that, at the time of contracting, were not subject to a third-party right or claim based on intellectual property rights (IPRs) of which the seller knew or should have known. In effect, the seller must indemnify the buyer against certain third-party claims against her with respect to intellectual property rights. The seller's obligation extends only to rights or claims that exist under the law of the state in which the goods will be used or resold, or, in the alternative, under the law of the buyer's own state, and the seller is not liable for rights or claims of which the buyer knew or should have known.

* * *

2.   What standard is meant by "could not have been unaware"?

This is the most difficult question Article 42 raises. The seller is liable for third-party claims of which she "knew or could not have been unaware." Because the language appears redundant, the phrase "could not have been unaware" must be a term of art.

The secretariat commentary states that "the seller 'could not have been unaware' of the third-party claim if that claim was based on a patent application or grant which had been published in the country in question." This appears to place an affirmative obligation on the seller to research the patent (and by analogy, copyright and trademark) registries of the country in which the buyer will use or resell the goods. The secretariat commentary reinforces this view by stating further that "[T]he seller is in a position to ascertain whether any third party has industrial or intellectual property rights or claims. . . ." The legislative history, however, does not support the Secretariat's view. The International Chamber of Commerce (ICC) commented to the Diplomatic Conference that the Secretariat's view was incorrect. But there is no indication that this criticism was accepted or even debated, nor is there an indication of the standard that the ICC would have applied.

* * *

The most logical interpretation is that "could not have been unaware" places a duty on both seller and buyer to not be negligent about information that is reasonably at hand at the time they form a contract, especially if the other side is not likely to have the same information. The buyer's burden of proof is fairly heavy, perhaps close to gross negligence. Thus, the seller's liability may be limited to situations in which circumstances make it impossible for a judge to believe that seller did *not* know of the information at issue. * * *

Because intellectual property law is highly territorial, there will usually be no claim until the goods are actually imported. The seller's liability, however, is limited to claims of which he has knowledge at the time of contracting. Thus, when the contract is made before the goods are imported, there can be no liability unless seller can "know" of a claim which has not yet arisen.

The best argument that Article 42 should be interpreted to impose liability in such cases is that the alternative would make the entire article meaningless except when the goods are imported *before* the sales contract is made. In such a case, however, the IPR holder would have a direct action against seller, so there would be little need for Article 42. This interpretation would also come close to violating the canon that a legal provision should not be interpreted so as to deprive it of all meaning. It is unlikely that the drafters intended to impose liability only in such exceptional cases.

Domestic law provides a useful analogy, but one that is imperfect because it does not involve the import question. The UCC provides that the seller's liability extends to claims related to patent or trademark that "*will* mar the buyer's title." By analogy, seller's liability should extend to claims which she "knew," at the time the contract was made, would arise upon import.

* * *

B.   "Gray Market" Imports to the United States.

"Gray market" refers to trade in goods for which the owner has licensed the trademark, copyright, or patent with respect to certain countries or other geographic areas, but which are traded within those areas outside the terms of the license. To the extent that a trademark, copyright or patent owner or licensee may prevent goods from moving into a licensed area outside of the terms of the license, the seller of gray market goods may be liable to the buyer under Article 42.

1.   Trademark

The leading case addressing gray market imports of trademarked goods is *K–Mart v. Cartier, Inc.*, which interpreted section 526 of the Tariff Act of 1930. *K–Mart* treated three gray market scenarios:

Case 1 involves a foreign manufacturer that licenses its trademark to a domestic U.S. firm, which then imports and distributes the trademarked goods in the United States. The question was whether such a licensee, which may have paid a substantial fee for the trademark license, may then prevent the foreign manufacturer itself or a third party from importing the trademarked goods and selling them in the United States in competition with the licensee. Congress passed section 526 to protect the U.S. licensee in this situation. As interpreted, the rule is that the U.S. licensee is protected so long as she has independently developed goodwill in the United States through service, warranty programs, advertising or the like. A U.S. third-party buyer of such non-licensed goods would thus be subject to a claim by the licensee based on the trademark license; Article 42 would give the buyer an offsetting claim against the overseas seller.

Case 2 involves a U.S. firm that imports and distributes in the United States, under a U.S. trademark, goods that are manufactured abroad by an affiliated firm. Variations include a U.S. subsidiary of a foreign firm (Case 2a), a foreign subsidiary of a U.S. firm (Case 2b), or an unincorporated overseas manufacturing division of a U.S. firm (Case 2c) importing the goods. *K–Mart* held that if the trademarked goods were sold abroad to a third party in a Case 2 scenario, the goods could be imported freely into the United States and sold in competition with the U.S. owner of the trademark; this ruling upheld long-standing Customs regulations denying protection in this situation. The apparent rationale is that the owner of the trademark, whether in the United States or abroad, can prevent such sales by refusing to sell to the third party in the first place. Because *K–Mart* denied the domestic trademark owner relief, this situation would not give rise to a third-party IPR claim under Article 42; raising no issue of liability for the foreign seller.

Case 3 involves a domestic trademark holder that licenses his trademark to a foreign manufacturer for use in a designated overseas territory. *K–Mart* held that the U.S. licensor is protected against imports of the foreign manufactured goods carrying the licensed trademark by either the licensee or a third party. A buyer importing such goods into the United States would be vulnerable to the U.S. licensor's IPR claim, and Article 42 would give him an offsetting claim against the licensee-seller.

2.   Copyright

K–Mart clarifies U.S. law with respect to trademarks, but it says nothing about copyright and patent situations. The copyright statute itself, however, is fairly clear. The general rule is that importing an item which is copyrighted in the United States, without permission of the copyright owner, infringes the copyright even if the item was lawfully manufactured abroad (presumably under license from the U.S. copyright owner). If the item is a pirate copy (i.e., manufactured without benefit of a license), Customs can stop it at the border, but if the overseas manufacture is licensed, the copyright holder's only remedy is an infringement suit after importation. Thus, the distinctions elaborated in *K–Mart* are not relevant to copyright; the copyright statute protects the copyright owner against gray market imports into the United States. A third-party copyright owner would have a claim against a buyer who, without permission, imports or subsequently uses or sells a copyrighted item manufactured abroad, whether done under color of license or not; Article 42 would generally give the buyer a claim against the seller for the resulting damages.

* * *

PROBLEM 3–12

Double Happiness, a Chinese producer of CDs of top artists, including The Rockers, agreed to sell one million Rockers CDs to Beers and Sawbuck, a high-volume, low-price retailer of music, videos and CDs throughout the eastern United States. The CDs were delivered and are being resold to retail customers in America. Beers has received two letter which create concern.

One letter was from DACCA, Inc., the owner of the copyright on all Rockers music, and the owner of the Rockers trademark. It stated that Double Happiness never had permission from DACCA to reproduce Rockers music or to use its trademark. The letter demands that Beers immediately stop all retail sales of the CDs, or DACCA will sue.

The second letter is from Rolling Records, a Hong Kong producer of CDs. It states that it does have copyright and trademark licenses from DACCA, and that it did produce the CDs which Double Happiness sold to Beers, but that Double Happiness "stole" the CDs from Rolling Records. It demands that Beers either pay Rolling Records the full sale price of the CDs, or that it cease all retail sales, withdraw the goods from the retail outlets and return the goods to Rolling Records in Hong Kong, freight paid. Rolling's letter states that, if Beers does not agree to do this, it will sue.

Beers immediately called Double Happiness to inquire as to these claims, and to notify Double Happiness of the possibility of nonconformities in the goods. Double Happiness responded that half of the goods had, in fact, been purchased by Double Happiness from Rolling. The check to Rolling had "bounced," due to "bureaucratic misunderstandings" at the Bank of China, but that a second check was "in the mail" to Rolling, and it was not expected to bounce.

The other half of the goods had been produced by Double Happiness under a license agreement from Rolling, which had assigned to Double Happiness a part of its license rights from DACCA. It is not aware of any clause in Rolling's license which prohibits such an assignment.

(a) Beers now consults you. Have Double Happiness' obligations under the contract been breached at this time? CISG art. 42. Note that neither DACCA nor Rolling has yet initiated any action in court. Is the filing of an actual lawsuit necessary to create a breach? See UCC § 2–312.

(b) If either DACCA or Rolling does actually commence an action in court, can Beers require Double Happiness to appear and defend its rights? Compare UCC § 2–607(5).

3. CURE

A seller whose contract is governed by the Sales Convention has the right to cure a non-conforming tender both before and after tender is due as agreed in the contract. If the time for performance has not yet elapsed, the seller may cure the tender by timely performance as long as this "does not cause the buyer unreasonable inconvenience or unreasonable expense." *See* CISG art. 37. By curing, the seller does not, however, escape the obligation to compensate the buyer for any damages suffered as a consequence of the non-conforming tender. CISG arts. 37 (last sent.), 74.

After performance is due, the seller may cure if the buyer has not avoided the contract. The seller must complete the cure without unreasonable delay and the cure may not cause the buyer "unreasonable inconvenience or uncertainty of reimbursement by the seller of expenses advanced by the buyer." *See* CISG art. 48. To clarify where the parties stand, the Convention authorizes the seller to ask the buyer to state whether or not the buyer will accept the proffered cure. If the buyer agrees or fails to respond, the seller may proceed and the buyer is barred from seeking an inconsistent remedy, such as avoiding the contract. CISG art. 48(2).

* * *

PROBLEM 3–13

Sector Corp, an Illinois manufacturer of quality control equipment, agrees to manufacture and sell a tablet-testing machine to Beva, SA, a French pharmaceutical producer. The contract requires Sector to deliver and install the tablet-testing machine by September 15. The contract specifies that the machine will be able to test 200 tablets per minute, or 12,000 tablets per hour, which is the speed of Beva's production line. Sector's employees install the machine by August 15. During the first two weeks of operation, however, the machine is able to test an average of only 9,000 tablets per hour rather than the 12,000 tablets provided for in the sales contract. Sector notifies Beva that it will repair the machine.

(a) If Sector notifies Beva that it plans to cure, may Beva refuse to permit Sector to cure? CISG art. 37.

(b) If Beva refuses to permit repair, what potential sanctions does it face? CISG art. 61(1).

(c) What other forms of cure may Sector offer? May it, for example, replace the machine rather than repairing it? May it offer a money allowance to cover the difference in value of the promised machine and the machine as delivered? CISG art. 37.

Legislation Note on UCC Provisions

UCC § 2–508(1) allows a seller who has tendered delivery before the contract delivery date to cure any non-conforming tender, if there is notice and cure can be accomplished before the contract delivery date.

* * *

PROBLEM 3–14

Suppose the tablet-testing machine is not delivered and installed until September 16. Again, however, the machine is able to test an average of only 9,000 tablets per hour rather than 12,000 tablets provided for in the sales contract. [Please assume that Beva does not "avoid" the contract under CISG art. 25, 49. We will explore the concept of avoidance more fully in Chapter 4 on remedies.]

(a) May Sector still cure its performance? CISG art. 48.

(b) What form may cure take? May Sector, for example, replace the machine rather than repairing it? May it offer a money allowance to cover the difference in value of the promised machine and the machine as delivered? CISG art. 48(1); *cf.* CISG art. 37.

(c) If Sector notifies Beva that it plans to cure, may Beva refuse to permit Sector to cure? CISG art. 48(2). Where does this leave the parties?

Legislation Note on UCC Provisions

UCC § 2–508(2) gives a limited right to cure to the seller even after the contract delivery date. It is available only if the seller had "reasonable grounds to believe" that the non-conforming tender "would be acceptable" to buyer, even though defective. If so, seller must notify buyer of the intention to cure, and then may "substitute a conforming tender" within a reasonable time of the contract date.

* * *

PROBLEM 3–15

The tablet-testing machine is delivered and installed, and Sector has repaired the machine. After Sector has performed all the repairs, however, the machine is able to process an average of only 11,800 tablets per hour rather than the 12,000 tablets provided for in the sales contract. Has Sector "performed its obligations" under CISG arts. 35 and 48?

UNILEX CASE D. 1995–29

Hungary: Chamber of Commerce and Industry Court of Arbitration, 1995.

Abstract

A Hungarian seller concluded a master agreement with an Austrian buyer for the supply of waste containers to be produced by the seller. The parties agreed that the buyer would supply part of the materials necessary for such production to the seller. A dispute arose between the parties as the buyer did not pay the invoices issued by the seller for the delivery of several containers. The seller commenced arbitration proceedings claiming payment of the price. The buyer counterclaimed for reduction of price and damages.

The sole arbitrator found that the contract was an international sales contract governed by CISG as the materials supplied by the buyer did not amount to a substantial part of the materials necessary for the production of the goods (Art. 3(1) CISG). In the case at hand, the value of the materials supplied by the buyer amounted to approximately 10% of the total value of the containers to be produced.

As to the delivery of two containers, the buyer requested damages for defects concerning the painting. The sole arbitrator found that as the buyer had failed to give notice of the painting defects it had lost its right to rely on the lack of conformity of the goods (Art. 39 CISG).

* * *

With respect to another container, the buyer alleged to have discovered some defects after the time of delivery. According to the sole arbitrator, taking into consideration the speed in which the parties were used to carry on their relationship under the contract, the buyer had lost its right to rely on the lack of conformity of the goods as the seller received notice of their non-conformity 32 days after discovery of the defects.

* * *

UNILEX CASE D. 1992–10
Switzerland: Pretura di Locarno-Campagna, 1992.

Abstract

In 1988 an Italian seller and a Swiss buyer concluded contracts for the sale of furniture. The buyer sold a set of living-room furniture on to a customer who shortly thereafter complained that the goods were defective (by sitting on the sofas, the cushions slid forward). The buyer refused to accept the seller's offer to repair the goods by substituting the cushions' upholstery and declared the contract avoided. The buyer further claimed that another living-room set delivered by the seller was defective and, upon the seller's refusal to repair it, requested a refund of repair costs. The seller commenced legal action to recover the full price of all furniture sold.

The Court held that the contracts were governed by CISG, as the Swiss private international law rules led to the application of the law of Italy, a contracting State (Art. 1(1)(b) CISG).

With respect to the first set of furniture, the Court held that the buyer was not entitled to declare the contract avoided, as it had not examined the goods and given notice of the non-conformity in accordance with Arts. 38 and 39 CISG. In the opinion of the Court, as both parties were merchants, the buyer should have examined the goods upon delivery and, since the defect was apparent, it should have given immediate notice of the non-conformity, instead of doing so only following customer complaints.

The Court also observed that the buyer should have accepted the seller's offer to remedy the non-conformity by substituting the upholstery, in accordance with Art. 48 CISG.

* * *

PROBLEM 3–16

Ace Chemical Co., an Italian manufacturer, agreed to manufacture and sell Salzburger Vitriol to Bernard Broker, a German broker of chemical substances. Bernard then resold the vitriol to Hawkins Chemical Co., a Dutch manufacturer which would use the chemical in its manufacturing operations. When the goods were delivered to Bernard, he immediately had them forwarded to Hawkins. After they were delivered to Hawkins, it discovered that the vitriol did not conform to the contract terms because it had impurities in it. These impurities could be filtered out, but the process was expensive. Bernard notified Ace of the defect, and Ace offered to cure by having the goods redelivered to it in Italy, at Ace's expense, where Ace would reprocess them, remove the impurities and ship them back to Germany. Ace identified a carrier to make the redelivery to it in Italy. Must Bernard accept this offer of cure, or can it have the goods reprocessed in the Netherlands and make Ace pay the price of Dutch reprocessing? The cost of third-party reprocessing in the Netherlands will be significantly more than the cost to Ace of reprocessing in its own facilities in Italy. CISG art. 48(1).

* * *

PROBLEM 3–17

In Problem 3–16, Bernard agrees to Ace's proposed cure. One week later, Hawkins calls Bernard and states that replacement goods have not arrived, that Hawkins has no vitriol, and that it will therefore have to shut down its production line—at Bernard's expense. Bernard calls the carrier identified by Ace, and is told that the goods are still in the Netherlands. Please advise Bernard what he can do. He is facing financial ruin. Can Bernard now seek reprocessing in the Netherlands, or must it continue to await Ace's tender of conforming goods?

J. HONNOLD, UNIFORM LAW FOR INTERNATIONAL SALES UNDER THE 1980 UNITED NATIONS CONVENTION
319–21 (3d ed. 1999).*

Example 48A. Seller delivered a machine to Buyer. When Buyer tested the machine a defect in one of the component parts prevented the machine from operating. Only Seller had replacement parts for the machine. Buyer notified Seller that the machine had failed to operate. Seller offered immediately to replace the defective part but Buyer refused this offer and declared that the contract was avoided. The time required for replacing the defective part was not important to Buyer; his contention was that the machine had failed to function and that this constituted a fundamental breach of the sales contract (Art. 25) empowering him to avoid the contract (Art. 49(1)(a)).

In the 1978 Draft Convention, the provision allowing a seller to cure after the date for delivery (Art. 44(1) which became Art. 48(1) in the Convention) opened with these words: "Unless the buyer has declared the contract avoided in accordance with article 45 [now article 49] . . . ." At the Diplomatic Conference several delegates expressed their concern that, in situations like Example 48A, this "Unless" clause might be construed to authorize avoidance of the contract that would frustrate the seller's right to cure. There was widespread agreement that whether a breach is fundamental should be decided in the light of the seller's offer to cure and that the buyer's right to avoid the contract (Art. 49(1)) should not nullify the seller's right to cure (Art. 48(1)). However, it was difficult to find language that would clearly express the proper relationship between avoidance and cure. Finally, the Conference adopted a joint proposal prepared by delegates who had been anxious to protect the seller's right to cure. Under this proposal, the "Unless ..." clause of the 1978 Draft was deleted and replaced by the present cross-reference to Article 49.

In cases like Example 48A, the seller's right to cure could not have been frustrated even under the 1978 version that included the "Unless" clause; any other result would have nullified the Convention's narrow and specific provision authorizing cure.

The amendment to Article 48(1) leaves little room for doubt. The seller's right to cure should also be protected if, in cases like Example 48A, where cure is feasible, the buyer hastily declares the contract avoided before the seller has an opportunity to cure the defect. As was noted under Article 25, whether a breach is "fundamental" should be decided in the light of *all* of the circumstances. In cases like Example 48A, where cure is feasible and where an offer of cure can be expected, one cannot conclude that the breach is "fundamental" until one knows the answer to this question: Will the seller cure?

P. SCHLECHTRIEM, UNIFORM SALES LAW
75–78 (1986).*

Until the buyer has effectively avoided the contract—even after the deadline for delivery has passed—the seller can generally still "cure," that is, deliver the goods, make repairs, or replace parts or goods. However, he may not take an "unreasonable" (disproportionately long) time to do so or cause the buyer unreasonable inconvenience or uncertainty about the reimbursement of expenses advanced by the buyer (Article 48(1)). The buyer retains his right to claim damages caused by the delay, even if, as a result of his cure, the seller fully performs his obligations (Article 48(1) sentence 2). In addition to the right to cure under Article 48(1) sentence 1, which theoretically could be cancelled by the buyer's avoidance of the contract, Article 48(2) permits the seller, by sending a request (which is effective upon receipt) together with an indication of the date by which he intends to fulfill his obligations, to ask for clarification as to whether he the buyer will accept the cure. If the buyer does not respond to this request, he may not resort to any remedies inconsistent with performance by the seller before this deadline (Article 48(2) and (3)).

Article 48 was the subject of controversy in Vienna. The Federal Republic of Germany criticized the provision above all because the buyer's right to avoid the contract endangers the seller's right to cure. The West German delegation believed that the seller's right to a "second tender" should be ensured under the Convention. As a rule, however, the present version will not affect the seller's right to a "second tender".

* Copyright © 1986 and reproduced by permission from Manszche Verlag and Universitatsbuchhandlung, Wien.

Where the failure to meet a deadline in itself does not constitute a fundamental breach—in other words, when time is not of the essence—the seller's cure within a reasonable time after the due date will normally prevent the delay from constituting a "fundamental breach of contract" such as to permit the buyer to avoid the contract.

Domestic laws that permit the courts or arbitral tribunals to grant a seller in breach extra time to perform are expressly excluded by Article 45(3), both because such grace periods are inappropriate for international trade and because judicial discretion in their application could favor the party at home in the forum. Domestic rules favorable to the buyer, such as additional remedies, are also excluded. A Dutch proposal was rejected which would have excluded domestic remedies, such as avoidance for mistake, when the required notice of defects is not given. However, only one of the opposing votes was based on the belief that, because questions of contract validity are excluded from its sphere of application, the Convention should avoid them. Others approached the question from exactly the opposite direction, namely that domestic law is not applicable at all in these cases. The rejection of the Dutch proposal, therefore, should not be understood to mean that domestic laws permitting a contract to be voided on the basis of lack of conformity or rescinded for mistake are still generally applicable through Article 4(a). If they were, the goal of uniformity in the prerequisites and consequences of breach of contract involving the delivery of non-conforming goods would be greatly endangered.

B.　BUYER'S PERFORMANCE

1.　PAYING THE PRICE

PROBLEM 3–18

Able Co., a Chinese manufacturer of transistors receives an e-mail from Baker Co., a Virginia-based manufacturer of electronic equipment, stating: "We wish to buy 1,000 A7S transistors. How much are they?" Able replies by e-mail: "We can let you have them for U.S. $6 apiece." Baker's e-mail responds: "Good. Done. Be sure to send them by air so that they arrive here by Friday."

(a) If Able fulfills its obligation to deliver, must Baker accept delivery? CISG arts. 53, 60.

(b) What must Baker do to perform its obligation to "pay" for the transistors? CISG arts. 54, 57.

(c) Must Baker pay the air freight?

(d) When must Baker make payment? CISG arts. 58, 59.

* * *

UNILEX CASE

Austria: Oberster Gerichtshof, 1994

Abstract

An Austrian buyer ordered from a German seller a "certain quantity" of medium to good quality Chinchilla furs, at a price ranging from 35 to 65 German Marks apiece. The seller sent 249 furs, 239 of which were sold on by the buyer to an Italian customer. The buyer paid only 2400 Marks to the seller, who then commenced an action to recover the rest of the price due. Both lower Courts decided in favor of the seller; the buyer appealed to the Supreme Court.

The Supreme Court confirmed the lower Court's decisions and granted the seller payment of the sums it asked for. According to the Court, the buyer's proposal constituted an offer which was sufficiently definite as to the quantity of goods and as to their price, since it implicitly made provisions for determining both elements (Art. 14(1) CISG). The Court held that in order to ascertain whether an offer is sufficiently definite, it has to be interpreted according to the understanding of a reasonable person of the same kind as the other party in the same circumstances (Art. 8(2) CISG) and that in determining such understanding all relevant circumstances of the case are to be considered, including negotiations, practices established between the parties, usages and subsequent conduct of the parties (Art. 8(3) CISG).

As to the quantity of goods, the Court held that the request of "a certain quantity" of furs made the offer sufficiently definite in view of the subsequent conduct of the buyer, who immediately sold on almost all the delivered furs without complaints as to their quantity.

As to the price of goods, in the opinion of the Court the offer was sufficiently definite since the parties agreed on a range from 35 to 65 German Marks for medium to good quality furs, which made it possible to price each fur according to its quality. As the price was implicitly determined according to Art. 14 CISG, the Court left open the question whether in the absence of such a determination, reference can be made to the market price of the goods sold (Art. 55 CISG).

Finally, the Court held that in the absence of a contrary agreement between the parties, payment of the price was to be made at the seller's place of business (Art. 57(1)(a) CISG), and not at the place of delivery of the goods. The latter rule applies when payment is to be made against the handing over of the goods or of documents (Arts. 57(1)(b) and 58 CISG), and according to the Court it refers only to the situation where payment must be made to a carrier or a warehouse holder.

UNILEX CASE D. 1995–15.2
Germany: Amtsgericht Alsfeld, 1995

Abstract

A German buyer concluded a contract at a market fair with a standhostess who worked at the stand of an Italian seller of tiles. After the conclusion of the contract the Italian seller sent an invoice to the buyer. The hostess then collected the price for the goods from the buyer, but did not transfer the payment to seller. After the seller's Italian attorney sent a request for payment to the buyer, the seller commenced action against the buyer for payment of price and for recovery of the attorney's fees as damages. The buyer counterclaimed a discount on the price that had been agreed upon with the standhostess after the conclusion of the contract.

As agency is a matter not falling within the scope of CISG, the Court applied German law to determine whether the standhostess had authority to modify the contract terms after the contract had been concluded and consequently denied the buyer the discount on the price.

The Court stated that according to Art. 57(1)(a) and (b) CISG the buyer should have paid the price either at the seller's place of business or at the place where the goods were delivered, neither of which happened. Payment to the standhostess was not a valid payment under CISG. Therefore the buyer was obliged to pay the price to the seller under Art. 53 CISG.

Moreover, the buyer who has engaged a third person for payment bears the risk that the seller does not receive the payment, when the requirements for exemption from liability set forth in Art. 79 CISG are not met, as in the case at hand.

* * *

The seller was not entitled to recover the Italian attorney's fees. By requesting payment through an Italian attorney, the seller violated its duty to mitigate the loss (Art. 77 CISG), as it should have done it through its German attorney who then filed the suit in the German Court.

* * *

PROBLEM 3–19

Your client, Sam Silver, of Houston, Texas, consults you about a contract for the sale of 100,000 electronic calculators that he has just negotiated with a buyer in Argentina, Señor Bolivar. Sam shows you a piece of paper signed by both Señor Bolivar and himself. The paper is labeled "Contract" and contains all the necessary terms for a sales contract, such as price, description, quantity, and quality of the electronic calculators to be delivered. The contract does not state whether the sale is for cash or on credit, but it does have a "price/delivery" clause:

"U.S. $65,000.00—F.O.B. Houston (Incoterms 1990)." Sam asks for your advice on the following matters:

    (a) When is payment due?

    (b) Where must payment be made?

    (c) What form must payment take?

    (d) May Señor Bolivar inspect the calculators before paying?

* * *

PROBLEM 3–20

Charlie, a Maine manufacturer of rollers for pulp mills, agrees to manufacture and sell to Dietrich, a German paper manufacturer, four replacement rollers for use in processing pulp into paper. The delivery term is "CIF (Incoterms 1990) Hamburg" with shipment to be made from New York by July 1.

    (a) When is payment due?

    (b) Where must payment be made?

    (c) What form must payment take?

    (d) May Dietrich inspect the machine before paying?

* * *

PROBLEM 3–21

Good Luck Co, a Chinese manufacturer of electronic equipment, agreed to sell 3,000 TV sets to Bataan Dept. Stores, a Philippine retailer. In its offer to sell, Good Luck stated the price in Chinese currency, 1,000,000 Yuan. In its only response to that offer, Bataan stated the price in the then-equivalent amount of Philippine currency, 5,000,000 pesos. Good Luck expected to be paid in Chinese currency, and Bataan expected to pay in Philippine currency.

Between the date the contract was concluded and the date of delivery, the Philippines experienced an economic and financial crisis. The value of Philippine currency dropped by 80%. Bataan wants to know whether it can pay for the TV sets with 5,000,000 devalued pesos, or whether it must pay 1,000,000 Chinese Yuan, which is worth five times as much. What is your advice, counsellor? CISG art. 53, 54 and 57.

* * *

2. TAKING DELIVERY

Under article 60 of the Convention the buyer is obligated to take delivery of the tendered goods. This obligation extends to doing all acts necessary to make it possible for the seller to perform its obligation to deliver the goods. CISG art. 60(a). These acts will usually be spelled out in the contract itself, but the Convention does not require that the contract do so. As a consequence, article 60 may be evidence of a general principle that the parties must cooperate to fulfill the contract within the meaning of "general principle" in Article 7(2).

The duty to take delivery is related to the buyer's duty to preserve the goods while they are in its control. CISG arts. 86–88. Even if the buyer is entitled to avoid the contract and end its obligations under the contract, the buyer who has received the goods is bound to take steps to protect the seller's interest.

C. EXCUSED PERFORMANCE

J. HONNOLD, UNIFORM LAW FOR INTERNATIONAL SALES UNDER THE 1980 UNITED NATIONS CONVENTION
480–85 (3d ed. 1999).*

D. *The Standard for Exemption for Non-Performance*

Under Art. 79(1), a party who seeks exemption from liability for non-performance must establish (*inter alia*) that the failure to perform "was due to an impediment beyond his control." How high and impenetrable must an "impediment" be to justify non-delivery or non-acceptance? We shall address this question at § 432, *infra*. As background for this issue we now consider (1) The hazards of following diverse domestic law and (2) The possible relevance of contract patterns in international trade.

(1) *Domestic Law: Hazards; Comparative Law.*

Attention has been drawn to the danger that local tribunals may unconsciously read the patterns of their domestic law into the general language of the Convention—an approach that would be inconsistent with the Convention's basic goal of international unification (Art. 7(1)). And deliberate recourse to the exemption rules of a single domestic system would flagrantly violate the Convention. As we have seen, Article 7(2) permits recourse to "the law applicable by virtue of the rules of private international law" only as a last resort—*i.e.*, when questions are "not expressly settled" by the Convention and cannot be "settled in conformity with the general principles on which it is based". The fact that a provision of the Convention presents problems of application does not authorize recourse to some one system of domestic law since this would undermine the Convention's objective "to promote uniformity in its application" (Art. 7(1)). However, no such difficulty arises from a comparative law approach that seeks guidance from the prevailing patterns and trends of modern domestic law.

* * *

But contracts drafted jointly by sellers and buyers may be useful (along with modern patterns of contract law) to help solve problems of

---

* Copyright © 1999 and reproduced by permission from Kluwer Law International.

interpreting and applying the general standards of the Convention. A pattern of contracting that is "widely known to, and regularly observed by, parties to contracts of the type involved in the particular trade concerned" may constitute a usage that the parties have "impliedly made applicable to their contract." (See Art. 9, *supra* at §113.) In addition, contract patterns may be useful to inform a tribunal with respect to the practicability and suitability of competing interpretations of the Convention. Professor Nicholas notes that a crucial element in Article 79(1) is whether the party claiming exemption could "reasonably be expected to have taken the impediment into account at the time of the conclusion of the contract" and that patterns of contracting in similar transactions can bear on the "reasonable expectations" of the parties.

* * *

F. *"Impediment"—How Tough a Barrier?*

As we have seen (§ 427, *supra*), paragraph 1 of Article 79 embodies a decision that exemption from liability for a "failure to perform" should be confined to situations in which an "impediment" *prevents* performance—production or delivery of goods, transfer of funds to pay the price. Paragraph 1 also emphasizes that grounds for excusing failure to perform are strict. Thus, the party seeking exemption must prove that its failure to perform (1) "was due to an impediment *beyond his control*" and that the party (2) "could not reasonably be expected to have *taken the impediment into account*" when the contract was made or (3) "to have *avoided* or *overcome* [the impediment] or its consequences".

The nub of our problem is this: It is not practicable to enumerate the circumstances that will excuse a failure to perform. Instead, words must try to express a dividing point on a continuum between "difficult" and "impossible". Even domestic rules cast in terms of "impossibility" conceal questions of degree. Military blockade and government prohibition provide excuse on the grounds of "impossibility" although it may be possible to run a blockade or evade a law. However, the varying concrete results under diverse formulations of domestic law provide a point of reference. Tallon (*B–B Commentary* 592) on the basis of careful study, suggests that the Convention stands somewhere between the most strict and the most liberal of the domestic systems. See also Nicholas, *Parker Colloq.* (5–4 to 5–6: comparison of domestic approaches; 5–9: emphasis on Article 79(1)'s reference to what the party could "reasonably be expected" to take into account in the light of usages and contract practices in the trade concerned).

In spite of strenuous efforts of legislators and scholars we face the likelihood that Article 79 may be the Convention's least successful part of the half-century of work towards international uniformity This prospect calls for careful, detailed contract drafting to provide solutions to fit the commercial situation at hand. (Examples of standard contract provisions were set forth at § 431.) Those who are not able to solve the problem by contract must await the process of mutual criticism and adjustment by tribunals and scholars in the various jurisdictions. See the current decisions in the following section.

(1) *Economic Difficulties and Dislocations*

The Convention, as we have seen, narrowed the grounds for exemption in ULIS 74 by replacing exemption based on *"circumstances"* with a provision that failure to perform must be "due to an *obstacle*" (§ 423.3, *supra*). In addition to denying exemption for the delivery of defective goods, this change responded to concerns that the reference to "circumstances" could be a basis for excuse merely because performance became more difficult or unprofitable. However, the language of Article 79(1) seems to leave room for exemptions based on economic dislocations that provide an "impediment" to performance comparable to non-economic barriers that excuse failure of performance.

Assume that the supply of a material needed for performance of a contract unexpectedly becomes so reduced in quantity and inflated in price that only a minority of producers that need this material can continue in production. This situation clearly constitutes an "impediment" barring performance by most producers whose contracts overlap the onset of the shortage; requiring production by only one (or a minority) unfairly prejudices some in favor of their competitors. Comparable unfairness can result if extreme and unexpected currency dislocations make it impossible for sellers to continue to produce or for buyers to purchase at the monetary values stated in those contracts that overlap the dislocation.

Extreme price and (especially) currency dislocations may be sufficiently widespread to lead to laws or administrative regulations that require contract readjustment. The Convention (Art. 4(a)) does not interfere with such domestic rules on validity.

In sum, the application of Article 79 to unanticipated economic difficulties should be consistent with the general principles applicable to this provision: (1) Exemption is confined to barriers to performance (e.g., delivery or payment); (2) An "impediment" to performance may result from general economic difficulties and dislocations only if they constitute a barrier to performance that is comparable to other types of exempting causes.

UNILEX CASE D. 1996–3.4
Arbitration Award, 1996

Abstract

A German buyer concluded two separate but substantially identical framework agreements with two Hong Kong companies (the sellers), concerning delivery of goods produced in the People's Republic of China. Further to the agreements the buyer placed several orders on behalf of its customers. Price and time of delivery varied each time, taking into account that the buyer needed the goods at short notice. Payment had to take place within 90 days of delivery but in individual cases the buyer paid in advance or on delivery.

In the course of the business relationship the buyer ordered 10,000 units of product from one of the sellers. The latter asked for advance payment; later on it informed the buyer that its own Chinese supplier was undergoing serious financial and personal difficulties, and refused to deliver the goods unless the buyer paid all outstanding debts. The buyer refused. The seller brought an action before the Arbitral Court. The buyer declared the sales contract avoided and asked for damages deriving from breach of the individual sales contract in dispute and breach of the framework agreement.

As far as the individual sales contract was concerned, the Court held that it was governed by CISG because by agreeing on a German Arbitral Court the parties had implicitly chosen the law of a contracting State (German law) as the law governing the contract (Art. 1(1)(b) CISG).

In the opinion of the Court, the buyer was entitled to avoid the sales contract pursuant to Arts. 49(1)(b) and 47(1) CISG, because the seller refused to deliver without receiving payment for all outstanding debts deriving from past deliveries to the buyer. Such a request was inconsistent with a term in the sales contract providing for advance cash payment by the buyer, which by its nature implied that delivery should not be conditioned on payment of any amount due under previous contracts (Art. 8 CISG).

Even after declaring the contract avoided according to Art. 49(2) CISG the buyer was not deprived of the right to claim damages (Art. 45(2) CISG and 74 CISG). The Court awarded the buyer damages for non-performance including lost profits for the contracts already concluded by the buyer, which were considered to be foreseeable losses.

Moreover, the seller was not exempted for non-performance under Art. 79 CISG. According to Art. 79 CISG a party is not liable for a failure to perform its obligation if it proves that the failure was due to an impediment beyond its control and that it could not reasonably be expected to have taken it into account. As a rule, difficulties in delivery due to the seller's financial problems, or to financial problems of the seller's supplier (even when connected to the act of public authority in the supplier's country) are not to be considered an impediment beyond the seller's control but belong to the seller's area of risk.

UNILEX CASE D. 1995–34
I.C.C. Arbitration Award, 1995.

Abstract

In order to perform a contract with a third party, a Swiss buyer entered into a contract with an Austrian seller for the supply of chemical fertilizer. The seller in turn applied to an Ukrainian supplier to obtain part of the fertilizer. The buyer sent to the Ukrainian supplier the packaging to be used for delivery (sacks manufactured by the buyer under the seller's instructions). As the sacks sent by the buyer did not conform to the technical rules of the Ukrainian chemical industry, the supplier could not make use of them. Consequently, the goods were not delivered within the period of time fixed in the contract. The buyer asked the seller in writing when the goods would be delivered, expressly adding that, in the absence of a clear commitment by the seller, it would avoid the contract with respect to the part of the goods not yet delivered. Since the seller's reply was generic, the buyer had to make a substitute purchase at a higher price in order to be able to perform the contract already concluded with the third party. The buyer commenced arbitral proceedings demanding damages, including the cost of the sacks it had supplied as well as the loss deriving from the substitute purchase. The buyer also asked for interest, at the London International Bank Offered Rate (LIBOR) plus 2%.

The Arbitral Tribunal found that the seller had fundamentally breached the contract (Art. 25 CISG) as it had breached its duty to give the buyer the necessary instructions for the correct manufacture of the packaging.

Moreover, the seller was not exempted from performance pursuant to Art. 79 CISG, since the seller is responsible for non delivery caused by its supplier, as part of the seller's risk (Art. 79(2) CISG).

The Arbitral Tribunal furthermore held that though late delivery does not usually amount to a fundamental breach and entitles to avoid the contract only after the additional time fixed by the buyer has expired without performance by the seller (Art. 47(1) CISG), a relevant delay may constitute fundamental breach if it appears from the circumstances that the date of delivery is of particular significance to the buyer, and that the seller has knowledge thereof. In the case at hand the seller knew that the goods were to be delivered by the buyer to a third party and that, in case of late delivery, the buyer had to pay a contractual penalty as well as additional costs incurred by a substitute purchase of the goods.

The buyer was entitled to partial avoidance of the contract pursuant to Arts. 51(1) and Art. 73 CISG, being a contract for delivery of goods by instalments. As the buyer had sent a letter to the seller expressly saying that, in the absence of a clear commitment by the seller, the contract would be partially avoided, the Arbitral Tribunal considered the contract avoided even in the absence of an express subsequent declaration. Indeed, parties' declarations should be interpreted in conformity with what a reasonable person would have understood in the same circumstances: in the case at hand, it was reasonable to consider the contract avoided at the moment in which the conditions mentioned by the buyer came about.

According to Arts 49(1)(a), 74 and 75 CISG, the buyer was entitled to recover damages, including both the costs for the sacks it had supplied and the costs of the substitute purchase.

As far as the substitute purchase was concerned, the Tribunal held that the transaction concluded by the buyer was reasonable as required by Art. 75 CISG. According to the Tribunal, a transaction should be considered reasonable if the buyer acted as a prudent and careful businessman and the first condition for that is that the goods bought in replacement are of the same kind and quality as the undelivered ones. Small differences in the quality of the goods are of no importance. The price of the purchase should also be considered reasonable, as the short period in which the buyer had to buy the fertilizer in replacement in order to deliver it in time to the third party justified a higher price than the one that could have been obtained if the buyer had more time to negotiate.

* * *

PROBLEM 3–23

François Fermier is a French farmer and vintner who bottles his own wine under the label "François' Fizzy." François uses his own grapes and those of his friends and neighbors to produce François' Fizzy. François agreed to sell 1,000 bottles of François' Fizzy to Bowery Boutique, a New York restaurant and retailer. The contract was concluded on May 1, and the delivery date was one year later. The delivery term was DDP (Delivered Duty Paid)(Incoterms 1990), so François was responsible for U.S. import taxes.

Immediately after the contract was concluded, a terrible storm hit François' part of France. His entire crop of grapes was ruined, as was those of his friends and neighbors. However, for some strange reason, the grapes of his neighbors who were not friends remained unharmed.

In November of that year, a trade dispute between the U.S. and the EU culminated in the U.S. placing additional tariffs of 100% on many European products, including French wine.

On November 3, François notified Bowery that the May storm was "an impediment" under CISG art. 79 which would prevent the production of any François' Fizzy that year, and so none would be delivered to Bowery next May. Bowery is suspicious of the timing of this notice. Please advise it whether François' performance is, in fact, excused in this transaction. CISG art. 79.

J. HONNOLD, UNIFORM LAW FOR INTERNATIONAL SALES UNDER THE 1980 UNITED NATIONS CONVENTION
486–87 (3d ed. 1999).*

G.   *Performance Delegated to Third Party.*

Paragraph (2) [of art. 79] addresses cases where a party delegates performance to a third party who fails to perform.

Example 79A. Seller contracted to sell Buyer a machine to be built in accordance with specifications supplied by Buyer. Seller contracted with Electron to manufacture the machine. Electron had a good reputation for efficiency and responsibility but, in this case, mismanaged production so that it was unable to deliver the machine. At the time of Electron's default, Seller could not obtain the machine from another supplier and was unable to deliver the machine to Buyer.

Under the general rule in paragraph (1), Seller might be able to contend that Electron's failure constituted an "impediment beyond [Seller's] control," and that Seller would therefore be exempt from liability to Buyer. Paragraph (2) restricts exemption in situations like this in which a party (*e.g.* Seller) has engaged a third person (Electron) "to perform the whole or a part of the contract". The crucial question is posed by paragraph (2)(b): Would the third person (Electron) be exempt from liability to Seller under the rules of paragraph (1)? Here the answer is No. Consequently, Seller cannot be exempt from liability to Buyer. The net effect is that if Seller's default forces it to pay damages to Buyer, Seller must look to Electron for reimbursement. (Under modern procedural systems, if Buyer sues Seller, Seller would bring in Electron as a third-party defendant.)

On the other hand, assume that Seller's contract with Electron called for Electron to produce the machine at a specified manufacturing plant, and that, before the date for delivery to Buyer, Electron's plant was destroyed by flood or some other impediment that met the standards of Paragraph (1). Since Electron would be exempt from liability to Seller the barrier to exemption in Paragraph (2)(a) would not apply; Seller could be exempt from liability to Buyer under paragraph (1).

Problems comparable to those posed by Example 79A could also arise if the seller is obliged to deliver the goods to the buyer (as under a quotation *ex ship* Buyer's port) and thus is responsible for transit damage to the goods. If the goods are damaged in transit because of ordinary circumstances (water seepage, improper stowage, or the like), the seller would not only be responsible for the physical damage but also could be liable to the buyer for damages such as production interruption. On the other hand, if the goods were lost or seriously damaged as a result of a hurricane, embargo or similar impediment, the seller would bear the loss from physical damage (subject to insurance) but could be exempt from liability for damages to the buyer that resulted from (*e.g.*) interruption of production.

RAUH, LEGAL CONSEQUENCES OF FORCE MAJEURE UNDER GERMAN, SWISS, ENGLISH AND UNITED STATES LAW

25 Denv. J. Int'l L. & Pol'y 151, 151–64 (1996).*

I. INTRODUCTION

Long-term contracts, whether for the turnkey construction of a plant, the construction of works or installations, or for the periodic supply of goods, frequently face the problem that the economic, political and/or natural surroundings change far more than the parties contemplated or expected when they signed the contract. This is especially true for long-term construction contracts where a European or North-American contractor agrees to perform construction work in a third world country. Here, subsequent events which render the performance of the contractor's obligation radically different from what was originally contemplated occur much more often than in a domestic contract. The possible risks in the performance of such a long-term contract are so numerous that they cannot reasonably be considered when the contract is signed.

In view of these imponderable risks, the parties often agree to add a Force Majeure Clause. These clauses are worded much like the following:

In the Contract "force majeure" shall mean any occurrence outside the control of the parties preventing or delaying their performance of the contract.

Force majeure shall mean extraordinary events independent of the Parties' will that cannot be foreseen or averted by them even with due diligence, being beyond their control and preventing the Contracting Party/or Parties/ from fulfilling the obligation(s) undertaken in this Contract.

The expression "force majeure" shall mean circumstances which were beyond the control of the party concerned exercising the standard care of a reasonable and prudent operator.

Most clauses of this type require four essential criteria for an event to qualify as Force Majeure:

1) the event must be external;

2) it must render the performance radically different from that originally contemplated;

3) it must have been unforeseeable (objective standard) or at least unforeseen (subjective standard); and

4) its occurrence must be beyond the control of the party concerned.

These criteria are also required by the definition of Force Majeure under most national legal systems. In this respect the term Force Majeure is described as "Wegfall der Geschaftsgrundlage" (destruction of the basis of the contract—Germany and Switzerland), "frustration" (England) and "impracticability" (United States).

Parties often, however, pay less attention to Force Majeure clauses. These clauses are generally included under "Miscellaneous" and their wording as well as their structure is not as detailed and accurate as they should be. Quite frequently, the contractual Force Majeure Clause broadly articulates the definition of a Force Majeure event without delineating the legal consequences to follow the occurrence of a Force Majeure event. To remedy this omission, the parties would have to insert detailed and lengthy provisions dealing with the effect of a Force Majeure event on the contractual duties already and still to be performed, provisions responding to questions such as: on what basis is work already performed to be calculated if such work is of no further use for the employer? can the contractor claim compensation for investments already made but not yet visible for the employer? etc. Instead of dealing with these complicated questions, the parties hope that a Force Majeure event will not happen and leave the determination of its effects to the applicable law—to the principles developed in each of the jurisdictions with respect to Wegfall der Geschaftsgrundlage, frustration or impracticability.

This note will examine the effects of Force Majeure clauses under German, Swiss, English and American law, and how these effects greatly differ. [Author's Note: The references to Swiss and English law have been edited out.] The legal consequences of a recognized Force Majeure vary from a judicial adjustment for the altered circumstances to a division of loss to annulment of the contract.

II. PRESERVATION OF THE CONTRACT UNDER MODIFIED CONDITIONS

A. Alteration of the Contract by the Court

1. Germany

Under German law, not every destruction of the basis of the transaction results in per se legal consequences. The principle of pacta sunt servanda may only be breached if it is in general unreasonable to expect the obligor to fulfill the contract. In Machine Games, the Federal Supreme Court stated that the destruction of the basis of the transaction only has legal consequences where called for given the totality of circumstances and where necessary in order to avoid results which are intolerable and in general incompatible with law and justice. Consequently, "unreasonableness" has a double function: in addition to determining whether the basis of the transaction has been destroyed, it serves to determine the legal consequences.

If the relationship between the parties largely breaks down, then a modification of the contract for the changed circumstances is to be considered first. The primacy of adjustment follows from the principle of pacta sunt servanda, since an adjustment encroaches less severely on the contract. In this respect, the contractual relationship as such is maintained. Modifying the contract to the changed circumstances should ensure that continuing the contract is reasonable for both parties. Contract modification, because of its flexibility, is particularly suited to taking individual circumstances into account, and every possible restructuring of the contract can, in principle, be achieved. The following types are possible:

• comprehensive reform of the contractual relationship, which can go so far as to replace the original obligation with a completely new one.

• partial restructuring of the contractual relationship

• partial preservation of the contract

• alteration of the contractual obligation

• increase in the amount payable

• grant of additional equalization claim

• reduction of the contractual performance

• postponement of performance

* * *

[3] b.   Uniform Commercial Code § 2–615

Uniform Commercial Code § 2–615 does not make any express provision for the legal effects; it is evident from Comment 6 that this provision however does not exclude the possibility of adjustment:

In situations in which neither sense nor justice is served by either answer when the issue is posed in flat terms of excuse or no excuse, adjustment under the various provisions of this Article is necessary, especially the sections on good faith, on insecurity and assurance and on the reading of all provisions in the light of their purposes, and the general policy of this Act to use equitable principles in furtherance of commercial standards and good faith.

All the same, the overwhelming majority of decisions continue to proceed on the assumption that there are generally the two alternatives of preservation and annulment.

The first case in which the contract was adjusted was the ALCOA case. ALCOA had entered into a long-term supply contract for the conversion of minerals into aluminum (toll conversion service contract). The contract contained a price adjustment clause, whereby the parties chose the wholesale price index for industrial goods as an objective measure for the alteration of non-operation related production costs.

However, when OPEC began to raise the price of crude oil in 1973 and, in addition, unexpected environmental protection measures greatly increased ALCOA's electricity costs, the rate of increase of the non-operation related production costs considerably exceeded the rate of increase of the index.

* * *

After the court affirmed the existence of Force Majeure, it refused to terminate the contract since this would give the plaintiff's business an unexpected profit, because ALCOA could only conclude a contract on increased present prices. The court further stated that the completion of a long-term contract required a careful examination of the circumstances of the contract, the intent of the parties and the supervening event.

The court, no doubt impressed by the huge sum involved, admitted that in certain cases terminating the contract was the only appropriate option. The court further stated that if the defendant wished to secure a long-term supply of aluminum at a price which still allowed it to make a profit and if the plaintiff had a continuing interest in the contract based on its desire for the full use of its production capacities, then both parties had the same interest in a long-term relationship. The court held that an adjustment was the suitable legal remedy since it came closest to the intentions and expectations of the parties and avoided inequities.

On the basis of its superior expert knowledge the court even considered itself more able than the parties themselves to adjust the contract. The court declared that it possessed "information from hindsight far superior to that which the parties had when they made their contract." After considering the original contract and the expectations of the parties, the court drafted the following price clause:

For the duration of the contract the price for each pound of aluminum converted by ALCOA shall be the lesser of the current Price A or Price B indicated below. Price A shall be the contract ceiling price computed periodically as specified in the contract. Price B shall be the greater of the current Price B1 or B2. Price B1 shall be the price specified in the contract, computed according to the terms of the contract. Price B2 shall be that price which yields ALCOA a profit of one cent per pound of aluminum converted.

In addition, the court fixed the invoice arrangements and rules for mutual provisions of information (in part for up to two years after expiration of the contract).

* * *

B. Allocation of Loss

1. Germany

In some German cases a division of the loss comes into question as a legal consequence of the disappearance of the basis of the transaction. The assumption underlying the basic principle of determination of loss is that the loss resulting from the contractual breakdown is to be appropriately fixed and allocated between the parties with consideration given to the interests of both parties, their economic circumstances and the originally expected profits.

In a case which occurred under the equalization of burdens legislation, a seller who had sold a war-damaged piece of land with a house for the price of DM 8,000. demanded compensation from the purchaser in the amount of DM 10,000, which was granted to him by the competent equalization of burdens authority for the property. The Federal Supreme Court held that an equal division of the respective advantages and disadvantages between the two contracting partners was appropriate. The court granted the plaintiff DM 5,000 because the grant of such a claim for equalization would always be possible when the continued enforcement of the contract would lead to a result which was intolerable and no longer compatible with law and equity. An equal allocation of the loss is, by no means, a rigid principle; rather, all the circumstances of the case must be considered and valued to achieve an equitable and just equalization. This includes considering whether or not one of the parties has accepted a greater risk. Consequently, every possibility of allocation is open to the court.

2. Anglo-American law

Due to the general reluctance of Anglo-American courts to adjust the contract, it is not surprising that in only one case has the court allocated the loss. ***

C. Pro-rata Performance

Where a seller has concluded several contracts for the delivery of specific goods and the supply of those goods subsequently becomes restricted, the restriction frustrates the seller's ability to fulfil all his obligations to supply. The question then becomes how to distribute the remaining goods.

1.   United States of America

Both the Common Law and the Uniform Commercial Code § 2–615 provide for the allocation of available goods instead of dissolving one contract because of impracticability and declaring the other contracts capable of being fully performed. There is, however, no fixed allocation standard, so that the seller has some room for discretion in the distribution.

* * *

2.   Germany

German law also allows a pro-rata performance in cases where the basis of the transaction is destroyed. When the seller of specific restricted goods encounters difficulties in obtaining these goods without any fault on his part, and when these difficulties constitute an unreasonable demand on him such that he can no longer comply with his obligations, then he may reduce the supply to his customers proportionately. At the same time, he is exempted from claims for damages under § 242 of the German Civil Code.

In the Sugarbeet Seeds case, the Supreme Court of the German Reich permitted a seller, who had sold a specific amount of sugar-beet seeds for several years in advance, to allocate the seeds proportionately amongst all purchasers when events of nature reduced the harvest so that there were no longer sufficient supplies. The Federal Supreme Court said that in these cases, the seller's obligees represent a group of equally entitled persons who find themselves in a group with a common interest. The court added that it would be against the principles of good faith if one purchaser received more at the expense of the others. Since the court stressed that the claimants enjoyed equal contractual rights and belonged to a group entitled to raise the claim, only those claimants who have concluded a contract with the obligor, and not his regular customers, will benefit from the pro-rata allocation.

* * *

III.   ANNULMENT OF THE CONTRACT

Whereas a termination of all contractual duties is seen as the last option in both German and Swiss law, this is the primary remedy in Anglo-American law. Accordingly, the requirements for an annulment of the contract are different.

* * *

A.   Requirements for Contract Annulment

1.   Anglo–American law

Both English and American law, in the event of significant frustration, only annul the contract at the time of frustration: "[f]rustration brings the contract to an end forthwith, without more and automatically." The rationale for this is that the resulting contractual certainty should make cases of frustration predictable.

2.   Germany

In German law, contract annulment replaces contract adjustment where the adjustment alone is insufficient to avoid a result incompatible with the principle of good faith and where this aim can only be achieved by discharging the aggrieved party from the contract. This occurs when the adjustment of the transaction leads to an obligation on one or both parties which can no longer be justified.

In the Vigogne spinning case, one partner in a commercial partnership had entered into an obligation in favor of a third party in a preliminary contract, whereby, after the termination of the partnership agreement and in the course of the distribution of the partnership assets he would purchase a certain piece of property and sell it to the third party at a fixed price. During the distribution of the partnership assets inflation forced the partner to pay a much higher price than that fixed in the preliminary contract. On this basis, he refused to perform because the high rate of inflation had frustrated the fulfillment of the contract.

The Supreme Court examined whether or not the contract could be preserved with altered conditions. The Court said that the obligor could only be discharged from his obligations if further performance of the contract would significantly contravene the principle of good faith and continue to bind the obligor either because the factual situation would not permit an adjustment or because the obligee refused to consent to an adjustment.

C. DADOMO AND S. FARRAN, FRENCH SUBSTANTIVE LAW
42–46 (1997).*

Article 1148 C. *Civ.* expressly provides for the possibility of *force majeure*—or *cas fortuit*. *Force majeure* refers to circumstances beyond the contracting parties' control or power to prevent, which render performance of the contract impossible. It consists of three characteristics: (1) irresistibility; (2) unforeseeability; and (3) externality.

Irresistibility is understood to mean a force which is superior to that of man, making the execution of the contractual obligation totally impossible. This does not mean that only events which are natural phenomena will be considered: man-made occurrences are also relevant. The essence of the irresistibility lies in the contracting party's inability to do anything about the turn of events. This applies both to the events themselves and their consequences. This aspect is judged in an abstract sense, the judge's task being to consider whether any person placed in the same situation as the contracting party would have been similarly unable to overcome the obstacles presented.

Mere difficulty in meeting the obligations will not suffice, unless those difficulties are not only serious but insurmountable. Similarly, the fact that the burden of executing the contract has become more onerous than was originally foreseen does not qualify as *force majeure.* * * *

Unforeseeability means that the event must have been absolutely fortuitous. If it could have been foreseen, or even suspected, and the individual could have adopted measures to avoid or prevent the problem, then this aspect will not be met. A recurrent problem which has arisen in this context is the issue of strikes. During the 1960s the courts adopted a very restrictive approach and refused to allow that strikes could amount to *force majeure.* This approach has been modified following decisions of the *Chambre Mixte* of the Court of Cassation, in 1983, so that now it will depend on the circumstances. This aspect is judged objectively from the perspective of the reasonable man—*in abstracto*—but some reference may have to be made to the actual facts of the case—*in concreto.* The relevant moment at which this characteristic must be appreciated appears to be the moment at which the contract is concluded, rather than when it is entered into. However, the issue may also be relevant in the case of ongoing contracts—for example the supply of utilities such as electricity.

The externality of the event means that it must have come about through no action—direct or indirect—of the contracting parties. It must be not only outside the circumstances of the particular contract but also outside the parties' sphere of activity. Therefore, defects in products or vehicles used to carry out obligations cannot amount to *force majeure*, nor can the actions of employees, the poor construction of buildings, or the interruption of production processes due to liquidation of assets. Similarly, the intervention of administration authorities in the carrying out of a business—for example because a trader is acting outside the terms of his licence—will not amount to *force majeure* even though they are external to the contracting party.

These three elements should be read together, so that it may be the case that the circumstances make the performance of the obligation absolutely impossible, even though they are not strictly external to the contracting parties' activity. To insist on each element being established separately could lead to inequitable results—an example is where the long-term illness of an employee prevents his return to work, or a sudden strike stops a business from operating. Indeed at one stage the case law tended to merge the two aspects of *irrésistibilité* with *impossibilité*, on the grounds that if an event could be foreseen it would be possible to take steps to avoid it.

The doctrine is strictly interpreted in French law, and the circumstances must be such that performance of the contract is absolutely impossible in both a legal and physical sense. This will be a question of fact, so the matter rarely comes before the Court of Cassation. This concept includes both natural occurrences and human conduct. In neither case will all eventualities be regarded as *force majeure*. In the former, for example, avalanches, sudden violent thunderstorms or fallen trees may be recognised provided these are not normal or foreseeable occurrences in the circumstances. In the latter, the disruption caused by demonstrators to the transport of goods may amount to *force majeure*, but changes in public taste, or the introduction of new products on the market, or the intervention of administrative officials will not. *Force majeure* only applies to impossibility, it does not apply where there is a fundamental alteration in the nature of the obligation. The relevant impossibility is measured by referring to the express provisions of the specific contracts and considerations of reasonableness. Thus, impossibility may include economic and practical considerations.

* * *

The general consequences of *force majeure* are twofold: first, and most importantly, the debtor is released from the claims of the creditor. He is therefore liberated or exonerate absolutely from any obligation. The only exception to this may be where the impossibility is only temporary and execution of the obligation is possible after a reasonable delay. * * * Where *force majeure* is established, then no damages are recoverable for the non-performance of the contract. If only part of the contract is rendered impossible, then the rest of the contract must be carried out. If the circumstances giving rise to the *force majeure* are deemed to be only temporary, then the contract may simply be suspended.

Secondly, and less often, *force majeure* has the effect of safeguarding a party in the case of delay or proof. For example, the case law recognises that if a debtor or an owner of property is prevented from exercising his rights because of *force majeure*, the operation of any time-limits in exercising such rights will be suspended. In the case of proof, for example of title to land, Article 1384 C. *Civ.* dispenses with the need for written proof from a party who has lost his paper documents of title as a result of *force majeure.*

PERILLO, UNIDROIT PRINCIPLES OF INTERNATIONAL COMMERCIAL CONTRACTS: THE BLACK LETTER TEXT AND A REVIEW
63 Fordham L. Rev. 281, 291–92 (1994).*

VI. VALIDITY

While CISG states that it is not concerned with the validity of contracts, chapter 3 of Principles is entitled "Validity." It, however, disclaims any coverage of capacity of parties, authority of agents, or public policy. These are left to domestic law. It expressly provides, however, that neither consideration nor causa are required for the valid formation of a contract.

A. Existing Impossibility

It has been the rule in some civil law systems and a sometime dictum in common law cases and literature that if an agreement is impossible to perform at the outset, and this fact is unknown to both parties, the agreement is void. These statements are usually made in a context where goods have perished or never existed. This rule is discarded along with another obsolete rule that one cannot contract to sell that which one does not own—a rule that had made short-selling impossible.

* * *

X. FORCE MAJEURE AND HARDSHIP

The modern common law has developed the concepts of impossibility and impracticability. The dichotomy in Principles between force majeure and hardship does not replicate the common law division; rather, it is based on civil law notions. The obtaining or denial of licenses and permits is singled out for separate treatment.

* * *

The provisions on "Hardship" contained in the chapter called "Performance" should be compared with the provision on "Force Majeure," contained in the chapter on "Non-Performance." The rule of force majeure is draconian and unforgiving. Under the rule, nothing short of total impossibility will excuse non-performance or partial non-performance. Impracticability will not suffice as an excuse. Rather, impracticability as well as hardship far short of impracticability must be tested under the "Hardship" articles.

Hardship alone never forgives non-performance. It instead compels renegotiation and authorizes courts to "adapt" (reform) the contract to take the hardship into account. "[A]n alteration amounting to 50% or more of the cost or the value of the performance is likely to amount to a 'fundamental' alteration" justifying invocation of the doctrine. One illustration involves a ten-year contract for the sale of uranium at fixed prices in United States dollars payable in New York. The currency in the buyer's country declines to one percent of its value against the value that it had at the time of contracting. The buyer cannot invoke force majeure. Similarly, if the price is increased ten-fold because some Texans have almost cornered the market, force majeure is not present. Nonetheless, the buyer may have redress under the hardship provisions. Renegotiation is compelled if "the equilibrium of the contract" is "fundamentally altered" by events that occur or become known after contracting, the events could not reasonably be taken into account, the events are not within the party's control and the risk was not assumed. Consequently, in the two illustrations just described a prima facie claim of hardship is made out.

Compelled renegotiation and judicial reformation of the bargain are not in the mainstream of the common law. One case of reformation and one case of compelled renegotiation have been the raw materials for serious scholarly urging of more of the same. In a well-argued article, Professor Speidel has concluded that when a long-term supply contract is disrupted by changed conditions, "[a]t a minimum, the advantaged party should have a legal duty to negotiate in good faith. At a maximum, he should have a legal duty to accept an 'equitable' adjustment proposed in good faith by the disadvantaged party." His conclusion approximates the law in countries such as Argentina, Germany and Italy, and the provisions of Principles.

Professor Spiedel's solution does not receive a great deal of support from American case law or scholarly literature. One reason for the difference between the common law and the modern civil law approach is that the leading common law countries have not suffered from the unmanageable inflation that has ravaged much of the civil law world. However, American law should realize that international trade is different from domestic trade and the modern civil law solution formulated in Principles deserves support in international trade disputes. One reason is that sophisticated international trade agreements of long duration typically contain a renegotiation or other adaptation clause that provides flexibility to the relationship—so typical as to perhaps rise to the strength of a usage. The absence of such a clause may reflect that such a clause has been rejected by one or both parties, but is more likely to have been overlooked by unsophisticated parties or deliberately omitted by a sophisticated drafter. In the last two cases, the court should consider the contracts as having an omitted term and fill the gap with the help of *Principles*.

* * *

APPENDIX

UNIDROIT PRINCIPLES OF INTERNATIONAL
COMMERCIAL CONTRACTS

* * *

Section 2: Hardship

Article 6.2.1   (Contract to be observed)

Where the performance of a contract becomes more onerous for one of the parties, that party is nevertheless bound to perform its obligations subject to the following provisions on hardship.

Article 6.2.2   (Definition of hardship)

There is hardship where the occurrence of events fundamentally alters the equilibrium of the contract either because the cost of a party's performance has increased or because the value of the performance a party receives has diminished, and

(a) the events occur or become known to the disadvantaged party after the conclusion of the contract;

(b) the events could not reasonably have been taken into account by the disadvantaged party at the time of the conclusion of the contract;

(c) the events are beyond the control of the disadvantaged party; and

(d) the risk of the events was not assumed by the disadvantaged party.

Article 6.2.3   (Effects of hardship)

(1) In case of hardship the disadvantaged party is entitled to request renegotiations. The request shall be made without undue delay and shall indicate the grounds on which it is based.

(2) The request for renegotiation does not in itself entitle the disadvantaged party to withhold performance.

(3) Upon failure to reach agreement within a reasonable time either party may resort to the court.

(4) If the court finds hardship it may, if reasonable,

(a) terminate the contract at a date and on terms to be fixed; or

(b) adapt the contract with a view to restoring its equilibrium.

* * *

Article 7.1.7 (Force majeure)

(1) Non-performance by a party is excused if that party proves that the non-performance was due to an impediment beyond its control and that it could not reasonably be expected to have taken the impediment into account at the time of the conclusion of the contract or to have avoided or overcome it or its consequences.

(2) When the impediment is only temporary, the excuse shall have effect for such period as is reasonable having regard to the effect of the impediment on the performance of the contract.

(3) The party who fails to perform must give notice to the other party of the impediment and its effect on its ability to perform. If the notice is not received by the other party within a reasonable time after the party who fails to perform knew or ought to have known of the impediment, it is liable for damages resulting from such non-receipt.

(4) Nothing in this article prevents a party from exercising a right to terminate the contract or to withhold performance or request interest on money due.

Chapter 4

NON–JUDICIAL REMEDIES

If performance of the contract does not go as planned—the seller, for example, delivers nonconforming goods or the buyer fails to pay for the goods delivered—the "aggrieved" party will consider how to respond. Often, of course, the seller and buyer will work out their differences informally without the need for a lawyer. The seller might agree to reduce the contract price, or the buyer might agree that in future contacts it will pay by letter of credit. Informal adjustment is all the more likely if the parties have traded with each other before and hope to do so in the future. Sometimes the seller and buyer will have agreed that future disputes will be submitted to arbitration or mediation and in some trades there will be well-recognized arbitration procedures. In some cases the parties may have agreed on a liquidated damage clause or otherwise tailored the remedies to conform with the risks undertaken. Sometimes a party may conclude that the costs of working something out are too great and merely chalk up the contract losses to experience.

All of which is not to say that legal remedies are irrelevant. Even when the seller and buyer adjust their differences informally the strength of their bargaining position will reflect in part the relevant legal remedies available.

These legal remedies fall under three headings: (1) the right to call off the contract, (2) the right to specific performance, and (3) the right to recover damages in substitution of the promised performance. Consider, for example, the case of a seller who fails to deliver goods as promised. The buyer may wish to cancel the contract and look elsewhere for a more reliable seller. On the other hand, the buyer may really want the seller's goods because, for example, they are not readily available from other suppliers. The buyer may then seek a court's assistance in obtaining the promised goods. In either case, the buyer may also ask to recover money compensation for losses suffered in connection with the cancellation or enforced performance.

Both the U.N. Sales Convention and the Uniform Commercial Code include remedies that conform to these three alternatives. As a lawyer trained in the Common Law you will discover, however, differences in emphasis—at least on paper. The Convention, for example, appears to make it both easier to obtain the remedy of specific performance and more difficult to cancel the contract for breach by the other party. On the other hand, the damage formulas in the Convention and the Code are similar: both laws compensate a non-breaching party in the amount of the foreseeable loss of that party's expected gains, together with incidental and consequential damages.

To find the Sales Convention's remedy provisions you must look in three places. First, you will find remedy provisions immediately following the statement of the seller's and the buyer's performance obligations. CISG arts. 45–52 (buyer's remedies) and 61–65 (seller's remedies). These provisions are deliberately drafted in parallel so that one interpretative technique you should keep in mind as you read these articles is to construe the text of a buyer's remedy provision in the light of the parallel text of the seller's remedy provision. Second, you will find remedy provisions common to both seller and buyer at the end of Part III of the Convention. CISG arts. 71–88. You will refer most often to the general damage formulas, but you will also find provisions on anticipatory breach and installment contracts. Finally, several general concepts relevant to the Convention's remedy provisions are set out at the beginning of Part III. CISG arts. 25–26, 28. The most important of these key concepts is that of *fundamental breach*, a concept that reappears in several of the more specific remedy provisions.

When reading these Convention provisions you should remember that the seller and buyer may derogate from them or vary their effect, subject only to rules on validity found not in the Convention but in national law. CISG arts. 4(a), 6. Whether parties may agree, in other words, to a particular liquidated damage clause that would bypass the Convention will ultimately be tested by the rules on the validity of such clauses under the applicable national law. In this respect the remedy provisions are no different from any of the other provisions of the Convention.

FLECHTNER, REMEDIES UNDER THE NEW INTERNATIONAL SALES CONVENTION: THE PERSPECTIVE FROM ARTICLE 2 OF THE UCC
8 J. Law & Com. 53, 54–71 (1988).*

Article 2 of the U.C.C. contains two alternative remedial schemes. In one, the exchange contemplated by the contract of sale is completed despite a breach by one of the parties. The goods end up with the buyer and the seller receives the price, either because the breaching party voluntarily (although defectively) performs or because a court orders the breaching party to perform. Many damages compensate the aggrieved party for ways in which the completed exchange falls short of that contemplated.

In the other Article 2 scheme the exchange is not completed. The buyer does not end up with seller's goods and the seller has no right to the price from the buyer. Instead, the parties' obligation to complete the contemplated exchange is "cancelled." An aggrieved party can thus escape a bad bargain. If the exchange would have been favorable, the non-breaching party can recover a monetary equivalent in the form of damages measured by the difference between the contract price and either the cost of a substitute transaction (cover/resale damages) or the market price of the goods.

The Article 2 concept that usually dictates which of these two remedial schemes will apply is "acceptance." If a buyer receives and continues to "accept" the goods, the exchange will normally be completed despite a breach. Thus, except in rare circumstances, a buyer can retain accepted goods and a seller is entitled to the price for accepted goods. If the seller has breached, an accepting buyer can recover compensation for resulting loss—damages measured by, for instance, the difference in value between conforming goods and non-conforming goods which were actually delivered plus incidental and consequential damages. If an accepting buyer has breached, the seller's usual remedy is an action for the price plus incidental damages.

Alternatively, if the goods do not continue to be accepted—that is, if the seller has (rightfully or wrongfully) not delivered or the buyer has (rightfully or wrongfully) rejected or revoked acceptance of delivered goods—the basic exchange will normally not be completed. Thus if the buyer has not received and retained the goods, the non-breaching party can require literal performance by the other side only in those rare cases where an aggrieved buyer can obtain specific performance or replevin, or where an aggrieved seller can recover the price because the goods cannot be resold or have suffered casualty after risk of loss passed to the buyer. Where the goods do not continue to be accepted, therefore, the aggrieved party can escape an unfavorable bargain but normally must look to resale/cover damages or market price differential damages as compensation for a lost favorable exchange.

The Convention contains two alternative remedial schemes that correspond, in broad outline, to those in U.C.C. Article 2. The most important difference between the remedy systems of CISG and Article 2 is the sorting or channeling mechanism that dictates which of the alternative schemes will apply. Under the Convention, avoidance (or nonavoidance) of the contract performs the function that acceptance (or nonacceptance) of the goods performs under Article 2. Avoidance is the process through which an aggrieved party, by notice to the other side, terminates the contractual obligations of the parties. If the contract is not avoided, the Convention contemplates that the basic exchange of goods and price will be completed despite a breach, with damages or other remedies to compensate for defects in the exchange. If the contract is avoided, the contemplated exchange either will not occur or will be undone, triggering remedial provisions very similar to the Article 2 remedies that apply when goods are not accepted or acceptance is revoked. Thus a party who avoids a contract governed by the Convention can escape a bad bargain or look to resale/cover or market price differential damages to compensate for a lost favorable exchange.

The key to the Convention's rules regarding avoidance is "fundamental breach." If the other side has committed a fundamental breach, the aggrieved party can avoid the contract. Subject to one exception, if the other side has not committed a fundamental breach, the aggrieved party cannot avoid the contract. The Convention defines "fundamental breach" in terms of the materiality and foreseeability of its consequences—that is, a breach is "fundamental if it results in such detriment to the other party as substantially to deprive him of what he is entitled to except under the contract," provided this result is foreseeable.

For those schooled in Article 2 of the U.C.C., the Convention's use of avoidance/nonavoidance rather than acceptance/nonacceptance significantly changes the analysis of remedies. In some situations, the Convention's approach produces notably different results. * * *

* * *

Article 49(1) of the Convention permits a buyer to avoid the contract whenever the seller commits a fundamental breach or fails to deliver in response to a *Nachfrist* ultimatum under Article 47 Avoidance relieves both parties of executory performance obligations. It gives the buyer a right to restitution of amounts 'paid under the contract' and an obligation to return whatever the seller has "supplied ... under the contract." Thus if the seller has delivered goods, an avoiding buyer must preserve and return the goods, although it may retain them until reimbursed for reasonable expenses of preservation. Indeed, subject to certain broad exceptions, the buyer loses the right to avoid if it cannot return the goods 'substantially in the condition' in which it received them. The buyer will also lose the right to avoid unless it sends notice of avoidance within a reasonable time after it knew (or should have known) of the breach. Furthermore, the buyer will lose the right to avoid on the basis of non-conformity in the goods unless it sends notice "specifying the nature of the lack of conformity within a reasonable time after he has discovered it or ought to have discovered it" or, at the latest, within two years from the date of delivery. Successful avoidance entitles the buyer to damages measured by the market price of the goods or the price paid in a substitute transaction ("cover").

The buyer's power under the Convention to avoid after the goods have been delivered is strikingly similar to the buyer's power to reject or revoke acceptance under Article 2 of the U.C.C. A rejecting or revoking buyer, like an avoiding buyer, has a right to recover "so much of the price as has been paid" and an obligation to preserve and return the goods to the seller, subject to a security interest for reasonable expenses of "inspection, receipt, transportation, care and custody...." A buyer loses the right to revoke acceptance under Article 2 if the goods have undergone "any substantial change in condition" not caused by their own defects—a limitation similar to that in Article 82 of the Convention.

Article 2 requires a buyer to send notice of rejection or revocation within time constraints similar to those applicable to notice of avoidance under the Convention. By failing to specify "ascertainable" defects in the notice of rejection, an Article 2 buyer may waive the right to base rejection on such defects much as a Convention buyer may, under Article 39, lose the right to rely on discoverable defects by failing to specify them in notice to the seller. Where the seller has delivered, successful rejection or revocation is a prerequisite to the Article 2 buyer's claim for cover or market-price differential damages, just as successful avoidance by buyer is a prerequisite to those damage measures under the Convention.

* * *

If the aggrieved party has a right under the Convention to avoid the contract, it has the option to choose either avoidance or nonavoidance and thus the power to elect between the two distinct remedial schemes available under the Convention. A buyer that has suffered a fundamental breach, for instance, can opt either to terminate the exchange and recover market-price or cover damages, or to go forward with the transaction and claim remedies consistent with this choice. In certain circumstances an aggrieved Article 2 buyer has a similar election. Where a breaching seller has tendered, Article 2 often permits the buyer to choose between rejection/revocation of acceptance, which aborts the exchange and gives a right to cover or market-price damages, and acceptance, which triggers an obligation to complete the exchange (pay the price) and a right to recover damages under section 2–714. Where the seller refuses to tender, however, the Article 2 buyer normally has only the avoidance-type remedies of cover or market price damages.

An aggrieved seller's right under the Convention to elect between avoidance, which gives a right to restitution and damages measured by resale or market price, and nonavoidance, which gives a right to compel the exchange of goods for price, represents a significant departure from U.C.C. Article 2. Unless the buyer accepts, an Article 2 seller must look to the "avoidance" remedies of resale or market price damages except in certain narrowly-defined situations. If the buyer does accept, an Article 2 seller must normally look to its price remedy and cannot "undo" the exchange by recovering the goods except in certain narrowly-defined situations. For sellers, therefore, the Convention's remedy scheme is radically more elective than that in Article 2.

* * *

Articles 49(1) and 64(1) of the Convention state the prerequisites to avoidance of contract. These provisions allow avoidance if the other party has committed a fundamental breach, which is defined elsewhere as a form of material breach. If the other party's breach is not fundamental, the only path to avoidance is through the *Nachfrist* procedure in Articles 47 and 63. These provisions permit an aggrieved party to 'fix an additional period of time of reasonable length for performance' by the other side. If the breaching party fails to perform its basic contractual obligations (for sellers, delivery of the goods; for buyers, taking delivery or paying the price) within the period fixed in a *Nachfrist* notice, or if the breaching party declares that it will not perform those obligations within that period, the aggrieved party can avoid the contract.

A.   SUSPENDING PERFORMANCE

J. HONNOLD, UNIFORM LAW FOR
INTERNATIONAL SALES
426–28 (3d ed., 1999).*

This article [art. 71] addresses problems like these: (1) A seller has agreed to deliver goods on credit but, prior to the time for delivery, the buyer becomes insolvent or otherwise has manifested an inability to pay for the goods. (2) A buyer has agreed to pay before receiving the goods but, prior to the time for payment, the seller's insolvency or some other circumstance makes it apparent that the seller will not deliver the goods.

* * *

In limited circumstances, paragraph (1) authorizes a party to suspend the performance of obligations such as delivery of the goods (Arts. 31–34) or payment of the price (Arts. 54–59). Article 71(1) also has a broader reach. For instance, the contract may require the seller to procure or manufacture goods described in the contract; when it is apparent that the buyer will not be able to accept delivery and pay for the goods, the seller may suspend procurement or production. Similarly, when it appears that the seller will not be able to deliver the goods, the buyer may suspend required steps leading toward payment, such as the establishment of a letter of credit (Art. 54).

The contract and the Convention may require other preliminary steps leading to final performance. See, *e.g.*, Art. 32 (shipping arrangements), Art. 34 (handing over of documents), Art. 54 (required steps such as establishing a letter of credit), Art. 65 (supplying specifications for goods). Failure to take these steps may constitute a breach of contract, not merely a portent of a future breach; in some cases the breach may be sufficiently serious to justify avoidance (Arts. 49(1)(a), 64(1)(a)) or a *Nachfrist* notice (Arts. 47(1), 63(1)). However, if the aggrieved party is hopeful of obtaining performance or if grounds for avoidance are not clear, the aggrieved party will prefer a less drastic approach such as suspension of its own performance.

Article 71 does not authorize a seller to dispose of goods held for the buyer nor does it authorize a buyer to purchase goods to replace goods to be supplied by the seller; under Article 75, these remedies apply only when the contract is avoided. The point is significant since *avoidance* of the contract by one party because of prospective failure of performance by the other (Art. 72) is subject to standards that are more strict than the standards that Article 71 applies to *suspension* of performance.

B. NICHOLAS, THE FRENCH LAW OF CONTRACT
213–14 (2d ed. 1992).**

2. *EXCEPTIO NON ADIMPLETI CONTRACTUS*

This term, deriving from medieval Roman law (and meaning literally "defence of unperformed contract") is still commonly in use, though the Ministry of Justice has urged the courts not to use Latin expressions, mentioning among others, this one. The French translation is *exception d'inexécution*. The term is misleading in either language, since the word *exceptio* suggests a defence to an action, whereas an essential characteristic of this remedy is that the party exercising it need not go to court (though he may choose to do so).

The remedy, which is available only in the case of a contract in which the duties of the parties are concurrent, consists in the refusal by one party to perform his duty unless the other party performs his. The remedy was well established in the *ancien droit* and there are what can be seen as specific instances of it in the *Code civil*. Thus in a contract of sale the seller can withhold delivery if the buyer does not pay the price. The English parallel is the unpaid seller's lien. Similarly, the buyer can withhold the price if he is threatened by eviction, until the seller removes the threat or gives a surety. There is, however, no general text and, in view of the firmly rooted policy against self-help, it was not until this century that the courts made bold to apply it to all synallagmatic contracts. In so doing they founded it on the doctrine of *cause*: since each obligation is the cause of the other, the non-performance of one justifies the non-performance of the other. It is, however, essentially a temporary and provisional non-performance. The contract and the duties under it remain and the party making use of the *exceptio* (who will be referred to here as the creditor) must be ready to perform as soon as the other (the debtor) does so. This is obviously a situation which the creditor may find inconvenient. The unpaid seller, for example, will not wish to tie up for long goods which he can sell elsewhere. But if the creditor wishes to repudiate the contract altogether and recover his freedom of action, he must bring an *action en résolution* under article 1184. The point is illustrated by a case in which the creditor had given to the debtor for three years the exclusive agency for the sale of his boats, the debtor undertaking to sell nine boats a year. At the end of the first year, during which the debtor had sold none at all, the creditor gave notice that he was terminating the contract and granting the exclusive agency to a third party. It was held that the creditor was entitled to suspend performance of the obligation of exclusivity (i.e. to allow others as well as the debtor to sell), but that he could not give the exclusive agency to another. For this involved a total resolution of the contract, which could only be done by a court under article 1184.

UNCITRAL CLOUT CASE 238
Austria: Supreme Court, 1998

An Austrian buyer, defendant, ordered umbrellas from a Czech seller, plaintiff. The parties agreed to a reduction of the purchase price inasmuch as the goods were defective. However, the buyer did not pay for two subsequent deliveries. Upon the seller's request for payment, the buyer showed the seller a copy of a bank payment order. Then, the buyer cancelled the bank payment order without informing the seller. Lacking liquidity, the seller could neither produce nor deliver goods ordered. The seller, therefore, suspended performance of the contract and sued the buyer. The buyer notified the seller of its compensation claim arising from non-compliance with the contract.

The Supreme Court held that although the contract between the two parties had been concluded before the CISG had entered into force in the Czech Republic, the contract was governed by the CISG under its article 1(1)(b) since the parties had agreed to the application of Austrian law.

The Supreme Court further held that a seller who acts in conformity with a contract may choose between the remedies available under CISG articles 71(1)(a) and 73(2). Neither the fact that the buyer had not paid the purchase price for a number of deliveries nor the cancellation of the bank payment order indicated with a sufficient degree of probability a serious deficiency in the buyer's ability to perform the contract or in its creditworthiness in keeping with CISG article 71(1)(a). The seller's right, therefore, to suspend performance had not been established.

Accordingly, the Supreme Court overturned the decision of the appellate court and remanded the case to the court of first instance for consideration of other issues.

* * *

PROBLEM 4–1

Sneaker World, Inc., a Singapore–based company, agrees to manufacture and sell to Kids, Inc., a New York corporation located in Brooklyn, 10,000 pairs of athletic footwear. The parties' contract requires Kids to arrange for a letter of credit to be issued to Sneaker World by a date 30 days before the scheduled shipment date. Kids fails to obtain a letter of credit by this date.

(a) Assume that the reason Kids has failed to obtain the letter of credit is because the company is in such financial difficulty that it is a poor credit risk. May Sneaker World refuse to ship on the agreed shipment date? CISG art. 71(1).

(b) Alternatively, assume that the reason Kids has not acted is that there has been a change in management and the new managers have not yet caught up with the company's paper work. May Sneaker World refuse to ship on the agreed date?

(c) If, on learning the information set out in paragraphs (a) or (b), Sneaker World decides not to ship on the agreed date, must it inform Kids of its decision? CISG art. 71(3). What is the likely sanction for any failure to give notice?

(d) After Sneaker World informs Kids that the goods will not be shipped, Kids promptly responds by sending a copy of a letter from its bank stating that a letter of credit will be issued to Sneaker World next week. Must Sneaker World ship the footwear? CISG art. 71(3). If not, how long can Sneaker World continue to refuse to ship the goods?

Legislation Note on UCC Provisions

UCC Article 2 has provisions on a seller's ability to suspend performance in UCC § 2–702, but they are related to buyer's insolvency. Seller has more general rights to stop delivery under § 2–705(1), including a right to stop delivery for a "repudiation." Rights of "either party" to suspend performance are granted by UCC § 2–610 for an anticipatory repudiation which will substantially impair the value of the contract to the other party. However, the drafters of the UCC also hoped that any party who suspended its performance due to insecurity concerning the other party's performance, would seek assurances of performance under UCC § 2–609, rather than automatically scuttling the transaction.

BENNETT, ARTICLE 71
Commentary on the International Sales Law: The 1980 Vienna Sales
Convention 520–21 (C.M. Bianca & M.J. Bonell, eds. 1987).*

2.7. -Article 71(2) applies in a specific situation—where the threat of non-payment becomes apparent after the goods have been dispatched and before they have been handed over by the carrier. The seller is empowered in such circumstances to prevent the handing over of the goods to the buyer. Apart from this provision Article 58(2) enables a seller to dispatch goods on terms providing for them not to be handed over to the buyer except against payment of the price. Presumably, therefore, Article 71(2) will be resorted to only where the goods have not been dispatched on those terms.

2.8. -Paragraph (2) is expressly limited in its operation to "the rights in the goods as between the buyer and the seller". The carrier is accordingly not bound to comply with a direction of the seller not to hand over the goods to the buyer, and indeed where the buyer holds a document which entitles him to obtain the goods, the carrier may be precluded from withholding them from him by his obligations under municipal and international law. In such circumstances the effective operation of the paragraph could therefore be quite limited.

2.9.　-Paragraph (2) also needs to be read in conjunction with the statement in Article 4(b) that the Convention is not concerned with "the effect which the contract may have on the property in the goods sold". A third person may therefore acquire title to the goods from the buyer under the applicable domestic law which would then govern the question whether those rights were subject to the seller's right to prevent the handing over of the goods to the buyer.

F. ENDERLEIN & D. MASKOW, INTERNATIONAL SALES LAW
288 (1992).**

[Comments on Art. 71(2)]

6.　...　If the seller has already dispatched the goods he can only prevent the handing over of the goods to the buyer by giving relevant orders *to the carrier or forwarding agent in question.* To what extent the latter follows those orders in the first place depends on the contract concluded for carriage.... If the buyer's country has acceded to the CISG or if the domestic rules of that country also provide for a right to stop the goods in transit, the seller may try to enforce this right through the courts, e.g. by way of *distress or temporary injunction.*

7.　Hence even when the *buyer has obtained title in the goods* through the handing over of the documents.

8.　The right to stop the goods in transit, therefore, does not relate to the relationship between the buyer and his other partners if he has already resold the goods and a third party has obtained title in the goods.... Also *the relations between the buyer and his obligees remain untouched.* If an obligee of the buyer has the goods or if he has pledged title in the goods from a document, the rights of the seller are not governed by the CISG but by the otherwise applicable domestic law (cf. also Article 4 according to which property issues are not covered by the CISG; ...).

Finally, the right to stop the goods in transit does not touch upon the relationship between carrier and buyer. There are *no obligations for the carrier under the CISG* to respect the seller's request for stoppage. If he voluntarily stops the goods in transit he exposes himself to a claim for damages on the part of the buyer. The seller, on his part, could, because of the right to stop performance, request the buyer not to take measures against the carrier.

Because of the contractual relationship with the carrier the seller could perhaps give orders to the former thus exercising his right to stoppage. Otherwise, he would have to call in a court.

UNCITRAL CLOUT CASE 51
Germany: Amtsgericht Frankfurt, 1991

The plaintiff, an Italian manufacturer of shoes, demanded payment of the balance due under the contract with defendant, a German company. The contract provided for payment of 40% of the purchase price upon delivery and the balance within sixty days after delivery. The seller sent an invoice in September [1988] and shipped the goods in January 1989 but suspended delivery without notifying the buyer, who was forced to pay more than 40% of the purchase price upon delivery in order to obtain the goods.

The court held that the seller committed a breach of contract by suspending delivery without giving notice of the suspension to the buyer and set off the claim of the seller for the balance of the purchase price against the claim of the buyer for damages (art. 45(1)(b), 73(1) and 74 CISG).

SURVEY OF PREVIOUS DECISIONS BY GERMAN COURTS APPLYING THE CISG: SELECTED PASSAGES

14 J.Law & Com. 225, 228–29 (1995).*

AG Frankfurt/Main 32 C 1074/90–41, January 31, 1991

[Under the facts of CLOUT case 51,] the court need not decide whether, after the dispatch of the goods, reasonable doubts as to the solvency of the defendant [buyer] ... actually arose, which eventually could have caused the exercise of a right of stoppage [under CISG, Article 71(2)]; the right of stoppage, however, is connected with a duty to give notice under CISG, Article 71(3), pursuant to which the complaining party was obliged to inform the defending party of any doubts concerning the defendant's solvency if the plaintiff intended to invoke the right of stoppage. Appropriate notices, however, have not been submitted [to the court] by the plaintiff. Yet notice would have been a prerequisite for a justified exercise of the right of stoppage. The defendant, therefore, is entitled to damages for the loss of profit [suffered when the plaintiff interrupted delivery of the goods].

* * *

PROBLEM 4–2

Assume that in the preceding problem Sneaker World's shipping department did not learn that the letter of credit had not been opened until after the department had shipped the footwear.

(a) As between Sneaker World and Kids, may Sneaker World stop delivery of the goods while they are in transit? CISG art. 71(2).

(b) Does it matter whether, in accordance with the terms of the sales contract, the carrier has issued a negotiable bill of lading running

* Copyright © 1995 and reproduced by permission from the Journal of Law and Commerce.

to the order of Sneaker World? First, assume that Sneaker World still has possession of the document. May it stop delivery? Second, assume that Sneaker World had already transferred the bill by negotiation to Kids. May Sneaker World still stop delivery? CISG art. 71(2). Third, assume that, in accordance with the terms of the sales contract, the carrier issued a non-negotiable bill of lading naming Kids as the consignee. May Sneaker World still stop delivery?

(c) In any of the cases described in paragraph (b), if the carrier delivers the goods to Kids notwithstanding Sneaker World's stop delivery request, do the provisions in CISG require Kids to return the goods to Sneaker World? CISG arts. 71, 4(b).

Legislation Note on UCC Provisions

The UCC has provisions on "stoppage in transit" in § 2–705. They establish relatively clear end-points for this device. For example, § 2–705(2)(d) provides that "seller may stop delivery until negotiation of any negotiable document covering the goods." In relation to third parties, consider the situation where a judgment creditor of Kids has the New York sheriff levy the equivalent of a writ of execution on the goods as soon as Kids takes possession of the negotiable bill of lading? U.C.C. § 2–702 (3) provides that the seller's rights to the goods are "subject to the rights of a buyer in ordinary course or other good faith purchaser." Is there a comparable limit under CISG? CISG art. 71(2) states that its provision "relates only to the rights in the goods as between the buyer and the seller."

PROBLEM 4–3

Sneaker World has another contract to sell 10,000 pairs of blue athletic footwear. This second contract is with Runners, Inc., a California corporation. The contract with Runners does *not* have a letter of credit term, or any other payment term. CISG art. 58. The contract requires delivery to Runners to be completed by July 1. The goods are shipped to be delivered on July 1, but Sneaker World informs Runners that all the footwear it has shipped is colored pink instead of blue, because blue footwear is not available. Must Runners take delivery and pay for the goods, or may it suspend performance of these obligations? CISG art. 71.

B. AVOIDANCE: REFUSAL TO ACCEPT A NON-CONFORMING PERFORMANCE

ZIEGEL, THE REMEDIAL PROVISIONS OF THE VIENNA SALES CONVENTION: COMMON LAW PERSPECTIVES
International Sales, 9–12 to 9–14 (N. Galston and H. Smit, eds., 1984).*

The circumstances in which a buyer should be entitled to cancel a contract ("avoid" in Convention terminology) for breach by the seller has long been a matter for vigorous debate among common law scholars as well as among common law courts and legal practitioners. The Convention, reaffirming ULIS's position, has firmly thrown its support behind a uniformly applied test of "fundamental breach," regardless of when the breach occurs, and it applies the same test to breaches of the buyer's as well as the seller's obligations. There is only one important exception to this key concept. It is safe to predict that the Convention's seemingly simple and surprisingly little-debated solution will not put to rest the scholarly controversies.

The basic issue is simple to state. It is a matter of balancing the buyer's concern for predictability and certainty against the seller's need for protection against contracts canceled on minor or capricious grounds, particularly where the goods have already been tendered to the buyer and there is no readily available alternative market or they could only be disposed of at great cost to the seller. Although the question is easy to frame, the common law sales acts provide only complex and widely divergent answers. The British Sale of Goods Act still adheres to a system of *a priori* classification into conditions and warranties of the seller's implied obligations of title, description, merchantability, fitness for purpose and sale by sample, in which the conditions strongly predominate. So far as breaches of express terms of the contract are concerned, an earlier tendency towards an equivalent system of *a priori* classification has now been modestly leavened by a judicially added regime of innominate terms. A recent House of Lords decision makes it clear however that the *a priori* system of classification is far from dead.

The Uniform Commercial Code, as we know, ostensibly begins its provisions on the buyer's rights of rejection by embracing a "perfect tender" rule but then dilutes it with a substantial breach test in several important provisions and with an overriding, albeit uncertain, right-to-cure section. Curiously, with one exception, this leavening hand is totally absent in the Code's treatment of the consequences of the buyer's breach.

Given the divided voices within the common law world, the application of the Convention's avoidance provisions will, I am sure, be followed with particularly keen interest.

UNCITRAL CLOUT CASE 235
Germany: Bundesgerichtshof, 1997.

A German seller, plaintiff, delivered stainless steel wire to a Swiss buyer, defendant. The buyer gave notice to the seller that it was unable to work with the sub-standard goods delivered and placed them at the seller's disposal. The seller declared its intention to credit the value of the goods if the buyer's contention of lack of conformity was justified.

The seller sued the buyer for the unpaid purchase price. The buyer claimed set-off for expenses incurred with the refacing of a grinding machine, which was utilized for processing the defective goods.

The Court dismissed the seller's claim. The buyer was entitled to declare the contract avoided under articles 81(1), 49(1)(a) and 51(1) CISG. In fact, the buyer had effectively avoided the contract by communicating to the seller that it could not use sub-standard goods. The court left open whether the buyer examined the goods (article 38 CISG) and gave notice (article 39 CISG) within a reasonable period of time since the seller had waived its right to object by agreeing to credit the value of the non-conforming goods.

The impossibility of restoring the goods to their original condition did not disqualify the buyer from avoiding the contract under article 82(1) CISG. Both parties were aware that the goods had to be processed before any non-conformity could be discovered. Moreover, the buyer was entitled to declare the contract avoided if upon examination it was discovered that the goods had perished or deteriorated (article 82(2)(b) CISG).

UNCITRAL CLOUT CASE 7

Germany: Amtsgericht Oldenburg in Holstein, 1990.

A German fashion retailer and an Italian clothing manufacturer concluded a contract for the sale of fashion goods, with the specification "autumn goods, to be delivered July, August, September + - ". When a first delivery was attempted on 26 September, the buyer refused to accept the goods and returned the invoice on 2 October claiming expiry of the delivery period. The parties argued about the meaning of the above specification, relying on different additional factors allegedly known to both parties.

The court applied CISG as the law of the seller's country but took also into account German domestic law for filling gaps on questions of performance. The court awarded the seller the full sales price, including interest at the statutory rate in Italy plus additional interest as damages. The seller's claim was held to be justified since delivery was tendered during the agreed delivery period. Even if, as alleged by the buyer, during each of the three months one third of the goods had to be delivered, the buyer did not effectively avoid the contract by refusing acceptance of the goods without having fixed an additional period in the previous cases of non-delivery.

B. NICHOLAS, THE FRENCH LAW OF CONTRACT

241–43 (2d ed., 1992).*

RÉSOLUTION

(a) *Character of the remedy*

Where the contract is unilateral, the unsatisfied creditor has a choice between *exécution en nature*, where that is available, and dam-

* Copyright © 1992 and reproduced by permission from Oxford University Press.

ages. Where the contract is synallagmatic and the creditor has not yet performed his part, he may, as we have seen, resort to the *exceptio non adimpleti contractus*, but where he has already performed, or where he wishes to obtain a definitive release from his obligation in place of the temporary bar created by the *exceptio*, he has the further option of rescission (*résolution*) of the contract, with damages where appropriate. In a contract of sale of goods, for example, the unpaid seller, if he still retains the goods, can invoke the *exceptio* in reply to the buyer's demand for delivery, but if he wishes to sell the goods elsewhere, he must obtain *résolution*. If he has already made delivery, *résolution* may be advantageous if, for example, the market value of the goods is higher than the agreed price, or if there is a possibility of the buyer's becoming insolvent.

There is obviously a broad similarity of function between the remedy of *résolution* and the Common law remedy of rescission or avoidance for breach, but there are two marked differences. (i) Save in certain exceptional cases, the creditor must normally apply to the court for an order resolving the contract; he may not, as in the Common law, simply treat the debtor's breach as discharging the contract. (ii) There is no legal criterion for distinguishing those breaches which are sufficiently serious to justify the termination of the contract and those which are not. The matter lies in the *pouvoir souverain* of the trial judge.

* * *

(b) *The judicial discretion*

The option to claim the remedy is the creditor's, though the debtor can defeat the claim at any time, even during the course of appellate proceedings, by offering performance. Where the *inexécution* is total, the court will usually order *résolution* as of course, though it may accord a *délai* under article 1184 al. 3, particularly if it thinks that the creditor is seeking to take advantage of a temporary difficulty in order to escape from a bad bargain. Where the *inexécution* is other than total, the *jurisprudence* has held that the court has a discretion. This discretion relates in the first place to the assessment of the gravity of the breach.

* * *

PROBLEM 4–4

(a) Otto Start is a Mexican manufacturer of automobile batteries. It has contracted to sell 10,000 batteries to Ford's River Rouge assembly plant in Michigan. Otto Start delivers 10,000 batteries to the plant in Michigan on July 1, the contract delivery date. That same day, Ford inspects the goods and determines that 50% of the batteries have small scratches in the finish of the battery cases, usually on the underside of the battery. The batteries all perform to contract specifications, but Ford's sense of aesthetics is offended. The contract states the color of the cases, but is silent as to "scratches". Ford wants to "avoid" the contract and return the goods to Otto Start, and not pay for them. Would you advise Ford that it can avoid the contract? CISG arts. 49(1)(a), 25.

If not, what is Ford's remedy under CISG for the "scratches"? CISG art. 45. Is that effective?

(b) In a separate contract, Otto ships 20,000 automobile batteries to Ford's plant in Michigan. This time, Ford discovers that 50% of the batteries do not perform up to contract specifications and do not have enough electrical power to start an automobile. Would you advise Ford that it can avoid this contract?

If so, what are the obligations with respect to the goods after avoidance of the contract? CISG arts. 81, 82. What would you advise Ford to do with the goods? CISG art. 86.

(c) Would your advice in response to either of the previous questions be different if you discovered that the reason Ford wished to avoid the contract is that the market price for similar batteries has dropped 50% since the time the contract was signed? CISG art. 7(1).

Legislation Note on UCC Provisions

The most powerful informal remedy available to a buyer under the UCC is "rejection of the goods" under § 2–601. A buyer may reject the tender of the goods if the tender or the goods fail "in any respect" to conform to the contract; in other words, the goods may be rejected if they, or their tender, are not "perfect." As we saw in Chapter 3, CISG also requires that the goods and their tender conform to the contract; tender which amounts to substantial performance can create a breach. But CISG does not have an informal remedy provision similar to the rejection concept of UCC § 2–601. Instead, a buyer under CISG may have only the formal, in-court remedies (a suit for specific performance or damages) discussed in Chapter 5. The purpose of the problems in Section B of Chapter 4 is to determine whether, and under what circumstances, a buyer who receives a tender which is not "perfect" may use the contract "avoidance" provisions of CISG to obtain the functional equivalent of the power to "reject" goods under the UCC.

Once a buyer has "accepted" the goods under UCC § 2–606, it can no longer reject them. However, the buyer can later "revoke its acceptance" under § 2–608, if the non-conformity "substantially impairs" the value of the goods to buyer. A much-discussed topic is whether the UCC's "substantial impairment" test is the equivalent of the "fundamental breach" test under CISG.

GARRO, THE U.N. SALES CONVENTION IN THE AMERICAS: RECENT DEVELOPMENTS
17 J. Law & Com. 219, 232–33 (1998).*

The two Mexican decisions applying CISG were rendered by a government agency—the Mexican Commission for the Protection of Foreign Commerce ("Compromex"). * * *

* * *

2.   Conservas La Costeña, S.A., v. Lanin San Luis S.A., Agroindustrial Santa Adela, S.A., *29 April 1996, Dictamen de la Comisión para la Protección del Comercio Exterior de México ("COMPROMEX")*

In December 1992, a Mexican importer (*La Costeña* S.A.) placed a purchase order for 8,490 boxes of canned fruit with an Argentine seller (*Lanín* S.A.). Before the conclusion of the contract, *La Costeña* had approved the can and label samples furnished by *Lanín*. *La Costeña* furnished samples of the carton packages in which he wanted the cans to be contained and shipped. Payment of the purchase price was effected by a letter of credit opened by the Mexican importer. * * *

La Costeña claimed that the goods arrived in Mexico in a damaged condition and that the lack of conformity of the goods was the responsibility of the respondent sellers. As relief, *La Costeña* sought the return of the purchase price and damages. The Mexican importer made several allegations: that 63% of the cans were corroded due to humidity in the packages; that the colors of the cartons and labels were different than those agreed upon by the parties; that the mixture of fruits and the size of some of those goods were not in accordance with the specifications; and that there was a shortage in the number of boxes. In order to establish the lack of conformity of the goods, *La Costeña* submitted a document in which a Mexican Notary Public certified that the cartons and cans were in a damaged condition, and to which twenty-eight photographs were attached, showing the damaged boxes labeled *"La Costeña."* Attached to the notarial act, the Mexican buyer submitted a report by two technicians concluding that the cartons used by the seller were useful for wrapping but not for packaging the goods. A third document provided by *La Costeña's* production manager of packaging (Gerente de Producción de envases) reported that the cause of the damage was the seller's use of improper material for packaging.

* * *

Lanín's alleged breach of contract did not involve a failure to perform (as would be the case if it would have failed to deliver the goods to the buyer), but rather a defective performance consisting of lack of conformity of the goods to the express or implied specifications called for by the contract. Did the seller's failure to package the goods in such a way that would have allowed the buyer to receive the goods in satisfactory condition amount to a fundamental breach warranting the avoidance of the contract? Was the breach serious enough as to "substantially deprive" *La Costeña* of what it was entitled to expect under the contract? This determination required, *inter alia*, an assessment of whether *La Costeña* would have been able to make a reasonable use of the goods despite the alleged nonconformity, or whether the partial performance could have been remedied by partial avoidance of the contract, a reduction of the price, or damages. Thus, Compromex could have properly inquired whether the canned fruit could have been resold in the condition in which it was received. If the saleability of the fruit was not in jeopardy, *La Costeña* could not have avoided the contract in its entirety.

Otherwise, *La Costeña* could have fixed an additional and reasonable period of time for *Lanín* to comply with its obligations, or it could have required *Lanín* to deliver substitute goods. In the alternative, *La Costeña* could have declared the contract avoided and sought damages.

In its decision, Compromex found that the use of a packaging different from the one required by the contract was a determinant cause of the lack of conformity. However, the decision fails to provide any reason as to why such nonconformity amounted to a fundamental breach of the contract. *La Costeña* requested the payment of damages, but without furnishing any guidelines as to the criteria for determining the recovery of damages. It is not difficult to understand why Compromex refused to grant damages to *La Costeña*, which failed to provide any evidence of its losses. However, *La Costeña*'s right to interest should not hinge upon the buyer's indication as to how the interest is to be calculated.

BABIAK, *DEFINING "FUNDAMENTAL BREACH" UNDER THE UNITED NATIONS CONVENTION ON CONTRACTS FOR THE INTERNATIONAL SALE OF GOODS*
6 Temp. Int'l & Comp. L.J. 113, 118–24 (1992).*

A.   Structure and Legislative History of Article 25

Legislative history and literary structure lay the groundwork for gaining an understanding of the meaning of Article 25. The definition of a fundamental breach under Article 25 has two main components. The first is the detriment/expectation component and the second is the foreseeability component. Although the detriment/expectation component is what makes a breach "fundamental," liability for such a breach is limited by the affirmative defense of foreseeability. For a breach to be "fundamental," the breach must cause a "detriment" that substantially deprives the nonbreaching party of its reasonable expectations. This detriment concept developed out of what were perceived weaknesses of the revised text of the ULIS. Those weaknesses were replaced by a substantial detriment test for fundamental breach.

The CISG does not contain any definitions for the term "detriment." It also does not give any examples of a detriment that rises to the level of a fundamental breach. However, the unofficial commentary to the early drafts created after the development of the substantial detriment test does provide significant guidance as to its meaning and application.

The drafters' commentary stated that "[t]he determination whether the injury is substantial must be made in the light of the circumstances of each case, e.g., the monetary value of the contract, the monetary harm caused by the breach, or the extent to which the breach interferes with other activities of the injured party." From this comment, it is possible to conclude that the drafters simply and naturally intended the word "detriment" to be synonymous with monetary injury or harm, or of a consequential harm, and that the determination of a fundamental breach was to be made on a case-by-case basis.

* * *

The expectation interest term of Article 25 is central to determining whether a breach is fundamental. It is the object of the inquiry into whether the nonbreaching party suffered a substantial injury. Expectation interest developed out of the drafters' perceived need to add an objective criterion to define substantial detriment. The extent to which a party suffers an injury to its expectations will be found not only in the language of the contract but in the circumstances surrounding the contractual relationship of the parties. Since the parties' expectations dictate the degree to which they will suffer harm if a breach occurs, it is very important that both parties be aware of their respective interests, both monetary and nonmonetary.

The second part of Article 25 is its foreseeability component. The foreseeability component developed out of the former Article 10 of ULIS which completely based fundamental breach on the foreseeability of events. Article 25 adds objectivity into the determination of whether a breach is fundamental by asking two questions: (1) did the party in breach foresee the substantial detriment (i.e., loss of expectation interest) it caused to the nonbreaching party; and (2) would a "reasonable person of the same kind in the same circumstances" foresee that the breach of contract would cause the nonbreaching party substantial detriment. These two questions will require a finder of fact to view the transaction from the subjective perspective of the party-in-breach, as well as from the objective perspective of the reasonable merchant in the breaching party's position. In addition, the finder of fact will have to determine whether the nonbreaching party's expectation interests were and would be substantially injured by the breach.

Based on an analysis of the legislative history of the CISG, the burden of proving the foreseeability of loss is on the breaching party. The drafters did not wish to include language in Article 25 which would raise questions of civil procedure and, therefore, did not incorporate express language, other than the word "unless," that would indicate a shift of the burden of proof. However, there was a consensus that this burden should be on the party in breach because of the logical difficulty of requiring the nonbreaching party to prove what the party in breach actually foresaw or a party in its position could have foreseen.

Once the party alleging breach establishes that it has suffered a substantial loss of expectation interests, the breaching party can respond affirmatively. The first requirement for negating the claim for breach under Article 25 is purely a subjective one that focuses solely on whether or not the party in breach actually foresaw the harm done by the breach.

The actual foreseeability of the detriment caused by the breach will depend on the breaching party's knowledge of the facts surrounding the transaction. Factors such as the breaching party's (in)experience, level of sophistication, and organizational abilities should be considered in showing foreseeability of harm. These factors demonstrate the breaching party's ability to anticipate and recognize problems in the transaction. The nonbreaching party's experience, or lack thereof, may also be relevant. The manner in which the nonbreaching party performs may affect the ability of the breaching party to perform properly. It is possible that the nonbreaching party may not have provided material information or simply withheld such information which was crucial to properly completing performance.

The second requirement under Article 25 for negating the claim for breach is an objective one requiring the breaching party to show that a reasonable person of the same kind in the same circumstances would not have foreseen the injuries to the nonbreaching party. Since parties to contracts involving international sales are presumed to be merchants, a "reasonable person" may be construed as a reasonable merchant. A reasonable merchant would, therefore, encompass all merchants that satisfy the standards of their trade and that are not intellectually or professionally substandard. The phrase "of the same kind" refers to a merchant in the same business, doing the same functions or operations as the party in breach. The requirement that the reasonable merchant be "in the same circumstances" refers to the market conditions, both regional and worldwide.

A party alleged to be in breach has a difficult burden but if it can meet both requirements then the party claiming breach will not be able to avoid performance of the contract. If the alleged party in breach can prove that it did not foresee the substantial loss of expectation interest the breach caused the nonbreaching party, and can prove that a reasonable merchant facing the same market conditions would not have foreseen that the breach would cause a substantial loss of expectation interests, then there is no fundamental breach.

Article 25 does not address the point at which foreseeability is measured. Are facts and circumstances arising after the conclusion of the contract relevant for determining foreseeability? Or is the focus only on the facts and circumstances that occurred up to the conclusion of the contract? The drafters apparently believed that by leaving the timing issue open that Article 25 maintains its flexibility because of the varieties of circumstances that could arise and that relevant information may have been provided after contract formation. Parties to a contract may clarify the ambiguity surrounding the timing of foreseeability by expressly specifying the point at which information pertaining to the performance of the contract will no longer be considered. If the parties to the contract do not specify the timing, then in the event of litigation they will be leaving the determination to a tribunal.

UNCITRAL CLOUT CASE 6
Germany: Landgericht Frankfurt a.M., 1991.

A German retailer ordered in September 1989 from an Italian manufacturer through a commercial agent 120 pairs of shoes *"Esclusiva su B"*. After delivery in March 1990 and having resold 20 pairs, the buyer learned that identical shoes supplied by the Italian manufacturer were offered for sale by a competing retailer at a considerably lower price. Since attempts to enjoin the competing retailer failed, the buyer returned the unsold 100 pairs and cancelled the "order of March 1990" promising payment for the 20 pairs upon receipt of the credit.

The court, applying CISG as the relevant Italian law, held that a valid contract had been concluded at the latest at the time of delivery and that this contract had not been avoided under article 49 CISG. The cancellation of the "order of March 1990" was not an express declaration of avoidance of the order of September 1990 since it referred to another order. Even if a declaration of avoidance could be made impliedly (a point on which authors disagree), the buyer did not reject the entire contract as evidenced by the promise to pay for 20 pairs. Even assuming such rejection, the buyer was not entitled to avoid the contract for lack of a fundamental breach of the exclusive contract according to article 25 CISG. The manufacturer had no knowledge about the branches of its business partners, and any knowledge of the commercial agent could be imputed to the manufacturer only if the agent had acted as a closing agent.

CASE NOTE

The various notices required by CISG provisions have created large amounts of litigation. An example is CLOUT Case 3, where a notice from a German buyer to an Italian shoe manufacturer was held to be insufficient. The buyer had allegedly notified seller that the goods were of "poor workmanship and improper fitting." The court stated that such a notice "did not specify precisely the defect in the goods," and so failed to meet the CISG requirements.

Such cases raise two alternative questions: 1) If the buyer is advised by counsel, how much of a burden to investigate is placed on the aggrieved buyer? Must the nonconforming goods be taken apart and every flaw discovered and reported? 2) But most buyers will not seek specific advice from counsel in this situation. There is some sympathy for the buyer who receives shoddy goods and, in disgust, "calls them as he sees them"—relying on a lifetime of experience with such goods, but without spelling out the details. If shoes do not follow standard measurements, and thus fit poorly, what should the law expect a merchant-buyer to say about them? Are comparative measurements required? Customer-buyer complaints? Or, is the court in CLOUT Case 3 stating that general, non-specific objections to goods are not credible?

GERMANY: OBERLANDESGERICHT CELLE (20 U 76/94)
May 24, 1995.

[In 1992 a German dealer in used printing equipment concluded a contract with an Egyptian firm for the sale of five offset printing presses and four smaller pieces of equipment. The German seller agreed to deliver the items in two installments. The first installment was to include three of the presses and two smaller items, while the remaining equipment was to be sent in the second instalment. The purchase price included freight and insurance. The buyer agreed to pay the total purchase price as follows: 350,000 DM before shipment of the first installment, 130,000 DM against documents, 90,000 DM before the second shipment, and the last 85,000 DM against documents.

[Before the first installment the buyer paid the seller 464,000 DM, which covered the purchase price of the first three presses plus 70,000 DM. The buyer made this payment together with a request that the seller include in the first installment one of the small items that was to be sent in the second installment. The seller accepted the payment but responded that the additional item would mean finding another container and the seller did not have enough time to do so. As a consequence, the first installment included only the three presses.

[The seller then delayed sending the second installment. After some consultations, the seller informed the buyer on October 1, 1992, that the seller was unable to acquire the two presses not yet delivered but could deliver three of the smaller items. The buyer rejected the offer and asked for its money back. With the notice of rejection on December 4, 1992, the buyer sent a notice giving the seller until December 16 to perform. The seller did not perform within this period and after subsequent negotiations failed the buyer declared the contract avoided. The buyer brought a legal action to recover damages for the delay, for partial non-delivery, and for return of the 70,000 DM. The Landgericht rendered judgment for the buyer. The seller appealed.]

The appeal is rejected. The Landgericht correctly held that the buyer is entitled to restitution.

1. [The appellate court held that the CISG governed.]

2. The buyer's claim to restitution is based upon the CISG. The basis of the claim is Art. 81(2), which provides that a party who has performed the contract in whole or in part may claim restitution from the other party if the contract is avoided. This is what happened here, as long as the seller had not yet fully performed the contract by its partial deliveries.

2.1. With regard to the three small machines, the parties agreed to cancel the contract. The buyer informed the seller by his communication of October 22, 1992, that the three machines were no longer needed because the buyer's own buyer had canceled its purchase contract for those machines. The seller responded: "We thank you for your communication of October 22, 1992. As for your first point, we express our regret that we are not to deliver to you the machines, which we have kept ready for delivery to you." At the same time the seller offered the buyer two substitute machines. This communication was confusing and must have led the buyer to understand that the seller reluctantly agreed to rescission of the contract with respect to the three smaller machines. If the seller intended to say that he would stand upon the contract he should have made this unmistakably clear to the buyer (CISG art. 8(2)). The communications of October 28, 1992, should be read as an agreement to a partial avoidance of the contract.

2.2. The buyer likewise effectively avoided the contract with respect to the other machines which seller had not delivered. This was done at the latest by a communication of the buyer's attorney on January 26, 1993, which rejected any further delivery and demanded the return of the excess price already paid. The buyer was entitled to do so.

2.2.1. Pursuant to Art. 49(1)(b) the buyer may declare the contract avoided in the case of non-delivery if the seller does not deliver the goods within the additional period of time fixed by the buyer in accordance with Art. 47(1) or the seller declares that he will not deliver the goods within the period so fixed. Where the seller has already delivered part of the goods, this rule also applies to that part of the goods which are missing (Art. 51(1)). The buyer gave notice pursuant to Art. 47(1) by the communication of his attorney on December 4, 1992. Such a notice is authorized if the seller has not satisfied his obligations under the contract (Art. 45(1)(a)).

Where the contract fixes a period of time for delivery, the seller must deliver the goods within that period (Art. 33(b)). The seller failed to satisfy this obligation. The seller was obligated to deliver the missing machinery by no later than August. The lower court's finding that the first installment was due by the end of May and the second by the end of August is convincing. The buyer was entitled to give a notice fixing an additional period of time for the seller to perform.

There remains the issue of whether the period fixed was too short. The buyer fixed a period from the time of the notice on December 4 to the time fixed in the notice of December 16, a period which required shipment within 11 days.

With hindsight this period was possibly too short to organize carriage by sea from [X] to [Y], given that the seller was dependent on the schedule of the ship and the existence of free space for freight. This does not make the notice ineffective where the notice has merely extended a period of time (*von Caemmerer/Schlechtriem/Herber*, Art. 47, para. 12). In any case, when the buyer gave notice that the contract was avoided on January 26, 1993, a sufficiently long time (seven weeks) had elapsed. The buyer may declare the contract avoided even though the seller in the meantime has declared by its letter of November 22, 1992, that it is ready to deliver part of the goods. That letter offered to ship four of the machines originally ordered (for three of which there was an agreed partial avoidance) but it offered to substitute a different press for one of the presses originally agreed upon and the letter failed to mention (apparently by mistake, if one understands the seller's argument) the last of the machines ordered.

If the seller's offer to deliver conformed with the contract, the buyer would not have the right to avoid the contract unless he could show that a partial delivery was a fundamental breach and therefore the missing press entitled him to avoid the entire contract (Art. 51(2)). On the other hand, the seller's obligation of good faith (Art. 7(1)) required him to await the buyer's answer to his offer before shipping.

However, the seller's offer was not in accordance with the contract. The seller wanted prepayment for the total price of the machines offered. This did not conform with the terms of the contract, which provided that part of the price was to be paid upon the tender of documents. The buyer was therefore entitled to declare the contract avoided by the communication of January 26, 1993. The seller's subsequent announcement on February 3, 1993, that he would be able to deliver the original press, came too late. In any event, this latter communication again demanded prepayment of the purchase price.

* * *

PROBLEM 4–5

Osman de Lenta, a Syrian manufacturer of shoes, contracted to sell and deliver 10,000 pairs of high-fashion shoes to Gulchy Stores, SA., a retailer located in France. The shoes were designated standard Osman products, the assortment was specified, and the delivery date was July 1. It is now July 8, and no shoes have been delivered to Gulchy. May Gulchy avoid the contract? What are the conditions on Gulchy's right to avoid the contract? CISG arts. 49(1)(b), 47. Gulchy consults you regarding:

(a) When must it send any notice?

(b) What should such a notice say?

(c) How long should the additional time period be? Gulchy wants to display the goods during the July 14 holiday period, but transportation of the goods from Syria will take at least one week.

Legislation Note on UCC Provisions

The UCC, with its "perfect tender" rule under § 2–601, does not distinguish between delivery of non-conforming goods and failure to deliver the goods on time. Nor does the "substantial impairment" test of § 2–608 make this distinction for exercise of a buyer's right to "revoke its acceptance." However, there is substantial body of caselaw concerning whether "time is of the essence" under particular transaction fact situations.

* * *

PROBLEM 4–6

Osman de Lenta also has a contract with Glitzy Stores, Ltd., a retailer located in Singapore, to sell 20,000 pairs of high fashion shoes to Glitzy. These shoes are specially designed by Glitzy and are not standard Osman products, but must be specially manufactured for Glitzy. The delivery date is August 1. On July 15, before such manufacture has begun, the manager of Glitzy writes a letter stating that market prices for shoes have declined substantially and that Glitzy is "reluctant" to take delivery and pay for the shoes unless Osman is willing to make a similar reduction in the prices of its shoes. May Osman treat this letter as an anticipatory repudiation of the contract? CISG art. 71. May Osman suspend its special manufacture of the shoes for Glitzy?

That suspension may protect Osman for a short time, but Osman also seeks a long-term solution to its difficulties with Glitzy. Can it "avoid" the contract under CISG art. 72(1). If so, what are Osman's rights and obligations after an anticipatory repudiation?

KAROLLUS, JUDICIAL INTERPRETATION AND APPLICATION OF THE CISG IN GERMANY 1988—1994.
Review of the Convention on Contracts for the International Sale of Goods (CISG) 62–64 (1995).*

Several decisions have dealt with the question of fundamental breach. It is interesting that this question has arisen only in the context of the buyer's right of avoidance. Other CISG provisions that require a fundamental breach have not yet been considered by the German courts.

In one case, an Italian seller promised to deliver shoes within a particular geographic area exclusively to the German buyer. The seller delivered shoes to another merchant whose main place of business was outside the area reserved to the buyer but who had a place of business within the reserved area. The second buyer sold the shoes within the restricted area and in competition with the first buyer. Apparently, the seller did not intentionally violate his contractual obligation because the sale to the second buyer was organized by a commercial agent. The agent either intentionally violated the contract or was unaware that the second buyer had a secondary place of business in the area reserved for the first buyer.

Because the first buyer did not receive exclusive deliveries as promised, he declared the contract void under CISG Article 49(1)(a). However, the LG Frankfurt am Main held that the breach was not fundamental (presumably, the court would deny that there was a breach of contract at all). The court argued that the Italian seller could not have known where his German buyers had places of business, and that the knowledge of the commercial agent could not be imputed to the seller. These arguments are not convincing. A seller who has promised exclusive delivery to the buyer is obliged to organize his distribution such that it meets his contractual obligations.

Of course, the seller is not liable for the acts of his other buyers. The seller must, however, impose contractual duties on other buyers to prevent them from selling the goods in the area reserved for the first buyer, and he must stop further deliveries if they do not comply. In any case, the seller is liable if he enters into contracts with other buyers who would foreseeably sell the product in the reserved area. The result is not different if the commercial agent alone can foresee the interference, since a seller who engages commercial agents is liable for their actions under CISG Article 79(2) to the extent they concern his obligations.

In a second case, an Italian manufacturer promised to manufacture shoes with a trademark ("Marlboro"). The manufacturer was allowed to use the trademark only with special permission from the buyer. Nevertheless, the manufacturer displayed the shoes with the trademark during a fair at Bologna and did not remove them upon demand of the buyer. The buyer declared the contract void under CISG Article 49(1)(a). The OLG Frankfurt am Main decided that the manufacturer had committed a fundamental breach because his actions severely shook the buyer's confidence in the manufacturer's contract fidelity. The court held that violation of additional obligations could amount to a substantial breach. Therefore, the buyer could not be expected to cooperate further with the manufacturer. While this decision seems correct, it does not answer the question of how to distinguish the fundamental character of a present breach from expected future breaches. As to an expected breach, the requirements of Article 72 go beyond those of Article 25 and should take precedence.

* * *

Finally, the OLG München decided as to a contract for the sale of coke that the alleged breaches—minor lack of conformity and a direct sale to the contracting partner of the buyer—were not fundamental (in fact, it was not proven that the seller had committed a breach of contract at all). I agree as far as the minor lack of conformity is concerned. If exact conformity is a special requirement of the buyer, then the contract should contain an appropriate clause. As far as the direct sale is concerned, I do not agree with the OLG München. The direct sale should be regarded as a fundamental breach even if it did not cause present prejudice to the buyer. In effect, the seller tried to interfere with the business relations of the buyer. This is a severe breach of confidence and it is reasonable to expect further interferences in the future. There is no reason to treat this breach of confidence differently from the impermissible use of the "Marlboro" trademark.

* * *

PROBLEM 4–7

Société Export, SA, a French clothing manufacturer, contracted to sell five shipments of clothes to Bonaventure, Inc., whose offices are located in Delaware. The types of clothing, their numbers, sizes, quality and prices for each installment were specified in the contract. In the contract negotiations, Société Export emphasized that it was of crucial importance where Bonaventure would resell the goods, so as not to compete with any of Société Export's other distributors. Bonaventure stated to Société Export that it intended to resell the goods to a distributor in South America.

After delivery of the first installment, Société Export was informed that the goods were actually sold to a distributor in Spain. Since Société Export already had a distributor in Spain, it demanded that Bonaventure provide documentary evidence that the goods had actually been delivered to a distributor in South America. Bonaventure rejected this demand, stating that its resale actions were of no concern to Société Export. Société Export's Spanish distributor conducted further investigations and determined that the goods shipped to Bonaventure are in fact being offered for resale in Spain.

It is now time for Société Export to ship the second installment of the goods to Bonaventure. Instead, it wants to avoid the contract and refuse to make any further shipments to Bonaventure. What is your advice counsellor? CISG art. 73. Is Société Export permitted to avoid the remainder of this contract?

Legislation Note Under UCC Provisions

Under UCC § 2–612(2), the "perfect tender" rule of § 2–601 does not apply to installment contracts; at least it does not permit the aggrieved buyer to reject the goods for "any defect." Instead, buyer may reject the goods only if the non-conformity "substantially impairs the value of that installment and cannot be cured," or involves defects in required documents. Compare CISG arts. 49(1), 51(1) and 73(1).

As to breach of the whole contract, UCC § 2–612(3) provides that, if the non-conformity "substantially impairs the value of the whole contract," buyer may "cancel" (avoid) the whole contract. However, the primary purpose of this provision is to provide yet another exception to the "perfect tender" rule of § 2–601, rather than a special anticipatory repudiation rule for installment contracts.

WILL, ARTICLE 48
Commentary on the International Sales Law: The 1980 Vienna Sales
Convention, 356–58 (C. M. Bianca & M. J. Bonell, eds., 1987).*

3.2. -The second problem, probably of little practical consequence, was identified within UNCITRAL, but no longer discussed at the Vienna Conference. It concerns the relationship between the right to cure and the notion of fundamental breach. Specifically, does an offer to cure prevent a breach from being fundamental?

3.2.1. -It has been suggested that the question of whether a breach is fundamental should be decided in the light of all the circumstances including the effect of a rightful offer to cure. If this construction were correct, it would render meaningless the buyer's right to require substitute goods under Article 46 (2). For as soon as "cure is feasible and . . . an offer of cure can be expected, one cannot conclude that the breach is 'fundamental' ". Accordingly the buyer will be barred not only from avoiding the contract under Article 49 (1) (a), which makes sense, but will be barred also from requiring performance by replacement under Article 46 (2). The latter makes less sense, since the right to claim substitute goods would be restricted to the few situations where repair is impossible. Such a reduction was certainly not in the mind of the drafters, who had originally dedicated all of Article 46 to the right to require substitute goods.

3.2.2. -Another argument against this approach is that it would contribute to the further weakening of the notion of fundamental breach. The element to be taken into consideration is not very precise: is it a rightful offer received, which suddenly converts an otherwise fundamental breach into a non-fundamental one? Is it reliable news of an offer which was dispatched? Is it a mere expectancy?

* * *

* * * The same goal is just as well achieved when the fundamental breach is determined by lack of conformity only (without having regard to cure), and the existing right to avoid is merely suspended when a rightful offer to cure arrives. The same theory of a remedy merely suspended should apply under Article 46 (2).

<h2 style="text-align:center">F. ENDERLEIN & D. MASKOW, INTERNATIONAL SALES LAW</h2>
288 (1992).*

[Comments on Art. 71(2)]

6. . . . If the seller has already dispatched the goods he can only prevent the handing over of the goods to the buyer by giving relevant orders *to the carrier or forwarding agent in question*. To what extent the latter follows those orders in the first place depends on the contract concluded for carriage. . . . If the buyer's country has acceded to the CISG or if the domestic rules of that country also provide for a right to stop the goods in transit, the seller may try to enforce this right through the courts, e.g. by way of *distress or temporary injunction*.

7. Hence even when the *buyer has obtained title in the goods* through the handing over of the documents.

8. The right to stop the goods in transit, therefore, does not relate to the relationship between the buyer and his other partners if he has already resold the goods and a third party has obtained title in the goods. . . . Also *the relations between the buyer and his obligees remain*

---

untouched. If an obligee of the buyer has the goods or if he has pledged title in the goods from a document, the rights of the seller are not governed by the CISG but by the otherwise applicable domestic law (cf. also Article 4 according to which property issues are not covered by the CISG; . . .).

Finally, the right to stop the goods in transit does not touch upon the relationship between carrier and buyer. There are *no obligations for the carrier under the CISG* to respect the seller's request for stoppage. If he voluntarily stops the goods in transit he exposes himself to a claim for damages on the part of the buyer. The seller, on his part, could, because of the right to stop performance, request the buyer not to take measures against the carrier.

Because of the contractual relationship with the carrier the seller could perhaps give orders to the former thus exercising his right to stoppage. Otherwise, he would have to call in a court.

* * *

PROBLEM 4–8

Oscar Benz, GmbH, a German manufacturer of trucks, bought six "platforms" or truck beds, from Flat Motors, SA, an Italian-based manufacturer. Flat failed to deliver the platforms on the delivery date in the contract, and Benz duly sent a notice under CISG art. 49(1)(b), fixing an additional 30 days for delivery. Flat did deliver the six platforms 15 days after the original delivery date, but Benz found them to be non-conforming to the contract specifications. The non-conformities do not constitute a "fundamental breach" of contract. Can Benz now avoid the contract? Must Benz send any further notices to Flat? Compare CISG arts. 39 and 53 with art. 49(1)(b).

* * *

PROBLEM 4–9

Oscar Benz bought a second set of six platforms from Flat Motor Co. This time, Flat delivered the platforms on the delivery date in the contract, but five out of six were found to be non-conforming to the contract specifications. The defects in the goods did not constitute a "fundamental breach" of the contract. Benz sent a notice to Flat stating: "You have not yet delivered conforming goods under our contract. You have an additional 30 days in which to deliver conforming goods to me, or this contract will be avoided under CISG art. 49 (1)(b)."

If Flat does not deliver any further goods, can Benz avoid the contract 30 days later? CISG art. 47. Note that CISG art. 39 gives sellers a right to "cure" defects in delivered goods, but Benz is attempting to impose an obligation to cure on Flat.

C. NON–JUDICIAL PRICE ADJUSTMENT

BERGSTEN AND MILLER, THE REMEDY
OF REDUCTION OF PRICE
27 Am. J. Comp. L. 255, 255–57 (1979).*

Among the provisions which will be unfamiliar for most Common lawyers is art. [50], which provides the buyer with the right to reduce the price under certain circumstances. Because the remedy of reduction of price is similar to the remedy of damages in that both grant relief to the buyer measured in money, it is easy to confuse the two. * * *

Nevertheless, reduction of the price is a remedy separate from that of damages, both under the Civil law and the Draft Convention, and should not be confused with the right to set-off. * * *

* * *

Civil law origins

The remedy of reduction of price for the purchaser of defective goods derives from the *actio quanti minoris* in Roman Law. At the risk of considerable over-simplification, this action originated from an Edict of the Aediles which sought to "repress the sharp practices of sellers of slaves and cattle in the City markets." If a buyer became aware, after delivery, of certain specified defects which the vendor did not declare and which, had the buyer been aware of them at the time of sale would have led him to pay a lesser price, he could bring an action for reduction of price or for recission of contract. Defects which were evident at the time of conclusion of the contract were excluded from this remedy since the buyer should have taken them into account when calculating the price he was willing to pay.

The Roman law origins of the remedy are reflected in contemporary provisions in Civil law countries. For example, if the goods contain hidden defects, art. 1644 of the French Civil Code enables a buyer to recover part of the purchase price, the amount to be determined by experts, or to rescind the contract and recover the total purchase price. In the Federal Republic of Germany, § 459 BGB provides that if the goods lack promised qualities or contain defects which diminish the ordinary use of the goods or the use provided for in the contract, the buyer has the option of rescinding the contract or of reducing the price according to a formula set out in § 472.

It has been pointed out that in the Civil law, rescission and reduction of price are the normal remedies for a buyer who has been delivered non-conforming goods, and damages are, in principle, the exception. In

* Copyright © 1979 and reproduced by permission from the American Journal of Comparative Law.

large measure this is because damages can be recovered in the Civil law only if the non-performing party was at fault.

* * *

Although the most obvious difference between damages and reduction of price is the time at which and the means by which the monetary allowance will be calculated for defective performance, there are a number of other differences between the two.

One difference (more formalistic than substantive) is that, under the Draft Convention, the remedy of price reduction is effectuated by the unilateral declaration of the buyer. No further action by the seller, such as acquiescing to the reduction of price, or by a tribunal in confirming the reduction, is necessary. This can be compared with the remedy of damages in which the buyer may "claim" the damages from the seller but his claim is not liquidated until the seller or a tribunal has agreed to it. Interestingly enough, this aspect of the remedy appears to be unique to the Draft Convention since in at least French and German law something more than the unilateral declaration of the buyer is necessary to change the juridical situation.

Although the only other remedy under the Draft Convention which is effectuated by the unilateral act of a party, i.e. a declaration of avoidance of contract, is required to be made by notice to the other party, no such requirement is placed on the declaration of reduction of price. Presumably it must be done by means appropriate in the circumstances, but it may well be that one such means would be the statement of claim or defense in a law suit.

FLECHTNER, MORE U.S. DECISIONS ON THE U.N. SALES CONVENTION: SCOPE, PAROL EVIDENCE, "VALIDITY," AND REDUCTION OF PRICE UNDER ARTICLE 50

14 J. Law & Com. 153, 169–76 (1995).*

* * *

BRAUN V. ALITALIA-LINEE: REDUCTION IN PRICE UNDER ARTICLE 50

Another recent opinion by a federal court- S.V. Braun, Inc. v. Alitalia–Linee Aeree Italiane, S.p.A.—deals with an interesting aspect of Convention remedies: proportional reduction of price by a buyer who has received non-conforming goods. In 1990 S.V. Braun, Inc. sold a shipment of bathing suit material to the Nikex Hungarian Foreign Trading Co. Nikex claimed that the material was defective and that the shipment was short in quantity. The parties later settled their dispute by allowing Nikex to retain $35,000 of the purchase price. Braun then sued the carrier that had transported the material for tortiously misstating the weight of the delivery in the shipping documents, thus giving Nikex grounds for withholding payment. One of Braun's arguments was that Nikex had the right to withhold part of the price under CISG Article 50, which provides:

If the goods do not conform with the contract and whether or not the price has already been paid, the buyer may reduce the price in the same proportion as the value that the goods actually delivered had at the time of the delivery bears to the value that conforming goods would have had at that time.

The court rejected Braun's argument, explaining that

[t]he Vienna Convention may permit a proportionate reduction in price for non-conforming goods, but Braun has stipulated here that the goods delivered to Nikex were conforming. Accordingly, Nikex had no legal justification for withholding payment.

According to the court's statement, Braun stipulated only that the goods shipped to the buyer met the quality specifications of the contract ("the goods delivered to Nikex were conforming" (emphasis added)). But Article 35(1) of CISG—the first provision of the section of the Convention entitled "Conformity of the Goods and Third Party Claims"—states that "[t]he seller must deliver goods which are of the quantity, quality and description required by the contract. . . ." On the basis of this text at least one commentary declares that a failure of quantity constitutes a "nonconformity," and that reduction of price is therefore available when the goods are insufficient in either quality or quantity. If so, a stipulation going merely to the conforming quality of the goods would be insufficient to establish that Nikex could not justifiably reduce the price under Article 50. Elsewhere in the Braun opinion, however, the court indicates that the seller also stipulated that "full delivery had in fact been made." There is a textual argument, furthermore, that the phrase in Article 50 describing when the remedy applies—"If the goods do not conform with the contract"—refers only to situations where the goods fail to meet the quality obligations of the contract. Finally, it is worth noting that most commentators have not taken up the suggestion that price reduction is available when the seller ships the wrong quantity.

Many other aspects of Article 50 deserve careful attention from U.S. lawyers. It is a remedy distinct from the damage remedies with which we are familiar. Indeed, reduction of price is available even if the seller is exempt under Article 79 from liability for damages.

To date, English-language commentaries on Article 50 have focused on the provision's Civil Law origins; methods for calculating the amount of the price reduction; the distinction between damages governed by CISG Articles 74–77 and proportional price reduction under Article 50; and the tendency of common law lawyers to misperceive the price reduction remedy as a mere setoff provision. One of the more striking observations on Article 50, made by several commentators, is that in some circumstances the provision yields results inconsistent with a fundamental principle of common law remedies: protection of the expectation interest.

Indeed, the price reduction remedy of CISG operates in a fashion that cannot be justified by any of the remedial principles recognized in U.S. contract law. In other words, Article 50 is not designed to protect the expectation interest, the reliance interest, or the restitution interest. An example will illustrate. On April 1 Seller contracts to sell 100,000 barrels of oil with a sulphur content not to exceed 1% for $25/barrel, delivery on May 1. On May 1 Seller delivers 100,000 barrels with a 2% sulphur content, and Buyer elects to accept the shipment. By May 1 the market value of 1% sulphur oil is only $20/barrel, and the 2% sulphur oil actually delivered is worth even less-$15/barrel. If Buyer chooses to pursue damages, which it can do under Article 74 of the Convention, its recovery will be measured by the difference between the $20/barrel value that 1% sulphur oil would have had and the $15/barrel value of the 2% sulphur oil that was actually delivered. Thus Buyer is entitled to damages of $5/barrel, with the result that Buyer would end up paying $20/barrel ($25/barrel contract price less $5/barrel damages) for the 2% sulphur oil worth $15/barrel. Article 74 damages calculated in this fashion will (as the common law has long viewed the matter) put Buyer in the position it would have been in had Seller properly performed the contract.

If Buyer chooses to reduce the price under Article 50, on the other hand, it would pay only $18.75/barrel-$6.25/barrel less than the contract price. The reduction is calculated by multiplying the contract price by a fraction—the ratio of the value, as of the delivery date, of the goods actually delivered to the value of conforming goods on that date. Since the 2% sulphur oil was worth $15/barrel on the delivery date, and conforming (1% sulphur) oil would have been worth $20/barrel, the ratio is 15/20, or 3/4 . Multiplying the $25/barrel contract price by 3/4 yields $18.75/barrel. Obviously that result departs from expectation damages as calculated under Article 74. Nor does it correspond to a reliance-based or restitutionary recovery. If the market value of oil was higher than the contract price on the delivery date, the result under Article 50 would again differ from expectation damages under Article 74—although in that case the Article 74 damages would exceed the reduction in price under Article 50.

In other words, the amount of the price reduction under Article 50 seems to be based on a principle unknown to the common law. To phrase the matter in a fashion that echoes the traditional description of common law remedy principles, one could say that Article 50 puts an aggrieved buyer in the position she would have been in had she purchased the goods actually delivered rather than the ones promised—assuming she would have made the same relative bargain for the delivered goods. For example, if at the time non-conforming goods were delivered the contract price was 80% of the market price of conforming goods, the buyer can buy the non-conforming goods for 80% of their market value. Put another way, expectation damages are designed to preserve for an aggrieved party the benefit of her bargain; reduction in price under Article 50 attempts to preserve the proportion of her bargain.

* * *

There are many other issues surrounding Article 50. For example, although the provision specifies the time as of which the value of goods is to be determined ("the time of the delivery"), it is unclear where (i.e., in what geographical market) value should be measured. It is also unclear whether the Article 50 remedy is available against sellers who violate their obligations under Articles 41 or 42 to deliver goods free of rights and claims of third parties and whether a buyer is bound by an election of remedies if it avails itself of Article 50. For U.S. lawyers, however, the most pressing job is to apprehend the nature of the price reduction remedy—how it departs from the remedial concepts with which we are familiar, and how it establishes a new remedy principle of substantial potential significance in certain scenarios.

INTERAG CO, LTD. v. STAFFORD PHASE CORP.

United States District Court, S.D.N.Y., 1990.
1990 WL 71478.

HAIGHT, DISTRICT JUDGE:

* * *

Motion for Discovery

Interag's motion to compel Stafford to produce documents relating to the resale of the sweaters in the United States and to reexamine Eisner on that issue is granted.

It is disingenuous for defendant to suggest such documents and testimony do not constitute appropriate discovery, given the issues framed by the pleadings.

Interag sold and delivered sweaters to Stafford. Stafford mailed Interag two checks representing payment for 70% of the purchase price, but stopped payment on those checks, denies any obligation to pay Interag anything, and asserts a million-dollar counterclaim for damages resulting from Stafford's resale of the sweaters to third parties. It appears to be common ground that a resale of at least a portion of the sweaters occurred. Obviously Interag is entitled to discovery on the resale.

Defendant says the resale information is irrelevant because defendant bases its asserted remedies upon the difference "between the value of the good accepted and the value they would have had if they had been as warranted," § 2–714(212) of the Uniform Commercial Code (Sales); see also Article 50 of the 1980 United Nations Convention on Contracts for the International Sale of Goods (to which both the United States and Hungary are signatories), 15 U.S.C., Cumulative Annual Pocket Part at

48 et. seq. (1990). Stafford apparently proposes to prove this difference in value by expert testimony. However, it is well settled that the price obtained for defective goods on resale is probative of the value of the goods as actually received.

Stafford resists giving discovery on resale on the theory that "the Hungarians are notorious for stealing client accounts." This conclusory slur upon an entire nation is insufficient to foreclose plaintiff from discovering evidence of manifest relevance, particularly where the affidavits submitted on the motion indicate that Stafford in its prior dealings with Interag had made known the names and addresses of its third-party purchasers so that transactions might be completed.

In these circumstances, I make the following order:

* * *

2. Within sixty (60) days of the date of this Order, defendant Stafford shall produce to Interag all documents described in plaintiff's first request for production of documents, to the extent those documents have not already been produced.

3. Within ninety (90) days of the date of this Order, Arnold Eisner will again present himself for deposition by counsel for plaintiff and respond fully to questions on the subject of resale.

Non-compliance with paragraphs (2) and (3) above will result in striking of the counterclaim and entry of judgment for plaintiff in the amount demanded in the complaint.

Plaintiff is entitled to costs and attorney's fees under Rule 37(a)(4) insofar as its motion related to compelling discovery from defendant. Defendant's resistance to discovery concerning retail is untenable, and cannot be regarded as "substantially justified" under the circumstances of the case. As the Notes of the Advisory Committee to the 1970 amendments to the rule makes clear, the amendment is intended to require the awarding of expenses in the absence of substantial justification or other circumstances making an award of expenses unjust. In addition, counsel for defendant signed the response to the request for production of documents, so that Rule 11 is implicated as well. I award to plaintiff costs and fees in the amount of $500 to be paid by counsel for the defendant.

* * *

PROBLEM 4–10

Louie Vulture, an Italian manufacturer of shoes, contracted to sell and deliver 10,000 pairs of high-fashion shoes to Gross Stores AG, a German corporation and retailer. The contract specified that the shoes were to have silver rivets at the toe, and the average price of each pair was 100 DM. The shoes when delivered on the contract delivery date were found to have brass rivets instead of silver ones. They were still quite useable as shoes, but Gross decided that, any attempt to sell the shoes without the silver rivets would be detrimental to its self-proclaimed image. The rivets cannot be removed or replaced without permanent damage to the shoes.

The purchasing department at Gross estimated that at the time of delivery the shoes were probably worth about 50 DM per pair, and remitted 500,000 DM to Louie. The next day, Gross was able to sell the shoes to Payless Stores, an American retailer for 60 DM per pair. When Louie learned of the latter sale, it hired its own expert to determine a value for the shoes. After conducting a market study, the expert concluded that Gross could easily have sold the shoes to its customers for 75 DM per pair, and without diminishing its high-fashion image. The expert is prepared to state his conclusion under oath in any ensuing litigation.

Gross consults you, and tells you these facts. It wants to deal fairly with Louie, and neither overpay or underpay, but pay what the law requires. Louie is threatening to litigate unless it receives either an extra 250,000 DM or a very good explanation as to why the law does not require Gross to pay that amount?

What is your advice to Gross, and your explanation to both Gross and Louie? CISG art. 50.

D. STIPULATED REMEDY PROVISIONS

HARTNELL, ROUSING THE SLEEPING DOG: THE VALIDITY EXCEPTION TO THE CONVENTION ON CONTRACTS FOR THE INTERNATIONAL SALE OF GOODS

18 Yale. J. Int'l L. 1, 54–8, 80–85 (1993).*

* * *

[T]he provisions of the Convention generally displace article 2 of the Uniform Commercial Code in contracts for the international sale of goods. However, domestic rules remain applicable to some issues arising in such contracts. The rules of contractual validity, for example, are excluded from the CISG's scope, and thus subject to the laws of the applicable domestic jurisdiction.

Enormous tension exists between the international legal order, on the one hand, and the various domestic legal systems, on the other. Generations of international commercial traders have exercised their contractual freedom in hopes of creating an autonomous international commercial law (*lex mercatoria*) free from those "awesome relics from the dead past" that are embedded in domestic legal systems. Although the CISG arose from that tradition, it is not entirely autonomous.

Indeed, the Convention must occasionally yield to "important domestic policies that outweigh common international interests."

* * *

The exclusion of validity issues from the Convention's scope significantly limits the development of an international body of case law to guide adjudicators, traders, and their counsel. Article 4(a) poses a particular danger to the development of a coherent jurisprudence of international trade, because it gives adjudicators wide discretion to determine when to apply domestic law rather than the CISG to contracts for the international sale of goods. Therefore, how adjudicators distinguish uniform, autonomous Convention issues from issues of validity is critical to the success of the CISG.

* * *

The above analysis has referred frequently to mandatory law and to the problems of equating it with validity. The analysis suggested that equating the two would lead adjudicators to apply an overly-broad conflict of laws inquiry when interpreting article 4(a). Such an inquiry threatens to undermine the article 7(1) instruction to interpret the CISG in light of its internationalist object and purpose. This section brings together the arguments against an oversimplified conflicts approach to article 4(a) and in favor of a more balanced approach to the validity exception.

Throughout the drafting history of the CISG, delegates equated validity with mandatory law. For example, one delegate noted that "fraud and contract validity were matters of public policy regulated by mandatory provisions of national law." More recently, domestic rules relating to validity of contract and warranty disclaimers have been described as mandatory domestic laws that embody public policies. While there is some justification for equating validity with mandatory law, doing so is confusing at best and imperils the success of the CISG at worst. Therefore, the mandatory law interpretive approach to article 4(a) should be abandoned.

* * *

The general rule of party autonomy holds that parties are free to select the law which will govern their contract. However, the choice of law rules pertaining to validity issues such as capacity, form, consideration, vices of consent, and illegality, are more complicated. In a purely domestic transaction, these issues lie beyond the parties' freedom of contract. However, parties to an interstate or international contract *may* designate the law which will govern the issues of validity raised by their contract, subject to certain exceptions described below, and thereby avoid the application of the validity rules of the jurisdiction whose law they do not choose. Therefore, the fact that domestic rules of contract formation and validity are mandatory in domestic contracts, does *not* compel the tribunal to apply such rules to a contract for the international sale of goods when the contract is governed by a different body of law.

The situation of mandatory rules as more narrowly defined above— i.e., regulatory rules inspired by considerations of public policy or economic *dirigisme*—is rather different. This sort of domestic rule, such as a rule regulating contracts between parties of unequal bargaining power, has a more compelling effect in a conflict of laws analysis. A forum may be *obliged* to apply such a domestic rule, despite the fact that the contract is governed by a different body of law. Such mandatory (usually statutory) rules override the law that would normally apply and limit the parties' autonomy in international cases as well as in purely domestic cases. Such rules are internationally mandatory, that is, the parties may not derogate from them by selecting another law to govern their contract.

* * *

At the very least, article 7(1) requires courts to read their states' public policies narrowly in cases to which the Convention applies. It is realistic to expect that courts will do so. A similar requirement is familiar to tribunals accustomed to deciding claims brought under the public policy exception to the New York Convention on the Recognition and Enforcement of Foreign Arbitral Awards. In that context, the U.S. Supreme Court has demonstrated on several occasions its willingness to read domestic public policy narrowly when the dispute involves international commerce. It would not be surprising, therefore, to see the same reasoning applied to the validity exception where a contract is governed by the CISG.

* * *

It is important to examine whether domestic rules through which courts control unfair, unreasonable, or unconscionable terms apply to contracts for the international sale of goods. The judicial and legislative control of onerous contracts has grown significantly during this century. Efforts to control contractual fairness may be aimed at procedural defects in the bargaining process, which often inhere in standard forms, or at the substantive allocation of risks in the agreement itself.

Although the techniques of control differ, their underlying purposes are basically the same, i.e., to guard the party having a weak bargaining position from disadvantage. Such rules may be found in case law, in general statutory principles, or in special protective legislation. Of special interest here are provisions found in modern sales legislation, such as § 2–302 of the Uniform Commercial Code and § 36 of the Uniform Nordic Contract Act, and in statutes expressly regulating the use of standard form contracts, such as the U.K. Unfair Contract Terms Act, 1977 and the German Act for the Control of the Law of General Conditions of Business (AGB Law). As a practical matter, these domestic rules will most often come into play when a contract for the international sale of goods contains an exculpatory clause (disclaimer), i.e., a clause which modifies, limits, or excludes the warranty that would otherwise be provided by law, or that limits or excludes the available remedies.

Exculpatory clauses play an important role in commerce. The Convention itself does not restrict the parties' freedom to limit or exclude their liability under contracts within its scope. However, domestic laws invalidating unfair, unreasonable, or unconscionable clauses *do* limit the parties' autonomy. If such domestic rules apply to contracts for the international sale of goods pursuant to article 4(a), then there is an "unfortunate, if inevitable, conflict between the philosophy of freedom of contract generally enshrined in the Convention and a restriction on that freedom, governed by national law, which may proceed from much more protectionist sentiments." More concretely, the question is whether CISG, article 6 permits "the exclusion of obligations imposed under the Convention, however basic, even though such a disclaimer would be treated as unconscionable, and therefore unenforceable, under the applicable municipal law? Would this be a question of validity within article 4 or would article 6 take priority?"

The prevailing view is that domestic rules permitting courts to exercise control over unfair, unreasonable, or unconscionable contracts constitute rules of validity and thus apply to contracts for the international sale of goods pursuant to article 4(a). In other words, the autonomy granted to the parties under article 6 is subject to the limits imposed by the applicable domestic law. Thus, the question "whether the parties have validity ... derogated from any of [the Convention's] provisions falls outside the Convention and has to be solved by reference to a particular domestic law." This means that both U.C.C. § 2–302 and U.C.C. § 2–719(3), which permits parties to limit or exclude consequential damages unless the limitation or exclusion is unconscionable, constitute rules of validity, and therefore apply to contracts for the international sale of goods when the Uniform Commercial Code is the proper law to govern issues not governed by the Convention.

Whether article 4(a) also preserves the application of U.C.C. § 2–719(2), which limits the parties' freedom to modify or limit the remedy "[w]here circumstances cause an exclusive or limited remedy to fail of its essential purpose," is less clear. Professor Murray doubts that this limitation on the parties' autonomy raises a question of validity "since the circumstances giving rise to 'failure of essential purpose' arise after the contract is formed." Although technically correct, this narrow reading of subsection (2) is not justified when the policies behind U.C.C. § 2–719 are viewed in the context of CISG, article 4(a). The overriding purpose of U.C.C. § 2–719 is to permit a tribunal to evaluate the fairness of a limitation of liability clause in accordance with vague standards that embody public policy. The mere fact that U.C.C. § 2–719 provides two different standards to judge the effectiveness of contractual provisions excluding consequential damages or otherwise modifying the buyer's remedy—i.e., unconscionability (subsection 3) and failure of essential purpose (subsection 2)—does not detract from this underlying purpose, which is entirely consistent with the spirit of CISG, article 4(a).

However, not all commentators subscribe wholeheartedly to the view that such domestic laws apply to exculpatory clauses in contracts for the international sale of goods. Here, as elsewhere, some argue that the provisions of the Convention may displace rules of domestic law, such as where operative facts that trigger U.C.C. § 2–302 also invoke a rule of the Convention. Professor Honnold states that, "Domestic rules on validity—such as requirements of 'good faith,' *Treu und Glauben*,' 'conscionability,' or rules controlling contract clauses restricting responsibility for defective goods—may become inapplicable in certain cases."

The controversy revolves around the standards for evaluating a clause excluding or modifying a warranty, that is, an exculpatory clause limiting duties undertaken. CISG, article 35(2) states that the seller must deliver goods that conform with designated criteria, "[e]xcept where the parties have agreed otherwise."

* * *

PROBLEM 4–11

Société Ballard from Problem 3–7, pg. 194, agrees to manufacture and sell a bottle-capping machine to Bottling Company. The contract includes an express term stating that the machine will cap 10,000 bottles per hour. A separate term states that if the machine fails to meet the contract standards the seller, at its option, may repair the machine or replace it. The term goes on to state that this repair or replacement is the buyer's exclusive remedy.

(a) Assume that the delivered machine initially caps only 9,600 bottles per hour but Société Ballard promptly repairs the machine so that it caps 10,000 bottles per hour. Must Bottling Company accept the repaired machine? CISG arts. 46, 6.

(b) Assume that the delivered machine initially caps only 6,000 bottles per hour. Bottling Company is so frustrated with this performance that it insists that Société Ballard replace the machine rather than merely repair it. Must Société Ballard send a replacement, or can it insist that Bottling Company accept the original machine after it is repaired? Is CISG art. 46(2) relevant? If Bottling Company purports to avoid the contract before the repairs are carried out, has Bottling Company breached the contract?

* * *

PROBLEM 4–12

Société Ballard agrees to manufacture and sell a bottle-capping machine to Bottling Company. Again, the contract includes an express term stating that the machine will cap 10,000 bottles per hour. A separate term states that if the machine fails to meet the contract standards the seller, at its option, may repair the machine or replace it. The term goes on to state that this repair or replacement is the buyer's exclusive remedy.

(a) Assume that the delivered machine initially caps only 9,600 bottles per hour but Société Ballard promptly repairs the machine so that it caps 9,800 bottles per hour. Must Bottling company accept the repaired machine. Compare CISG arts. 45 and 45 with CISG art. 6.

(b) Assume that the delivered machine initially caps 9,900 bottles per hour and, when informed, Société Ballard refuses to attempt to repair the machine. What remedy, if any, does Bottling Company have? Would your answer change if the machine caps only 6,000 bottles per hour?

Chapter 5

JUDICIAL REMEDIES

A. INTRODUCTION

FARNSWORTH, DAMAGES AND SPECIFIC RELIEF
27 Am. J. Comp. L. 247, 247–53 (1979).*

[Professor Allan Farnsworth, who represented the United States at the 1980 Vienna diplomatic conference, wrote the following article before the conference. He cites and quotes from the 1978 draft UNCITRAL text rather than the final official text. Before relying on Professor Farnsworth's analysis you should examine the official text. See, in particular, the final text of article 28, which amends the 1978 draft in response to the criticism of Professor Farnsworth and others.]

* * *

No aspect of a system of contract law is more revealing of its underlying assumptions than is the law that prescribes the relief available for breach. In the following pages an attempt will be made to identify some of the underlying assumptions of the 1978 Draft Convention on Contracts for the International Sale of Goods through an examination of its provisions on damages and specific relief. The perspective is admittedly that of one familiar with the legal system of the United States.

The assumptions of that legal system in this respect are relatively simply stated and differ relatively little from those held in most Common law countries. Of concern here are five basic tenets. First, the law of remedies for breach of contract is directed at *relief* to the *promisee* to redress breach rather than *compulsion* of the *promisor* to prevent breach. Second, relief to the promisee is to be measured by his *expectation*, sometimes called "the benefit of the bargain," and the attempt is therefore to put him in the position in which he would have been had the contract been performed. Third, this attempt should take the form of *substitutional* relief, an award of money, rather than specific relief, whenever substitutional relief is adequate. Fourth, the award of substitutional relief should not include compensation for loss that might reasonably have been *avoided* by the claimant. Fifth, the award of substitutional relief should not include compensation for loss that could not reasonably have been *foreseen* by the party in breach at the time he made the contract.

Taken as a whole, these tenets are designed to accord with the goal of economic efficiency in a free enterprise economy. For the good of society, its resources should be efficiently allocated at every point in time. It is therefore in society's interest that each economic unit reallocate its resources whenever this would lead to greater efficiency. Even if a party is bound by a contract to allocate his resources in a particular way, the good of society requires that he break the contract and reallocate his resources whenever this makes him better off without making someone else worse off. Since reallocation through breach will not make the injured party worse off as long as his expectations are protected (the second tenet), and will, by hypothesis, make the party in breach better off, it is in society's interest that the contract be broken and the resources reallocated. This reasoning supports, for example, substitutional rather than specific relief (the third tenet), because such compulsion would discourage reallocation.

First Tenet: Relief

The tenet that the law of remedies for breach of contract is aimed at relief of the promisee rather than at compulsion of the promisor is admirably expressed by the Draft Convention in the first sentence of art. 71:

> . . . if, in a reasonable manner and within a reasonable time after avoidance, the buyer has bought goods in replacement or the seller has resold the goods, the party claiming damages may recover the difference between the contract price and the price in the substitute transaction and any further damages recoverable. . . .

The following article, which lays down the market price formula, makes it clear that no more than the aggrieved party's actual loss is recoverable. He cannot inflate his damages by using that formula if he has actually covered or resold.

Although the Draft Convention makes no provision for punitive damages, it is always open to the parties themselves to include an express provision for a penalty in the event of breach. There are polar views on the validity of such penalty clauses. Many legal systems find nothing inherently objectionable in them. Others, notably those based on the Common law, draw a distinction between a provision for a "penalty," which is not valid, and a provision for "liquidated damages," which is valid. Since this condemnation of penalty clauses is rooted in public policy, it is untouched by the Draft Convention which is not, according to art. 4(a), concerned with "the validity of the contract or of any of its provisions." An inquiry into the validity of a penalty clause will continue to involve an exercise in choice of law to ascertain the governing law whenever jurisdictions with these polar views are involved.

SECOND TENET: EXPECTATION

The second tenet is that relief to the promisee is to be measured by his expectation, that is, by "the benefit of the bargain," and is not limited to the extent of his reliance losses. Although this is nowhere stated in so many words, it seems implicit in a reference to the promisee's "loss, including loss of profit" in the first sentence of art. 70. The word "loss" alone might be read narrowly to refer to out-of-pocket reliance expenditures, but the mention of "loss of profit" makes it clear that this is not what is intended.

THIRD TENET: SUBSTITUTIONAL RELIEF

The third tenet, that relief should be substitutional rather than specific, runs into heavy weather in the Draft Convention. This is scarcely surprising in view of the (proposed) preference of Civil law systems for specific relief on doctrinal grounds, buttressed, in the case of countries with planned economies that lack markets for substitute transactions, by a preference on economic grounds. What is more surprising is that it has not been possible to work out a compromise that would be satisfactory to countries with other legal traditions and different economies.

The rights of both buyer and seller are stated in absolute terms. Under art. 42, the buyer may not only "require performance by the seller of his obligations," but he may, in some instances where the goods do not conform, "require delivery of substitute goods." Under art. 58, the seller "may require the buyer to pay the price, take delivery or perform his other obligations." Articles 41(a) and 57(a) give the respective parties the power to "exercise the rights" so conferred.

Such "compromise" as there is appears in art. 26, which provides:

> If, in accordance with the provisions of this Convention, one party is entitled to require performance of any obligation by the other party, a court is not bound to enter a judgment for specific performance unless the court could do so under its own law in respect of similar contracts of sale not governed by this Convention.

To begin with, the words "judgment for specific performance" suggest that the provision does not apply to a suit in which the seller tenders the goods to the recalcitrant buyer and claims the price. Such a suit, traditionally one at law rather than in equity, is not commonly thought of as one for "specific performance," even though it gives the seller relief that might accurately be described as "specific." Furthermore, even as to a buyer's suit against the seller for what is unmistakably "specific performance," a Common law court is not relieved of the obligation to render such a judgment if it "*could* do so under its own law in respect to similar contracts of sale." This is a very different test from that permitted under a reservation of ULIS (art. VII) which relieves a court from the obligation to render such a judgment "except in cases in which it *would* do so under its own law in respect of similar contracts of sale." The law relating to equitable relief in any Common law system is sufficiently discretionary that, given appropriate facts, a court *could* render a judgment of specific performance in respect of many types of contracts although it *would* render such a judgment in respect of very few. The rewording of the language has produced at best a sham compromise.

* * *

The conclusion is inescapable that, under the current version, neither seller nor buyer is free to reallocate its resources even if the other party has a ready market on which it can cover or resell as the case may be and even if that party is fully compensated for any resulting loss. This would not, perhaps, be a significant matter if it offended only the sense of pride of those Common law countries whose history dictates a contrary rule. Its importance lies in its disregard of fundamental notions of economics. It may be that both buyers and sellers will choose to ignore their rights to specific relief and seek damages based on cover or resale. Should that be so however, it will be in spite of the Draft Convention and not because of it.

FOURTH TENET: AVOIDABILITY

The requirement of avoidability is stated in art. 73:

> The party who relies on a breach of contract must take such measures as are reasonable in the circumstances to mitigate the loss, including loss of profit, resulting from the breach. If he fails to take such measures, the party in breach may claim a reduction in the damages in the amount which should have been mitigated.

* * *

The most common step to be taken in avoidance of loss under a contract for the sale of goods is a substitute sale or "resale" to another buyer in the case of breach by the buyer and a substitute purchase or "cover" from another seller in the case of breach by the seller. The rule that results from applying the general rule on avoidance to these situations is the market price formula stated in art. 72(1): * * *.

This provision parallels UCC 2–713(1), which ties buyer's damages to "the market place at the time when the buyer learned of the breach." It departs from UCC 2–708, which ties seller's damages to "the market price at the time ... for tender." The Draft Convention proceeds on the assumption that the aggrieved party, whether buyer or seller, can be expected to protect himself by a substitute transaction as soon as he has the right to free himself of the original contract. This seems unexceptionable and, as to anticipatory repudiation, accords with UCC 2–723(1), which ties both buyer's and seller's damages to "the time when the aggrieved party learned of the repudiation." Under art. 72(2), "the current price is that prevailing at the place where delivery of the goods should have been made." There is no counterpart of UCC 2–713(2), which allows the buyer to base damages on the market at the place of arrival where the goods have already reached their destination before the buyer's failure to take or keep them.

* * *

Fifth Tenet: Foreseeability

The requirement of foreseeability, known throughout the Common law world as "the rule of *Hadley v. Baxendale*," appears as the second sentence of art. 70:

> Such damages may not exceed the loss which the party in breach foresaw or ought to have foreseen at the time of the conclusion of the contract, in the light of the facts and matters which he then knew or ought to have known, as a possible consequence of the breach of contract.

Any such formula is inevitably imprecise. It comes close to blending Restatement of Contracts § 330, which allows recovery for "injuries that the defendant had reason to foresee as a probable result of his breach when the contract was made, and UCC 2–715(2)(a), which allows the buyer recovery for "any loss resulting from general or particular requirements and needs of which the seller at the time of contracting had reason to know." Although the use in art. 70 of "*possible* consequence" may seem at first to cast a wider net than the Restatement's "*probable result*," the preceding clause ("in the light of the facts . . .") cuts this back at least to the scope of the Code language.

A more significant difference goes to damages for breach of warranty. In the case of injury to person or property, UCC *2-715(2)*(a) has a separate formula for damages allowing recovery for injury "proximately resulting from any breach of warranty." It thus applies to such claims the more generous measure of damages for tort rather than the less generous one of damages for breach of contract. The Draft Convention has no such separate formula to claims for breach of warranty, which are governed by the less generous contract formula of art. 70. If the difference reflects the relatively favored status of the personal injury claimant in the United States, it is impractical to hope that the [rest] of the world could be brought to accept the broader separate formula of the Code.

B. NICHOLAS, THE FRENCH LAW OF CONTRACT
211–13 (2d ed., 1992).*

Remedies for non-performance

1   GENERAL

A French work will not usually have a chapter exclusively devoted to this subject. Treatments vary in detail, but they broadly reflect the arrangement of the Code. As we have seen, what English law classifies as remedies for breach are classified by the French lawyer among aspects of the effect of contracts or of obligations. The effect of an obligation is to constrain the debtor to perform what he has undertaken; if the debtor does not do so voluntarily, the law, in principle, provides the means of compelling him to do so. It is only if those means are for some reason not available or not effective that a question of non-performance (*inexécution*) arises, and in that event the law provides a substitutionary relief in damages. This difference between the two systems is partly a mere matter of arrangement, and as such it is of no great importance once the arrangement is understood, but it also reflects a significant difference of emphasis or approach. From the point of view of the French lawyer the creditor's primary recourse is in principle to have the contract performed, whereas for the Common lawyer the primary remedy is damages. In practice, it is true, as is explained in more detail below, the remedy of specific enforcement is less important than principle suggests, but the attitude of mind remains.

This attitude of mind is seen more fundamentally in the contrast between the Common lawyer's emphasis on remedies and the French lawyer's emphasis (which is that of the Civil lawyer in general) on rights and duties. We have remarked before that the French lawyer sees law as a system of rules, in principle complete, for the conduct of life in society. The courts will, or should, enforce the rights and duties which these rules create, but this is a logically secondary matter. Mr Justice Holmes's well-known assertion that "the duty to keep a contract at common law means a prediction that you must pay damages if you do not keep it—and nothing else" is an exaggeration, but, as well as pointing to the primacy, already noted, of the remedy of damages, it does correctly reflect the fundamental approach of the Common lawyer, which is to ask, not "is there a duty?", but "will a court give a remedy?". This is not to say, of course, that the lawyer's commercial client will have regard only to this question, but the duty which will weigh with him will be a matter of commercial practice and commercial reputation. Holmes's remark does indeed point to a more fundamental difference of approach. Just as in matters of mistake and of *réticence dolosive* French law takes a moral stance while English law emphasizes the security of transactions and economic efficiency, so also French law treats breach of contract as a form of moral wrongdoing, while the Common law looks more to commercial considerations. This is exemplified in the readiness of some Common lawyers to embrace the concept of "efficient breach".

This fundamental difference of approach no doubt reflects the fact that the case-law of the Common law systems in the field of contract has been concerned to a far greater extent than French law with commercial transactions.

B. SPECIFIC PERFORMANCE

J. HONNOLD, UNIFORM LAW FOR INTERNATIONAL SALES
305–06 (3d ed., 1999).*

A. *The General Rule for "Requiring" Performance*

Paragraph (1) of Article 46 lays down the general rule that the buyer may *"require* performance" by the seller; the seller's package of remedies (Ch. III, Sec. III) has a parallel rule (Art. 62) that the seller may *"require* the buyer to pay the price." Both articles reflect the principle, embedded in civil law theory, that an aggrieved party may "require" the other party specifically to perform its contractual obligations.

The rule of paragraph (1) that the buyer may require the seller to perform its "obligations" may be invoked in a wide variety of circumstances. The most common example is when the seller fails to procure or produce the goods or to deliver them at the place (Art. 31) or date (Art. 33) provided by the contract. In addition, subject to restrictions stated in Article 46(1) & (2), a buyer may require the seller to deliver goods that are in conformity with the contract (Art. 35). Under Article 46(1) the seller may also require the seller to perform its obligations under Articles 41 and 42 to deliver goods free from any right or claim of a third party; we have considered the use of Article 46 to require the seller to remove such claims or to defend them on behalf of the buyer. It is not possible to itemize all of the applications of Article 46 (or of the seller's parallel remedy under Article 62) since these provisions apply generally to the parties' "obligations" under the Convention and the contract (Arts. 6, 30, 53).

B. *The Concession to the Rules of the Forum: Article 28*

Article 28 states that even though the Convention's general rules provide that a "party is entitled to require performance," a court "is not bound to enter a judgment for specific performance unless the court would do so under its own law in respect of similar contracts of sale not governed by this Convention." As was noted under Article 28, this concession to the procedures of the *forum* was granted by ULIS (1964) in response to the objection that common-law systems compelled ("specific") performance only when alternative remedies (*e.g.,* damages) were not adequate. Comparative research also revealed that some civil law systems would not always compel performance by the coercive measures, such as imprisonment for contempt, that may be available in "common law" systems; as a consequence flexibility based on Article 28 is not confined to common law jurisdictions.

(a) Requiring Performance by the Seller at Common Law. "Common law" restrictions on requiring (specific) performances of sellers' obligations are sometimes exaggerated. It is true that common law courts will not ordinarily compel a seller to deliver goods that the buyer can readily acquire; common examples are standard raw materials—wheat, cotton or the like. In these cases the courts usually find that the buyer's only loss is the added cost of purchasing the goods—a loss that can readily be ascertained and compensated by awarding damages. However, if substitute goods can not readily be obtained because of shortages or their unique character the buyer's loss may not be readily measured or compensated by a damage-award. Other examples include a seller's repudiation of a long-term contract; in this and similar situations the buyer's loss may be difficult to ascertain. In these and many other situations where damages do not fully compensate the buyer one may expect a favorable response to an action to require ("specific") performance.

BEARDSLEY, COMPELLING CONTRACT PERFORMANCE IN FRANCE
1 Hastings Int'l & Comp. L. Rev. 93, 93–96, 101 (1977).*

ARTICLE 1142 of the Code Napoleon declares that "[e]very obligation to do or not to do shall be resolved in damages in case of nonperformance by the obligor." Specific performance, the draftsmen seemed to say, is not to be had where a contract imposes this kind of obligation. But Article 1142 was arguably intended and has certainly been interpreted, primarily as an expression of the maxim *nemo potest praecise cogi ad factum* which in turn could be seen as prohibiting the use of force to compel performance rather than as the consecration of a damages-only rule on remedies. The courts and doctrinal writers were in agreement that in principle the disappointed promisee was entitled to performance where it could be obtained without physical coercion.

The difficulty lay not in the principle but in its implementation. French courts do not possess the power to fine or imprison the contemnors of their civil judgments. Their sole weapon is the judgment itself adorned with an executory clause *(formule d' exécution)* addressed to the *hussiers de justice* and officers of the police and *gendarmerie* ordering them to lend their assistance in its execution. The execution of a money judgment is accomplished by levy on the debtor's property and a subsequent judicial sale. If the judgment requires the debtor to deliver specific moveable property, the performance of this obligation "to do" can similarly be accomplished through seizure of the property by the *hussier* with the assistance, if needed, of the police. The need alone does not suffice to assure police assistance, despite the language of the executory formula. There has long been a notorious reluctance on the part of the administrative authorities to provide police assistance in the execution of civil judgments. Where the performance ordered is not the delivery or surrender of property, the problem of the availability of coercive forces rejoin that of the legitimacy of such coercion in light of Article 1142. Using force to separate a debtor from property is one thing; compelling him by physical coercion to perform some agreed task is quite another. For, as it is customarily explained, to do so would infringe his liberty.

The problem of specific performance of contracts in France was thus twofold. On the one hand, it was a matter of finding a substitute for coercion where the requisite State assistance was not forthcoming. On the other hand, it was to devise a form of compulsion or inducement capable of reaching at least some of those situations in which direct coercion was excluded either by Article 1142 or by broader scruples not unlike those which have led Common Law jurisdictions to refuse to order the specific performance of personal service contracts. A solution had to be built around the money judgment, the only sanction available to the courts. The Civil Code itself offered one possibility: the contractual penalty fixing a liability in excess of probable damage in case of failure to perform. The other approach, the *astreinte,* was devised by the courts without statutory support. Both methods rely on the threat of a money judgment substantially exceeding provable damage. Both have been the subject of recent legislation which, with the evolution of the case law on the *astreinte,* has substantially changed what may be called the law of specific performance in France.

The *astreinte* is a money judgment imposing upon the non-performing debtor a liability of a fixed amount per day (or month or year) for every day which passes without performance by the debtor after the date fixed by the judgment. As it was shaped by the case law and the doctrinal writers, the *astreinte* might be either "definitive" or "provisional." In either case, a further judicial decision was required to "liquidate" it by fixing the cumulative amount before execution could be obtained. The definitive *astreinte* took the form of a final judgment whose "liquidation" involved nothing more than a simple multiplication operation. The provisional *astreinte,* on the other hand, was not cast as a final judgment and was subject to revision by the judge at the time of liquidation. On the basis of a further examination of the circumstances, extenuating and otherwise, surrounding the debtor's failure to perform, the provisional *astreinte* could be liquidated at an amount quite different from that originally fixed. The utility of the device in either form as a means of compelling performance obviously depends in very large part upon credibility of the threat to impose a financial liability on the debtor greater than that to which he would be subjected by a judgment awarding actual damages to the creditor. The central problem in the development of the *astreinte* was precisely whether a civil tribunal could ever impose liability for a sum in excess of actual damages.

* * *

With the adoption of the Law of July 2, 1972, the *astreinte* has undergone a complete renewal. It may be considered as effective as a money judgment can be for compelling specific performance of a contractual or other obligation. The judge may impose the *astreinte* on party application or on his own initiative. He may either fix the amount definitively or leave it open to redetermination upon liquidation. The *astreinte* has now been statutorily characterized as a coercive measure the amount of which is not in any sense restricted by the actual damages suffered by the beneficiary of the *astreinte*.

TALLON, REMEDIES; FRENCH REPORT
Contract Law Today; Anglo-French Comparisons.
263–288 (D. Harris & D. Tallon eds. 1989).*

41. To the external observer, it appears that English law does not place all the remedies on the same level. The normal remedy is the award of damages, even if the famous dictum of Holmes[65] should not be taken literally. Specific performance is considered to be an exceptional remedy. Rescission seems to be somewhat marginal. In English law, the ranking of remedies is a question of principle; in French law, it is more a question of the circumstances—the remedy best suited to the situation will be adopted. Undoubtedly, French law is committed to the notion that the primary objective is performance of the contract, as is confirmed by a number of legal solutions: judicial assessment of the severity of the breach, to justify rescission; the role of the *astreinte*, but also the requirement of a *mise en demeure*, conferring on the debtor a last chance to perform (analogous to the *Nachfrist* in German law); the validity of penalty clauses (though subject to judicial control since 1975—see article 1152, *Code civil*); rejection of the doctrine of *imprévision*; and perhaps even the terminology which regards an award of damages as a substitute for performance. At the heart of all this is discernible a commitment to the principle of the binding quality of contracts: the "law of the parties", in the words of article 1134 must be respected like the law of Parliament.

42. The pre-eminence of performance should not, however, be exaggerated. It is not reflected in legislative provisions, indeed rather the reverse: article 1184 (the only general provision which refers to the three remedies) confers a free choice on the creditor, "either to compel the other to perform . . . or to claim rescission with damages". The choice is not circumscribed, once the conditions for each remedy have been

65. "The duty to keep a contract at common law means a prediction that you must pay damages if you do not keep it—and nothing else", dictum cited by Nicholas, who nevertheless regards it as exaggerated.

satisfied. And performance "by substitution" plays a residual role. It will always be possible if the other measures prove to be ill adapted to the circumstances or cannot be applied. So, in a case of defective performance not justifying rescission, the contractual equilibrium is re-established by the award of damages.

43. Further, there is a provision in the Civil Code which seems considerably to limit the role of specific performance: article 1142, which prescribes that "every obligation *de faire* or *de ne pas faire* gives rise to damages, in the event of breach by the debtor". Taken literally, the provision asserts a principle denying specific performance except in the cases envisaged in articles 1143 and 1144 and where the obligation is to transfer (*donner*)—an obligation no longer important in a legal system where property may be transferred by pure agreement.

In reality, the provision is ambiguous. Today, specific performance is no longer regarded as exceptional. * * *

* * *

51. As we have observed, there is no legal hierarchy of remedies. In the light of the creditor's choice and the judge's control, may we envisage a factual hierarchy? The opinions of writers are divided. Some speak of enforced performance usurping the role of substitute performance, having regard to the evolution of *astreinte*. For others, judicial rescission remains the primary remedy for breach committed through fault, even though a decline in judicial rescission is also recognized. Such diversity of opinion, suggests that knowledge of the phenomena is inadequate; in any event, there are no obvious answers to the questions posed. The opinions expressed are based only on impression. In my view, more adequate data are required before a conclusion can be sensibly reached. Further, to obtain a complete picture of the problem, contractual provisions as to remedies (penalty clauses, limitation clauses) would also have to be studied.

ZIEGEL, THE REMEDIAL PROVISIONS OF THE VIENNA SALES CONVENTION: COMMON LAW PERSPECTIVES

International Sales 9–9 to 9–12 (N. Galston and H. Smit, eds., 1984).*

Article 46 of the Convention confers on the buyer a strong right to demand specific performance of the seller's obligations subject only to the following qualifications: (i) the buyer is not entitled to demand it where he has resorted to a remedy inconsistent with the remedy of specific performance; (ii) where the seller has delivered non-conforming goods, the buyer may only require the delivery of substitute goods if the lack of conformity constitutes a fundamental breach of contract; (iii) the buyer may not require the seller to remedy a non-conformity by repair if this would be unreasonable having regard to all the circumstances; and

* Copyright © 1984 and reproduced by permission from Matthew Bender.

(iv) pursuant to article 28, the buyer is not entitled to specific performance at all "unless the court would do so under its own law in respect of similar contracts of sale not governed by [the] Convention." * * *

To a common law mind it may seem puzzling that civilians are still so attached to a remedy that is inefficient economically, at any rate in those cases where damages would adequately compensate the buyer. I am not sure the civilians are as strongly committed to it as we think—it may be more a case of unwillingness to renounce a long familiar remedy simply because it is uncongenial to common law lawyers. In any event, the common law is less than consistent in its own position. Commonwealth courts at any rate regularly enforce specifically contracts for the sale of commercial realty even where damages would be an adequate substitute. Still more significant is the action for the price permitted the unpaid seller under section 49(1) of the British Sale of Goods Act even where the buyer has refused to accept the goods. This is surely an action for specific performance in all but name even if it can be rationalized on historical and somewhat dubious conceptual grounds. Again, for what it is worth, economists are not all agreed that specific enforcement involves a misallocation of economic resources, and there is evidence that the remedy is gaining ground among judges in the sales as well as non-sales areas. * * * First, since the rules of specific performance differ widely even among civil law jurisdictions, the results of such an action will depend on the geographical location of the court before which the action is being brought. This seems regrettable even if it is unavoidable. Second, when article 28 invites a tribunal to consider whether a "similar" contract would be specifically enforceable under its own law, presumably it is not the contract alone but *all* the surrounding circumstances, including the subject matter of the contract and the identity of the parties, that the court is entitled to take into consideration.

* * *

PROBLEM 5–1

On June 1, François Fermier, a French farmer and vintner who grows his own grapes, bottles his own wine, and sells it under the name François' Fizzy, agreed with the Wine Import Board of Russia to produce and sell 50,000 bottles of François' Fizzy to the Wine Import Board. The contract requires François to ship the goods by December 1. In September, the wine critic of the New York times "discovered" François' Fizzy and wrote a rave review about it. Subsequently, François has been inundated with orders offering to pay twice as much as the price in the contract with the Wine Import Board. It is now December 6, the Board knows that François has 50,000 bottles in its inventory, but is afraid that François will ship the wine to fill the higher-priced orders.

(a) If the Russian Wine Import Board commences legal proceedings in France, may it obtain a court order compelling François to ship the goods? CISG art. 46(1).

(b) If Frank, a New York farmer and vintner had made the same contract with the Wine Import Board, failed to ship, and the Board had brought suit in New York, could the Board obtain a court order compelling Frank to ship the goods? CISG art. 28. Is a New York court required to order specific performance under UCC § 2–716, set forth in the Documents Supplement? Would that court be prohibited from ordering specific performance if it would not do so if the transaction were purely domestic? Would it matter whether Frank's wine had also been "discovered" by wine critics, and that caused the failure to ship?

(c) Would your previous answers be different if the Wine Import Board knew that the seller did not have 50,000 bottles in its inventory?

Legislation Note on UCC Provisions

In contrast to Civil Law concepts (see the excerpts from Tallon), the UCC provides for specific performance in only a limited number of circumstances under UCC § 2–716. Specific performance "may be decreed" if the goods are "unique" or "in other proper circumstances." The "may be decreed" language is susceptible to a statement which gives courts: 1) limited authority but no requirement, or 2) a limited requirement, but no limitation on their authority. However, a court which wishes to order specific performance will usually find that there are "other proper circumstances" for such an order. The Comment of 2–716 specifically lists output contracts and requirements contracts as a "typical commercial specific performance situation," and states the unavailability of covering goods is strong evidence of "proper circumstances."

* * *

PROBLEM 5–2.

Société Ballard, the French company, agrees to manufacture and sell a bottle-capping machine to Bottling Company of Brooklyn, New York. Assume Société Ballard delivers and installs the machine but that the machine caps only 9,600 bottles per hour. Attempts during the following month to adjust the rate of output are unsuccessful. As a consequence, the four other machines used in the company's bottling cycle are not used to capacity. According to Bottling Company's accountants, the resulting lower production rate will decrease the company's projected profits by 10%. The contract is silent about cure of non-conformities. Bottling Company writes a letter to Société Ballard informing it that the machine fails to meet contract specifications and requesting a replacement machine. Must Société Ballard comply with the request for a replacement? CISG arts. 25, 39(1), 46(2).

* * *

PROBLEM 5–3.

Assume that in the preceding problem Bottling Company asked Société Ballard to repair the machine, rather than to replace it. Société Ballard does not have mechanics in New York and would have either to send mechanics from France or to hire mechanics in New York to do the work. With the detailed information given in the letter from Bottling Company, Société Ballard estimates that (i) it would take between two weeks and one month to complete the repairs, during which time the machine could not be used; (ii) the likelihood of increasing output somewhat is 90% but the likelihood of meeting the contract specifications is only 70%; (iii) that the probable cost to Société Ballard to make the repairs would reduce the company's profit on the sale of the machine by 60%; and (iv) it would be less costly to replace the machine. Must Société Ballard comply with the request? CISG art. 46(3).

COMPELLING BUYER TO PERFORM

The usual problems concerning specific performance issues arise when a buyer attempts to compel a seller to perform its obligations. Can they also arise when a seller attempts to compel a buyer to perform? Read on.

* * *

PROBLEM 5–4.

Schmitthoff's Vodka, a Russian manufacturer with offices in France, agrees to manufacture and sell 24,000 bottles to Merchandise Market, a Delaware corporation, with offices in New York. The parties' contract requires Merchandise Market to arrange for a letter of credit to be issued in favor of Schmitthoff's Vodka by a date 30 days before the scheduled shipment date. Merchandise Market fails to obtain a letter of credit by this date.

(a) Assume Schmitthoff's Vodka brings suit in New York asking the court to order Merchandise Market to obtain a letter of credit. Is Schmitthoff's Vodka entitled to such an order? CISG arts. 62, 28.

(b) Assume that Schmitthoff's Vodka brings suit in France asking the court to order Bottling Company to obtain a letter of credit. Is Schmitthoff's Vodka entitled to such an order? Reread the Tallon excerpt at the beginning of this chapter.

(c) How likely is it that Schmitthoff's Vodka will bring a suit asking for specific performance in New York, France or Russia?

* * *

PROBLEM 5–5.

As in the previous problem, Schmitthoff's Vodka agrees to manufacture and sell 24,000 bottles to Merchandise Market. However, this time the goods are sold C.I.F. New York, but there is no letter of credit term. Between the time it entered into the contract and the time for delivery, the public's taste in alcoholic beverages has changed, and Merchandise Market decides that it will have great difficulty in reselling the goods in the U.S. When the documents are tendered pursuant to the terms of the contract, Merchandise Market refuses to accept them or pay for them.

(a) May Schmitthoff's Vodka require Merchandise Market to accept tender of the documents? CISG art. 62.

(b) May Schmitthoff's Vodka require Merchandise Market to accept delivery of the goods when they arrive in New York? CISG arts. 62.

(c) May Schmitthoff's Vodka require Merchandise Market to pay for the goods notwithstanding its refusal to accept them? CISG arts. 62, 28.

Legislation Note on UCC Provisions

The UCC has separate provisions on specific performance of the contract and payment of the price. An action for payment of the price is set forth in UCC § 2–709 (not § 2–716), and is limited in scope. Thus, a seller has an action for the price, rather than damages, for: 1) goods accepted by the buyer, 2) goods lost or damaged after the risk of loss has passed to the buyer, and 3) goods which seller cannot resell. Otherwise, the aggrieved seller is supposed to resell the goods and sue for damages.

Is the UCC remedial limitation engrafted onto CISG actions litigated in the U.S. through CISG art. 28, or is CISG art. 62 the only applicable provision? That is what the debate between Honnold and Farnsworth is all about.

C. DAMAGES

FLECHTNER, REMEDIES UNDER THE NEW INTERNATIONAL SALES CONVENTION: THE PERSPECTIVE FROM ARTICLE 2 OF THE U.C.C.

8 J. Law & Com. 53, 97–107 (1988).*

Damages Upon Avoidance

A lawyer conversant with Article 2 of the U.C.C. who successfully travels the unfamiliar pathways of avoidance of contract under the Convention, including the sometimes unexpected turnings of its rules on restitution, will discover recognizable landscape at the end of the journey. Article 75, for instance, permits an avoiding party to recover damages measured by the difference between the contract price and the price in a reasonable substitute transaction. The aggrieved party can claim further damages as measured by Article 74. This provision, which will be discussed in more detail in connection with nonavoidance remedies permits an avoiding party to recover consequential and incidental damages.

Provisions comparable to Article 75 are found in U.C.C. section 2–706 (sellers' resale damages) and U.C.C. section 2–712 (buyers' cover damages), both of which also permit recovery of consequential and/or incidental damages. For sellers, the major difference between U.C.C. section 2–706 and Article 75 of the Convention is that the latter neither requires notice of the substitute sale nor regulates the details of resale beyond requiring that it be made "in a reasonable manner and within a reasonable time after avoidance." For buyers, Article 75 appears almost indistinguishable from U.C.C. section 2–712. Article 75, however, does not specify the adjustment mentioned in both U.C.C. section 2–706(1) and U.C.C. section 2–712(2) for expenses saved by the party claiming damages as a result of the breach. Under the U.C.C. language, items such as transportation expenses saved by the aggrieved party in a substitute transaction are deducted from cover or resale damages. A similar result can be reached under Article 75 of the Convention by construing the phrase "price in the substitute transaction" to permit such adjustment. Equitable considerations demand this construction, given that increased transportation costs and similar items of extra expense associated with a substitute transaction would constitute losses suffered "as a consequence of breach" and thus would be recoverable under CISG Article 74.

Article 76(1) of the Convention permits a party that has not entered into a substitute transaction to claim damages measured by "the difference between the price fixed by the contract and the current [i.e., market] price." The comparable provisions in U.C.C. Article 2 are section 2–708(1) (seller's market-price damages) and section 2–713 (buyer's market-price damages). The manner of measuring market-price damages under the Convention, however, differs in several significant respects from the method in the U.C.C.

CISG Article 76 damages are generally measured by the market price "at the time of avoidance"; if the aggrieved party avoids the contract after "taking over the goods," however, the reference point is "the time of such taking over." The latter alternative prevents an avoiding buyer who has received delivery from manipulating the time of avoidance in order to increase the seller's liability. Under U.C.C. Article 2, the seller's market-price damages are normally measured at the time for tender and the buyer's damages are usually measured as of the time the buyer "learned of the breach." If the breach was an anticipatory repudiation and the action comes to trial before the repudiator's performance is due, however, U.C.C. market-price damages are measured at the time the aggrieved party learned of the repudiation. Thus suppose the seller contracted to deliver goods at a price of $10,000 on June 1, at which time the market price was $8,000. If the buyer wrongfully rejected the goods, the seller's market- price damages under U.C.C. section 2–718(1) would be $2,000 (assuming no "expenses saved" because of the buyer's breach). The damages under Article 76 of the Convention, however, would depend on when the seller declared the contract avoided. If avoidance occurred on June 15, when the market price had risen to $9,000, the seller's market-price damages would be $1,000.

Under Article 76(2) of the Convention, market price is measured "at the place where delivery of the goods should have been made." This language refers to the place of tender, at which the U.C.C. also measures market-price damages for sellers and, in many circumstances, buyers. The Convention and the U.C.C., therefore, often point to the same place for measuring market-price damages. Where an aggrieved buyer has rejected or revoked acceptance after the goods arrived, however, U.C.C. section 2–713(2) measures the market price at the place of arrival. Suppose goods that were sold and delivered under a shipment contract (i.e., a contract in which the seller tenders by placing the goods with the first carrier) turn out to be seriously defective. Under the Convention, if the buyer rejects the goods by avoiding the contract, its market-price damages would be measured by reference to the price prevailing at the place of tender—where the seller delivered the goods to the carrier for shipment. Under the U.C.C., the rejecting buyer's market-price damages would be measured by the price at the place where the goods arrived.

Most commentators on Article 2 of the U.C.C. agree that an aggrieved buyer or seller who has in fact entered into a substitute transaction should not be permitted to claim market-price damages more generous than those produced by the resale or cover damages formula. There is, however, contrary opinion and the text of Article 2 does not provide clear guidance. Article 76(1) of the Convention resolves this issue in part by providing that an avoiding party can claim market-price damages only if it "has not made a purchase or resale under article 75." A party that has entered into a substitute transaction within the meaning of Article 75, therefore, must proceed under that provision and cannot claim damages under Article 76. An attempt at resale or cover that does not meet the requirements of Article 75 (e.g., because the substitute transaction did not occur within a reasonable time after avoidance), however, does not prevent the aggrieved party from claiming market price damages under Article 76. To avoid over-compensating the aggrieved party, nevertheless, such substitute transactions should be deemed to establish an upper limit on the amount of damages recoverable under Article 76, although the text of the Convention does not mandate this result.

A seller who is deprived of sales volume by the buyer's breach will be fully compensated only if it can recover the profit on the lost sale to the buyer. The U.C.C. deals with this situation in section 2–708(2), which permits an aggrieved seller to recover lost profits where the market-price damage formula "is inadequate to put the seller in as good a position as performance would have done." Although the Convention contains no specific provision comparable to U.C.C. section 2–708(2), both Articles 75 and 76 permit an avoiding party to claim further damages recoverable under Article 74. Article 74, in turn, permits an aggrieved party to recover "the loss, including loss of profits," caused by a breach. This provision will permit a volume seller to recover damages to compensate for the lost sale.

Where a lost profits recovery would yield lower damages than other formulas, however, results under the Convention and the U.C.C. may differ. One court has restricted an Article 2 seller's damages to lost profits under U.C.C. section 2–708(2) where market-price damages measured by section 2–708(1) would have been more generous. The holding is consistent with the expectation-based principles behind U.C.C. remedies and is supported by at least one commentary. This result, however, may be difficult to reach under the Convention. Unlike U.C.C. section 2–708(2), which is cast as an alternative to market-price damages under U.C.C. section 2–708(1), the CISG provision that permits recovery of lost profits (Article 74) is structured as a supplement to the resale/cover or market-price damage provisions available to avoiding parties. The text of Articles 74–76, therefore, argues against limiting damages to lost profits where the contract has been avoided. Furthermore, the result under Article 2 of the U.C.C. is supported by the general statement of expectation principles in U.C.C. section 1–106(1). Although the Convention's remedial provisions reflect a policy of protecting an aggrieved party's expectation interest, there is no overt statement of this policy and at least one remedy—the buyer's right to reduce the price under Article 50—will in some circumstances violate expectation principles.

* * *

Nonavoidance Damages

Remedies other than damages which are available to a party that has not avoided the contract—i.e., the seller's price remedy and the buyer's right to specific performance, substitute goods, repair, or reduction in price—have previously been described. To the extent these remedies do not fully protect the aggrieved party's expectations under the contract, Article 74 of the Convention authorizes recovery of damages measured by "the loss, including loss of profit, suffered ... as a consequence of the breach." Damages under this provision, which are also available where the aggrieved party has avoided the contract, are subject to familiar limitations involving foreseeability and mitigation of damages.

Thus if the seller fails to deliver, a buyer who elects not to avoid the contract and who seeks specific performance under Article 46(1) can also claim damages under Article 74 for losses caused by the delay in receiving the goods, provided the losses were foreseeable when the contract was formed and could not have been avoided by reasonable attempts to mitigate. A buyer can also recover Article 74 damages if it reduces the price under Article 50, seeks substitute goods under Article 46(2), or demands repair of defective goods under Article 46(3). In these circumstances, Article 74 performs the function of the U.C.C. Article 2 provisions that permit an aggrieved buyer to recover consequential damages, which (under U.C.C. section 2- 715(2)(a)) must be foreseeable at the time of contracting and not reasonably avoidable "by cover or otherwise."

Suppose, however, that a seller delivers non-conforming goods and the buyer can neither avoid the contract nor demand substitute goods because the defects do not satisfy the fundamental breach standard. Suppose further that the buyer cannot require the seller to repair because that would be "unreasonable having regard to all the circumstances." Under Article 74 of the Convention, the buyer can claim damages measured by its losses from the defects. In these circumstances, Article 74 performs the function of U.C.C. section 2–714(2), which authorizes a buyer who has accepted the goods to recover damages for breach of warranty. Damages under the U.C.C. provision are measured by the difference between the value of the goods delivered and "the value they would have had if they had been a warranted." The same measure is available under Article 74 of the Convention.

DELCHI CARRIER SPA v. ROTOREX CORP.

United States Court of Appeals, Second Circuit, 1995.
71 F.3d 1024.

WINTER, CIRCUIT JUDGE:

* * *

In January 1988, Rotorex agreed to sell 10,800 compressors to Delchi for use in Delchi's "Ariele" line of portable room air conditioners. The air conditioners were scheduled to go on sale in the spring and summer of 1988. Prior to executing the contract, Rotorex sent Delchi a sample compressor and accompanying written performance specifications. The compressors were scheduled to be delivered in three shipments before May 15, 1988.

Rotorex sent the first shipment by sea on March 26. Delchi paid for this shipment, which arrived at its Italian factory on April 20, by letter of credit. Rotorex sent a second shipment of compressors on or about May 9. Delchi also remitted payment for this shipment by letter of credit. While the second shipment was en route, Delchi discovered that the first lot of compressors did not conform to the sample model and accompanying specifications. On May 13, after a Rotorex representative visited the Delchi factory in Italy, Delchi informed Rotorex that 93 percent of the compressors were rejected in quality control checks because they had lower cooling capacity and consumed more power than the sample model and specifications. After several unsuccessful attempts to cure the defects in the compressors, Delchi asked Rotorex to supply new compressors conforming to the original sample and specifications. Rotorex refused, claiming that the performance specifications were "inadvertently communicated" to Delchi.

In a faxed letter dated May 23, 1988, Delchi cancelled the contract. Although it was able to expedite a previously planned order of suitable compressors from Sanyo, another supplier, Delchi was unable to obtain in a timely fashion substitute compressors from other sources and thus suffered a loss in its sales volume of Arieles during the 1988 selling season. Delchi filed the instant action under the United Nations Convention on Contracts for the International Sale of Goods ("CISG" or "the Convention") for breach of contract and failure to deliver conforming goods. On January 10, 1991, Judge Cholakis granted Delchi's motion for partial summary judgment, holding Rotorex liable for breach of contract.

After three years of discovery and a bench trial on the issue of damages, Judge Munson, to whom the case had been transferred, held Rotorex liable to Delchi for $1,248,331.87. This amount included consequential damages for: (i) lost profits resulting from a diminished sales level of Ariele units, (ii) expenses that Delchi incurred in attempting to remedy the nonconformity of the compressors, (iii) the cost of expediting shipment of previously ordered Sanyo compressors after Delchi rejected the Rotorex compressors, and (iv) costs of handling and storing the rejected compressors. The district court also awarded prejudgment interest under CISG art. 78.

The court denied Delchi's claim for damages based on other expenses, including: (i) shipping, customs, and incidentals relating to the two shipments of Rotorex compressors; (ii) the cost of obsolete insulation and tubing that Delchi purchased only for use with Rotorex compressors; (iii) the cost of obsolete tooling purchased only for production of units with Rotorex compressors; and (iv) labor costs for four days when Delchi's production line was idle because it had no compressors to install in the air conditioning units. The court denied an award for these items on the ground that it would lead to a double recovery because "those costs are accounted for in Delchi's recovery on its lost profits claim." It also denied an award for the cost of modification of electrical panels for use with substitute Sanyo compressors on the ground that the cost was not attributable to the breach. Finally, the court denied recovery on Delchi's claim of 4000 additional lost sales in Italy.

On appeal, Rotorex argues that it did not breach the agreement, that Delchi is not entitled to lost profits because it maintained inventory levels in excess of the maximum number of possible lost sales, that the calculation of the number of lost sales was improper, and that the district court improperly excluded fixed costs and depreciation from the manufacturing cost in calculating lost profits. Delchi cross-appeals, claiming that it is entitled to the additional out-of-pocket expenses and the lost profits on additional sales denied by Judge Munson.

DISCUSSION

The district court held, and the parties agree, that the instant matter is governed by the CISG, *reprinted at* 15 U.S.C.A. Appendix (West Supp.1995), a self-executing agreement between the United States and other signatories, including Italy. Because there is virtually no caselaw under the Convention, we look to its language and to "the general principles" upon which it is based. *See* CISG art. 7(2). The Convention directs that its interpretation be informed by its "international character and ... the need to promote uniformity in its application and the observance of good faith in international trade." *See* CISG art. 7(1). Caselaw interpreting analogous provisions of Article 2 of the Uniform Commercial Code ("UCC"), may also inform a court where the language of the relevant CISG provisions tracks that of the UCC. However, UCC caselaw "is not *per se* applicable."

We first address the liability issue. * * *

Judge Cholakis held that "there is no question that [Rotorex's] compressors did not conform to the terms of the contract between the parties" and noted that "[t]here are ample admissions [by Rotorex] to that effect." We agree. * * *

Under the CISG, if the breach is "fundamental" the buyer may either require delivery of substitute goods, CISG art. 46, or declare the contract void, CISG art. 49, and seek damages. * * * Because the cooling power and energy consumption of an air conditioner compressor are important determinants of the product's value, the district court's conclusion that Rotorex was liable for a fundamental breach of contract under the Convention was proper.

We turn now to the district court's award of damages following the bench trial. * * *

Rotorex argues that Delchi is not entitled to lost profits because it was able to maintain inventory levels of Ariele air conditioning units in excess of the maximum number of possible lost sales. In Rotorex's view, therefore, there was no actual shortfall of Ariele units available for sale because of Rotorex's delivery of nonconforming compressors. Rotorex's argument goes as follows. The end of the air conditioner selling season is August 1. If one totals the number of units available to Delchi from March to August 1, the sum is enough to fill all sales. We may assume that the evidence in the record supports the factual premise. Nevertheless, the argument is fallacious. Because of Rotorex's breach, Delchi had to shut down its manufacturing operation for a few days in May, and the date on which particular units were available for sale was substantially delayed. For example, units available in late July could not be used to meet orders in the spring. As a result, Delchi lost sales in the spring and early summer. We therefore conclude that the district court's findings regarding lost sales are not clearly erroneous. A detailed discussion of the precise number of lost sales is unnecessary because the district court's findings were, if anything, conservative.

Rotorex contends, in the alternative, that the district court improperly awarded lost profits for unfilled orders from Delchi affiliates in Europe and from sales agents within Italy. We disagree. The CISG requires that damages be limited by the familiar principle of foreseeability established in *Hadley v. Baxendale.* CISG art. 74. However, it was objectively foreseeable that Delchi would take orders for Ariele sales based on the number of compressors it had ordered and expected to have ready for the season. The district court was entitled to rely upon the documents and testimony regarding these lost sales and was well within its authority in deciding which orders were proven with sufficient certainty.

Rotorex also challenges the district court's exclusion of fixed costs and depreciation from the manufacturing cost used to calculate lost profits. The trial judge calculated lost profits by subtracting the 478,783 lire "manufacturing cost"—the total variable cost—of an Ariele unit from the 654,644 lire average sale price. The CISG does not explicitly state whether only variable expenses, or both fixed and variable expenses, should be subtracted from sales revenue in calculating lost profits. However, courts generally do not include fixed costs in the calculation of lost profits. This is, of course, because the fixed costs would have been encountered whether or not the breach occurred. In the absence of a specific provision in the CISG for calculating lost profits, the district court was correct to use the standard formula employed by most American courts and to deduct only variable costs from sales revenue to arrive at a figure for lost profits.

In its cross-appeal, Delchi challenges the district court's denial of various consequential and incidental damages, including reimbursement for: (i) shipping, customs, and incidentals relating to the first and second shipments—rejected and returned—of Rotorex compressors; (ii) obsolete insulation materials and tubing purchased for use only with Rotorex compressors; (iii) obsolete tooling purchased exclusively for production of units with Rotorex compressors; and (iv) labor costs for the period of May 16–19, 1988, when the Delchi production line was idle due to a lack of compressors to install in Ariele air conditioning units. The district court denied damages for these items on the ground that they "are accounted for in Delchi's recovery on its lost profits claim," and, therefore, an award would constitute a double recovery for Delchi. We disagree.

The Convention provides that a contract plaintiff may collect damages to compensate for the full loss. This includes, but is not limited to, lost profits, subject only to the familiar limitation that the breaching party must have foreseen, or should have foreseen, the loss as a probable consequence. CISG art. 74.

An award for lost profits will not compensate Delchi for the expenses in question. Delchi's lost profits are determined by calculating the hypothetical revenues to be derived from unmade sales less the hypothetical variable costs that would have been, but were not, incurred. This figure, however, does not compensate for costs actually incurred that led to no sales. Thus, to award damages for costs actually incurred in no way creates a double recovery and instead furthers the purpose of giving the injured party damages "equal to the loss." CISG art. 74.

The only remaining inquiries, therefore, are whether the expenses were reasonably foreseeable and legitimate incidental or consequential damages.[2] The expenses incurred by Delchi for shipping, customs, and related matters for the two returned shipments of Rotorex compressors, including storage expenses for the second shipment at Genoa, were clearly foreseeable and recoverable incidental expenses. These are up-front expenses that had to be paid to get the goods to the manufacturing plant for inspection and were thus incurred largely before the nonconformities were detected. To deny reimbursement to Delchi for these incidental damages would effectively cut into the lost profits award. The same is true of unreimbursed tooling expenses and the cost of the useless insulation and tubing materials. These are legitimate consequential damages that in no way duplicate lost profits damages.

---

2. The UCC defines incidental damages resulting from a seller's breach as "expenses reasonably incurred in inspection, receipt, transportation and care and custody of goods rightfully rejected, any commer-cially reasonable charges, expenses or commissions in connection with effecting cover and any other reasonable expense incident to the delay or other breach." U.C.C. § 2–715(1) (1990).

The labor expense incurred as a result of the production line shutdown of May 16–19, 1988 is also a reasonably foreseeable result of delivering nonconforming compressors for installation in air conditioners. However, Rotorex argues that the labor costs in question were fixed costs that would have been incurred whether or not there was a breach. The district court labeled the labor costs "fixed costs," but did not explore whether Delchi would have paid these wages regardless of how much it produced. Variable costs are generally those costs that "fluctuate with a firm's output," and typically include labor (but not management) costs. Whether Delchi's labor costs during this four-day period are variable or fixed costs is in large measure a fact question that we cannot answer because we lack factual findings by the district court. We therefore remand to the district court on this issue.

The district court also denied an award for the modification of electrical panels for use with substitute Sanyo compressors. It denied damages on the ground that Delchi failed to show that the modifications were not part of the regular cost of production of units with Sanyo compressors and were therefore attributable to Rotorex's breach. This appears to have been a credibility determination that was within the court's authority to make. We therefore affirm on the ground that this finding is not clearly erroneous.

Finally, Delchi cross-appeals from the denial of its claimed 4000 additional lost sales in Italy. The district court held that Delchi did not prove these orders with sufficient certainty. The trial court was in the best position to evaluate the testimony of the Italian sales agents who stated that they would have ordered more Arieles if they had been available. It found the agents' claims to be too speculative, and this conclusion is not clearly erroneous.

CONCLUSION

We affirm the award of damages. We reverse in part the denial of incidental and consequential damages. We remand for further proceedings in accord with this opinion.

UNCITRAL CLOUT CASE 237
Arbitration Institute of Stockholm Chamber of Commerce, 1998.

(Abstract prepared by Peter Winship)

A manufacturer in the United States contracted with a joint venture in the People's Republic of China to sell a press. The contract guaranteed that the press was made of "the best materials with first class workmanship, brand new and unused." During manufacture, the seller substituted a different lockplate for the lockplate described in the design documents given to the buyer. The seller did not inform the buyer of this substitution or of the need to install the lockplate properly. The seller shipped the disassembled press from the United States to China and when the buyer reassembled the press in China the lockplate was installed improperly. Slightly more than four years after the seller shipped the press, the lockplate broke, causing significant damage to the press. The buyer immediately notified the seller. When the seller rejected any liability for the breakdown, the buyer requested arbitration.

The issues before the arbitral tribunal were whether the U.S. seller made a non-conforming tender of goods and whether the Chinese buyer's claim of non-conforming goods was timely.

The arbitral tribunal found the seller liable for damages for the failure of the press. The tribunal concluded that the tender of the press did not conform under article 35(2) CISG. The seller was aware of the possibility that the substitute lockplate would probably fail if it was not properly installed. The seller, nonetheless, failed to inform the buyer of the need to install the lockplate properly. The mere inclusion of an express guarantee in the contract did not exclude the obligations set out in article 35(2) CISG. The tribunal further found that the buyer was not negligent when it installed the lockplate or later maintained the press.

A majority of the tribunal also found that the buyer's claim was timely because under article 40 CISG the seller was not entitled to rely on the time limits set forth in article 39 CISG. The tribunal stated that it did not matter whether the non-conformity resulted from breach of the contract guarantee or breach of article 35 CISG. Even if articles 38 and 39 CISG were concerned only with examination and notice of non-conformity under CISG, article 40 CISG states a general principle that applies to contractual obligations by virtue of article 7(2) CISG. The majority of the tribunal concluded that article 40 CISG excused notice by the buyer because the seller "consciously disregarded facts which were of evident relevance to the nonconformity".

J. BELL, S. BOYRON & S. WHITTAKER, PRINCIPLES OF FRENCH LAW
348–57 (1998).*

Despite the widespread availability of orders for specific enforcement of contractual obligations, damages remain a very important feature of French practice. In some cases, an order for specific enforcement is meaningless (for example, in the context of personal injuries), but in many others the injured party will have lost confidence in the quality of any performance which would be tendered by the other party. As in English law, damages are in principle available to compensate the injured party's loss caused by non-performance, this being termed *réparation par équivalent*.

* * *

The starting point of French law for the assessment of damages in both contract and delict is that the injured party should receive full compensation (*réparation intégrale*) for his losses and this may be supported in the case of contract by article 1149 of the Civil Code, which allows recovery of both losses incurred and profits denied as a result of breach. We therefore do not find in French texts elaborate discussions of the "heads of damage" which may be recoverable in an action for breach of contract, for all, including *dommages morales* (mental distress, lost reputation etc.) are recoverable. Indeed, for a common lawyer there is remarkably little law on the issue of quantification of damages and this is to be explained by the fact that this issue is in principle within the "sovereign power of assessment" of the *juges du fond*. In particular, French lawyers do not in this context distinguish between recovery of an injured party's reliance and expectation interests. Two important issues remain.

First, the Civil Code recognizes two tests of remoteness of damage for contractual damages, so that in general a party in breach is liable only for those losses which were foreseen or could have been foreseen at the time of making the contract, but where that party is guilty of *dol*, here meaning bad faith and in particular deliberate non-performance, then he will be liable for all losses which are the "immediate and direct consequence" of his breach and the Cour de cassation intervenes to make sure that these provisions are properly applied. Thus, for example, in the case of an "innocent breach", it has made clear that the requirement of foreseeability applies to the extent as well as to the type of loss suffered by the injured party, but not to its monetary value.

Secondly, the courts may reduce an injured party's damages on the grounds of his contributory fault (*faute de la victime*), whatever the content of the obligation on the breach of which he relies, whether *de résultat* or *de moyens*. The extent of the reduction lies in the "sovereign power of assessment" of the *juges du fond*. This has two principal significances. First, an injured party's negligence or other fault may contribute to his initial harm, for example, a driver's careless driving contributing to an accident which was also caused by the car's defective steering. Here, then, it functions rather like the English defence of contributory negligence (to the limited extent to which it applies to actions for breach of contract). Secondly, however, French law sometimes relies on the injured party's contributory fault to perform the function which in English law would be played by the so-called duty to mitigate. Thus, if an injured party fails to take the necessary steps to reduce his own losses flowing from the other's breach, then any losses coming after that failure may be said to be caused by his own fault, rather than the defendant's. However, French law's attitude here is distinctly ambiguous. For its starting point is that an injured party is *not entitled* to go into the market and obtain a substitute performance on his own authority, but must first seek the court's approval for "performance by a third party" at the other party's expense, though no approval is required in commercial sales nor cases of urgency, as long as it is done as cheaply as possible. What this means in practice is that an injured party may without authorization obtain substitute performance, but if he does so he risks a later court telling him that he should have asked first and/or that the price at which the substitute performance was obtained was too high.

* * *

PROBLEM 5–6.

FibreTex, a Texas enterprise, sells to Norgrain, a Norwegian buyer, 100 tons of grain for a total price of $50,000 DES Oslo (see p. 165). When delivered, the grain had more moisture in it than allowable under the contract description and, as a result of the moisture, there had been some deterioration in quality. After taking possession of the grain Norgrain had it dried at a cost of $1,500. If the grain had been as contracted, its value in Oslo would have been $55,000 at the time of delivery, but because of the deterioration caused by the moisture the grain had a value of only $51,000 after it was dried.

(a) If it keeps the grain, how much may Norgrain recover in the form of money damages? CISG art. 74.

(b) Was Norgrain required to dry the grain? CISG art. 77. Would your answer be different if the undried grain had a market value of $50,000 at the time Norgrain decided to dry the grain?

(c) Assume that the undried grain had a value of $45,000 at the time of delivery but would have had a value of $55,000 if the grain had conformed to the contract requirements. By how much may Norgrain unilaterally reduce the contract price? CISG art.50. Is Norgrain better off reducing the price under article 50 or seeking damages under article 74?

[This problem is taken, with modifications, from Example 70D of the UNCITRAL Secretaritat's *Commentary*.]

* * *

PROBLEM 5–7.

François Fermier, the French farmer and vintner, agrees to produce and sell 6,000 bottles of François' Fizzy to Ace Liquors, U.S. beverage distributor. Assume, however, that François fails to deliver the wine and Ace avoids the contract. Ace now wishes to assert a claim for damages. You are asked to determine these damages. Your investigation reveals the following data.

— The contract price was $50,000 CIF New York.

— At the time the delivery was supposed to be made the cost of insurance and freight from Cherbourg to New York was 2,000.

— At the time the delivery was supposed to be made, 6,000 bottles of a commercially equivalent wine would cost $55,000 in France (for delivery in France) and $58,000 in the United States (including, however, costs of delivery to Ace's warehouse in Brooklyn).

— If Ace Liquors purchases an equivalent French wine, delivery of the replacement wine could not be made for two months, during which Ace would lose significant sales to competitors; which its accountant's value at $8,000.

(a) If Ace purchases 6,000 bottles of equivalent wine from France for $55,000 FOB Cherbourg, how much may Ace recover as money damages? CISG arts. 74, 75.

(b) If Ace purchases 6,000 bottles of an equivalent American wine in the U.S. for $58,000 FOB Ace's warehouse, how much may Ace recover as money damages? CISG arts. 74, 75 *supra*. If this amount is higher than the damages recoverable when purchasing an equivalent French wine, must Ace buy the French wine? CISG art. 77.

(c) If Ace decides not to buy any substitute wine, how much may it recover as money damages? CISG art. 76. Must Ace have a "good reason" for not buying any substitute wine?

(d) Assume Ace buys substitute American wine for $56,000 FOB Ace's Warehouse because the seller gives an implicit discount in the hope for future business from Ace. May Ace recover damages under article 76 notwithstanding its cover purchase?

* * *

PROBLEM 5–8.

Vitex is engaged in the business of chemically shower-proofing cloth for duty–free importation into the United States. For this purpose, Vitex maintains its offices and plant in Lesotho and is entitled to process a specific quantity of material under the United States quota system. Caribtex is in the business of importing shower-proofed cloth in to the United States.

In the fall of 1989, Vitex found itself with an unused portion of its quota but no customers, and Vitex closed its plant. Caribtex found some potential U.S. buyers for such cloth, and the parties entered into a contract in which Vitex agreed to sell to Caribtex 125,000 yards of shower-proofed woolen material at a price of 50 cents per yard F.O.B. Cape Town.

Vitex proceeded to re-open its Lesotho plant, ordered the necessary chemicals, recalled its work force and made all the necessary preparations to perform its end of the bargain. However, before any cloth was bought or processed, Caribtex repudiated the contract, apparently because Caribtex was unsure that the processed wool would be entitled to duty-free treatment by the customs officials. Vitex then brings suit to recover its damages for Caribtex's breach.

Vitex figures that its lost profit on the sale was $15,563, computed in the following manner: the contract price which would have been due for the processed cloth was $62,500. The unprocessed cloth would have cost $31,250. Vitex expenses to re-open its plant, order the necessary chemicals and recall its work force was $387. Its costs for labor, chemicals and energy to complete processing of the goods would have been about $9,750. If the contract has been completed, Vitex would (under normal accounting rules) have allocated $5,550 of its expenses for executive and clerical salaries, property taxes and general administrative expenses to this contract. Its accountants would, therefore, have recorded profit of $15,563.

Vitex has a series of questions for you. Advise Vitex.

(a) Can Vitex sue for the contract price of the processed cloth? In particular, Vitex wants to know whether it should now purchase unprocessed cloth, process it and ship it to Caribtex. If it did so, could it recover from Caribtex the contract price of $62,500?

(b) If Vitex does not purchase the unprocessed cloth, must Vitex sue for the contract price of the processed cloth less the market price of such processed cloth (which is probably at least $62,500)? If so, Vitex probably recovers nothing.

(c) If Vitex does not purchase the unprocessed cloth, can Vitex sue for the contract price of the processed cloth ($62,500), less the cost of the unprocessed cloth ($31,250), *i.e.* "expenses saved in consequence of the buyer's breach"?

(d) Alternatively, can Vitex sue for the "lost profit"? Is that lost profit equal to $15,563 or is it more?

[Problem 5–8 is loosely adapted from *Vitex Mfg. Corp. v. Caribtex Corp.*, 377 F. 2d 795 (3d Cir. 1967)].

* * *

NOTE ON PRE-AWARD INTEREST

One of the most-litigated issues in CISG cases is pre-award interest. The issue arises because, although the breach may occur in 1999, the courts may not schedule the case until 2004, and award the aggrieved party $500,000 actual damages then. Should the aggrieved party receive only the $500,000, or should it receive more because of the delay in the court's award. The CISG provision which deals with the issue (art. 78) is remarkably ambiguous, which is part of the reason for the significant amount of litigation on the topic. The issues relate to whether interest should be added to the damages award, during what time period, and at what rate should the rate be a "legal rate," or a market rate—and if the latter, which one? In particular, in an international transaction, the legal and market rates in buyer's notion may be quite different from similar rates in seller's notion, due to different rates of inflation or the quality of the local currency. A separate decision in the *Delchi* case considered these issues, and is critiqued below.

DARKEY, A U.S. COURT'S INTERPRETATION OF DAM-
AGE PROVISIONS UNDER THE U.N. CONVENTION
ON CONTRACTS FOR THE INTERNATIONAL SALE
OF GOODS: A PRELIMINARY STEP TOWARDS AN
INTERNATIONAL JURISPRUDENCE OF CISG OR A
MISSED OPPORTUNITY?
15 J.Law & Com. 139, 148–50 (1995).*

The second U.S. court application of CISG occurred in 1994 in the
Northern District of New York and is the subject of this comment. The
court in Delchi Carrier, SpA v. Rotorex Corp. interpreted the damage
provisions of CISG, namely articles 74–78, and discovered gaps that it
filled in a variety of ways. The nonchalance of the court's determination
that CISG was the applicable law is striking. Furthermore, the opinion is
more noteworthy for the dearth of analysis and the methodology utilized
to support the conclusions than for the actual reasoning employed.

* * *

3.   Pre-Judgment Interest

Article 78 of CISG authorizes recovery of interest on the payment
price or any sum in arrears. Under CISG, it is not clear whether a party
is entitled to recover interest on an unliquidated amount, which was the
case in Delchi. Given the international controversial nature of interest,
the final language of Article 78 entitling a party to interest on "any . . .
sum . . . in arrears" was a compromise among the states. Honnold
discusses two situations that fall within the scope of Article 78: when a
buyer delays paying the seller, and when a seller delays refunding the
purchase price for defective goods. Neither of these two scenarios were
presented in Delchi.

Honnold also discusses the question of liquidated sums and observes
that some jurisdictions do not recognize interest accruing until the
amount in arrears is made certain. The U.C.C. makes no mention of the
ability to recover interest on incidental damages. A U.S. federal court
has commented on the wide availability of pre-judgment interest as
follows: "[u]nless there is a statutory provision to the contrary, the court
has broad discretion in deciding whether to award pre-judgment interest."

Thus, the Delchi court followed the domestic tradition of discretionary awards of pre-judgment interest of unliquidated sums. However, it is
far from clear that the drafters of CISG intended that interest on
consequential loss, including lost profits, be awarded and calculated at
the rate of the debtor's country.

Even if recovery of pre-judgment interest was warranted, there still
remains a question of what rate should be utilized. Noting that Article

78 does not specify an applicable interest rate, the court, "in its discretion," awarded interest at the rate established by U.S. federal law for the award of post-judgment interest. The court made no reference to Article 7, which provides a uniform application for gap-filling. Nor did it examine the legislative history of the Convention or refer to scholarly opinion. Ironically, the court, which was so receptive to scholarly authority on the issue of lost profits, does not follow Sutton's recommendations for interpretation of the gap in Article 78, which were made in the same journal article that the court cited to earlier in its opinion.

During the drafting of CISG, there was much debate over Article 78, making it one of the most controversial articles. A rule on interest was omitted in earlier drafts of the CISG. Thus, there is no commentary to allow insight on its development as is provided for in other articles. However, a 1976 draft included a provision for interest awards to the seller. Article 58 of this draft provided for interest at the rate of the country of the seller's [principal] place of business.

Since Article 78 of CISG extends interest recovery to the buyer as well as to the seller, it can be analogized from previous drafts that the appropriate interest rate would be the interest rate of the country where the injured party has its place of business, since this is the cost of credit. While a court is not bound to the rationale employed in previous drafts of the convention, it would be wise to examine these drafts in order to determine intent.

In addition, foreign courts have addressed the interest issue, albeit in fact scenarios where the buyer was the breaching party due to nonpayment. Applying a conflict of law analysis, German courts have held that the law of the aggrieved party's country should be applied when determining the interest rate. The International Court of Arbitration applied the law of the place of payment to determine the interest rate owed on an unpaid balance to the seller.

Determining the method of calculation of interest by a domestic conflicts of law analysis should be the last resort of a court. Pursuant to Article 7(2)(ii), domestic law should only be applied once general principles of the Convention cannot be ascertained. In conformity with the general principles of the Convention, specifically those from Article 74 which strives to award recovery of suffered losses, and Article 75 which calculates compensation by the cost of the substitute transaction, interest should be calculated by the cost of credit faced by the injured party.

By applying the U.S. federal rate, which is the rate of the country of the breaching party, the Delchi court did not promote the uniformity that is the goal of the Convention. Furthermore, the court was incorrect to apply a federal statute rather than a state statute to determine the rate of interest.

KISER, MINDING THE GAP: DETERMINING INTEREST RATES UNDER THE U.N. CONVENTION FOR THE INTERNATIONAL SALES OF GOODS
65 U. Chi. L. Rev. 1279, 1288, 1302–04 (1998).*

One function of interest rates is to preserve the time value of money for the injured party. All else being equal, money today is worth more than money tomorrow because it can be invested today for some positive return. Consequently, the deferred receipt of funds should be compensated by some interest on those funds. Two other factors affect money's value in international trade: inflation and depreciation, or a currency's decline in value relative to other currencies. Nominal rates protect against the former by providing an inflation premium. Using nominal rates that apply to a particular currency protects against any loss in that currency's value from depreciation.

Basic contract principles suggest two purposes for awarding interest—compensation and restitution. Rates that reflect the creditor's cost of capital are compensatory; they ensure that the injured creditor's delayed payment maintains the same value it would have but for the debtor's breach, ensuring the injured party the benefit of the bargain. Conversely, rates that reflect a debtor's cost of borrowing are restitutionary; they aim to prevent the debtor from unjustly enriching herself at the creditor's expense by taking what amounts to an interest-free loan from the creditor. Depending on whether a compensatory or restitutionary approach is chosen, appropriate rates come from a variety of sources.

* * *

Adjudicators should "customize" the rate by awarding actual borrowing costs when a party incurs them, and an average investment return, such as one for a certificate of deposit for the currency in which the transaction is denominated, when the creditor does not borrow. This solution puts the injured party in the position he would have been absent the late payment by compensating him for actual out-of-pocket expenses incurred, while guaranteeing a reasonable return when he does not borrow.

Awarding actual borrowing costs would mimic what the parties would have bargained for when negotiating the contract had they recognized that the creditor would borrow to cover for the delayed payment and selected a rate. The rule is also consistent with the CISG's general principles. First, it ensures that the creditor is put in the position she would have been but for the debtor's breach by compensating her for her additional costs, consistent with Article 74, the CISG's general damage provision. Second, by using this principle from the CISG as a guide, the rule avoids using national laws to fill the gap. While some national courts have reached the same result by first determining the appropriate rate using conflict of laws rules and then adjusting the rate to match the rate at which the creditor actually borrowed, not all national laws recognize interest as an element of damages. Thus, relying on the national law approach to fully compensate the injured creditor may not guarantee this element of compensation. Third, the rule promotes uniformity in the CISG's interpretation by using the same substantive principle—ensuring the benefit of the bargain—to make awards in individual cases. Finally, because many traders do borrow when financing international transactions, awarding the cost of replacement funds reflects a common international trade practice, consistent with Article 9. In sum, it fulfills the principal objective for interpreting gaps under the CISG's Article 7: encouraging uniform and international solutions.

One might argue that ensuring an award of borrowing costs may encourage parties to borrow recklessly. However, this possibility can be policed by adjudicators, who can review the reasonableness of any borrowing that seems suspect. An adjudicator can rely on CISG Article 77, which obligates an injured party to mitigate her damages, to constrain unreasonable borrowing by requiring information on a party's creditworthiness. For example, one German court denied an Italian creditor his actual costs because they were excessive compared with other borrowing options. While this will require adjudicators to review transactions more thoroughly (thereby increasing decision costs), it may also promote the development of a common practice. Furthermore, any incentive for a creditor to borrow recklessly may be constrained by the fact that recovery of interest remains uncertain until after adjudication.

When a creditor cannot demonstrate specific substitute lending, however, she should be awarded not a lending rate, but rather a savings rate. A savings rate, such as a certificate of deposit for the currency of payment, provides a uniform way for adjudicators to settle interest rate disputes with low decision and error costs. In order to put a creditor in the position she would have been but for the breach, the court would have to award her weighted average cost of capital, which reflects the opportunity cost of her funds. In practice, however, calculating a creditor's weighted average cost of capital involves high decision costs, requiring adjudicators to synthesize an enormous amount of financial information. In contrast, a rule awarding a savings rate, such as the rate on a certificate of deposit, is easy to apply, reducing decision costs. Moreover, this rule will also reduce error costs by acting as a penalty default. If a creditor knows that she will not have to borrow to cover a shortfall caused by delayed payment, she will have an incentive to reveal this information during the negotiations. This rule will encourage her to specify in the contract an interest rate that will adequately compensate her, reducing both decision and error costs should a dispute arise.

NOTE ON STATUTE OF LIMITATIONS ISSUES

In addition to the U.N. Convention on Contracts for the International Sale of Goods (CISG), there is also a U.N. Convention on the Limitation

Period in the International Sale of Goods (Treaty Doc. 103–10). The latter Convention was separately drafted in UNCITRAL and separately ratified by the United States in 1993.

The Limitation Convention addresses the following problem: when there is a dispute between parties to an international sale, how long can the parties wait before they are barred from enforcing their claims? American business trading abroad now face wildly-divergent limitation periods and foreign legal concepts. The Convention provides the following uniform, understandable, and certain rules.

— The Limitation Convention will provide U.S. traders more certain legal rules on when claims can no longer be made. It is a truism in the commercial world that more certain legal rules allow entrepreneurs to determine risk allocation more definitely and to plan accordingly.

— Application of the Convention will usually reach similar results to those that would result if U.S. law were applicable.

— The basic four-year period provided by the Convention is a reasonable period to require commercial record keeping. This period is the same as that provided by the U.S. Uniform Commercial Code (U.C.C. § 2–725).

— The Convention's uniform rules should decrease the incentive to shop for a forum that will hear the case. The costs of "forum shopping" are well known.

— When the Convention is applicable, costs of legal research will decrease over time. Unnecessary legal costs are, of course, an impediment to the growth of the trade.

— Sellers and buyers are free to agree that the Convention will not govern their sales contracts. They may do so, e.g., when they can predict what limitation period will apply. Like most rules of sales law, the Convention provides "supplementary" rules for parties who leave gaps in their agreement.

Many of these points are illustrated in the hypothetical case set forth below.

One difference between the Convention and the U.C.C. should be noted: the Convention does not permit the seller and buyer to agree to *reduce* the time period to less than four years, while the U.C.C. permits parties to reduce the period to not less than one year. However, sellers and buyers who wish to reduce the time period may do so effectively by agreeing that the Convention will not apply. The Convention permits them, moreover, to agree on the time within which notice of breach must be given.

LIMITATION CONVENTION

HYPOTHETICAL CASE

A Rhode Island corporation agrees to sell equipment to an Argentinean enterprise. Six years after the equipment is delivered to Argentina it breaks down. The Argentinean enterprise claims that the breakdown is a result of alleged defects in the quality of the equipment. The Rhode Island corporation asks: Are we responsible for the alleged defect?; Is the complaint too late?

The first question can be answered with confidence. Both Argentina and the United States are parties to the 1980 U.N. Convention on Contracts for the International Sales of Goods ("CISG"). Unless the seller and buyer have chosen to have a domestic sales law apply, the Sales Convention will govern. CISG art. 1. That Convention, however, gives precedence to the parties' contract. CISG art. 6. Therefore one must first determine what the parties agreed to. Only if the contract is silent or incomplete may the Convention be consulted. It states that the seller's obligations as to quality are similar in content to those found in the U.S. Uniform Commercial Code ("U.C.C."). CISG art. 35.

If the United States was not a party to the Limitation Convention, the second question could not be answered—whether the complaint is too late—with the same confidence. Instead, the answer requires detailed and complex analysis. It will turn in part on where the Argentinean enterprise brings its legal complaint: in Argentina or Rhode Island (or any other place where it can obtain jurisdiction); before a court, arbitral tribunal, or administrative body. The four-year *statute of limitation* provided by U.C.C. § 2–725 differs from the ten-year *prescription* period provided by Article 4032 of the Argentinean Civil Code.

However, because the United States is now a party to the Limitation Convention this second question can be answered with much greater confidence: the claim against the Rhode Island corporation is too late.

This answer results from the following analysis. The Convention applies because the United States has ratified the Convention. Argentina is also a party to the Convention and therefore the seller and buyer would have places of business in two different States party to the Convention. Limitation Convention arts. 2, 3. The Argentinean enterprise's claim that there is a defect would accrue (i.e., the limitation period would begin to run) when the equipment was actually handed over six years ago. Limitation Convention art. 10(2). The Convention's limitation period of four years would have elapsed at the time of the complaint. Limitation Convention art. 8. As a consequence, the Argentinean enterprise's claim would not be enforceable—whether it made the complaint in Argentina or in the United States. Limitation Convention art. 25(1).

If this had been a domestic U.S. sales transaction, the result would be the same. The buyer's claim would have accrued "when tender of delivery is made" and would run for four years. U.C.C. § 2–725(1), (2).

D.   STIPULATED DAMAGES PROVISIONS
(Including Liquidated Damages and Penalty Clauses)

HARTNELL, ROUSING THE SLEEPING DOG: THE VALIDITY EXCEPTION TO THE CONVENTION ON CONTRACTS FOR THE INTERNATIONAL SALE OF GOODS
18 Yale. J. Int'l L. 1, 79–80 (1993).*

There is no disagreement that CISG, article 4(a) preserves the effect of domestic rules avoiding illegal or immoral contracts. These are the classic "regulations of a police character or for the protection of persons" which the drafters intended to leave untouched by the uniform law. In this area, it is practically impossible to draw a line between validity and public policy (*ordre public*). As such, no degree of unification seems possible. The categories of illegal and immoral contracts are too extensive to discuss here, beyond reference to a few commercially important issues.

International contracts frequently "contain clauses which provide for the payment of a specific or ascertainable sum of money in the event a party is late or otherwise fails to comply with his contractual obligations." CISG, article 6 permits such liquidated damages clauses, subject to any domestic law prohibiting penalty clauses that are applicable by virtue of article 4(a). For example, U.C.C. § 2–718(1) contains a "condemnation of penalty clauses . . . rooted in public policy . . . [that] is untouched by the [CISG]." Not all countries prohibit such clauses, however. Some efforts have been undertaken to unify the law governing such clauses, but they have not been successful to date.

KONERU, THE INTERNATIONAL INTERPRETATION OF THE UN CONVENTION ON CONTRACTS FOR THE INTERNATIONAL SALE OF GOODS: AN APPROACH BASED ON GENERAL PRINCIPLES
6 Minn. J. Global Trade 105, 141–45 (1997).**

B.   Liquidated Damages

The subject of liquidated damages is not explicitly covered in the Convention, although there was considerable support for the idea that the Uniform Law should regulate liquidated damages clauses. The Committee felt that such regulation is particularly desirable because the rules on liquidated damages vary widely, and it would be a practical contribution to international trade to bring uniformity in their application. The Committee again could not agree on proper language that would avoid the technical problems associated with the proposed draft.

As a result, the basic principle underlying the liquidated damages provision was not rejected in the Convention. Accordingly, a liquidated damages clause agreed upon by the parties should be given full effect under the Article 6 principle of contractual freedom to derogate from the Convention.

At least two courts misunderstood the provision and misinterpreted it, casting doubt not only on the future of liquidated damages clauses under the Convention, but also on the court's ability and willingness to comply with the Article 7 mandates of international interpretation of the Convention. When an Austrian seller and a Bulgarian buyer entered into a contract for the sale of goods, they specifically agreed to limit their damages to a certain percentage of the contract price, regardless of who failed to perform. After noting that the CISG did not expressly address liquidated damages, an arbitration court applied Austrian domestic law to determine if the liquidation clause was valid. The court held that the seller should recover all damages suffered, in spite of the specific agreement to limit the damages by a penalty clause. The parties seemed to have been commercially sophisticated and their agreement should have been respected. The court ignored the Article 6 provision that the parties may derogate from or vary the effect of any of the provisions of the Convention. There was no inquiry needed to determine the validity of the liquidated damages clause. The only inquiry should have been whether the parties were behaving in good faith as provided under Article 7(1). Thus, this ruling seems to be unwarranted.

Should the result be different if the buyer agreed to pay a "compensation fee" that amounts to thirty percent of the contract price even in a force majeure situation? One arbitrator held that even though there was a "construction difficulty" of the term "compensation fee" and that the phrase is "not usual in legal vocabulary," the wording of the clause was not "precise enough" to be construed as a liquidation clause which would foreclose any claim for other damages. The arbitrator focused on the condition that the buyer agreed to pay the "compensation fee" even in the condition of force majeure situations and interpreted to mean that the fee was "money payable in consideration of the termination of the contract independently of any damages suffered by Seller." The seller was awarded storage costs under Article 77 ("mitigation" costs), seller's costs in modifying the equipment for a substitute buyer, the lost profit resulting from the substitute sale (Article 74 damages), the "compensation fee" of thirty percent of the contract price, and interest on all the amounts due.

Given the ambiguity of the provision, the arbitrator had to choose between granting or denying the thirty percent "compensation fee." Even though the Convention does not address the "compensation fee" issue, the issue could have been analyzed under the general principles of the Convention, namely, the principles of freedom of contract, fair dealing and good faith observance, and full compensation. The seller was fully compensated with all the damages under Articles 74, 75, 77 and 78. Even though the principle of contractual freedom requires that the fee provision should be respected, it is nonetheless subject to the principles of good faith and fair dealing. Both parties were merchants and were presumably dealing at arm's length. But the seller's provision required that in case of seller's breach, the buyer would get only his down payment back, with no interest. The seller seemed to have made a substitute sale in a short time but only for approximately fifty percent of the contract price, which raises the question of whether the sale was done "in a reasonable manner and within a reasonable time" under the Convention. Moreover, the seller asked for the higher interest rate of Italy, whereas the contract money was to be paid in German marks. These facts raise an issue of unfair dealing.

This case would have been an ideal opportunity for the court to interpret the contract and the Convention under the Article 7 mandate of promoting observance of good faith in international trade. Most likely the seller drafted the contract, and the seller should have borne the consequences of any resulting ambiguity. The court should have ruled that, after the plaintiff is fully compensated, claims for additional sums must meet the test of good faith. Or conversely, it is reasonable to assume that a high (thirty percent) "compensation fee" indicates the nature of the risk the buyer assumed in case he defaulted and that was all the seller is entitled to recover. Thus the court's ruling casts doubt on the ability of courts to interpret liquidated damages clauses in a manner that promotes observance of good faith in international trade.

When a contract has been validly avoided, both parties are required to make restitution concurrently. When the buyer in another case placed the goods at the seller's disposal, the seller failed to take delivery and refused to refund the price. The court stated that this matter is not expressly covered by the CISG and that Article 31, which deals with the delivery of the goods by the seller, is not applicable by analogy. After stating that it could find no applicable general principles of the Convention, the court applied domestic law. Instead, the court should have imposed on the seller an obligation of good faith and an obligation to mitigate his losses. The court should have stayed within the Convention rather than referring to domestic law.

* * *

PROBLEM 5–9.

A French seller and a buyer located in the U.S. concluded a contract for the sale of steel bars. The contract contained a clause obligating buyer to pay an additional 30% of the price as a penalty, if buyer failed to take delivery or pay for the goods in a "timely manner." When the invoices were not paid at the time of delivery, the seller formally notified buyer that payment was due within 30 days of delivery or the penalty clause would be enforced. Buyer paid the purchase price, but only 60 days after delivery of the goods. The seller seeks your advice. It wants to commence an action claiming damages under the provisions set forth in the contract. Does it matter whether the action is brought in a French court or an American court? CISG arts. 4(a), 6, 7.

Legislation Note on UCC Provisions

UCC § 2–718 allows the parties to stipulate the amount or measure of damages due to a breach by either party, but with several restrictions on their ability to do so. First, the stipulated damages must be "reasonable in light of the anticipated or actual harm," taking into account evidentiary difficulties and costs and likelihood of obtaining any remedy.

Second, although stipulated damages which are too small are given no special treatment, stipulated damages which are "unreasonably large" are "void as a penalty." This Common Law concept is discussed in the excerpt from Farnsworth, below. Does such a penalty clause raise issues of "validity" under CISG art. 7?

E. ALLAN FARNSWORTH, CONTRACTS
935–37 (2d ed., 1990).*

§ 12.18 Liquidated Damages, Penalties, and Other Agreed Remedies. To what degree is the law of remedies for breach of contract amenable to contrary agreement by the parties? Compared with the extensive power that contracting parties have to bargain over their substantive contract rights and duties, their power to bargain over their remedial rights is surprisingly limited. The most important restriction is the one denying them the power to stipulate in their contract a sum of money payable as damages that is so large as to be characterized as a "penalty."

The advantages of stipulating in advance a sum payable as damages are manifold. For both parties, it may facilitate the calculation of risks and reduce the cost of proof. For the injured party, it may afford the only possibility of compensation for loss that is not susceptible of proof with sufficient certainty. For society as a whole, it may save the time of judges, juries, and witnesses, as well as the parties, and may cut the expense of litigation. These advantages are of special significance when the amount in controversy is small.

If, however, the stipulated sum is significantly larger than the amount required to compensate the injured party for its loss, the stipulation may have quite a different advantage to that party—an *in terrorem* effect on the other party that will deter breach by compelling performance. Enforcement of such a provision would allow the parties to depart from the fundamental principle that the law's goal on breach of contract is not to deter breach by compelling the promisor to perform, but rather to redress breach by compensating the promisee. It is this departure that is proscribed when a court characterizes such a provision as a penalty. Since it is the *in terrorem* effect that is objectionable, the proscription applies only if the stipulated sum is on the high, rather than the low, side of conventional damages, although a provision stipulating an unreasonably low sum as damages may be attacked as unconscionable. How did this hostile judicial attitude toward penalties come about?

The attitude can be traced back to the development of equitable relief in cases involving penal bonds, which were used to secure performance under contracts. A penal bond, originally a sealed instrument, took the form of a promise to pay a stated sum, coupled with a provision that this obligation was "null and void" if the promisor rendered the required performance under the contract. The common law courts enforced such bonds literally and, if the promisor had not strictly performed as required by the contract, would give judgment against the promisor for the sum fixed in the bond, regardless of the amount of loss caused the promisee by the breach. However, by the latter part of the seventeenth century, it had become settled that equity would enjoin collection of the penal sum by the promisee and send the case to trial at law for determination of the amount of actual loss caused by the breach. This equity practice led to the enactment of statutes in both England and the United States, requiring the promisee at common law to state the promisor's failure to perform and allowing the promisee recovery only for damages actually proved. The principles developed in connection with penal bonds were later extended to contractual penalties of all kinds. In this way a distinction grew in contract provisions stipulating the amount of damages between those characterized as "penalties," and therefore condemned, and those characterized as "liquidated damages," and therefore permitted. If a provision is condemned as a penalty, it is unenforceable; but the rest of the agreement stands, and the injured party is remitted to the conventional damage remedy for breach of that agreement. If the provision is sustained as one for liquidated damages, both parties are bound by it, and it displaces the conventional damage remedy for breach, whether it provides for damages that are larger or smaller than would otherwise have been awarded. The same distinction is now often applied to clauses providing that a sum of money deposited as security shall be forfeit in the case of breach.

BEARDSLEY, COMPELLING CONTRACT PERFORMANCE IN FRANCE
1 Hastings Int'l & Comp. L. Rev. 103–07 (1977).*

* * * In approving the penal clause and sheltering the amount of the penalty from judicial scrutiny, the draftsmen of the Code were faithful to the principle of freedom of contract expressed in Article 1134's celebrated declaration that "agreements lawfully entered into make law for the parties." * * *

The Court of Cassation has consistently held that penal clauses are to be given full effect, however extravagant they may appear. Neither the plaintiff's failure to prove actual damage nor considerations of "justice and equity" justifies refusal to enforce the full penalty. *Force majeure* or impossibility might suffice to avoid the penalty on the ground that performance of the principle obligation was thereby excused, but only where the parties clearly did not intend the penalty to apply to *every* case in which the agreed performance was not rendered. Article 1231, permitting reduction of the penalty where the defendant had performed part of the obligation, provided relief in some cases, but only where the parties themselves neither provided for a scaling down of the penalty where the creditor had received some value prior to default, nor made it clear that the full penalty was payable notwithstanding part performance.

* * *

Apart from some hesitation over the application of Article 1231, the Court of Cassation held firmly to the immutability and full enforceability of penal clauses throughout the period of controversy running from the late 1960's until Articles 1152 and 1231 were modified by legislation * * * The amendments did not disturb Article 1152's prohibition of a damage award in an amount different from any amount agreed upon by the parties, but added the following qualification: "Nevertheless, the judge may reduce or increase the agreed penalty, if it is manifestly excessive or derisory. Any stipulation to the contrary shall have no effect." * * * The new texts clearly mark the abandonment of the rigid enforcement of penal clauses which has for so long been a distinctive characteristic of French contract law. It seems likely, however, that the texts themselves will cause difficulty for it is far from clear precisely what mandate is now given to the judge who is called upon to enforce a contract penalty. There is no doubt that the new Article 1231 overturns the Court of Cassation's ruling that the parties can by agreement preclude application of the moderating power of the judge. Article 1231, as well as the new language in Article 1152, has been made a matter of *ordre public*.

UNILEX CASE D. 1992–10
Switzerland: Preturia di Locarno–Campagna, 1992.

Abstract

In 1988 an Italian seller and a Swiss buyer concluded contracts for the sale of furniture. The buyer sold a set of living-room furniture on to a customer who shortly thereafter complained that the goods were defective (by sitting on the sofas, the cushions slid forward). The buyer refused to accept the seller's offer to repair the goods by substituting the cushions' upholstery and declared the contract avoided. The buyer further claimed that another living-room set delivered by the seller was defective and, upon the seller's refusal to repair it, requested a refund of repair costs. The seller commenced legal action to recover the full price of all furniture sold.

The Court held that the contracts were governed by CISG, as the Swiss private international law rules led to the application of the law of Italy, a contracting State (Art. 1(1)(b) CISG).

With respect to the first set of furniture, the Court held that the buyer was not entitled to declare the contract avoided, as it had not examined the goods and given notice ofthe non-conformity in accordance with Arts. 38 and 39 CISG. In the opinion of the Court, as both parties were merchants, the buyer should have examined the goods upon delivery and, since the defect was apparent, it should have given immediate notice of the non-conformity, instead of doing so only following customer complaints.

The Court also observed that the buyer should have accepted the seller's offer to remedy the non-conformity by substituting the upholstery, in accordance with Art. 48 CISG.

With respect to the second set of furniture, the Court found that the buyer was entitled to a reduction of the price, calculated as provided in Art. 50 CISG (in the same proportion as the value the goods actually delivered had at the time of delivery bears to the value conforming goods would have had at that time). The Court held that, in the absence of evidence to the contrary, the value that conforming goods would have had is determined by the price agreed upon in the contract. The Court further specified that the sum by which the price is to be reduced may not correspond to the repair costs actually suffered by the buyer.

*

INDEX

References as to Pages

References as to Pages